When Journalism was a Thing

When Journalism was a Thing

Alexandra Kitty

Winchester, UK
Washington, USA

First published by Zero Books, 2018
Zero Books is an imprint of John Hunt Publishing Ltd., Laurel House, Station Approach,
Alresford, Hants, SO24 9JH, UK
office1@jhpbooks.net
www.johnhuntpublishing.com
www.zero-books.net

For distributor details and how to order please visit the 'Ordering' section on our website.

Text copyright: Alexandra Kitty 2017

ISBN: 978 1 78535 654 4
978 1 78535 655 1 (ebook)
Library of Congress Control Number: 2017936411

A CIP catalogue record for this book is available from the British Library.

Design: Stuart Davies

Printed and bound by CPI Group (UK) Ltd, Croydon, CR0 4YY, UK

We operate a distinctive and ethical publishing philosophy in
all areas of our business, from our global network of authors to
production and worldwide distribution.

Contents

To the two women in my life, past and present:
my grandmother and my mother.

I thank Andrea Sierer for her gracious generosity in editing my book. In a world filled with uncertainty, your kindness is never in doubt.

"Here is a lie. I know it's a lie, but I must print it because it is spoken by a prominent public official. The public official's name and position make the lie news. Were the source some unknown person, I could and would gladly throw it in the wastebasket".

Oliver K. Brovard.

An open letter to journalists, particularly those in North America

You are working in a dead profession that you all had a part in killing. The time for denial is over. Journalism has been dead for a very long time. Deal with it.

The list of your sins is too long to place in a single volume of a book, but you have much to answer for.

For starters, you openly lie to each and every news consumer with your every story by cribbing from press releases and parroting whatever tidbit you hear from public relations hacks, and pretend it is original research.

That is your first lie and everything else begins from there. You have done no research on how to better do your jobs. You have the nerve to run to focus groups and market researchers to tell you what the public is thinking, and how to better pander to them with your deceptions.

You have caused wars. People have died and been falsely imprisoned thanks to your ignorant propaganda. You have spread lies that have forever altered and ruined lives, and no, there is not a single story you can cite that can make up for the countless deaths that you are responsible for. The lives you purported to save cannot nullify a single one your irresponsible ways have caused.

You have spread hate. You have spread prejudice. You have spread fear. You have spread absolute panic. You have spread lies. You have turned ordinary people into targets to be reviled for life. You have constructed false pecking orders, rewarding psychopaths and narcissists who have contributed nothing to society, causing untold damage. You have confused running a Bedlam with being journalists, rigging coverage with loaded language, distorted videography, and selective reportage.

You have no moral high ground to take, and you have proven

to be unteachable.

You have incited the populace to treat their fellow human being as monsters. You have perpetuated countless stereotypes, an ironic twist as it was the journalist Walter Lippmann who coined the term.

You have plagiarized and stolen ideas. You have smeared the reputations of countless lost souls as you cheered on grifters, swindlers, liars, rapists, psychopaths, and murderers who appealed to you. You have let lies go unchallenged as you stalked and hunted anyone who does not think just like you, and then pretended as if your xenophobic tendencies did not exist. You have fabricated stories or allowed others to do it for you.

You have become shrill, irrational, paranoid, and deluded monomaniacs as you threw your countless childish temper tantrums in public. You have pretended to go through war zones, even as your own video footage gives your choreographed games away. You are not fooling those with a working mind. Grow up.

You have sexually harassed employees and generously employed a casting couch as you drank too much and snorted even more on the job — and then went out and condemned those who play in the same gutter as you.

You have ignored stories that mattered because they involved the poor, the foreign, the disabled, and the uncharismatic time and again. You have ignored genuine rape victims as you fawned over the liars. You have cost the economy billions of dollars as you extolled the brilliance of con men such as Kenneth Lay, Tyler Cassity, and Bernie Ebbers. You have bankrupted hard-working people. You have cost those people jobs, their homes, their dignity, and peace of mind forever because the notion of actual work and research repulsed you. You have been clueless, racist, sexist, homophobic, and xenophobic, all while trying to pretend you extol something that resembles progressive values. Stop believing your own hype. It is as fake as your concern for humanity.

2

Because your newsrooms have been stubbornly white and male. The way you spin your yarns have always been and continues to be misogynistic patriarchal in structure. You have set up false divides as you demanded that civilians be bombed in the name of morality, but of the real tyranny in the world, you have seen it, but kept unrepentantly quiet.

Your logic is nonexistent. You liberally appeal to authority, stoop to personal attacks as you commit strawman fallacies, and the confirmation bias. You have made fun of the mentally ill and bullied people you deemed unhip, poor, and homely. You fill up your pages and newscasts with celebrity garbage and troll social media instead of getting off your backsides to do actual work.

Your sophistry is childish, yet treacherous. You look down on others as you boast, gloat, and puff your way up the ladder.

You have destroyed the industry with arrogance, deceit, and immaturity, and now expect a single soul other than your mothers to actually believe a word you say.

There will always be the lost and the fearful who think they need to hear lies and insults to hide from reality and truth — the two most important goals to reach for any journalist, yet both are routinely ignored in lieu of fluff.

The last handful of journalists who still do their jobs cannot keep a dead profession going. Media concentration is out of control, and do not look to Canadians for a clue as their own journalists have become paupers holding their tin cans, asking their government whether they have a dime — and had they done their jobs and paid attention, they would already know the answer is their government is as broke as they are.

You have become mudslingers covered in the stench of your own laziness. There will be those forever ruined and traumatized thanks to your games.

And now you have been reduced to the vile and uninspired bullying of the President of the United States because he played you and you never saw it coming. He was the love of your shallow life, and if it weren't for your decades' long drooling over him, he would not have made it further than any of you ever will.

When he was aligned with the Left and the Democrats, none of his practices or beliefs bothered you or got you to expose his ways — he is a product of your side of the fence, but now you scream and writhe in agony. When he was one of yours, you cheered him on. Do not think for one second that you can fool all of the people all of the time.

And now you are praying that your own country implodes to prove he should not have been president, and your petty and sick games are causing instability, and millions of people will suffer because you cannot face how ugly and disgusting you have become as a profession. That is sick and pathological. Stop sabotaging the very people you vowed to protect by liberating truth from lies. The last president praised you as his regime flattered you, and many of you got plum patronage appointments as a result all the while press freedoms were being actively eroded by that same regime, and now you know there is no cushy landing for any of you under the *current* regime. You are not as cunning as you fancy yourselves to be.

Where were you when young people were being recruited by terrorists in their own schools?

Where were you when countless women were being beaten and tortured in their own homes?

Where were you when pedophiles were getting positions of power and luring in their prey for decades uninterrupted?

Where were you when the poor were destroyed and denied their basic human rights?

Where were you when people and institutions who promised to right wrongs, merely gave themselves paper crowns as they took the money for themselves?

Where were you when the robber barons of the modern age were actively hoarding money as they destroyed industries, privacy, and personal freedoms?

You were too busy ignoring them as you drooled over Kardashian backsides because you have been kissing any backside that comes from money, and obliviously parroting what those manipulative people told you to think.

It does not matter if you fancy yourself as a liberal or a conservative, you all do the same rotten thing, day in and day out.

You are not the smartest or most cunning people around. You are not shrewd. You are not impressive. You never were and you never will be. Your conniving and calculated lies have become too transparent to swallow. There is no denying it. There is no justifying it. There is no deflecting attention away from your gross incompetence by attacking those who see what you have done and remember every single transgression.

For those of us who seen first-hand what you have done, we will neither forget, nor keep silent.

You did not like when the President told you that you were all fake news for one reason: because the truth *hurts*. He knows that truth because he made a very enviable and viable career knowing who you all really were all along.

So, to each and every one of you:

Shame on you. Shame on you for your lies, manipulations, prejudices, and vendettas. You can continue to justify your rot, but you cannot turn it into anything else.

It is rot and it is a reflection on your broken soul.

My heart aches for every person who you willfully killed or destroyed by pen or by microphone just so you could pretend you had a scoop and a story for a cocktail party or memoir. None of you are worthy or trustworthy enough to change your ways because you will always try to justify every horrible thing you ever did as you mulishly misuse your destructive and antagonistic narrative templates that always cast you as some sort of hero no one could possibly survive without, regardless how villainous you have repeatedly proven yourselves to be.

Your lofty degree or position cannot nullify your iniquities. Your posh New York City address cannot hide the fact you are bigoted thieves, followers, enablers, and vultures with a limited understanding of the world or your fellow human being, and must resort to reading a script to know what to think.

You cannot keep banking on everyone being afraid of you, or fretting they won't get fawning coverage, or worse, being the victim of a relentless character assassination. Some of us do not care what the desperate and cowardly think because it is the sum total of your actions that have caused the world one crisis too many. Some people can stand alone as they stand up to you, and can see reality and truth despite your spiral into a void of your own making. You may be groping in that dark, but not everyone has fallen into that abyss.

Like a philandering spouse who brings home disease, lies, excuses, and disrepute on those who believed those vows, you have squandered your goodwill. You cannot deny what you have done. You cannot sweet talk those harmed by your disloyalty to truth into giving you another chance.

You can no longer make threats that the world cannot leave and survive without you.

Because there is one truth you cannot face: that the world survived just fine without journalism for centuries before, and it — and democracy — will continue to progress even better without your meddling and presumptuous attempts at social engineering. No one is obligated to indulge in your grandiose fantasies, now or ever again. Enough is enough.

May whatever discipline that takes your place keep your lazy and malicious arrogance out of their ideology, and never look back because a bad media creates a bad world.

And that bad world has put up with your self-absorbed inhumanity long enough.

Alexandra Kitty

Preface

As a journalist who wrote about the business of journalism, its ethics, and its groupthink, what I saw perpetually *disturbed* me. There was a certain cocky obliviousness that was slowly killing the profession, and my work and research at the time proved it: ownership of newspapers was no longer stable or was in many hands, and editors and publishers, who once reigned for years in the same coveted spot, were now lucky to survive a couple of years in the position.

I saw it all first-hand. I saw the ideological stagnation. I saw the disdain and contempt for "the common folk" who were the news consumers. I saw the cluelessness of how to retain audiences, let alone expand the base. Writing hard news stories for youth was shunned. I saw the structural sickness all around me, and by 2005, I had my first book published, *Don't Believe It!: How lies become news.*

The book was more than just a guide on how to spot dishonest and deceptive news stories: it was about how and why those problems ended up in the news in the first place. I felt as if I were a doctor who was diagnosing a critically ill patient, but there was a cure and a rigorous treatment available; so long as the patient understood there was a sickness, and took steps to get better. The patient, however, insisted that there was nothing wrong, and was the model of perfect health.

Sadly, the patient did not see the depth of seriousness of the precarious condition, and in November 2016, passed away.

And now I am writing about my profession once again; this time feeling as if I am a coroner. It is a very unsettling notion, yet the standard of quality since my last foray into writing about the news media at length is shocking.

There was a single man who felled the press: a US businessman by the name of Donald J. Trump. I had not intended to mention this improbable press slayer in this book; though, circumstances compel me to include the one person who took on an entire profession — and *won*. The press, not just in the US, but globally, are still in shock that the US reporters' collective best efforts proved to be no match for a man with no political experience — but since the 1970s, was a master without peer in controlling the press.

If the news media has taken a hysterical and childishly petty disdain for him, it is merely a case of a one-sided love affair that soured. Once upon a time, Trump shamelessly and vigorously courted the press, and they, in turn, shamelessly and vigorously threw themselves at him, writing stories about him that had no business being covered, because there was no story there at all. They heaped on the accolades on "The Donald" and they were his greatest fans.

The relationship turned over time, and when Trump discovered that Twitter — which "was like owning *The New York Times* with no overhead", as he reportedly likened it — could help him completely bypass the media, he promptly dumped them. The scorned and the jilted were furious at the slight, vowing to malign him and openly support his rival for the US presidency. Hillary Rodham Clinton had previously been the object of the press's cruel coverage, as she had many insufferable faults, an oblivious hubris that sabotaged her at every turn, and no bubbly personality to charm them; however, suddenly, Clinton was the belle of the press's peculiar and twisted farce of a ball, and efforts to bury their one-time love, Trump, were in overdrive. But they could do nothing to stop him.

They had a very good track record at derailing careers in US politics: stopping one-time candidate Gary Hart from vying for office with a single photograph, which hinted he was not all that into marital monogamy. Richard Nixon's position as president was no match for two young reporters, either.

But with Trump — a man who they knew all too well — they

were powerless against him, and their narrative that they were always the righteous protagonist winners turned out to be mere spiteful fantasy.

They did not see Trump's rise or that it meant their fall was just around the corner, but he was not the architect of their irrelevance in modern society: it was journalists themselves who made their profession one to distrust and ignore.

Even as a twenty-something journalist, I saw the cataclysm coming. I saw it, and did what I could to snap the profession out of its slumber, but journalists long-ago forgot how to see their surroundings, and hence, could not see their own downfall approaching.

This book chronicles the demise of journalism: not only how and why it came to be, but also what its replacement needs to do in order not to fall into the same vortex that destroyed a once seemingly invincible profession. Society not only needs data to progress and grow, but it also needs proper context. Throwing a barrage of random facts is not enough — we need to be able to make sense of those facts by trained minds, and this is the precise reason journalism has always been a crucial calling.

We must find ways to gather facts, and carefully interpret truth and reality as they are, not as we wish them to be. Journalism is not the medium. It is the art and science of finding and verifying information before disseminating it to the public.

It can be done. It must be done, but it cannot happen until we open ourselves to the truth and reality we now face. Journalists are unwilling to face it, but citizens must not follow their lead of being in denial, and hoping a few cosmetic changes and abandonment of ideals will do it for them.

One important note to reading this book: I have taken many case studies to illustrate my points, but this is not a comprehensive encyclopedia of every journalistic sin ever committed, nor was it ever intended to be one. If a particular strain of virus is not chronicled here in print, it does not mean I have not taken it into my equations. I have selected certain stories and issues that most realistically reflect the key factors that contributed to the fall of journalism, and tried to keep it as current as possible. If I were to take such an epic undertaking, there would be hundreds of volumes, and there is no need to belabor a point.

And now, let us begin at the end.

Part One

A Requiem for a Noble Profession

Chapter One

What was journalism?

It was a special edition of the syndicated version of *Who Wants to Be a Millionaire* and it was "Hometown Heroes" week: the contestants were the three US soldiers who stopped a terrorist on a bus in France and their $100,000 question was: Which of the following groups did not make *Time* magazine's Person of the Year: 1984: Republicans, 1975: Women, 2002: Whistleblowers, or 1960: Scientists?

The group used interesting logic to get to the right answer: it could not be the Republicans, as a news magazine would not take an ideological side. They are to remain neutral; hence no political party could expect such a lofty honor.

In an era where overtly partisan news operations such as the Fox News Channel have replaced fact with opinion, the function of the press has morphed from information-gatherers and disseminators to cheerleaders and enablers. These days, media outlets can openly applaud political parties without feeling fraudulent and unprofessional. It is a different world, but one that came at a price: the press had large audiences, most of whom did not have a college education, but despite the fact that there are now a record number of university-educated citizens with graduates and even doctorates, journalism consumption is at an all-time low. Newspapers, once the heart and soul of a community, have been shuttered, television and radio ratings are in decline, and even Internet news sites are suffering financial losses and are cutting staff as their audiences are losing interest in their listicles.

The anarchy has had its consequences, and the first is that journalism has lost its place. In the 2016 US presidential election, the press took sides, deciding that the Democratic candidate

Hillary Rodham Clinton was the shoo-in over her Republican rival Donald John Trump. She had all the positive press, as the media decided she was the logical and more rational choice. There once was a time when the press would have stayed out of such matters, yet they banked on their perceived power to guide the electorate to Clinton.

It was a peculiar decree, given that Clinton wasn't always blessed with positive media coverage. In fact, she had received negative press coverage for decades, from the moment her husband Bill Clinton ran for US president, to her stint as Secretary of State. Her press before Trump ran for president was consistently negative and often personal. While Trump repeatedly complained that the election was "rigged", Hillary Clinton claimed that a "vast right-wing conspiracy" was trying to destroy her husband, when his affair with White House intern Monica Lewinsky was exposed.

When she first ran to be on the Democratic presidential ticket in 2008, she was seen as inferior to the highly endearing, sociable, and charismatic Barack Obama, who eventually won the nomination and two terms in the White House. She failed to inspire then, and even at her second go, she still played second fiddle to rival Bernie Sanders, who electrified younger crowds and she narrowly eked out a victory.

She was hardly ever a media darling, but when Trump blew into the campaign, suddenly Clinton's image fortunes radically changed. Trump had publicly toyed with running for president once before, in the late 1980s, but as a Democratic candidate, yet his past as a more liberal-thinker had been buried and his press also changed, and as a result of which he faced uniformed media scrutiny.

But on Election Day, all the journalistic decrees were ignored and Trump won. The press was shut out and of all the media players from print to the Internet, only Matt Drudge had a pulse on the mood of Americans.

How did journalism fall from being king-maker, gatekeeper, agenda-setter, and fate-sealer, to becoming irrelevant?

Some in the profession, such as Ian Gill, theorize the news producers should be publicly funded with tax dollars, but that theory misses the point: if journalism was truly useful and connected to audiences, they would buy it voluntarily, and not be forced to fund it against their will, even if it does not provide any use to them.

That line of thinking completely ignores the fact that if journalism were doing its job, there would be no need for charity, as people would willingly tune in or read the product.

Worse, and more disgraceful to the profession, is that journalists are those who are supposed to know the mindsets, problems, and realities of the world they observe and cover for a living: if they have no pulse on the public they report on and report to, then they have no business being in the profession. It means what they are presenting is inaccurate or untruthful. It is tantamount to being a fraud.

If there is one profession that cannot use ignorance of the zeitgeist or ortgeist as an excuse, it is the profession that chronicles the times and places that are made up of people from every walk of life. Journalists are part fact-gatherers, part storytellers: to do either with competency, one must be aware of truth, reality, and the perception of both in the general public. To be a journalist is to be a historian, psychologist, anthropologist, criminologist, economist, and psychologist.

In other words, a journalist is the eye of reason amid the chaos, anarchy, unrest, destruction, and zealousness. They are to provide facts and evidence so people can make the right, productive, rational, and sensible choices according to their own wants, needs, beliefs, and circumstances. It is not a pulpit to preach or tell people how to think or what to do. If something is not working properly, it is the journalists who are to let people know. It is not about passing judgment or talking down to audiences.

Yet journalism has been misused to belittle groups, push agendas, misrepresent people, and gossip with propaganda and manipulation. Audiences could see it and began to tune out.

If the traditional press had taken a turn downward, online journalism did not pick up the slack or improve the product. The tone was always smug, sanctimonious, and snarky, but it also has a distinctly partisan bent: Left or Right, balance is nowhere in the equations, yet print had also been openly partisan during the Penny Press era. That is, until technology improved and wire services made it more financially beneficial to replace the rhetoric with objective reportage; hence, journalistic liberation began.

When online journalism emerged, however, it took decided steps back to a partisan spin. Technology made it simple to get audiences searching for validation and reassurance that their biases were truth. It seemed foolproof, yet despite the seemingly popularity of sites such as *BuzzFeed* and *Politico*, their power is not all that it seems, as they are tethered and their audiences restricted.

Nowhere has journalism's — and social media's — diminishing clout shown to be fact than the otherwise improbable Trumpian Rise to president. The media had been unrelenting in highlighting and stating that Republican candidate Donald J. Trump was too crude and unqualified to be in the Oval Office, while the Democrat contender Hillary Clinton was hyper-qualified. Trump did not fit the pattern of a president; ergo, he would lose. He was the inept and boorish villain to Clinton's faultless and sensible heroine, and every major media outlet projected a Clinton win by a comfortable margin.

So certain were journalists that Clinton would be victorious that they made their predictions public with authority. Both traditional and online journalists and commentators used bold authority to make their decrees.

Californian Professor Philip Seib certainly did so on July 30, 2016 in the *Huffington Post*, when he erroneously postulated that Hiilary Clinton would win. He held this view because voters, male and female from both political stripes, would be compelled to vote for the first female president, even if they did not like her, and that Trump could not get his voters compelled to go out and mark their ballots.

He was hardly the only one who did not grasp the reality around him. Cliston Brown, writing in the *New York Observer* (a property owned by Trump's son-in-law, interestingly enough), made the same prediction on November 7, 2016, proffering that an "unprecedented Latino turnout" would propel her to the White House. While Trump was closing the gap, it meant very little, as other elections of the past showed similar narrowing of support, only to see the candidate to lose, assuming that all factors of past elections were the same as this one.

The Canadian and UK press were also in complete lockstep with their US counterparts, as *The Guardian*'s Martin Kettle did in his October 27, 2016 piece, assuming the pre-election polls were representative and had no confirmation bias. Taking Trump's campaigning in states such as North Carolina and Utah as a sign that he would "defend [his] own territories rather than attack in Clinton's" missed the point that there may have been another reason to shore up strongholds. This is because Clinton had lost states such as Michigan and Pennsylvania, where it was assumed voters there would stay loyal. There were assumed safe states, where Clinton had not visited for months during her campaign, and the results were catastrophic for her bid for president.

It was also catastrophic for the press as their role of barometer. Almost none in the press saw the obvious discontent brewing in the election: it was class warfare with the well-heeled, university-educated big-city citizens supporting Clinton, while the financially-struggling blue-collar Americans backed Trump (referred by the degrading euphemism "populist"), with many of those voters stating their feelings of discontent. The problem was that journalists ignored their voices and dismissed them as racist, sexist, and unimportant.

If reporters were scientists, they would have conducted a bad study. Their sample size was skewed and not representative of the group they were studying. It is not just the limousine liberals and their champagne socialist children who knew how to get to a voting station and mark their choice on a ballet. The willful ignorance did not just cost Clinton a victory, it showed that the press had lost its clout and competence.

There were signs screaming that Clinton was not going to grab that brass ring: there was no sign that the Democrats were going to gain the majority in The House or The Senate, hinting that the notion that the country was moving in a liberal direction was highly unlikely. It was also unlikely that the argument that "it was Hillary's turn" to be president was going to sway enough voters to give in to anyone's sense of entitlement, particularly to those voters who were in fear of becoming homeless and destitute because they believed an anemic economy would keep them jobless. Those voters were repulsed by celebrity gossip and entertainment news *TMZ*, a site that chronicled celebrities such as Miley Cyrus telling them how to vote as they sipped champagne, and bragged about their mansions and designer shoes, as those stars had their more literate assistants write their Tweets for them. The dispossessed had a way to protest by ballot. While journalists fawned over those celebrities and gave them all the free advertising they could, they could not see that the pendulum was swinging the other way, ready to hit them — and Cyrus like a wrecking ball. A haughty and clueless Clinton decreed that those who supported her rival were a "basket of deplorables", and the equally arrogant and ignorant press forgot to turn on their critical thinking skills and took it as permission not to do their jobs. Only after the election did many in the press concede that it wasn't "rednecks" with a fear of lattes and Pilates who voted for Trump.

The press was also guilty of forgetting the golden rule of US politics: whoever looks like they would be the most fun at a cocktail party wins The White House.

While Clinton suffered an epic defeat, it was the news media that lost their final battle, and with the covertly elegant victory of Donald Trump, they lost the war.

After all, those in the business of chronicling reality's big picture never saw the tsunami of desperate rage coming at them. They did not just lose credibility — the one thing no journalist can afford to lose — but also face.

It wasn't always like this. Once upon a time, the press could create or destroy people, governments, companies, and entire countries. CEOs resigned in shame. Actress Barbara Payton was once one of Hollywood's comeliest and highest paid actresses, but after bad publicity, her career had been so badly derailed, she literally became a prostitute who worked the streets, dying at age 39. Ohio Congressman James Traficant lost power and ended up serving a prison sentence. Richard Nixon was the president forced to resign after two young journalists exposed Watergate. There was no limit to how far and lasting a journalist's narrative could permanently influence the history books.

The press dictated how people were to think and people had once happily complied. One of the most stunning examples of the herd mentality was the naming a group of popular young actors *Brat Pack* in the 1980s. David Blum wrote a cover story for *New York* magazine on June 10, 1985 that pigeonholed and confined a group of twenty-something thespians, as he brought them to task for not graduating from college, but having the audacity to admire publicly, and be influenced by actors who did.

Blum cruelly skewered these actors, despite the fact they were still successful in their careers without it. The author of the piece looked down on his subjects, and his own prejudices had serious long-term consequences for their careers, infantilizing them needlessly. The entire career was made-up labels, and smug assessments and predictions that mostly did not come true, but there was a time when such amateur tactics were taken seriously in the public domain. While the structure of journalism hasn't changed, the impact has been diminished.

Despite its constant presence, the influence of the press is now negligible. It is a shocking fall from grace that is hard to imagine for those who saw titans fall when the press turned on them, exposing their dirtiest sins.

Watergate marked just how powerful journalism could be: two young *Washington Post* reporters Bob Woodward and Carl Bernstein took down a president with their methodical and solid reportage. Now, hundreds of reporters could not see the cagier Trump best Clinton as they reported about the election non-stop; nor did their decrees convince unhappy voters that Clinton was the only option on the ballot.

For a profession that makes its way into people's homes, its methods and ways are poorly defined. Journalism was always murky with its terms such as objectivity, balance, and fairness, let alone what made a person a journalist. Despite its one-time power, it was a profession of the shadows. We can cheer or mourn its demise, yet what we are cheering or mourning eludes many. So what was journalism?

Journalism was more than a profession: it was an ideal. It was the idea to inform society of the world around them, because knowledge is power. It is liberating and essential. You cannot find the right solutions on instinct alone. You cannot find the right solution if you have lies. Journalism was the simple solution: have those who dig by asking questions to bring light in the darkness. It has survived numerous forms over the ages and has managed to survive in its various forms, each with its own set of unique variables:

- Print was the First Medium, and of all the media, it has the most liberties to allow more facts in stories.

- Radio was the Second Medium, and it humanized stories as it is still about voices and sound, and can be heard anywhere without distraction, even if it cannot provide facts the same way print can.
- Television was the Third Medium of vision, putting a face on a story. Print has pictures, but television's moving pictures puts people in news consumers' living rooms. It is highly personalized, but at the expense of details.
- The Internet is the Fourth Medium, the one that blended the other three together as it broke the stranglehold of the gatekeepers. Now, anyone could broadcast to a world-wide audience. The news cycle became shorter, and articles became tainted with trivial news of pseudo-celebrities, press releases, and partisan vitriol, as there were no checks and balances to weed out lies and hoaxes.

Yet none of these media have been able to change radically the fortunes of journalism. Not one has altered the game. Not one sees the depth of seriousness of their fall, and the current strain of journalism has veered to an extremist form of partisan reportage: it has become demonizing propaganda where the object is to feign morality while making the most disturbing and unfounded of comments. It is completely devoid of facts, but filled with vitriol of the worst sort.

For example, former *Politico* scribe Julia Ioffe (who had written three articles for *Columbia Journalism Review* as well, among other publications) had written a vile and obscene tweet regarding the relationship between President Trump and his eldest daughter Ivanka in December 2016. The disturbing jab had negated any pretense of Ioffe being a genuine journalist, and while *Politico* had distanced themselves from her remarks and severed their ties with her, *The Atlantic* chose to have the bitter tantrum-thrower on their roster instead. Once upon a time, journalists had enough dignity, talent, and sensibility to ever stoop to playing in the gutter. Now, national outlets employ those who are incapable of reflecting rationally without resorting to childish propagandistic smears as they have become oppressively intolerant in any worldview that deviates from their own.

Ioffe is hardly the only journalist who could not comprehend that a vicious worldview was not a desirable trait for someone in the news business: *Daily Mail* columnist and LBC broadcaster Katie Hopkins had also lost all perspective in a May 2017 tweet after the Manchester terrorist attack by suggesting the answer to the violence was a "final solution". The backlash of her use of a Nazi phrase resulted in her losing both of her positions. Neither Ioffe nor Hopkins could see reality as their narratives stood in the way, making their utility as news producers highly questionable.

Even the media's post-mortems of the 2016 Election were completely oblivious to reality. It is difficult to imagine a single profession with such a lack of self-awareness as they march lockstep while they destroy their own industry. As journalist icon Walter Lippmann had written in 1913, "Where all think alike, no one thinks very much", yet journalists have not taken those words to heart, and opt to mere parrot one another as they refuse to think critically or think for themselves, mimicking the majority of test subjects in psychologist Solomon Asch's famous experiment. It is as if they have no idea what they are supposed to do as journalists and hope repeating someone else's words will hide their ineptitude, yet it is their own unthinking words that expose them.

For example, *New York* magazine's Jonathon Chait's May 11, 2017 piece entitled "Donald Trump Tries to Explain Economics to *The Economist*. Hilarity Ensues". was a typical propagandist diatribe worthy of a Saul Alinsky rule for radical — save that President Trump's lowest earnings far exceeded that of the wealthiest *Economist's* journalist's paycheck — and perhaps being able to explain *economics* is less important than proving one can apply it in the real world.

For another, the *Washington Post*'s Margaret Sullivan did not exactly see the light in her November 9, 2016, media column about why the news media failed to see a Trump victory. She discussed how no reporter "seemed to believe it in their bones" and that "journalistic conventional wisdom" pegged Clinton to win. She discussed how their erroneous predictions would force reporters to "eat crow", for perhaps years, and the worst was that "the media helped to give Trump his chance".

The press did not help Trump at all, not even inadvertently: they were *ignored* and voters did not vote out of spite. Sullivan fails to grasp just how irrelevant the media has become. It is white noise. But in the drive to rationalize willful blindness, Sullivan tried to put a positive spin on journalistic snobbery, assuming that, while journalists used the mask of cynicism and pretended to be "hard-bitten", but they could also "be idealistic, even naïve". Sullivan stated that journalists were desperate to think that the US was too decent and civil to vote for "someone so crude, spiteful, and intemperate", and that she couldn't fault her fellow journalists for their beliefs.

Journalists weren't being naïve — they were being gullible, conniving, arrogant, uninformed, lazy, and sloppy. They still did not hear the millions of voters who openly stated they were not voting as silly hero-worshipping fans: they voted for a candidate who made their biggest problem — their economic quagmire — his top priority. It was a pragmatic choice, with limited and uninspiring candidates. If Sullivan did not have the bravery or sense to fault journalists for their limited thinking, millions of news consumers do.

Fortune magazine was also thick when it came to the true value of the media's power, claiming that the news media were "forced to lend Trump legitimacy" to stay financially viable and that journalistic ideas about objectivity compelled them to give him a platform, "regardless of the ridiculousness of his claims". Reporters were hapless and blameless victims forced to "entertain" Trump, even if to disprove his claims, further trapping them "in the quagmire known as 'false equivalence'."

There are several problems with this part of sophistry: journalists are not babes in the woods or mindless victims. There is no shortage of things going on in the world at any given time, and reporters can not only pick and choose what they cover, but they can also choose to report what really goes on at canned events, such as election campaigns. They can tell the world the deals and demands public relations firms make for reporters to gain access to their clients. They can cover what happens behind the scenes instead of keeping silent. There is no "false equivalence": the press had been covering Trump since the 1970s without a hiatus, knowing full well most of the coverage was not newsworthy. It was cheap and easy filler and it was the reporters' choice to give him free publicity for decades. Trump was not the new kid on the scene, and reporters had behaved no differently toward him during the election than they did on his first day out in the public eye.

It did not matter if the press gave Trump legitimacy or ignored him: he largely bypassed the press as he traveled the country, stumping in town halls and rallies. He may have used Twitter, but it was his face-to-face dealings with people that sealed the deal: Trump was humanized to potential voters and he proved he was not too important for them; he was the sympathetic billionaire wearing hardhats and baseball caps as he spoke directly to the poor, who were willing to give him their vote in exchange for a better life. For the unemployed small-town dispossessed, seeing the fabulously wealthy Trump in their hopeless corner of the world did more than any Tweet ever could — or fawning newspaper story ever could. The press underestimated the power of being in the same room as your audience. They were glued to Facebook and Twitter, thinking that was the equivalent to going out in the streets to feel the shifting times. Besides, Trump was courting the poor who had nothing to lose, the very audience advertisers and the press ignore, and their classist beliefs came to annihilate the last of their relevancy.

Even months after Trump's victory exposed the press's chronic tone deafness, those in the business could not see it. Just how oblivious were they? Jack Shafer may have been one of the worst offenders in his May 2017 *Politico* article when he hinted that those in the business knew nothing about it. He was in denial that the confirmation biased blinded those such as him: "But the knowing-bias charge never added up: No news organization ignored the Clinton emails story, and everybody feasted on the damaging John Podesta email cache that WikiLeaks served up buffet-style. Practically speaking, you're not pushing Clinton to victory if you're pantsing her and her party to voters almost daily" before deciding that, "The national media really does work in a bubble, something that wasn't true as recently as 2008". His article comes a quarter century too late, and even then, offers no incite of value.

Shafer may use painful and unhip slang gratuitously, but what he does not do is realize that the media had been in decline long before 2008. The press does not live in a bubble: they live in an alternative reality. The fact that Shafer must ask "What went so wrong? What's *still* wrong?" speaks volumes as the very questions indict the news media on every level: the press has no clue what is happening in their own world, their own profession, or inside their own heads, making any of their observations useless; ergo, journalism has gone from being a critical part of society to white noise.

Shockingly enough, not everyone has come to grips that journalism used to be a thing. It has become nothing: it is as devoid of utility as any teenager's vanity blog or Facebook page.

There is no question that journalism is essential for society to progress and flourish, as it helps stop problems from remaining hidden, causing a systemic breakdown. The problem is why has an entire profession itself had a series of breakdowns that brought it to its near extinction — and how to rebuild it from scratch.

This is the book that chronicles the decay of a once-powerful profession, how it came to be, and why it happened. This is your guide to understanding the purpose and essence of journalism: why it exists, its power, its limitations, and how to create it to inform, express, and to find truths in relation to reality. It will show the ways it can be rebuilt so that it can be something again — something that is truthful, credible, reliable, valid, informative, honest, realistic, and helpful to all, both individually and collectively.

But to know how to reinvent journalism, it is critical to examine how it exists and why it collapsed in the first place.

Chapter Two

The seeds of destruction

Scandal is a concept that is linked to another concept: publicity. Without others knowing the problem, there is no scandal. Publicity is also a concept linked to another concept: the mass media, particularly the news media. It is not enough to make wrongdoing a scandal: one needs a credible vessel that can reach enough people who agree that what has transpired was malicious wrongdoing.

Not all wrongdoing results in scandal. Some are permanently hidden; some gain too little attention; some gain too little credibility; and some are not seen as malicious enough, if at all.

Journalism was the art of specific information dissemination: letting the public know where there were breakdowns in society, government, business, cities, nations, religions, and anywhere else. It was the vehicle to turn malicious wrongdoing into scandal: someone overtly paying for ads does not have the same effect than if the same information is verified and then validated by a disinterested third party. There is no agenda, and they have experience sifting through information and know what is a fact, opinion, truth, and lie.

Journalism is a peculiar profession as it is an ideal: credible fact-gatherers verify information by using credible sources, and reliable and valid techniques. They face threats and obstacles, and though there would be conflicts and dangers, reporters would have the know-how to dodge those landmines and deliver the goods to their audiences. They could stand up to tyrants, turn down bribes, and their specialized knowledge gave them the edge in finding sources, databases, and files in war and in peace.

That was the theory, at least. The model did not take into

account public relations firms, image consultants, or publicists. It did not consider focus groups, market research, or big data, either. It did not take into account that experimental psychologists and scientists could use biometric technology to measure how audiences reacted to what they read, saw, or heard on the news and then refine their messages to take full advantage of their knowledge, while journalists did not keep up with the competition. As Media Sociologist Aeron Davis, a professor of Political Communication at Goldsmiths-University of London and author of the book *The Death of Public Knowledge?* notes: "When you cut to the bone so much, [reporters] can't do the sorts of things they need, leading to a cut and paste form of sourcing. No one leaves their desks anymore". The sourcing is very often press releases from corporations and governments.

It is not to say that it is a Big Brother world where every paranoid conspiracy theorist is right on the money but, as we have seen with social media sites liberally collecting Big Data and using personal information to target individuals for stealth advertising, one would think news producers would be trained, or at least, actively aware of spotting and countering against such an unfair advantage. While there is Data Journalism — a method of using large statistical data with computers to find patterns — it is not a method to take into account how companies take personal information and then find ways to tailor their media campaigns and strategies.

Journalism has not improved its methods for several reasons, but the biggest is that with declining revenue and audiences, they have fewer resources to catch up, let alone get ahead with their investigative tactics and strategies. The divide widens, and we see the effects of the imbalance. In his life, Steve Jobs graced the cover of *Time* magazine eight times, and each time served as an advertorial for one of Apple's products, from the iMac to the iPad. It was million-dollar free publicity in prime real estate, where over 4 million readers were presented a product plug as hard news. A corporation received fawning coverage, while other scandals or problems needed to be exposed to those 4 million readers. It is one thing to profile technology, but quite another to relinquish repeatedly the front page giving uncritical praise for a product.

The accolades gave Apple an edge and raised the profile of Jobs to futurist visionary, but it did nothing to stem the hemorrhaging circulation numbers (though executives' salaries did not decrease, despite their impotency): in 1997, when Jobs made his second cover appearance about Apple finding a lifeline via Microsoft, *Time* had 4.2 million readers. In 2016, there were just 3 million. *Time* was the magazine that set the agenda, but now cannot keep up with the Silicon Valley lords they lavishly praised in their glossy pages. So how did journalism fall behind?

The short answer is that journalists could not see the reality they were given access to chronicle. Or, as Barry Richards, Professor of Political Psychology at Bournemouth University in the UK, said, "commercial pressures, the rise of social media, and the partial collapse of the liberal public sphere of which journalism was a key component" had a role in its current state of affairs.

It is an odd oversight for a discipline whose credibility hinges on accurately reporting on reality. Then again, this is a profession with no governing body, and press councils and broadcast regulators either have no teeth, or choose never to use them. Misaligned reportage eventually alienates news consumers, and they begin to disengage from the press. Some take personal offence when a member of their group is portrayed poorly, but often, many who believed what they heard in the press made decisions that turned out to bring them misfortune.

But the press did not pay much attention to the disenfranchisement, as they took the outrage as a sign they were doing their jobs properly, essentially inoculating themselves from feedback. They could play favorites, having darlings and devils without much worry of the consequences of their rigged games.

Yet on the surface, there seems to be very little to be rigged in the journalistic model. The methods are simple and mundane. Reporters in legacy media outlets are either assigned stories by editors, get tips from both the public and officials, or choose stories they wish to pursue on their own, either through their sources or by scrolling through social media sites such as Facebook or Twitter; though, a few may venture out to the Dark Web to find a nugget. They receive press releases of varying sleekness from different public relations firms or departments, and the chances are good that those in PR may have, at one time or another, been a colleague or at least a fellow journalist.

Governments release statistics and reports, from employment rates to their reactions to various world events. Some events, such as election campaigns, will have automatic fodder from gaffes, promises, debates, and canned events of the photo op variety. Businesses do the same, as do celebrities. There will be ad campaigns, court cases, protests, and stunts to go along with victims of corporate greed or tyrannical criminals, employers, or neighbors. They will conduct interviews, find supporting documentation, evidence, and experts to tell them a story, and then relay the information to audiences through words, photographs, or video or audio footage.

They will attend press conferences. They will ambush people who refuse to give them an interview. They will debate with other panels, offer opinions, and interview regular citizens about their reactions to events.

They may go to court to lift publication bans or argue they have rights to release classified documents to the public. They will interview people in person, over the phone, by video link, or by email.

Once they have collected the information, it will be vetted by an editor or producer, who may ask for additional information.

Fact-checkers may be employed to verify the information in the story, but once the editor and journalist are satisfied the information is ready for public consumption, it is released to the public and is then considered a story with a beginning, a middle, and an end, and there will be roles, from a hero or winner, to a victim, a villain, or an oddball.

Some news will be considered hard; others soft. Hard news revolves around government, justice, law, the economy, and any other facet that impacts daily life for citizens or regions. Soft news is not in the realm of need to know, but want to know, such as fashion, music, entertainment, cooking, automobiles and technology.

Then there is the divide between news and opinion, with columnists and pundits telling the public what they think of the facts reporters have uncovered. Journalists are supposed to keep their opinions out of their product and let the truth of reality speak for itself. This might be reality such as a disabled child being shut out from getting a medical scan because the clinic did not think to invest in an accessible one, or it might be a sea of bodies who were felled because a terrorist drove into them with a transport truck.

For decades, Western countries used this model of journalism to gather and disseminate information. It is a straightforward way of conducting affairs in an industry that serves a general public to keep them informed of a wide array of topics of varying degrees of complexity. It was a given that when dealing with a broad audience on a diverse number of topics, disagreement over what was published and how it was presented would be natural.

Yet disagreement can also come from other motives besides differing opinions. One group of people may be badly betrayed and misunderstood. A reporter may have an agenda and be driven by prejudice. An advertiser may have undue influence on an outlet. A PR firm may have shaped the coverage. A reporter or source may be merely lying. There are still no reliable checks and balances in place to stop any of these problems.

For a fact-based profession, how journalists gather and assess the information they receive has always been murky. When a press release is reprinted verbatim in a newspaper, it is proof that the standards of information verification are anything but vigorous. Credulous journalists have repeatedly reported hoaxes as news with no learning curve: professional media tricksters such as Joey Skaggs and Alan Abel could repeatedly pull a media stunt without suspicion, such as the time he convinced reporters of an old man who put an ATM machine on his tombstone. Sometimes the hoax is a mild one, such as the plight of Balloon Boy, 6-year-old Colorado resident Falcon Heene, who supposedly flew away on a giant helium-filled gas balloon as police and the press tried to find him. The press believed the yarn, despite the glaring red flags that it was all a publicity stunt.

But other times, false information sparks wars when false claims of atrocities are reported as real. Both US-led wars in Iraq had been supported by the media: the first time when false claims of Iraqi soldiers killing Kuwaiti infants was reported as real, and the second when it was claimed Iraq had weapons of mass destruction. Both times, evidence was threadbare, yet the media behaved as if the evidence was definitive. Only after the wars did the truth come out.

Business journalists were also vulnerable to con men, with disastrous results. Claudio Osorio was a Florida-based businessman whose schemes with his company CHS Electronics was nothing more than $40 fraud scheme. *The Miami Herald* and the *Sun-Sentinel*, for example, did not question Osorio or CHS.

In 1996, for example, *The Herald* had covered CHS with positive articles, but what the article did not bother to outline was whether CHS was a genuine company or a scam. A rapid rise was seen as a sign of health, not a red flag of trouble brewing. In a November 18, 1997 *Sun-Sentinel* story, CHS was reported to have purchased "six smaller rivals" and the paper described the plans as putting, "'CHS in a good position to stay at the top', said William E. Cage, an equity analyst at J.C. Bradford in Nashville". Reporters appealed to authorities, but did not look deeper for facts. In a May 9, 1998 article the paper used an identical formula to describe three other acquisitions, noting that "'CHS Electronics treats its acquisitions as subsidiaries and refers to its international operations as an army of entrepreneurs', said Robert C. Damron, principal and equity analyst for Cleary Gull Reiland & McDevitt, based in Milwaukee, Wis".

A reporter would copy information from a press release and then find an authority to put a positive spin on the information. However, the formula used by the *Sun-Sentinel* has failed time and again with grifters being exposed as liars, as journalists are exposed as being useless in spotting the feints and ruses early on.

The crippling blow was a spate of fabricating journalists who were exposed over a twenty-year period: Janet Cooke, whose Pulitzer Prize story in the *Washington Post* entitled "Jimmy's World" was based on a non-existent child drug addict; Stephen Glass, a *New Republic* darling whose majority of his articles were pure fiction; *The New York Times'* Jayson Blair, *USA Today's* Jack Kelley, the *Boston Globe's* Mike Barnicle and Patricia Smith, and NBC's Brian Williams fabricated his valor in covering the Gulf War, and others such as Kim Stacy, Jonah Lehrer, Christopher Newton, Brad Everson, Juan Thompson, Michael Finkel, Catherine Porter, and Francois Bugingo, to name a few.

In 2004 alone, the *National Post*, a Canada-wide daily, fired no less than three reporters for various journalistic transgressions: Everson for fabricating parts of his medical stories; columnist Elizabeth Nickson for plagiarism; and Gillian Cosgove, for "intentional misrepresentations". The paper's rival, *The Globe and Mail*, decided to keep its serial plagiarizer, columnist Margaret Wente, on their payroll despite her record for lifting others' work as her own (just as CNN continues to employ serial plagiarizer Fareed Zakaria, who has been caught, by some reports, in over three dozen cases of thought stealing).

Yet notwithstanding the cascading catastrophe that was tearing down the profession, no one thought to rethink their methods or revise the checks and balances. Glass had previously worked as fact-checker and knew how to bypass their system to peddle out-and-out lies that perpetuated stereotypes of the poor, and infected the public discourse — but also confused our knowledge of what is a lie and what is a fact.

Glass's outright deceptions were not the only thing pushing our regression to know what is fact. Outlets such as the Fox News Channel, that completely traded fact for opinion, made it acceptable to dismiss any fact that went against our opinions. Sophistry that became a confirmation bias shielded those from having to deal with evidence contrary to their ideology. But while Rupert Murdoch's crown jewel enabled the ideologues on the Right, the ones on the Left were no better off, as they had their own enablers masquerading as reporters.

US journalism has thrived in narratives of xenophobia, whether it was the Right-leaning outlets that had openly distrusted those from the Middle East from the Left-leaning outlets that currently distrust anyone from Russia. Fabulists such as Glass often get away with their deceptions, as they understand latent fears and misconceptions of the gatekeepers, and exploit them with seeds of destructive practices.

The fear may have been the fertile lands, but the seeds could never have taken root and grown if journalism was not static in their ways of creating news. There is no science or refinement of the theories of how to create a better news product.

Those seeds took root, as there were no real consequences for reporting propaganda as truth. Not a single reporter, editor, or media baron was arrested or fined for spreading lies that resulted in the death of thousands of innocent civilians, such as the case in both Gulf wars. Journalists could be sued for defamation, but aside from the UK, where the laws make such lawsuits easier to file and prove, most Western countries are far laxer with their libel laws. Few suits, such as former wrestler Hulk Hogan (funded by billionaire Peter Thiel, who had been outed as gay by *Gawker* years earlier) against the website *Gawker*, have actually succeeded in shutting down a major publication or program. There are lawsuits that can impede the financial health of an outlet, however, and it is these instances that journalists point to as proof that they are doing their jobs correctly — and that the assaults are tantamount to a "chill" that discourages news producers from pushing for the truth.

In the *Gawker* case, its employees were quick to blame Thiel for destroying their once powerful online brand. As *Gawker*'s Nick Denton opined on the site's final missive:

> Peter Thiel has gotten away with what would otherwise be viewed as an act of petty revenge by reframing the debate on his terms. Having spent years on a secret scheme to punish *Gawker*'s parent company and writers for all manner of stories, Thiel has now cast himself as a billionaire privacy advocate, helping others whose intimate lives have been exposed by the press... But in dramatic terms, it is a fitting conclusion to this experiment in what happens when you let journalists say what they really think.

Yet journalism is *not* about what a journalist *thinks*. It is not about what a journalist feels, either. It is about *senses*. What does the journalist see or hear? What are the facts? What is the evidence? What is the situation? What are the dangers, the problems, the traps? What is the reality? What is the *relevant* truth?

In the case of *Gawker*, it was a short December 19, 2007 article by Owen Thomas, entitled "Peter Thiel is totally gay, people", that had revealed his sexuality without his consent as the author then went on to speculate how Thiel's sexuality influenced his business philosophy, stating: "I think it explains a lot about Thiel: His disdain for convention, his quest to overturn established rules... That frees him or her to build a different, hopefully better system for identifying and rewarding talented individuals, and unleashing their work on the world". Despite the "it's okay to be gay" coda, the article's necessity was never properly addressed, as Thiel's proclivities had no relevance to his business ventures.

Had *Gawker* been a more useful publication, they may have benefitted from looking into the way Thiel dealt with rivals and opposition. Was he cutthroat and vindictive? Did he treat employees in a certain way if they behaved in a way he did not approve? Had they focused on relevant truths, they would have been better informers giving helpful information — and in this case, they would have been in a better position to help themselves. In the end, they were left flinging anemic insults to the man whose cunning bested them, using yet another irrelevant article about a faded wrestler's sex tape to do it.

The post in question came in 2012, when *Gawker* released the tape of Hogan having an affair with a woman. The reason for the release was explained by A. J. Daulerio:

Because the internet has made it easier for all of us to be shameless voyeurs and deviants, we love to watch famous people have sex. We watch this footage because it's something we're not supposed to see (sometimes) but we come away satisfied that when famous people have sex it's closer to the sex we as civilians have from time to time.

Journalists and those who merely labelled themselves as such often have a pathological tendency to be unable to admit that anyone in their profession could possibly be wrong. In a May 26, 2016 blog entry on the *Huffington Post*, Michelangelo Signorile went into overdrive as he took exception to Thiel telling *The New York Times* that *Gawker* had a tendency of "bullying people even when there was no connection with the public interest".

Signorile failed to grasp the obvious: there are true horrors in the world, from economic terrorism in its infinite forms to corruption, yet *Gawke*r chose to make a man's private life public in such a flippantly derogatory manner. It was not reportage, but petty village gossip readily heard in high-school halls from those too young and inexperienced to know the ramifications of their actions as they let their grade-point average slide and give in to the bullies who lord over them. *Gawker* was clueless to their own surroundings, nor did they have even a rudimentary ability to think about the future, and paid the price. Gossip is personal in nature by definition, and they began a gratuitous spat with someone who retaliated in the same way. Had they exposed corruption or malfeasance, it would have been justified. Instead, they chose to discuss trivialities in a snarky manner, and their actions made them vulnerable to destruction without sympathy. It is a lesson the press seems unable of grasping, as they believe anything they broadcast is newsworthy and sacrosanct by default. It is not.

When a real publication is felled by its own smug insistence of revealing gossip of the utmost unimportance, they become vulnerable to their own trivial pursuits. There were countless cases of those in power abusing their underlings with threats, poor working conditions, sexual harassment, and other true tyrannical forms of sexual skulduggery from the BBC's Jimmy Savile to Bill Cosby or CBC's Jian Ghomeshi, yet *Gawker* had not noticed a single outrage until they found themselves in the hot seat, and then saw only their own struggles as they blamed others for them. Their narrative was they were chroniclers of truth without a single flaw, yet their body of work suggested they were gossips who were the architects of their own demise. They, like many online publishers, rode on the outdated reputational coattails of traditional media outlets and then counted themselves with those of a bygone era.

Though they took easy pot shots at trendy people, as "culture critic" Lili Loofbourow of theweek.com bemoaned, "*Gawker* developed a form of journalism that privileged transparency — especially when it comes to reportorial sausage-making — and *voice. Gawker* posts could be absurdly detailed investigations into Taylor Swift's feud with Katy Perry or 60-word throwaways, but they were always coming from *someone* — a snarky soul with peculiar enthusiasms they were encouraged to chase". But what they did was encourage distractions of disposable entertainers, instead of bypassing those throwaway pseudo-celebrities in the first place.

But not every outlet obsesses with the by-the-numbers sexual romps of the rich and famous, yet they, too, have their own set of problems. For example, wars are particularly problematic for journalists to cover, but there are no specialty schools for students to learn to cover chaos and anarchy effectively. How does one find the truth amid lies and propaganda, especially if a reporter is not fluent in the language, customs, geography, or history in a hotbed of destruction?

Some reporters become vectors of lies and destructive narratives as they merely quote US Senator Hiram Warren Johnson, when he was quoted to have said, "The first casualty when war comes is truth". Whether or not he said it that way, another way, or ever said it at all in 1917 or 1918 was never established one way or another, however. It is shorthand to tell those seeking truth when it is needed the most to suck it up and be content with whatever lies reporters feed them that day.

Some other journalists, such as disgraced former *USA Today* reporter Jack Kelley, seemed to have no problem finding distressed foreigners in unfamiliar lands taking time out from being bombed to give him concise quotes for his newspaper articles. Yet other reporters covering mundane events during peacetime in their own countries struggled to find people who could be as pithy and profound.

Of course, the reason for Kelley's ability was simple: those people existed only in his imagination. He made up names that did not actually exist in any form, showing his cultural ignorance and refusal to conduct even rudimentary research, but his editors did not spot the childish ruses for years.

For years, editors did not need to spot them, either, as those who pointed out errors did not have a wide audience or control of their image, and would be dismissed for being disgruntled, paranoid, jealous, spoiled, insane, naïve, ignorant, evil, or just silly. A reader pointing out that Kelley was making up names and having factually questionable anecdotes in his reports would have been seen as a crank and forgotten.

But when the Internet began to become part of everyday life, those who knew the truth had a new platform that could bypass the gatekeepers. They could start their own blogs — chronicling the errors and lies — and chat forums, and then use social media to put forward their knowledge, observations, and theories, with many of those individuals succeeding in proving those trained professional news producers got it wrong. It would be this alternate pipeline that would prove to be a crippling blow to the traditionalists who once could keep a tight lid on dissent, and framing how to view those who objected to their reportage.

The factors that contributed to journalism's demise are plenty, from its ideals and base assumptions to its lack of scientific experimentation to improve its product, but the profession willfully tethered itself to unproven beliefs and became stuck in the past by its own ideology. The journalistic narrative thrives in a Manichean universe where someone who is labelled a "villain" has no redeeming qualities, while those designated a "hero" or "victim" are seen as above reproach and could not possibly commit the same sins as the designated villain. The narrative remained firmly in place, from the treatment of President Trump versus failed contender Clinton, to more dangerous stories such as making cases for more violent conflicts.

It is an absolutely ridiculous and toxic strategy, as people do not behave like angels when there is war: for example, who is guarding the prisons where rapists and murderers were serving their sentence?

No one, of course — those criminals are on the outside, committing atrocities to their hearts' content. Imagine if there was war in a region and all the prisons were emptied out with no policeman in sight. How safe would an average citizen feel knowing that fact?

Now imagine foreign psychopaths seeing an opportunity to get away with murder by sneaking in to join in the fun.

That is precisely what happens during violent conflicts. Western journalists have repeatedly and conveniently remained ignorant of these truths, just as they were willfully ignorant of the white tents PR firms set up in the areas, spoon-feeding narratives to reporters who then pretended to gather facts from the war zone.

The civil conflict in the former Yugoslavia represents a dark age for the press: it was a war based on economic strategy, not nationalistic sentiment. Public relations firms had spun the narrative that few reporters had the sense or courage to challenge. The Serbs were seen as the aggressors, even though it was other provinces who had declared their independence without regard whether or not other ethnicities in their region preferred to keep the status quo. The Western media took none of the complexities into their accounts, causing misperceptions that haunt the region to this day.

PR firms hired by the fledgling Croatian and Bosnian regimes were constantly sending media outlets press releases and video news releases (VNRs). No one covering the war can deny they were not influenced by the siege of propaganda and be telling the truth.

The lies often went against all logic. A *Time* magazine cover story in 1992 ("Must it go on?") discussed the alleged unfettered evil of the Serbian people and then to illustrate the point, they showed a mass grave, implying that all those people who were murdered were either Croats or Bosnian Muslims.

There was just one problem: the grave markers were all *crosses*, meaning that those were not Muslims buried there, but Christians, perhaps Catholic, as were the Croats, or Eastern Orthodox, as were the Serbs (though many Western journalists covering the war could not understand that Serbs were *not* Greek Orthodox, a very different subset of Christian Orthodoxy).

But the crosses were written in Cyrillic and that meant those were not Croatian casualties as they used the Latin alphabet. By simple process of elimination, the hundreds of dead were Serbian.

Yet *Time* magazine seemed completely oblivious to the fact that each faction may have had different markers for their dead. This oversight is neither justified, nor something one would expect from a journalist covering a civil war.

The press also seemed oblivious to the extent of public relations involvement in the coverage, though the ignorance strained credulity as O'Dwyer's *PR Newsletter* had reported on it (as they are equally reticent on the extent of research such firms had done or commissioned to improve the potency of their product, while journalists have spent nothing on experimental research how to combat their influence). *New Statesman*, a UK publication, wrote about it. Anyone scouring US Justice Department filings would know it, too, as foreign countries who hired US companies were required by law to register. Several European outlets let the information through, such as French journalist Jacques Merlino, who wrote the book *The Truth About Yugoslavia is not Coming Out. Intelligence Digest*, a UK trade newsletter chronicling all matters of international intelligence gathering, also wrote about it.

In other words, if there was a journalist or news producer who did not know who was sending journalists press releases or setting up those handy white tents, it was because the reporter in question did not want to know.

Of course, the media know full well who was feeding them information and misinformation, because the email addresses and the letterheads would be from those public relations firms. They were friends with many of those people who worked there, as many were former journalists and colleagues of those reporters, editors, and producers. So why do reporters fake ignorance?

If you don't know something, you cannot be held responsible for its ramifications. It is a game of optics, where denial is seen as an excuse to push an agenda that contradicts the facts. Take out the facts, and your faulty argument seems logical and natural.

During the Civil War in the former Yugoslavia in the 1990s, there was no shortage of journalists and columnists who condemned the Serbs for wanting to stay in Yugoslavia; yet those civilians wished to break away from a breakaway republic, though those in the industry failed to grasp the significance of it. The war brought fear, resentment, and anxiety to the region on all sides, yet the forced dichotomy of good guy versus bad guy was too much for the press to resist. Conversely, when it came to their own nations, many journalists took a different view of the same problem. The double standard was not unnoticed, and those who felt alienated could easily find an audience of those who felt the same way, courtesy of the Internet. While that war happened on the eve of the Fourth Medium becoming an everyday force accessible to billions of people, the US-led wars in the Middle East that came after and the results gave opponents a platform to be heard. This made spinning traditional narratives more challenging, especially as smartphones and Twitter give average citizens their own amateur breaking news outlet, allowing eyewitnesses to out-scoop the *Washington Post*, or the

Guardian.

This civilian liberation would prove problematic for journalists. Journalists were used to playing God. They could frame mass interpretation of people, nations, companies, and events in very rigid and specific ways, regardless if their interpretations did not square with either reality or truth. They never had to wonder what permanent damage it brought to innocents.

The seeds of destruction began when journalism's power was shown to make and break careers, fortunes, and even lives. It had the power to destroy careers, such as it did with 1950s Hollywood actress Barbara Payton. Though she had her own personal demons, the press had taken a promising career and ruined it, as she died at age 39 as a toothless and destitute street prostitute. Despite having a tumultuous love life and issues with alcohol, her life was no different than countless other starlets save for one aspect: the press did not expose the lives of those starlets, but did so relentlessly with Payton.

But Payton was a minor casualty who is, at most, a footnote. The press had also rightly exposed corruption and swindles, and with each fallen titan, the news media gained more than power: it gained the trappings of having the power of shaping public opinion and keeping the powerful in place. A single whistleblower who found the right reporter could take down corporations who were engaged in dangerous and illegal practices. Governments fell. When they hit their stride, the press was the single most powerful weapon to ensure that no one got too big or out of control.

Yet for all the power it once wielded, journalism is not an academic discipline. It never was. It was the way to disseminate important information to the public. Despite being published at universities, both the *Columbia Journalism Review* (CJR) and the *American Journalism Review* (AJR) merely publish the musings, laments, and self-congratulations of journalists and editors without academic experimentation and research. Furthermore, both have seen their fortunes fall: reporters have lost their credibility, and hence, reason for existence, while the *CJR* and the *AJR* have also lost their relevance. The publication frequency of both has substantially dropped (*CJR* went from being a bimonthly publication to a biannual one, while *AJR* folded its print edition in 2013 before completely ceasing its online publication two years later). Neither publication had offered the profession any sort of roadmap of how to bring a scientific approach to rejuvenate the profession. With articles such as "Newspaper Hunt for New Readers on Instagram" and "Happily, News Orgs Find Success With Humorous Video", it is no wonder *AJR* had no value to the thousands of people losing their news-producing careers as they lost touch with the sifting reality and their mandates.

Without an empirical map giving those in the profession a clue how to do their work in a changing world, the profession began to flounder, believing reporting on the sudden ample cleavage of once flat-chested C-list celebrities would invite the right readers in the right numbers and save the profession. The Internet provides that free of charge, as there is no shortage of willing ambitious exhibitionists. The hard questions were not asked, let alone answered, making the profession a nonfunctioning one. How does a reporter dodge a sophisticated propaganda campaign? What is the best way to interview traumatized children who witness an important hard-news story, such as war or a sex-slavery ring? Why is it important to know how various psychological disorders impact their assessments and interpretations of people and events?

Yet those in the profession are still in the dark about the level of ill-will they have created in the public over the years. A November 30, 2016 *CJR* article written by Philip Eil entitled "Remember, America: Hating the press is not American" did not question why or how the press had alienated its audiences. The article did not wonder how strategists managed to read the press in order to manipulate them or even bypass them. Instead, the article looked down on those supporters who openly distrusted the press as they voted for Trump, as it angrily compared them to fascists who supported Adolf Hitler.

It was true that while there were rightist extremists who supported him; there were many more who were not. They had repeatedly stated in interviews their support for him had nothing to do with anything else, save their fear for the economy. Despite the open and unequivocal endorsements that the press gave to Trump's rival Clinton, millions of voters had other ideas, yet the press did not see how little their opinions mattered.

Eil, like other chroniclers, missed the point in his diatribe: disliking the way an industry comports itself has nothing to do with being "American" or "un-American". The freedom to feel the communications industry in your own nation is failing you does not make you guilty of sedition or treason. Belief-shaming cannot mask the reason why people hold negative beliefs toward the press. The press made Trump an irresistible rebel bad boy, who became more attractive the more authority figures belittled and insulted him. The US press made a former reality show star forbidden fruit, and the article was akin to a meddlesome mother telling her daughter it is un-American to be annoyed by her nagging parents. Eil focuses on the US Bill of Rights and the importance of a free press, but back then, the Internet did not exist. The concept that there would be an alternative to the press that was freer than the gold standard could not have crossed the founding fathers' patriarchal minds.

Eil, and those in the profession, do not understand that freedom of speech may even include propaganda, bias, lies, and outright distortion. However, it does not mean the public will respect those who have allowed bad information to corrupt the information stream, and the public has the same right to express their views of journalism freely as do journalists. Free speech includes expressing disgust with journalists.

Journalists are not above being called on the carpet for their chronic negligence, and it is not "hypocrisy", as Eil fumes, to find them to be unreliable sources of information. The denial does nothing to rebuild credibility with a disillusioned public: journalists are dependent on the public for their survival; not the other way around in an age where Trump, even before he officially took office, could blast a single tweet, and alter the plans of both federal government bodies and multinational companies immediately. He needs no press release, press conference, or press secretary to make his opinions public knowledge. He needs no press. Nor does the public need the press to tell them what a world leader thinks or does.

Eil's misguided arrogance is a shocking attempt to shame the public into ignoring their distrust and discontent with journalists. A September 2016 Gallop poll revealed that only 32% of Americans had a "great" to "fair" amount of trust with their press. With two-thirds skeptical of the news media — the problems of credibility have reached critical levels. In an April 2016 survey, the American Press Institute found that only 6% of respondents had a "lot of confidence in the media". More people distrust the information they hear than believe it, and the increasing skepticism has its consequences.

On August 9, 1974, two young journalists took down a US president. By November 9, 2016, hordes of journalists could not stop a former game show presenter from becoming president.

The loss of journalistic power in less than half a century, particularly in the US, is breathtaking. They are used to presidents bowing to them to get publicity, not happily snubbing and mocking them on the path to victory. One would think reporters writing in a journalism review publication would question their very beliefs and core assumptions, to see why and how they became irrelevant to the functionality of civic life. Instead, they chose to assume their flaws and weaknesses were signs of their absolute perfection, and opted to shoot the messengers; in this case, an increasingly discontent and disillusioned public who were fed up with those very flaws and weaknesses that had led them astray one time too many.

This tunnel vision has slowly eroded the press in critical ways. As Daniel Hallin, Professor of Communication at the University of California, San Diego, notes, journalism has experienced a "collapse of the business model of news organizations, which has to do with the multiplication of channels, the fact that advertisers now have a much more advantageous position relative to media in the market, and the fact that advertising revenue is siphoned off by tech companies like Google and Facebook". Aeron Davis agrees: "The funding model is broken since the Internet came along. The core advertising has migrated elsewhere, but it has not been replaced on the online versions" of traditional outlets.

That seed of arrogance had turned into a toxic weed that poisoned the mindset of an entire profession. In an April 10, 2017 piece, the *Los Angeles Times* still believed there was a difference between the traditional press and the newer partisan propaganda offshoots as it made shallow lines of distinction in coverage of yet another fleeting and nebulously cynical national story revolving around their president. There is no difference: not in mindset, not in purpose, and not in structure. People cannot assess the flaws and shortcomings of others until they admit their own. Journalists cannot see how far they have fallen and so continue to slide straight into oblivion.

Chapter Three

The credibility problem

When Donald Trump gave his inaugural speech on January 20, 2017, there had been those in the press who had not been impressed with it because, as Jay Michaels, one Toronto radio news presenter complained, "It was not flowery".

It is a peculiar complaint to make, yet modern journalism often veers not only into the flowery, but also color. Many editors insist that their journalists give them more than *mere reportage,* but also color.

What is color? Simply put, it is the use of extraneous details to put a "human touch" on a story. How a singer twirls her hair during an interview is an example of color, especially if the article is not about her nervous ticks or recent diagnosis of Obsessive Compulsive Disorder. For example, Evan Osnos' sensational January 30, 2017 article for *The New Yorker* is a case in point. The article in question was about, as the title blared, "Doomsday Prep for the Super-Rich": those Silicon Valley robber barons who seemed to have too much money and free time on their hands and allegedly indulged in survivalist pastimes, such as building bunkers and the requisite training should an Apocalypse arise. "[Co-founder and CEO of Reddit Steve] Huffman, who lives in San Francisco, has large blue eyes, thick, sandy hair, and an air of restless curiosity; at the University of Virginia, he was a competitive ballroom dancer, who hacked his roommate's Website as a prank".

It was a set-up to some dystopian tale of excesses and sophistry, yet the article itself never gave a reason why it was necessary to write about it in the first place: so what if a group of wealthy snowflakes allegedly partake in paranoid behavior? Are they merely indulging in what they believe to be posh, and giving them a façade of toughness? Why is it necessary for them to express it in this manner? Have they conducted their affairs in such a way that if their practices were to be exposed that there would be such an outrage from the public that these tycoons' lives would be in danger by means of revolt and revolution? Is this canard even real, or it a throwback to a 2003 US-television news report entitled "Hunting for Bambi", where naked women could be "hunted" by paying customers with paintball guns? The story was equally sensational, but was later proven to be false.

We do not know the answer to any of the questions, as the author makes no case for any scenario, nor can a news consumer be certain the story is real or mere fabrication. As it stands, it is an article about the sanctioned insanity of those who can afford it, nothing more. Without context, there is only color and gossip, giving the reader no interest, or motive, to read further. There are no facts with color, only hints of how a news consumer should be feeling about the information given. It is a form of nudging readers or viewers covertly, while reducing the number of facts needed to persuade them based on logic.

For such an article to be effective, it all hinges on one thing: journalistic credibility. News consumers must have trust in those giving them information. They must believe the journalists who tell them to believe, think, and feel in a certain way. If journalists do not have credibility, they have nothing.

They had the power to take down world leaders — once, but for that power to sustain itself, reporters needed something else from the public: goodwill. Power is an illusionary concept and requires the benevolence of one side to give the other the leeway to do their jobs and fulfill their mandates. The public asked that journalists tell them the truth and find facts, and in exchange, they would be guided by those truths and facts.

When journalism lost face one time too many, a spell was broken. Reporters took too many gambles with the truth, telling the world Iraqi soldiers took Kuwaiti infants out of hospital incubators to die. They tagged the Iraqis again over a decade later, boldly declaring they had weapon of mass destruction. They sparked wars and were victims of a seemingly never-ending stream of hoaxes, from the benign Balloon Boy hoax to the lurid aforementioned Hunting for Bambi hoax. A *New York Post* reporter interviewed a Washington, DC lawyer named Robert Fisk, believing the man was a predecessor to prosecutor Kenneth Starr during then President Bill Clinton's impeachment trial. The trouble was he was not Robert *Fiske,* who *was* the prosecutor in question. Fisk decided not to correct the reporter, giving an outrageous interview, and the reporter was left humiliated for his half-effort.

The mistakes kept piling up as reporters proved to be unteachable. Grifters feigning illness convinced journalists they were in need of fundraisers, and the press obliged. People in positions of power who got there by plagiarizing were touted as capable people of integrity. Pyramid scheme conmen were presented as titans of industry. Innocent people were portrayed as killers, and found themselves sentenced for crimes they did not commit.

Sometimes, it was the journalist who committed those transgressions, yet the problems did not end there. They began to write extensively about the latest happenings on reality shows over the abuse institutionalized children endure, such as the shocking case of the BBC's one-time iconic presenter, Sir Jimmy Savile. This presenter's savage and extensive sexual abuse of children had gone unchallenged, and though his employers were in the business of watching the world around them as they exposed predators and abusers, they did not use the same vigilance when it came to exposing one of their own. It was the same in the case of CBC's radio personality Jian Ghomeshi, who had harassed female employees, who complained, but were ignored. When the BBC's program *Newsnight* planned to air a story about Savile's dark side, the story had been nixed by management, making a deplorable situation one of true revulsion.

It was not always the sins of commission that eroded the credibility of the profession. Sometimes, it was journalists' lack of foresight that also contributed to their professional demise. US journalists did not see a Trump presidency, and it was the final nail in the profession's coffin. Journalists had loudly declared that they would take on the forty-fifth president, yet for all of their chest-thumping, their myopic understanding of their surroundings still fail them in the present. Their sources have so far failed them when it comes to keeping up with the unpredictable commander in chief, making them sound more as if they were obsessed jilted ex-lovers bent on making the world hate their ex, than serious reporters in tune with reality in order to find the truth.

When the Brexit side won the referendum in the UK months earlier, the outcome stunned journalists around the world, who had been blindsided by the results. For one, their reliance on polling companies proved to be an error: neither group had a real pulse on the outcome, an odd oversight considering both are supposed to be experts in reality. But as journalists are supposed to cover their surroundings by observing it, their failure to see the outcome is more troubling.

The pollsters told them the UK would vote to stay in the EU, but wouldn't their daily interactions with the public give them a clue that perhaps the pollsters were not reading the right signs? While there have been a variety of explanations as to why pollsters erred (design flaws being on the top of the list), no such plausible excuse exists for reporters. They might have *teams* covering a single issue, yet they failed to *feel* the pulse of the very people who not only watch them, but are also the voters who opted for an exit. They did not see their discontent in the papers or on the newscasts.

The news consumers were also the newsmakers in this case, yet they saw the divide between journalists' perceptions of reality and reality itself. That chasm cannot be too far apart for reporters to maintain the link of trust they have with audiences. The blow was noted globally by many other foreign reporters, including those in the US; however, they would soon find themselves making the same grave error in judgment.

Editorials in both the UK and the US had been out of sync with how the majority of Brexit voters had *felt*. It was more than the polls that deepened the chasm: it was the sentiments expressed on newscasts and in the newspapers. As Aeron Davis puts it, "journalists lost authority and connectedness" with the public. Somehow, there was a lack of ideological diversity with regard to Brexit and the presidential victory of Donald Trump. Some in the press began to speak about the rise in "populism", a euphemism for what was once dubbed as the Great Unwashed. Trump supporters had been portrayed as uneducated rubes, when exit polls showed it was the white college-educated voter who had voted for the real estate magnate and former reality show host.

Some in the US press had assumed UK's errors could not possibly happen to them, as they saw themselves as authorities who had experts tell them that a Clinton victory was the only possible outcome. They did not heed the words of justice secretary Michael Gove who famously (or infamously, depending on your perspective) said that in the UK, "people in this country have had enough of experts".

For example, on June 24, 2016, *The New York Times'* Nate Cohn's column "Why the Surprise Over 'Brexit'? Don't Blame the Polls" had begun with the opening salvo: "Here we go again. Yet another failure in the world of election forecasting", yet his predictions over his own country's presidential election could be summed up with the headline of his October 17, 2016 piece: "Fewer Polls This Year, but They Point in Same Direction:

A Clear Clinton Lead". Cohn, whose political decree in their own headline to be "*New York Times'* new young gun on data", was firing blanks like the rest of the press. The new breed is as oblivious to reality as are the veterans — neither of which has an excuse to be so.

The insensitivity to their world has made their decrees meaningless. No credibility translates to no goodwill or trust, making journalism in its present form obsolete. How did lies, rumors, spin, and even propaganda destroy media credibility? It is best seen as a bad marriage between news producers and news consumers: the former had made its vows to society, who believed them and trusted them on their word alone.

Slowly, one journalistic transgression rocked audiences, but the press always made an excuse, localizing the error or negligence to a case of a single reporter lapsing — and the rest always promising to change and not repeat the error again. Yet with the next scandal, news producers made sure it was known that without them, democracy and freedom were in peril. They were the breadwinners of facts, and a slip-up here or a lie there was a small price to pay for being guarded.

The scandals kept coming, from *Washington Post's* Janet Cooke fabricating a child drug addict — winning a Pulitzer for her deceptions — to Stephen Glass fabricating stories and backup material for his numerous articles, to *The New York Times's* Jayson Blair also making stories up from whole cloth. There were numerous US columnists who fabricated their wares.

Some of those dishonest journalists went on to be accused of more felonious undertakings. Juan Thompson, who was a journalist for the online publication *The Intercept*, had been caught fabricating parts of his stories and used other deceptive means on the job, and was subsequently dismissed by the publication. On March 3, 2017, he was arrested for making at least eight bomb threats against several Jewish cantors, but not before he tried to pin the threats on a former girlfriend. Thompson was destructively troubled and by accounts, anti-Semitic, yet he managed to make it all the way to *The Intercept*. His background was so troubling, that it is a wonder a muck-raking publication would have ever hired him in the first place.

He was not the only journalist with a volatile nature. R. Foster Winans, a *Wall Street Journal* reporter who used his position to indulge in a little insider trading, was discovered, and convicted of securities fraud in 1985, serving nine months in prison for his misuse of his position.

Perhaps most shocking of all, was Vester Flanagan, a former television journalist for a CBS-affiliate in Roanoke, Virginia who was dismissed in 2013 after repeated run-ins with colleagues. He apparently sought a belated vengeance and shot and killed his former colleague Alison Parker and cameraman Adam Ward on live television on August 26, 2015, before he eventually turned the gun on himself — but not before he posted his crime on social media. He had accused Parker of making racist comments and filed an unsuccessful complaint against her, though reports had shown he had issues with several colleagues and had other "performance issues" that he failed to resolved before his firing.

Most troubled journalists were never homicidal in nature, but their transgression of choice is the standard fabricating stories, from a May 1991 television news story from reporter Wendy Bergen's false dog-fighting story (she had a cameraman film the fake anonymous footage that resulted in her being convicted of conspiracy and dog fighting), to *Details* magazine senior editor Bob Ickes who was blamed for not only fabricating an entire August 2002 article entitled *Dudes Who Dish,* but went so far as to put another journalist's name — Kurt Anderson — on the byline, though Anderson knew nothing of the piece or that his name would be on an article he had nothing to do with.

And if reporters weren't the ones lying, they were the ones believing ridiculous canards, from reporting the babies and incubators hoax that spurned the Gulf War to the weapons of mass destruction that proved to be anything but. Eventually, the erosion broke the spell with audiences, especially after someone else came along to make a new promise of greater freedom: online journalism was younger, hipper, more attractive, and promised to give a greater say to audiences in how they got their news, as well as provide them a platform to give their opinions. Traditional journalism did none of those things: they were the ones who gave the opinions, were more autocratic, and rarely gave a voice to citizens, save for an occasional Letter to the Editor, or guest column.

The new partner was a swaggering and confident player, and traditional journalism could not compete, as they had allowed one lie too many to get past their gates. Their promises for a better world were in dispute, but they would still insist the world could not function without them. This was despite the fact that the younger model was assuring them that not only would the world keep spinning, but audiences would also finally have their voices heard throughout that world unfiltered and unedited.

It cannot be emphasized enough the damage the double blow took to the profession: had journalists been more vigilant, the Fourth Medium would not have made the damage to the profession that it did. The Fourth Medium would have enhanced the profession, not made it a hindrance to the health of society.

As technology improved and altered our world, it seemed there were no shortage of journalistic scandals to destroy the profession's credibility. News Corps' UK newspaper arm found itself in a global scandal when it was revealed the newspaper, the *News of the World*, had hacked phones to get scoops on the Royal family and murdered teenaged girls. The *Boston Globe* fired Mike Barnicle and Patricia Smith — both high-profile columnists, when it was revealed they both had fabricated parts in their column. Canada's *National Post* had to rid themselves of no less than three columnists within a single year because of their dubious behaviors. The scandals were large and disturbing, particularly those in the US, which seemed to suggest the profession was one of neglectful anarchy. From *USA Today*'s Jack Kelley who made it a habit to fabricate his stories, to the *Owensboro Messenger*-Inquirer's Kim Stacy whose columns chronicled her bogus illness to readers, there is no shortage of reporters who disseminate untruths.

Their motives were not to inform the public. They wished attention, pity, envy, and a paycheck, but an interest in a functioning society did not cross their minds.

The public eventually took notice and began to drift away.

Some countries have seen a greater and more rapid deterioration of their media landscape. In 2016, Canada found itself in the midst of a complete media collapse that has no relief in sight. Daily newspapers, such as the *Guelph Mercury* and the *Nanaimo Daily News*, have been scuttled after well over a century of reportage, as had *Saturday Night* magazine, a news publication in business since 1887, also seen its last by 2005. Its spiritual replacement, *The Walrus*, has not lived up to the original, and had been scandalized in 2014. The Ontario government's crackdown on the illegal use of unpaid interns exposed the publication's secret to staying afloat in a time where circulation was in a free fall and online versions were not making up for the slack.

Canadian journalists began to panic, and in response, the Public Policy Forum (which, according to its website, touts itself as "an independent, non-governmental organization dedicated to improving the quality of government in Canada through dialogue among leaders from all sectors of Canadian society") put out a report entitled "Shattered Mirror". It was a melodramatic and simplistic pitch for taxpayer support, to enable their broken models of news-gathering and dissemination. The solution according to the report was for private enterprise to be paid for by the government, regardless of whether or not the public was rejecting journalistic products in droves (see Chapter Five for a more detailed discussion of the report). The cash infusion would do nothing to stop the reasons why the public no longer trusted the press.

Nevertheless, the analogy of a shattered mirror was appropriate: the press for too long had only looked at themselves, becoming increasingly unable to see the world around them as their audiences became enraged at the arrogant neglect and tuned out. When the mirror shattered, the press could no longer see themselves for what they had become.

Canada is not the only Western nation clueless to who they are: *The New York Times* sent a blast email to subscribers in January 2017, with the message "Discover the truth with us", as if it were recruiting faithful to a religion rather than a serious information-dissemination industry. The problem is journalists have lost sight — they have been running on their hamster wheels, assuming they were moving forward or even upward, but they have stayed static as the world began to change and look for their information elsewhere. They distrust the current middleman, and now have decided that they can better find what they need themselves.

After all, readers of Canada's *Maclean's* magazine had been greeted with a March 20, 2017 article from Andrew Potter, a former editor at the *Ottawa Citizen* and Director of the McGill Institute for the Study of Canada that was marketed as an essay on the problems suffered by the province of Quebec as evidenced by the "mass breakdown in the social order that saw 300 cars stranded overnight in the middle of a major Montreal highway during a snowstorm last week".

The reason those motorists were stranded, Potter claimed, was not poor government planning or leadership, but "the essential malaise eating away at the foundations of Quebec society".

How exactly the episode proved his thesis was anyone's guess, but Potter continued his singular attack, by stating that, "Compared to the rest of the country, Quebec is an almost pathologically alienated and low-trust society, deficient in many of the most basic forms of social capital that other Canadians take for granted". The facts and figures used to prove this hypothesis was not offered, but Potter claimed that the "absence of solidarity manifests itself in so many different ways that it becomes part of the background hiss of the city". He also noted without proof that Quebec was "a place where every restaurant offers you two bills: one for if you're paying cash, and another if you're paying by a more traceable mechanism", and that "bank machines routinely dispense fifties by default".

The backlash was swift and deafening as Potter began to retract much of what he wrote. For his troubles into exaggeration, unsubstantiated claims, and Francophobia, he resigned from his post as director, while the magazine was forced to admit there were flaws in the piece and noted it removed the references that "all" restaurants gave two checks and that "routinely" dispensed fifty dollar bills "by default". While many journalists defended him as did the editors of *Maclean's* as they made claims of academic censorship as Potter resigned his post, his supporters could not grasp that he had chosen opinion over crafting a coherent argument based on facts. How one snowstorm proved that the province was suffering from a lack of solidarity and malaise was never proven, but the role of a news producer is to explain a situation based on evidence, not on mere diatribe.

Journalists still do not see where they have failed. As Daniel Hallin notes:

> The special authority journalists' enjoyed in their "golden age": had to do with special conditions—their monopoly over the channels of communication, but also political conditions that made it easier to claim authority as "neutral" professionals.

They have lost their status as gatekeepers, along with their goodwill and credibility — but it is the loss of authenticity that has been one of the greatest blows of all.

Chapter Four

The authenticity problem

When the *National Enquirer* crowed in its November 28, 2016 edition that it was one of the few publications that predicted Trump's presidential victory, it did so by taking the low road, making repeated jabs to the "lamestream media". The superlatives were fast and furious. They "scooped the nation's media 'powers' and proved we alone were listening to the unheard majority". It "wasn't until President-Elect Donald Trump's landslide victory on Nov. 8 that our clueless rivals FINALLY caught up with reality!" (printed despite the fact that he *lost* the popular vote by nearly three million). However, there were two points that it had correct: one, that their endorsement of Trump was the first the publication had ever opined on such matters in its ninety-year history, and two, fifty-seven newspapers endorsed Hillary Clinton for president, while *three* endorsed Trump: the *Las Vegas Review-Journal,* the *Florida Times-Union* — and the *National Enquirer.*

Both Bloomberg News and *Vanity Fair* magazine openly speculated whether or not the *Enquirer* was "in bed" with Trump. However, no such articles pondering which publications may have been "in bed" with his rival, or whether a faded tabloid's endorsement meant anything in an age where salacious celebrity gossip has been co-opted by countless online websites, such as *TMZ, Perez Hilton, POPSUGAR, Gawker,* and *Radar Online* that all skew younger and have become more relevant and influential than the forefather. Most of these publications were far more vocal with their disdain and downright repulsion of Trump. The question is not so much whether the *National Enquirer* is in bed with Trump, but why a chorus of hip and trashy sites could not crush an unlikely candidate. Trump seemed like the stern and unsympathetic man who was marrying a woman with children, and he had made no secret that their undisciplined and Bohemian ways were about to be a distant memory on their wedding day.

Far from being influencers, both the soft and hard news sites are not forming society as first envisioned. Like the Wizard of Oz, the men and women behind the curtain may bluster and thump their chests, but their grunts and screeches have fallen on deaf ears, and with that, the unthinkable has happened.

The press has been grappling with an authenticity problem for many years: while they imply what they present is genuine and disseminated with the noblest of intentions, reality disproves their assertions time and again. News is highly processed, and often, it is PR companies that supply most of the fodder: from experts' quotes on video footage, and photographs, to press releases and press conferences.

In 2004, Karen Ryan, a former reporter who opened her own PR firm, had been hired by the US government to promote Medicare — and she provided media outlets with VNRs that had her pose as a reporter. However, in fact, it was paid advertising. It was a government body — not a news outlet — that had exposed the wrongdoing. The unmarked ads were deemed to be "propaganda" — journalists and editors saw it as good enough to be labelled *news*.

The use of video news releases (VNRs) as real news is common in celebrity reporting, especially during movie promotions with actor interviews that are not conducted by members of the press, but by publicity companies. It is these companies who send the advertorials to news shows, with the actor sitting beside a large movie poster of the vehicle they are promoting. We often forgive the practice with something as trivial as another disposable outlet being shilled, but when a government partakes in the same scheme, perhaps it is wiser to prevent all such forms of false reportage from ever being labeled as news.

But the omission is understandable: there is no clear definition of what is news. Is it about a singer's halftime show at a sporting event? Is it about a failed reality show contestant being charged with a misdemeanor? Is it about a Tweet an average citizen wrote in reaction to a local sports team firing a coach? None of these stories is authentic news. They are mere filler with no cultural, political, social, or economic benefit, let alone artistic or scientific relevance. Yet the press prefers to disseminate trivialities over the substantial, as each of the above have been repeatedly presented as information worthy of journalistic interest.

The line between yellow journalism (a term coined in the late 1800s to describe sensational stories appealing to basest of topics) and the mainstream has vanished with only previous reputations separating the two. Both engage in the same tactics, and have the same structure of thinking patterns: a dichotomy where one side is absolutely good, with the other is absolutely bad by default, and the confirmation bias is rampant. Hillary Clinton was said to have, "hit back" at Trump, accusing him "of spreading 'dark conspiracy theories' taken from the pages of supermarket tabloids". She was not brought to task by publications that supported her presidential bid of claiming on national television that a "vast, right-wing conspiracy" was out to smear her then-President husband Bill for accusing him of having an affair with a twenty-something White House intern in the mid-1990s. The allegations were all too true. While both candidates had much in common, the press had treated them differently, and had found differences where there were similarities.

It no longer mattered. By 2016, the *Enquirer* mattered in journalistic discourse, and, in a peculiar way, finally *arrived* as a legitimate source of political news. This was only because the old guard and the online press had faltered repeatedly in their own coverage, mistaking inciting mass hysteria with genuine reportage.

The *Enquirer* had made an impact on political discourse long before the arrival of Trump. It began in 1987, when the broadsheet published the notorious photo of then presidential candidate Gary Hart sitting with his comely fling, Donna Rice, on his lap. By 1992, it switched its focus on then-candidate Bill Clinton's fling, Gennifer Flowers. By 1998, it switched yet again to his fling Monica Lewinsky. And by 2007, it revealed that then North Carolina Senator John Edwards had produced an out-of-wedlock child with his fling, Rielle Hunter. When it came to exposing the tawdry sex scandals of powerful men, the *Enquirer* got the job done. However, journalists working for more respectable publications and broadcasts were also not only following the same stories, but would also use the *Enquirer* for information.

The difference was supposed to be that the *Enquirer* published scandalous gossip about celebrities, while the mainstream press reported important truths about the world. Over time, the lines become increasingly blurred until the tabloid began to best the once venerable press.

That journalism fell to the same standards is troubling. A downward harmonization was never supposed to happen, but why it happened is still a matter of debate. Declining circulation means declining revenue, and hence, resources to pursue worthy and difficult stories, yet there is more to the problem than money.

Journalism was more than just about stories: it was, and still is, about narrative, and narrative is a problematic concept in storytelling. A story with a protagonist begs for an antagonist, for instance. A hero or even victim must evoke sympathy, and hence, can never be blamed for any misfortune that has befallen them, often causing journalists to omit or downplay troubling information about those who are chosen as either role in their stories.

It also prevents information that disproves or weakens the narrative. Should a man who saves lives be revealed also to be a thief? Should a woman convicted of embezzlement be condemned even though she fostered stray animals, as it could have been a mere ruse to deflect attention away from her darker deeds — or are people more complicated animals?

The problem is that news stories are simple structures with little room for debate. It is all too easy to lose an audience with either a complicated story or one that runs counter to their life theories. Journalists cannot veer into certain territory, as readers lose interest. They have already proven themselves to be oversensitive and offended when their own life theories are challenged, or worse, disputed.

To prevent offending news consumers, journalists often have no qualms offending a newsmaker, causing them untold grief. Richard Jewell was hired as a security guard during the 1996 Summer Olympics in Atlanta, Georgia. When a bomb detonated during one of the events, it was his actions that contained the tragedy. At first, the press had been happy to cast Jewell as a hero without question — until police began to suspect Jewell of being the bomber, as he did not fit the accepted profile of a hero.

The moment it was collectively decided that he was the villain, the entire narrative shifted. It was proven that Jewell had nothing to do with the bombing, and that he was, indeed, a hero, but the damage had been done. The press particularly the *Atlanta Journal-Constitution* were relentless in portraying a mundane man as a monster, yet there had been no reason for the about-face.

On the other hand, the press had fawned over Kenneth Lay — who had been the head of the Enron Corporation. The press, who had lavished press on the chairman and CEO with reckless abandon, did not detect his security-fraud scheme. He was a corporate titan, and hence, incapable of wrongdoing. Journalists saw him as an authority, and promptly appealed to him to guide them on how to present him to the public, even going so far as dubbing him an "energetic *messiah*".

There are limits of narrative in nonfiction; namely, reality is not a fantasy and life does not come with preset guarantees of any sort. Good things can happen to bad people and bad things can happen to good people. Yet the compulsion to present a happy ending or resolution drives journalists to distort truths to fit the narrative.

Narrative is a filter, and there are distinct roles in the journalism product: victim, villain, and hero. These roles greatly confine what can be considered newsworthy and how stories can be presented, meaning breakdowns happen, and they happen often. Richard Jewell was maligned and suffered. Kenneth Lay was given a cover where he could hide his sins. Yet both men died young under intense stress. As conservative commentator George Will once quipped, "live by the press, die by the press", whether or not you wished to live by it.

Narrative is not authentic; ergo, the interpretation of reality will always be *off* in nonfiction storytelling.

Often, authenticity goes beyond a reporter doing his job — to how he uses or misuses it. Canadian broadcaster Mike Duffy had been a fixture in federal politics, and had openly lobbied for a senate position, which he received from then Prime Minister Stephen Harper. Duffy had lobbied hard before, and according to former Canadian Prime Minister Jean Chretien, Duffy's hard sell gave him pause as he recounted to one newspaper: "When he was in the lobby of the House of Commons, he would say, 'Hi, Prime Minister. I'm ready, I'm ready.' He must have said that a hundred times". Chretien rebuffed him.

Duffy would be tried, and acquitted of misusing his position in an expense scandal that tainted him — and his fellow colleague Pamela Wallin (like Duffy, a former high-profile journalist turned senator who also faced similar accusations; though, she was never formally charged). Duffy had used his position to lobby for a patronage appointment, and his naked ambition would come back to haunt him later.

That the press scrapes the bottom of the journalistic barrel should not be a surprise to news consumers in Canada: in March

22, 2017, for instance, *Globe and Mail* columnist Leah McLaren wrote about her attempt to breastfeed a politician's newborn infant without the parents' consent when the scribe was in her mid-twenties (as she was childless at the time, it was not as if she could do so), but had been stopped when the father walked in. Aside from the questions of whether this was an assault or even sexual abuse, the newspaper yanked the column off its site days later. There were several chronological inconsistencies with the yarn, though the politician in question called the incident "odd, no doubt, but not of any real consequence". (though why there were timeline problems at all, given the politician's seeming confirmation of the incident is not clear — whether it was misremembering key details, or a more troubling reason to obscure a timeline as McLaren implied it happened a decade ago, though it seems to have occurred a couple of years after was not determined).

Aside from the self-indulgent and reckless behavior of McLaren, whether the incident happened as described or was altered or fabricated in parts is disturbing as the paper made excuses, citing it "accidentally" posted the column, and then suspended McLaren even though it had saw fit to publish something the newspaper acknowledged was not fit to print in the first place. Journalists also made reaching excuses for her, with one *Toronto Star* column waxing sophistry about the "perils of writing personal journalism" (how a journalist's navel-gazing over her banal and unproductive existence could ever be considered journalism in the first place was not addressed in the piece. It is not as if McLaren pushed for the rights of the oppressed or fought to change laws that made a difference in society). McLaren lives a life of no consequence, reduced to unsuccessfully sticking a non-lactating breast into the mouths of forgettable politician's children. However, despite the unconvincing justifications, it was not the first time her self-entitled ways had exposed her as not grasping the fundamentals of her job.

In a September 20, 2012 article in the same newspaper, McLaren had written an article selling her house, a clear conflict of interest that the paper's public editor acknowledged, though no one at the paper had been reprimanded for the peculiar oversight.

Those incidences would hardly be the only scandals in Canada — CBC had several named journalists, including business correspondent and presenter Amanda Lang, whose paid speaking gigs placed them in a conflict of interest. Then there was Leslie Roberts, a *Global News* presenter and journalist who was forced to resign in 2015, when it was revealed that a PR firm where he had an equity stake was using his program to flog guests. This meant his clients were being interviewed by him in his role of journalist (though he was not a journalist per se, CBC radio presenter Jian Ghomeshi was fired for sexual misconduct, and was arrested, tried, and acquitted of sexual assault. However, it was revealed during the course of his public woes, that, he too, managed singing talent, and several of his clients were placed on his show, getting publicity under the guise of him merely conducting an average radio interview). Evan Solomon, also a former CBC presenter and political journalist, was fired after it was discovered that he had misused his position to broker art deals with newsmakers he was interviewing.

Both Roberts and Solomon, far from being forced out of journalism, were both hired by Bell Media to host radio talk shows (Roberts in Montreal, and Solomon in Ottawa) after their scandals. Solomon also penned a column for *Maclean's* magazine — a publication that had earlier written about his "downfall", yet had no trouble hiring a tainted commodity to discuss politics, a topic that requires a news producer to be free of conflict of interest.

In Canada, there is no such thing as a disgraced journalist who cannot find work, even after the reporter has been exposed as a duplicitous betrayer of this once noble profession. US television news also took a prolonged beating with their own high-profile journalistic scandals, aside from the never-ending stream of journalists who deliberately lied in their stories.

Dan Rather, once a CBS News anchor, had seen his fortunes plummet on September 8, 2004, when his *60 Minutes* segment on then US President George W. Bush's service in the Texas Air National Guard had proved to have used fake documents, and both Rather and his producer, Mary Mapes, lost their positions at CBS as a result.

CBS's Lara Logan also made headlines when her 2013 Benghazi report was revealed to have used a discredited source Dylan Davies, but she was reinstated back into *60 Minutes,* despite her amateur lapse in judgment (though the lapse was not as bad as colleague Lesley Stahl, who once interviewed political titans before being relegated to the advertorial interviewing Muppets, as she did on the March 19, 2017 broadcast). That Davies' narrative had obvious holes and could have been unraveled with ease (as others had shown with ease shortly after the fateful broadcast) seemed to conveniently fly pass Logan. Though she maintained that she had done her due diligence, her narrative has little to do with the reality of the facts, especially as Davies' interview coincided with the planned released of his book *The Embassy House* published by Simon and Schuster, a subsidiary of CBS and broadcaster of *60 Minutes,* meaning the actual "report" was not a news story, but an advertorial shilling the release of one of its own products.

NBC News anchor Brian Williams had been caught in an act of sheer inauthenticity of a different sort. He engaged in puffery, and tall tales, repeatedly recounting a yarn about how the helicopter he was flying in during the 2003 Gulf War had been "hit and forced down by RPG fire"; yet those soldiers in attendance of the alleged event debunked his story.

While he was fired from the anchor chair, he was still retained for CNBC.

The UK has not been immune to journalistic skulduggery. James Forlong, a Sky News reporter, was forced to resign over faking a report during the 2003 Iraq War by using archive footage of a firing missile; though, he ultimately took his own life at age 44. Johann Hari, a star *Independent* columnist, was caught as a serial plagiarizer in 2011.

Most of these tarnished figures were not fired for their transgressions: some were suspended, while others were demoted. The indifference toward those who have made gross errors implies that news producers do not care about their audiences or their profession — so long as there is filler for pages, airwaves, and bandwidth, anyone will do.

In 1994, ABC News' Cokie Roberts used a fake backdrop of Capitol Hill, and claimed to be standing outside, even going so far as to wear a coat to make it appear genuine. In 2000, CBS began to superimpose its logo on a billboard in the background scenery during the *Evening News*. It was a peculiar gambit, yet there have been journalists such as *Sacramento Bee's* Jim Van Vliet, who reported on attending a sporting event live, even though he did not actually attend it in person, but watched it on television. Ruth Shalit, once an up-and-coming young journalist, saw her fortunes fall when she was caught plagiarizing in the *New Republic* in 1995 — the same publication that employed Stephen Glass, whose own journalistic transgressions made Shalit's pale in comparison. The list is hardly exhaustive.

Yet news producers still do not understand the consequences of their serial disrespect for truth. While *Vanity Fair* and *The New York Times* have tried to capitalize on the buzz concept of "fake news" in their ad campaigns, they are ignoring the bigger picture: that fakery has plagued journalism for a very long time. The way it is put together is inauthentic, and it is this inauthenticity that has made serious problems in the profession.

When *Rolling Stone* magazine published *A Rape on Campus* in

November 2014, its author, Sabrina Erdely, had been lavishly praised by fellow journalists for her chronicle of "Jackie". Jackie was a young freshman at the University of Virginia who had been horrifically gang raped by seven men on top of broken glass at a frat party, but the university administration did nothing to bring her justice. Her article sparked protests, suspension of frat activities — but it also sparked a *Washington Post* story calling into question the story itself, finding so many discrepancies, that the university successfully sued both the magazine and the author for defaming the university's dean with malice, and by June 2017, reached a confidential financial settlement with both the fraternity and the associated dean, the latter who had been inaccurately portrayed in the discredited story.

Erdely had done an enormous disservice to more than merely real rape victims, victims of false accusations, and women's reputations in general: she made women look unreliable. How difficult was it to find a genuine victim of a campus assault? Of all the people to profile, she found the one who was lying, implying there were no genuine victims in the vicinity. For misogynists who do not believe rape exists, because they think it is their right to abuse women any way they choose, she handed them fodder to throw in the face of women for years.

But Erdely also drove a nail in the coffin of the journalism profession itself. If it was her intention to give victims a voice, she managed to plant a seed of doubt with their every word, doing more damage than any men's rights campaign could ever hope to do themselves.

However, those covering the debacle missed the point that is at the crux of journalists' authenticity problem; namely, that what journalists seek is often the source of all of their troubles. Should journalists seek examples of over-the-top stories, or opt for more subdued examples, allowing the facts instead of fear-mongering guide readers? Reporters do report on the smaller cases, and frequently, but often the lure of getting attention and a scoop compels journalists to go for dishonest sources. It is these sources who must then guess how it is to suffer a tragedy, and then guess on the side of narrative extravagance. After all, knowing that the nature of the profession itself prefers sensational stories over the more realistic. This means those who deceive by exaggeration will be believed over those who tell their story honestly.

The system is rigged to give deceptive people a bigger platform than those who state reality truthfully and modestly. Superlatives — the speaking style of the huckster — will be rewarded over more modest and realistic stories and cases. It is not enough for a woman to be raped by someone she trusted enough to go out on a date, according to the media logic — she must have been raped by a horde of ravenous psychopaths for her to get any media attention at all.

This rig does several things to the journalistic product:

1. It entrenches and encourages a confirmation bias in different ways to different groups. Those who are inclined to believe a victim's side without question will see it as more proof of some sort of war on women. While the side who are inclined to believe an accused side without question will see it as more proof of some sort of war on men. Both sides become unrealistic, strident, and extremist ideologues and propagandists by proxy. They become incapable of revising their own life theories and are unteachable, making their own views tainted and unhelpful to both social and academic discourse. The Left becomes as corrupted as the Right, and they cancel one another out, making both unreliable interpreters of reality. When a lie is first believed as a truth, those who support the lie use it as evidence of their perspective, but when it is revealed to be a hoax, the ones who supported it become blind to the real examples. Those actual abuses

remain ignored as a result, and polarized sides are blind and oblivious to both the reality of a situation, and the truth of their own emotional and logical failings.

2. It encourages believing deception to the point of news producers no longer being able to spot *truths*. They will compare the milder, if more accurate and truthful versions, and find them wanting.

3. Narratives form habits, and habits form expectations to the point that a sexual assault in everyday life seems "not that bad" in comparison. The real victims are colonized, and made to be "secondary", meaning their voices are shut out of public discourse — resulting in policies and solutions that can never work as lies are believed and truths are *dismissed*.

When journalists connive and contrive to enhance their stories, they infect the public as they muddle and misalign their own perceptions of reality and truth, and replace them with ideas, arguments, and information that are neither true nor realistic. With the transgressions and ruses piling up at an alarming rate, it is no wonder that the profession's credibility with the public has become near nonexistent.

Part Two

The Autopsy of Benign Corruption

Chapter Five

Sophistry and other verified facts

Former Fox News Channel's presenter Megyn Kelly's defection to NBC had mesmerized her fellow news producers, and the hype over her career move fascinated those in the business more than audiences. She was a telegenic blonde and former attorney, and for her debut performance on NBC in June 2017, she chose to take on Russian President and Left's convenient bogeyman Vladimir Putin. The end results were lackluster ratings and a mediocre interview where the former KGB head easily wiped the floor with the sheltered American without breaking a sweat. He had no challenge, and hence, treated Kelly as pesky fly who could be flicked away without thought. It was another pathetic low for US journalism.

Broadcast news in the US, particularly on a national level, is mere show. The façade of intrepid determination and gritty competence is akin to watching a stage magician, and assuming he has the gift of levitation and teleportation, when the truth is mere sleight-of-hand games with a dose of misdirection could deceive the senses. Only when a magician is ill-prepared, does the audience see the method of deception.

The Putin interview fiasco failed to mesmerize the crowds for the reason that Kelly is a stage performer who excels at the art of theatrics more than the science of truth-finding or reality-reconstruction. Yet Kelly is not alone in the game of optics. For a profession that preaches transparency and honesty, it adheres to neither when creating a newscast. Broadcast titans, such as the late Mike Wallace, who had made his name as a *60 Minutes* stalwart, had once made his living as an actor and game show presenter. Even modern-day talking heads, such as Lara Logan, who worked as a swimsuit model before resorting to Plan B of becoming a reporter. National presenters only need to *act* the part, not be the part.

Kelly's dismal and shallow bout in the ring with Putin had been cringe-worthy — so much so, that director Oliver Stone had pointed out the obvious; namely, that Putin "knew his stuff and [Kelly] didn't".

Kelly, like most national broadcasters — male and female — are comely, winsome, and are expected to draw in audiences on shallow charm more than substance. As Stone bluntly mused: "I think she was attractive and she asked hardball questions, but she wasn't in position to debate or counter him, because she didn't know a lot of things".

He was correct in his assessment as he stumbled upon one of the critical reasons journalism has collapsed: the weight of truth cannot be held on foundation made of paper, even if the paper has bricks painted on the front.

But those in the profession cannot take the slightest criticism, even when they have resorted to insults in lieu of actual reportage. NBC News President Noah Oppenheim had decided to dismiss Stone's remarks with the reply: "no one here is interested in Oliver Stone's unsolicited thoughts on Megyn Kelly's appearance or his ill-informed opinion of her journalism".

However, as Kelly's ill-informed responses to Putin proved, news producers no longer take the time to conduct the deep and necessary research to take on world leaders in any capacity. To be interested in feedback requires an understanding of reality, and that every system needs constant non-biased self-assessment; Oppenheim preferred to unleash a tantrum, and continue with the status quo, even as Kelly's vehicle failed to make any sort of contribution or impact to the journalism product. Had Kelly been an actual news producer, she would have found the facts to engage in a meaningful interview. She merely used the standard tricks and techniques to dazzle a crowd, and ones that previously worked on the partisan Fox News Channel, where there was never a pretense of unbiased news-gathering, but in a more substantial venue, she missed her mark when it was critical to deliver.

Finding facts is an expensive undertaking. Interviewing reluctant sources, finding information, and fighting institutions bent on suppressing ugly truths and dangerous realities takes money.

Opinion, on the other hand, is cheap, even free. You can deny the existence of facts without a shred of proof, which requires no money, thinking, logic, or research. It takes no training. It takes no reasoning, common sense, sensitivity, morality, or even sanity. Everyone has an opinion, but very few people have facts.

When the Fox News Channel (FNC) debuted in the US on October 7, 1996, it made its mark that it did news differently; namely, forgoing traditional methods of fact-finding and muck-raking to offer partisan opinion in lieu of actual reportage. The ideological hold was entrenched and kept consistent by the FNC. Then the executive vice president (VP) of Fox News Channel's-editorial John Moody's regular talking-points memos to his staff ensured they kept on point. He instructed editors, producers, and journalists on what issues to cover and how to cover them. In one April 6, 2004 memo, Moody reminded news producers that when it came to covering the Iraq war:

Err on the side of doing too much Iraq rather than not enough. Do not fall into the easy trap of mourning the loss of US lives and asking out loud why are we there?

In one April 28, 2004 memo, he ensured on-air talent understood to be mindful of subtext when referring to US soldiers: "... let's refer to the US marines we see in the foreground as 'sharpshooters' not snipers, which carries a negative connotation."

What the reality or truth of the actual situation was, was not the driving concern. What matters in the news world is that it has found itself unstable and fleeting, and it is about maintaining audiences at all costs. In North America, it has meant a dramatic shift from reporting facts to presenting opinions that are made to seem to be facts — and logical conclusions.

So how did opinion become confused with fact? It is a complicated answer; though, the strongest culprit is economic reasons. It is far cheaper to present opinions than to dig for truths. Opinion requires no knowledge or research: facts require mining databases, transcripts, articles, people, books, and going off to witness events firsthand. We can see smartphone footage of regular citizens recording an event; however, even then, there may be more going on than what a shaky mobile is revealing. Perhaps the footage is a hoax, or it gives a distorted view of what actually transpired. Finding those who recorded and witnessed the event — even in an age where social media makes billions of people instantly accessible — is still a time-consuming affair, especially when it comes down to verifying identities and whereabouts.

Interestingly enough, the history of journalism began not with facts, but with opinion. The ideals of objectivity were not in place. The pre-penny press era was a brazen propagandistic gambit of news producers to curry favor with elites. When wire services were born, their owners soon realized neutrality ensured more newspapers carried their product. When newspapers also caught on that increasing objectivity and reducing opinion also brought in more readers, a new era was born, one where journalism finally had its purpose to reach a broad audience to inform them about their surroundings.

Yet the profession did not bother to test or codify its philosophy in academic halls or laboratories. Debates over concepts such as fact and objectivity were philosophical, not scientific debates, meaning comprehension of the profession's ideals were run on the honor system: proclaim to be objective, and balanced, and we will believe you are both.

Somehow, it was enough to inspire audiences to support the enterprise, and journalists gave readers, then listeners, and finally viewers, facts they needed. Corrupt businessmen were exposed. Child abusers were hounded. Unscrupulous practices could no longer remain hidden.

In the US, Watergate proved the basic model worked. A couple of young reporters, who abided by the journalistic code, brought down a president from investigating a seemingly mundane *break-in*. They followed the facts they uncovered. As a model, it was simple, but it did the job unfailingly.

The reportage of Bob Woodward and Carl Bernstein did not veer into opinion, sophistry, or narrative (though they told their story in the book *All the President's Men* after their job was done). Yet they did not resort to speculation or telling readers what to think or how to think it: the facts spoke for themselves without propping them up.

Over time, opinion became more prevalent. It seemed more entertaining than fact. With audiences still tuning in or reading, opinion seemed to give context, especially as those who were allowed to opine were seen as experts in the field — from researchers to politicians to veteran reporters.

But as news consumers slowly began to drift away and new generations were not targeted by news producers, the drift began to eat away at resources, meaning the ratio of opinion to fact skewed in the former's favor at the latter's expense. From *What has a newsmaker done?* to *What do you think the newsmaker will do?* was shifting from the tangible to the intangible. As Barry Richard noted:

> Amongst broadcast media, the pattern of cynical reporting on politics has contributed to public cynicism and disengagement. It has probably also weakened journalism, as audiences will be less interested in news about something they feel distanced from, and reporting feeds into an overall

culture of suspicion and cynicism about everything.

As news consumers were given more opinion over time they, too, wished to be heard, as it seemed unfair that only those who knew the landscape were the only ones to weigh in with their feelings. Social media arrived, giving an outlet to armchair pundits who had more opinion than fact, and now could be a tiny broadcasting outlet on the cheap. This provoked their own controversies and attention, while relying on news feeds to give them basic fodder for them to express how they see the world.

The rise of these mass micro vanity presses would spell serious trouble for journalism. They could not compete, and yet, they continued without questioning their mandates or sloppy and ill-defined methods and concepts. They did not separate themselves from the public's reenactment of a news outlet where their lunch and unflattering selfie would be their front-page story, and hence, set themselves up to lose in the competition every time.

When journalists began losing their jobs in large numbers beginning in the 1990s, particularly in Canada, panic did not immediately set in. It was assumed things would "turn around". At first, hope was placed on the newest media owners as the 1990s saw a flurry of media acquisitions in the US and Canada. When the new boss turned out to be the same as the old boss, technology and focus groups were seen as the salvation. They, too, did not turn things around; yet journalists and other news producers were stumped for an answer to their woes.

The Canadian media landscape is unique in that media concentration is higher than it is in the US or the UK. Various levels of government also funded the press, but no solution; audiences are shrinking.

By 2016, the panic at the journalistic reality set in on different fronts: in February, columnists sounded the alarm that inquiry was needed; in August, Ian Gill had the book *No News is Bad*

News: Canada's Media Collapse—and What Comes Next published, though it came out about a decade too late. By January, 2017, the think tank Public Policy Forum came out with a report of over 100 pages on the matter, entitled *Shattered Mirror: News, Democracy and Trust in the Digital Age*. In both cases, each came to the same conclusion: shaking the government down for funding was the solution (the Forum's own press release seemed to buy their own hype: "After six months of study and discussions with close to 300 people, the report proposes a series of bold recommendations aimed at ensuring the news media and journalists continue in their role as the watchdogs over our elected representatives and public institutions and the connective tissue within our communities" without wondering whether the watchdogs themselves were in trouble because of their own bungling that has caused the public serious harm over the decades).

So oblivious to reality were they that the authors of the report stated:

...we encountered resistance to the very notion that public policy be applied to the news. While any case for doing so must be utterly compelling and delicately designed to safeguard press freedom, it is important to remember that Canada has always pursued public policy to ensure there is journalism by Canadians for Canadians.

If Canada had "always pursued public policy" with journalism, and is now in a state of dysfunction, then is continuing the same route the answer to solving the problem? Both the CBC (the outlet that had lost a libel case against one Dr. Frans Leenen in 2002 and was forced to pay a record near one million dollars in damages) and those publications that receive government funding have not benefitted from public policy — had they, they would no longer need state meddling, but now require *more* of it. The myopic desperation allows passivity — journalism's greatest problem — to continue to go unchallenged.

But as Canada had deep opposition to the election of Trump — why entrench the link between government and the press when whoever is in charge of the country may just take a drastic stand and do with the press whatever he finds convenient?

The report repeatedly appeals to authority, as it makes assurances that press freedoms will fare well with government funding — all without actual proof and without defining the most basic of terms and concepts. As the report states:

> Those who fear the state will take up residence in the newsrooms of the nation should realize it has been well ensconced there for a long time — although generally at a safe distance from the journalists.

What is a "safe distance"? How is that distance achieved or measured? The authors of the report do not concern themselves with the idea. Nor do they consider that the press — the ones who are mandated to know what is happening in their surroundings — are failing to grasp what is happening as they alienate themselves from the very public they proclaim to inform. This means public funding would only reward the continual ignorance gripping the news media.

This is same media who failed to grasp the mood of the very people they were covering. In 2010, some of that very same journalistic disconnect would transpire in the coverage of the mayoralty race in Toronto. There were two men who vied for the same political position. It was a battle between self-admitted cocaine and "party drug" user, the former Liberal provincial cabinet minister George Smitherman (who assured voters that he was a recovering addict), and confirmed alcohol and marijuana user, and the city councilor Rob Ford (who was in trouble with the law over the years with offences related to those substances as well those of the domestic variety). By accounts from the *Toronto Star*, Smitherman was far ahead in the polls, and he was portrayed as being far superior to Ford, even though their personal backgrounds were equally troubling, as their professional accomplishments were more substantial. Their resumes may have been impressive (and they *were* impressive), but their private lives meant both candidates would have to face the fact that profoundly embarrassing information about them would emerge, despite the savvy nature of their handlers who were trained to clean up unsightly messes.

Politics attracts the same sort of people who flourish under the same set of rules, and the choice was a coin toss that would bring the same outcome, only in a mirror image. If Smitherman won, the Left would have been happy, while the Right would have dug up dirt to show his personal life was in bigger disarray than he let on, and the distractions would have made the rule in office a messy one. If Ford won, the Right would be happy, and the Left would have dug up dirt to show his personal life was in bigger disarray than he let on. Again, the distractions would have made the rule in office a messy one. Both men had an equally dark past, mired by their reputed tastes for certain substances that would have to bring them near criminals. By definition, no law-abiding person can sell coke, meth, or weed or even possess it (at least at the time of that election).

Smitherman appealed to people in Toronto proper, as many in the city were secretly dependent on government services, and spending to subsist, as the elites of their town preferred that the little people foot their bill. Ford, meanwhile, appealed to those whose cities were annexed years before to be folded into Toronto — those of the suburbs who really did not want their taxes to keep going up. This election was about amassing city money, and control of how and where to spend it.

While Ford was a rotund married man who came from wealth and whose family was savvy in the optics of goodwill,

Smitherman was a modern gay married man who also was savvy in the optics department, except each man appealed to the other side of the fence. Smitherman was the Left's Rob Ford while Rob Ford was the Right's George Smitherman. Both portrayed themselves as family men, but either the behavior of their spouses or their own pasts strongly hinted that all was not as warm and fuzzy as the family portraits. It was those problems that could come back to bite them at inopportune times should either candidate become mayor.

Yet those at the *Star* took it upon themselves to decree that Smitherman was on his way to becoming mayor of the playground.

Except that Ford won by a crushing margin — 47.11% — and an unprecedented one in *North America* at that (second-place Smitherman eked out 35.61% and the third-place finisher Joe Pantalone nabbed 11.73%). The Family Ford (big brother Doug was also on City Council) resonated with those who recoiled at the thought of paying more taxes, and were at odds with voters living beyond their means in a city they could not afford to live in, and needed tax dollars to keep their unviable plans alive.

It was a territorial battle with blaring bottom line economic overtones. While each candidate addressed one side by telling them the story they wanted to hear, they did so at the expense of the other side that they all but ignored, making each candidate dangerously deficient in the exact same way.

Either man was a living recipe for a city's reputational disaster. Like a mirror image of the other, the two candidates were only superficially different, yet were identical in every way that counted the most — they knew how to exploit as they pandered to a certain psychographic. Both that looked to others to solve the problems of their own making without regard of the consequences to other people, as each man stumbled his way through interpersonal relationships.

However, the *Star* at first served as cheerleader for one

before their endorsement fell on deaf ears. Once upon a time, a newspaper's coronation would serve as a massive boost to a candidate's fortunes; yet their best shading and enhancing of certain established facts backfired. Hence, the decent into a self-righteous cult-like folly at the *Star* began.

They took facts into their stories — not the facts that counted, but the ones they created with their stalking and meddling. They took issue with the mayor's heavy frame, probably alienating every reader whose body mass index (BMI) did not reflect one of an Olympian.

The stories became increasingly vindictive in tone. The Ford Brothers stuck together, and hit back with their brand of measured folksy charm. They held events on their property, dubbed Ford Fest. They hosted a weekend radio program called *The City* on *Newstalk 1010*, a major station. Their followers, dubbed Ford Nation, stuck together as the tone of the *Star's* pieces became shriller in tone — openly pondering how to remove an elected official out of office — one, who was voted in by a wide margin, by voters who made their decision known. It is the same narrative the US Left have used on President Trump as well, in a nearly identical fashion. They have learned nothing from the Toronto media, who never managed to oust him or break his core supporters, despite their relentlessly vindictive and personal coverage).

Suddenly, the *Star* was something that worked against the very tenets of democracy — writing fawning stories over those who tried and failed to have the mayor removed from office as if it were all a logical forgone conclusion. Rumors of Ford's personal vices were already known to the voters long before Election Day and they chose their tipsy man all the same. The *Star* aimed for power above what their own citizens had agreed upon: the influence to oust a democratically elected official out of office — and to then encourage the powers that be to select their choice to replace him — and then spin it all to get citizens to approve all of the changes.

Should someone like Rob Ford be in power? Canada has had its share of mayors who have been arrested or were forced to resign based on illegal activities (from London, Ontario mayor Joe Fontana to Montreal mayor Michael Applebaum to Laval mayor Gilles Vaillancourt) — most involving misappropriation of public monies or shady dealings related to their office. Neither scenario is one that plagued the late Ford. He was a man who has had his share of demons, but hardly the first in Canada's history to possess them.

Canada's first Prime Minister, the beloved Sir John A. MacDonald, was a raging alcoholic, yet still graces the country's ten-dollar bill and has schools named after him. (The celebrated fable goes that he once was so drunk during one election debate, he threw up during his opponent's speech before he claimed his rival's prattle was what actually made him sick.)

Besides, the other front-runner had openly admitted doing the same damage to his own body and brain with the same substances, and yet the Star cooed all over him without a grain of irony. Perhaps the drugs Smitherman admitted ingesting were more beautiful and moral than the ones Ford inhaled. (Although, Smitherman's record as Ontario's Minister of Health and Long-Term Care was not without its horrendously expensive and irresponsible problems, as it was under his watch that serious troubles with eHealth and ORNGE ballooned. He certainly wasn't on something at the time — mostly, just not on the ball.

But Rob Ford was turned into a troll and a monster — a "thug" was the word of choice by the equally thuggish journalists, who became obsessed with their increasing journalistic impotency.

They were reduced to childish tattling that the mayor was spotted at a Kentucky Fried Chicken when he claimed to be on a diet. There may have been a child porn ring going on somewhere else in the city that day. (Canada's largest child porn ring that began in Toronto and affected almost 400 children in various countries was exposed November 14, 2013, but Project Spade took a backseat in the news to the mayor's vulgar verbal comeback regarding his marital relations, when he denied allegations that he was seen in the company of an escort.) Or there could have been a high-powered boss demanding another degrading sexual favor in exchange for a meager promotion, but they would have to be ignored, because of the possibility Mayor Ford ate a Double Down when he should have eaten something George Smitherman would have. They even thought it was newsworthy to go on his property and stalk him repeatedly, before indignantly reporting as hard news that he did not like this tactic, and was openly testy about it.

This was the absolute best reporting the scribes at the *Star* could muster.

Nothing seemed to stick until an alleged player in the drug trade went to *Star* reporters — they did not find him based on their own investigations. Nothing could be construed as investigative journalism. The source came to them, and reportedly played a cell phone video of the mayor with known drug dealers inhaling what appeared to be crack cocaine all while still serving as mayor. According to City Hall beat reporter Robyn Doolittle in the Wednesday, November, 6, 2013 edition of the *Toronto Star* someone else did her homework for her:

It was 9 a.m. Easter morning. I was lying in bed, trying to sleep in, when my cellphone started to ring. I grimaced. No one but my dad would be calling so early on a holiday... "Robyn speaking," I muttered. "I need to meet with you," said a deep voice I'd never heard before. "Okay. What about?" "I have some information I think you'd like to see," he said. "I don't want to talk about it on the phone."

Despite stretching out the details with an overload of superfluous color in a tedious attempt to build up suspense, it is clear all of the reportage was done in a haze of submissive slumber. When journalists become mere and obvious conduits for criminal cartels to disseminate their video news releases to the public, there is no longer a legitimate argument that the profession still exists.

Perhaps the underworld felt smug pity for them, and threw them a lifeline, as the scribes certainly did not have deep or reliable connections within the Toronto Police, since officers knew of the mayor's actions for a long time and did not divulge a word of it to journalists. So much for having a pulse on the town or playing a wily game to smoke out the smoking gun.

The mayor denied the allegations until he held a press conference in November, 2013. He then openly admitted that he couldn't remember smoking crack, because he was in a "drunken stupor" at the time.

The newspaper went further, paying 5,000 dollars for another video, where a seemingly intoxicated Ford made some blowhard threats against an unknown person. The second video served no purpose other than to confirm what had been confirmed before the man was elected into office — that he seemed to drink too much, and has something of a temper when he is intoxicated.

Real evidence of legally questionable behavior would have to be found by the grown-ups at the police, while the paper contented themselves with overpriced footage of the mayor acting like a man-child.

Regardless, the frenzy in the gutter made the mayor look like a hip villain in a Quentin Tarantino movie. Self-serving city councilors, meanwhile, threw choreographed fits as they salivated for the chance of free publicity, and to destroy Ford strategically, to further their own mayoralty aspiration. This succeeded in turning the city's municipal players into incompetent bottom-feeders.

In the years of disparaging the Fords, the *Star* has, in fact, done zero original factual investigation or reportage. None. It is all smoke and mirrors and hyperbole to mask the fact that the paper has a staff where people brazenly pretend to be journalists instead of gossipmongers and tattlers. What they do is mindlessly rattle off lists of sins put together and then disseminated by other people. That is not journalism, but stenography in its most deceitful form.

Moreover, the paper's older and up-the-pay scale columnists found no new information about Ford, merely choosing instead to connect the dots for less swift readers. Furthermore, they repeatedly reminded them that it was a bad thing to like the mayor.

What was known about the extracurricular proclivities of Ford was easily found in law enforcement records long before he was elected mayor. Every other detail is a redundant permutation of the same underlying single fact that Ford seemed to have prolonged substance abuse issues.

That is the sum total of factual information presented by their entire, and alleged, investigative team. It is the same team who has miraculously managed to stretch a single old fact into a career as if his personal travails were kept hidden from the electorate. This constituency has repeatedly stated on the record that they prefer a stoned Ford than a sober politician of the *Star's* choosing.

But that is the way of the once mighty titan of Canadian journalism: newspaper has shriveled and become impotent. They bluster with trash talk, stalking overweight middle-aged men in their fantasy games, and accuse them of using the same vile mudslinging strategies they freely use on him. Yet the reporters at the *Star* seem quite proud of their manipulations; after all, they participated in a public forum hosted by the website *Newsana* that was advertised as follows:

Toronto's Watergate? The inside scoop on how the media exposed Rob Ford... Meet the journalists responsible for the biggest story to ever come out of Toronto City Hall. Hear how they did it and what's next. This will be a lively panel discussion followed by a Q&A.

A comparison to Watergate is a peculiar point to argue in lieu that Ford's alleged substance abuse issues were public knowledge from the start. With Watergate, Bob Woodward's source Mark Felt (the former FBI Deputy Director, who was known to the public for years only as Deep Throat) was someone Woodward knew, and tested before the presidential scandal unraveled in the pages of the *Washington Post*.

So were the rock star antics of Ford Watergate worthy? Did the *Star* prove that the mayor accepted bribes or use public monies to buy drugs? No. Or that the mayor used dirty tricks or rigged votes? No. Did he stalk and record the doings and dealings from rivals and enemies? No. Finding those facts would have made their diatribes Watergate-worthy coverage, but that would take work and research to uncover.

What do we know about *Star* reporters' journalistic abilities from this escapade?

1. Unless someone with ties to the criminal underworld personally calls them at home directly, reporters are incapable of finding any pertinent information.
2. Unless the police or court system disseminates evidence to them directly, reporters are incapable of finding any pertinent information.

Journalism in Canada has been reportage by *stenography*: reporters are not the foot soldiers roaming and patrolling their surroundings, finding problems and then informing the public; they are accustomed to press releases and individuals, who take the initiative in telling journalists what to think and how to think it.

Perhaps the most peculiar blindness of the Public Policy Forum's January, 2017 report was the authors' initial question: "Imagine for a moment a community without news: how atomized and dysfunctional it would be".

The authors do not see that citizens have imagined that world and has chosen it over the one where journalism used to be a thing. It is akin to a wife leaving a husband, and then happily going on with her life as he repeatedly threatens her that her life without him will be miserable. She has already done her calculations, decided the risks and negatives were less than the ones she endured before with the status quo, and has chosen a life without him.

But buried in the end credits of the report was a thank you to Peter Donolo — the one-time Director of Communications in the office of Prime Minister Jean Chretien, Hill+Knowlton Strategies vice-chairman — not just any public relations firm, but one responsible for representing several high-profile radioactive clients. This resulted in the PR firm needing to rehabilitate its own image as a professional devil's advocate. The government could fund a passive industry whose members who have never acknowledged their own role in their current precarious state (though the federal, provincial, and even municipal levels already fund). It could also create a stronger conduit for spin doctors to manipulate public perceptions without challenge.

Nowhere does the report look *inward* to why journalism lost its connection and place in society. Amid the various scandals in journalism in Canada (from serialized plagiarists continuing to write columns to brazen conflict of interest), trust has been compromised. The base assumption that the institution has not erred, and repeatedly so, has not made the public forget its grievances against the once trusted institution.

Journalists are responsible for providing content, and what content they provide is supposed to be factual in nature. For decades, many journalists provided facts that guided and progressed society. Dangers from illness to wars were the fodder for reports that saved countless lives over time. Deceptive doctors were exposed. Toxic practices of corporations were revealed. Predators were unveiled. When journalism is at its best, society can make plans, and feel confident those plans will work toward removing obstacles and reaching goals. As media expanded, more content had to be found, even if too much information would become a hindrance, and turn information into white noise.

But all the same, content must still be provided, even if original reportage fails to deliver facts, evidence, and logical conclusions. Opinion is the simplest way to fill up a newscast or newspaper. Pundits and columnists have blurred the lines between the factual and the interpretation of it. Once facts were considered important, but with a never-ending stream of outlets to fill, the shift was inevitable. The now-defunct *Gawker* was not just openly partisan toward the Left; it reveled in picayune gossip, such as how dislikable singer Taylor Swift's parents are to them, or whether or not the latest movie adaptation of Batman had a costume with nipples. When it veered into hard news territory, it was to condemn those with a different ideological viewpoint under the *Bad Ideas* category. This led to headlines such as "Why Be a Neocon? Because You Like Being Very Wrong About Everything" intermixed with humiliating stories of people getting their genitalia caught in some unlikely place.

The *Daily Caller* is the Right's mirror image of *Gawker*, though that online publication is still in existence as of this writing. It saw House Speaker Paul Ryan's January 31, 2017 comments to CBS congressional correspondent Nancy Cordes, as a "shut down", when she attempted to challenge the White House's executive order to ban Muslims from entering the country, with the chilling retort, "We're not here to debate. We're here to answer your questions".

In another article the same day, the headline read, "Boy Scouts

Of America Totally Caves, Will Allow Transgenders Now", declaring, "Henceforth, the Boy Scouts will ignore biological facts entirely."

It is not just online publications that skew a smattering of information one way or another. CNN and the Fox News Channel had also taken sides, and kept close to the script. CNN had done much to promote Clinton as the unbeatable candidate, while that Fox News Channel portrayed the 2003 Iraq War bloodless. Its propagandistic approach to the conflict made it seem breezy and morally unambiguous.

Newspapers have also veered into twisted justifications and sophistry, explaining away questionable behavior of public officials. For example, the *Washington Post*'s David Weigel weighed in on WikiLeaks's release of Clinton's campaign hacked emails. He decided that the directive to "dump all those emails" meant her campaign wished to make her emails public, chastising Matt Drudge of suggesting it meant erase to hide their existence. Weigel was the one who erred.

It is not the job of the press to come up with excuses, nor is it their job to condemn those who have different life requirements. While CNN may have a left-wing bias, it is not constructive for the conservative website *Daily Wire* to call CNN *Hitler* or spewing homophobic slurs against anchor and journalist Anderson Cooper accusing him of being a part of a so-called *Gaystapo.*

The cannibalization of the press, particularly the US, has been fierce, as have attempts to lionize the press to keep it relevant in the public eye. For example, CNN anchor Jake Tapper is either a brilliant protector of the public, or a propagandist for the Democrats, depending on which media outlet discusses him. When WikiLeaks released a 2013 email of Tapper's to Democrat John Podesta — "Congratulations on the pending appointment ... I don't suppose you'd want to come on my show on CNN to talk about what you hope to accomplish?" — right wing outlets were quick to jump on the attack, but several months later, left wing outlets lauded his "scathing critique of Spicer's attempts to downplay President Donald Trump's executive order on immigrants and refugees".

Speaking of CNN and cannibalization, the network took a plunge into the desperate when Reza Aslan partook in eating human brains with a Hindu sect for a March 2017 series called *Believer with Reza Aslan,* though it is not hard to believe the cable newser would stoop to man-meat for a ratings push, though they could not even get half of Fox News Channel's numbers; however, Aslan is the same pseudo-journalist who stooped to calling the US president a "man baby", excrement, and an "embarrassment", in separate June 3 tweets, though his own disturbing and desperate actions and words prove he is the far worse moral offender. Aslan represents a strain of pseudo-journalist who mistake moral masturbation and gratuitous stunts as reportage.

In Canada, there is still great denial among the press that they could possibly be at fault for their decline, while in the US, there is acceptance that those news producers on one side of the political spectrum are completely to blame for all of the profession's woes, while the other side is completely flawless and hence, blameless.

The skewed logic has veered into irrational defense mechanisms and logical fallacies, from confirmation bias to personal attack to appeals to authority, and the mindset has warped the way news is being presented. It is no longer about facts, but philosophy. We can no longer have a news report about a fatal mugging: it becomes a blame game of whether it is poverty, racism, government social services or police incompetence that has brought tragedy. It is understandable: we wish to find meaning, big pictures, and solutions, and often we feel it is not enough to merely report on what is happening. The trouble becomes that we cannot find meaning, big pictures, or solutions unless we have the facts as they are: raw, truthful, honest, accurate, and realistic. Once facts were the journalist's domain, they no longer care about reporting them, as they cannot see their own facts as their profession rapidly disintegrates.

Chapter Six

The unreliable narrator

Journalism is about exposing the corrupt, yet it is all too easy to confuse vindictive ambition as being a driven crusader. MSNBC's presenter Rachel Maddow is a case in point. Her program did not have a large following — typical for a non-FNC all-news cable program, but once Donald Trump won the presidency, her fortunes began to radically change. Her daily monomania diatribes spoke to the flock, and she had finally found her audience, managing to beat perennial ratings king *The O'Reilly Factor* as her ratings more than doubled pre-Trump. Like talk show presenter Stephen Colbert, Maddow got a reprieve thanks to disgruntled liberal voters looking for someone to vent on their behalf.

What she had not found was factual information that corresponded to her level of ire. It was typical of other by-the-numbers opinion-based news programs of the era: knee-jerk reactions to the story of the day with pundits and experts opining and making their various snarky digs as well.

When she promised viewers that she had explosive information about the President's 2005 tax returns on March 14, 2017, it seemed as if she turned a corner from ideological re-assurer to someone who understood the importance of journalism: finding new and important information to keep news consumers informed with something other than vitriol. She announced that she "believe[d] this is the only set of the president's federal taxes that reporters have ever gotten ahold of".

It was the talk of traditional news, its online cousins as well as social media: what did MSNBC have? Was it real or another come-on common for the era (Boy gives his mother a mysterious box — you will never believe what was inside!).

The White House pre-empted the program by releasing the returns in question, by showing that the president paid thirty-eight million US dollars in income tax on one hundred fifty million in earnings.

But did Maddow have a smoking gun, despite the commander in chief's first strike? Would she be the one who brought Donald Trump down?

No to both questions. After a twenty-minute rambling opening, Maddow presented the same information, courtesy of journalist David Cay Johnston, who made an already humiliating episode even worse by speculating without proof that the anonymous source who gave him those returns could be Trump himself. He did not come across the returns through digging and investigation; he merely took the returns he "found" in his mailbox and ran with it. He was vague on every detail, from when he received them, and did not seem concerned that he knew nothing of the returns provenance, yet it was one of Maddow's most anticipated programs with the episode being compared to Geraldo Rivera's Al Capone's Vault special where an empty room greeted the one-time investigative journalist who saw his own credibility plummet after the hype. Even sister station CNBC conceded the returns were "not a huge deal". In fact, it was no deal at all.

If David Cay Johnston could not verify who gave him the information, then why report it in the first place? If he passively disseminated information of unknown origin, why did Maddow allow him on the program with such cocky hype? But even after the balloon deflated, there were journalists who still tried to insist there was news in the tax returns as they too speculated, without a single piece of independent research, what an over decade-long tax return meant about the current finances of Trump. For example, the *Washington Post* insisted Maddow (it was David Cay Johnston, not Maddow who had received the returns) had a "decent scoop", yet that scoop did nothing to connect the conspiratorial dots detractors insist were true about Trump (i.e., that he does not pay taxes, he has ties to Russia, he is not in fact rich). There was no scoop, and, if spurious and irresponsible speculation is to be believed, the scoop only came because Maddow was Cay Johnston's proxy, who himself was Trump's proxy — and being the proxy of the target of your attacks is not a scoop at all. The news world fell down the rabbit hole and their logic was warped and fragmented ever since. Blind insanity has hijacked all journalistic reason, yet the news media are the very last to know.

The episode exposed every problem modern journalism now faces: unreliable narrators disseminating information for public consumption. It is about a childish and malevolent pre-set narrative, not about facts.

Finding the subtext inside a narrative is not hard to uncover: there is a "right" and "good" side that is exclusively in the realm of the protagonist hero, and a "bad" and "wrong" side that is exclusively in the realm of the antagonist villain. The lines are clearly drawn in the sand. There are base assumptions in any narrative; often justified, but other times, there is room for debate, even if the narrator gives the appearance that it is absolute.

Sometimes, those questionable narratives assumed that a woman demanding pay equity was ignorant, vile, insane, silly, or even dangerous. These days, that narrative has shifted radically. It is a vestige of the Partisan Press Era: make the facts fit the narrative, not the narrative to explain the facts. A narrative to tell nonfiction stories often primes readers into accepting a certain mindset as the Truth. The narrator (the journalist) makes a value judgment and then lays out the facts that support the narrative, and downplays or omits the facts that may refute it. The news consumer cannot make a judgment himself, weighing the facts of the narration because there are none. Even when there are "two sides" presented, it is always presented as an antagonistic dynamic rather than two sides that have conflicting issues that need to be resolved in other ways.

In partisan reporting, the narrator is unreliable: there will always be crucial facts that are omitted because it does not fit the shading. The companies such as Enron, Tyco, or WorldCom had benefitted from unreliable narration of the press that heaped praise on their executives — until it became clear that praise was the last thing they earned.

Times have not changed and the lessons were not learned. As Daniel Hallin, Professor of Communication at the University of California, San Diego notes, "Partisan media thrive, in part, when media markets are fragmented. Cable TV and the Internet created a lot of fragmentation. But political factors are also important, particularly the growing polarization of society." In modern online journalism, while the technology may be future-focused, the structure is a throwback to older days where it is a boutique partisan buffet depending on how far-Left or far-Right you wish to be. Here, the same facts and events mean different things depending on which side of the linear divide you are. There is no debate or middle ground. A person is either a saint or sinner, but nothing in between. It is a peculiar twisted sophistry where devil's advocate seems to muddy the intellectual waters, giving us pause on the one hand, but then seem absolute in another.

Take, for instance, the coverage of comedian Bill Cosby. For decades, he was seen as a trailblazer with a clean-cut image, and media stories and profiles about him were laudatory. Then, when the accusations of drugging women and sexually assaulting them came to light, the unreliable narration of the past proved that journalistic practices were left wanting: did journalists know all along, but kept truths to themselves at the expense of a tight and hard-to-question narrative?

Journalists, regardless of the medium, are notoriously set in their ways, whether it is ideology or even technology. However, the only place where technology piques editorial curiosity is the use of algorithms in creating news stories (one company, called Narrative Science, touts itself as an outfit whose algorithms can mine data to find the story). Yet it was that same kind of mechanical and emotionless adherence to a single formula that not only does not give context or nuance, but also makes journalism prone to propaganda. It is binary, and shuts down a wider understanding of a person, event, or issue. Only after a skewed narrative is proven to be false or an out-and-out hoax, does its true machinations become evident. When Private Jessica Lynch, a US soldier who was injured in Iraq, went missing during the 2003 US-Iraqi War, her rescue spawned a front-page *Washington Post* story, claiming Lynch valiantly fought enemy soldiers with an action hero zeal. The article cited anonymous government officials and completely believed them, until the truth came out that Lynch was badly injured in a harrowing ordeal, Iraqi personnel looked after her, and saved her life. Though Lynch had no role in her lionization (she had said in one interview: "I'm still confused as to why they chose to lie and try to make me a legend when the real heroics of my fellow soldiers that day were legendary"), journalists seemed to believe that her survival was lacking and spiced up the tale with their unreliable narration.

Despite the risk of exposure, however, there are strategic advantages to the binary: it is easy to rouse a large enough readership or viewership who agree with one side over an another, with bonus points if audience loyalty is used as flattery with high intelligence or morals. There is no better way to hook in a crowd than to stroke the egos of an audience, particularly at the expense of another person or group. The "us versus them" dynamic is one we are primed to believe. It is in the marrow. Assure the audience that they are intelligent, enviable, superior, blessed, wise, and shrewd, and they will come back for more.

Politicians have understood this feint and have carefully crafted their messages during campaigns as reporters disseminate those words without much of a challenge. For example, the simple designation of a desirable socioeconomic status is all that it takes to perk up audiences who identify with it, whether or not they actually belong. Upwardly mobile is popular, but it is the middle class that captures audiences and gets politicians voted into office. While, for instance, those in the UK who earn on average $60,000 per annum (in the US, it is about $53,300, and in Canada, it is $70,000) can be considered "middle class", often politicians do a very good job of convincing those well outside those boundaries as being members of the group. In Canada, one revealed that almost 65% percent of respondents thought they were middle class, even if they were well below — or above — the poverty line. When a group falsely believe their socioeconomic status is above or below what it truly is, they will support policies and ideologies that are, in fact, detrimental to them as they internalized a false narrative as their own.

Journalism is a hopelessly sloppy profession, compounding the troubles with unreliable narration, making it seem as if post-truth or alternative truths are genuine concepts and not delusions, psychic fortresses, and mirages. Quantities are measured by "ish" rather than concrete, easily verifiable and falsifiable methods or scientifically reliable and valid experimentation that give precision and make it harder to use an unreliable narration in nonfiction. Yet precision is frowned upon and it is easy to see why so many lies and scams can be reported as fact: the less precise a story is, the easier it is to make a false narrative seem logical, and superlatively so.

But even when the facts found are truthful, valid, reliable, and relevant, their dissemination is often tainted with faulty logic, and separating the facts from the logic can be a tricky proposition.

The problem starts from the top and the beginning: most

academics conduct experiments to discover truths about their profession. Journalism could learn a lot from experimental psychology — the discipline that tests which ways people understand and misunderstand information; instead, journalism school (j-school) professors teach presentation, while media companies pay independent consultants to quiz focus groups about how they want their information given. That information should be refined in j-school programs, where professors test new ways of information verification and dissemination. The disconnect is baffling to say the least, and without a deeper understanding of information-gathering, it is difficult to have precision or reliable narration. The modern reality is that journalists cannot shake off their tendency to talk *at* an audience rather than *to* them.

It would also help if professors conducted experiments on the problems with journalistic logic, starting with the owners on down to the reporters themselves. The profession is not one that looks within, and if you do not understand how *you* see the world, there is little chance you can then understand how *others* see the world and why.

Those in the news business have an innately uppity attitude — they see themselves as the ones who enlighten the masses rather than merely offering the most current facts for their customer base to use in their everyday lives. Journalists and their bosses will frame their professional narrative in such a way that their dynamic with their audience is unequal. This results in the profession looking *down* on the world they are covering instead of seeing themselves as equals who walk among those they observe and then report their findings of their daily investigations. The narrator does not float from above as a god, but walks among the mortals who are his kind. That troubling arrogance is a very real beast lurking within the profession, and the logical carnage it creates is a serious problem.

The North American press has a pathological inability to

grasp how much damage they have done to their own brand with their biases, distortions, gullibility, deceptions, and most of all, hubris. They have been reduced to shrill mudslinging as they gang up to decimate a target, but then are genuinely surprised they are viewed with disgust by the public.

The *Los Angeles Times*, for instance, completely lost all insight with their April 2, 2017 editorial temper tantrum simply entitled, "Our Dishonest President". Sounding more like a spurned lover than information-gatherers, their irrational propagandistic primal scream begin in this blatantly arrogant way: "Donald Trump was a narcissist and a demagogue who used fear and dishonesty to appeal to the worst in US voters." The *Times* called him unprepared, and unsuited for the job he was seeking, concluding that his election would be a "catastrophe". Their own narcissist demagoguery had tainted their piece from first word to last. The reason for their tear-stained dissent into oblivion was simple: they made their majestic decrees that fell on deaf ears in November, and they would stop at nothing to make their own nation as miserable and dysfunctional as possible. So filled with uncontrolled vitriol, the editorial spanned *days*. They could not get over their loss of power, clout, credibility, and face. The *Times* obsessively repeats the same refrain in every page, praying for a different outcome, unaware they lack the goodwill, humanity, morals, and credibility for that to ever happen again, nor do they see that if Trump is a narcissist, it is the press's singular obsession over him that would enable such lofty selfassessments in the first place.

They are hardly the only ones parroting hatred on a job that requires complete reason. The *Toronto Star* may very well be Canada's worst offender in this regard. On February 5, 2015, the *Star* published an ominous front-page investigative article entitled, "A wonder drug's dark side", claiming the Gardasil anti-cancer vaccine posed serious physical side effects to young women. The story had no evidence to back up their claims, and misused a database from which it reached its conclusions. When critics pointed to the flaws of the story, the newspaper's editor-in-chief Michael Cooke went on a derogatory rampage, telling one critic on Twitter "try not to be an idiot", and told a *Vox* reporter, "Stop gargling our bathwater and take the energy to run yourself your own, fresh tub."

After Dr. Jen Gunter used her own website to outline the glaring flaws of the *Star's* claims, the paper's columnist Heather Mallick haughtily dismissed the physician's facts with a peculiar personal attack: "Here's a tip: don't read a website run by a rural doctor whose slogan is 'wielding the lasso of truth'", as if a medical degree lost its cache depending on the location where the doctor chooses to practice, yet Dr. Gunther has a license to practice in both Canada and the US, had been published in numerous academic journals and newspapers, holds four US board certifications, and won numerous research awards — all achievements an uppity Mallick does not have the caliber to ever achieve herself. Most mystifying to Mallick's poorly-researched attack, Dr. Gunter works in San Francisco.

When the newspaper could no longer hurl insults and explain away the mounting pie of evidence that discredited the piece, only then did the newspaper acknowledge they seriously erred.

The episode caught the attention of the International press, with the *Los Angeles Times'* Michael Hiltzik saying the *Star's* reputation was now "in tatters".

But there was no understanding how badly the *Star* behaved and how many people it had alienated for the long-term. When *Star* scribe Daniel Dale complained in a March 26, 2017 that there were Americans who put up with President Trump's lies, he failed to understand that the press had already primed the populace to tolerate deceptions and distortions. He noted that "The challenge for Trump opponents is not merely that many Trump supporters believe his false claims. It is that supporters are willing to explain away the claims they don't think are fully accurate", without a hint of irony that the press has not stopped explaining away their own deceptions.

He went on to write that "Trump supporters' scant faith in institutions, actively encouraged by Trump himself, makes them skeptical of the people who have called him out on the wiretapping lie: news outlets, Democratic leaders, even law enforcement". The North American press turns up the personal attacks against the one man who they could not best, still not understanding that they have been proven dishonest and now are the boys who cried wolf.

Let us take a simple example of an inherent logical fallacy that impedes the functionality of one magazine right at its roots. *The Walrus* is an 11-year-old publication based in Toronto that touts itself as a refined read. However, in 2014, the publication found itself facing a crude sweatshop scandal when the Ontario government enforced their law against using free labor. The publication relied on the work of unpaid interns, and their methods of enlightening the Canadian public boiled down to a very disrespectful practice.

The editorial at *The Walrus* did not take the turn of events very well. They did not apologize for making people work for free as they basked in the accolades, fund-raising parties, and all the perks of the well-heeled. *The Walrus* editorial responded with their own narrative on March 27, 2014, by claiming that its unpaid program "…assisted many young Ontarians — and Canadians — in bridging the gap from university to paid work and in, many cases, on to stellar careers".

That was considered acceptable journalistic narrative, and a good argument until we examine it. Many unpaid interns work for *months* without pay (four to six months, a third to a half year of their lives) five days a week for a 35-hour working week, translating to up to *600 hours* without financial remuneration for any *single internship*. (We are assuming a six-month internship at the standard 35-hour work week with no overtime included.)

Is working hundreds of hours for free the only way to break into publishing? No, but many publications cut corners by doing so.

No media internship should last longer than a couple of weeks and even then, there should be a paycheck at the end of the escapade. Journalism is not rocket science and neither is magazine production. No one *needs* an internship, except companies who are trying to get labor without having to pay for it.

So there are other ways to crack into the business, meaning interning is not the absolute necessary evil it is made out to be — it is being marketed as some sort of sure-fire shortcut to getting on the fast-track to success. But the statement is nebulous on every level — one that relies on an unreliable narrative.

Let's look at the numbers — or what is supposed to be construed as numbers. "Many cases" — what does this phrase *mean*? What percentage is "many"? Ninety percent of unpaid interns? Fifty percent? Five percent? If the number had been substantial, the rebuttal would have said so — the fact that the author of the piece does not quantify it means the phrase is a dodge to hide the fact that "many" means not that many at all.

Then there is the phrase "stellar careers". What is considered to be stellar? Does this mean full-time work with a salary that more than makes up for the 600 hours spent toiling for nothing? Journalists don't make that much money, save for a few US television journalists and anchors with national exposure.

When we try to clarify an author's terms, we can immediately see how *little* information we are actually being given (how unreliable it is). However, while the diatribe is short on facts (as in *nil*); there is plenty of logic, attitude — and narrative that we can examine.

In essence, the argument presented is that the magazine cannot run without unpaid interns and that interns cannot get paid employment unless they submit to giving away their labor.

In this case, those who run the magazine are entitled and see themselves as superior to both their employees and their public, who they believe will buy their excuse without question.

We can also look at what sort of logic is missing, namely a direct comparison. So are the publishers also forgoing the paycheck? Absolutely not; they are not working class, but well-to-do *elites*, who use the pages of their magazine to push various points of view on to the public.

That model of flawed logic was not exclusive to *The Walrus*. Another Ontario-based publisher St. Joseph Media had "twenty to thirty" unpaid interns at the time of the scandal (odd that a company would not know exactly how many free laborers they had at their disposal). The argument for having free labor was that it helped keep the publishers viable and made economic sense.

But does it?

If St. Joseph Communications had thirty unpaid workers and if they all worked for six months for 35 hours a week, then the company benefitted with up to 18,000 *hours of free labor in a six-month period*. The minimum wage for this period was $10.25 an hour (being raised to $11 Canadian in June 2014), meaning the total savings would be ... about $184,500 for *six months or $369,000 a year* (excluding any other expenses the employers would have to pay, so the savings would obviously be far greater).

We can quibble about the numbers — some people may have worked four months at twenty hours a week, and there could have been 20 interns rather than 30 (but since both *The Walrus* and St. Joseph Communications were deliberately vague with their figures, it is more prudent to err on the side of the uppermost figures proffered). However, once you have real and hard numbers you can plug in, a vastly different picture — and narrative — emerges. But how much do the publishers, editors, and owners of these publications make a year? Were they taxed on their windfall (they may claim poverty all they want, but imagine saving that much money a year — even half the amount)?

While owners defended their practice of brazen wage theft, their use of dodgy terms hints that they are very well aware that their logic — which drives their methods of information gathering and dissemination, as well as their operational practices — leaves much to be desired. If their narratives of their own misdeeds are nebulous and wanting, then their narratives for other events are also called into question.

(As a side note, the Ontario government estimated that up to 300,000 people in the province were working as *unpaid* interns at any given time. If they all put in 35 hours a week, that means the consumer economy is losing *$5,100,000,000* a year (5.1 billion). This means people would have disposable income to spend to support other businesses, spurring the economy, including magazine subscriptions — and this is assuming that every one of these jobs were minimum wage jobs, which may not be the case.)

Yes, the numbers cited here could be lower, and yes, you can juggle numbers to suit your own agenda, but even if the number is 3 billion, that amount is no chump change for any one province's citizens to lose.

By early May 2014, *The Walrus* managed to secure funding from the Montreal-based Chawkers Foundation (started by Walrus' co-founder Ken Alexander's father, Charles, which gave about 5 million to the magazine in its first few years, but came to the rescue once again) to pay their interns. Yet genuine business savvy or even crowdsourcing could have done the deed instead.

In other words, Canada's highest-profile high-brow magazine that prides itself on its long-form journalistic think pieces that instruct readers how to think cannot seem to grasp that nifty little trick for themselves.

The reason for the perpetual myopia is not hard to find as the February 24, 2013 edition of the *Toronto Star* quoted editor John Macfarlane:

As a not-for-profit operation supported by a foundation dedicated to long-form journalism and short-form fiction, and to educating the Canadian public about our country and its place in the world, it's not subject to the kinds of economic pressure and forced editorial decisions that burden traditional magazines that are dependent almost entirely on advertising revenue.

Macfarlane then insisted they were "not smarter than" their contemporaries; however, the publication was facing the same economic problems as everyone else, yet their decision to make their budgets by exploiting the industry's most vulnerable showed they were the ones in need of an education and being put in their place.

But news logic taints the product from top to bottom and beginning to end. It does not matter if the publication is highbrow or lowbrow, left-leaning or right-leaning, or even grassroots or the mainstream — the same underlying logical flaws choke the final product.

The example cited here demonstrates that facts are elusive and are kept deliberately *murky*. It is hard to argue with ballpark figures and rough estimates. Because facts are sparse, journalists must rely on other tools to prop up their news stories. While color and opinion are rampant, they still need a *glue* to hold them together with the facts and the narrative, and that glue has a name: logic.

What this means is bias is not as detrimental to the credibility of a news story as faulty logic. Bias can be identified and separated from the facts, which can still be valid and useful, but should those facts be held together with bad logic, ideas can be harder to evaluate.

If the news gave you real, truthful, and accurate information, but then was presented with a left-wing bent on those facts, you could merely shrug off the spin and go to the evidence; however, when the underlying logic is faulty, putting those facts in the right context becomes more difficult.

For example, the Jessica Lynch story was such a case: here was a US private who was injured and then held by the enemy camp during her time in Iraq — the *Washington Post* appealed to authority, and stated with certainty that Private Lynch had valiantly fired her weapons against Iraqi soldiers, and suffered a heroic, if harrowing ordeal at the hands of her captors. With no way of knowing how the story was verified, the facts are hard to judge. When Private Lynch was rescued and recovered, she gave a vastly different account — she was badly injured and her captors saved her life and treated her humanely as they tended to her injuries.

Often, it is the confirmation bias that destroys a report's credibility; though, it is often hard to tell when the narrative guides our thinking. Simply put, we often look for evidence that seems to *confirm* our theory, while ignoring the evidence that *refutes* it. While most of us commit the error time and again, journalism is not the vehicle to carry such toxic cargo. Information is disseminated like seeds — spreading a distorted point of view carries long-term and significant consequences.

Human nature is a frightfully predictable entity that seems more diverse than it truly is, but the differences are usually shallow ones. An anorexic and a steroid abuser may manifest their dysfunctions in different ways, but their underlying self-obsession with shaping their bodies to extreme and unhealthy versions of an unobtainable ideal are the same. The difference in physique is the misdirection — their repetitive and abnormal actions toward the same goal are identical. The narrative they use to justify their lethal behaviors cannot mask the damage they do to themselves.

Alcoholics and drug addicts do not see what the problem is, even if they end up homeless as a result of their consistent and constant need to self-medicate. Those who live in poverty may talk themselves into believing they are middle class because they have cable and a smartphone. Anorexics abuse their bodies as they try to outwit those who attempt to stop their own destruction, going so far as to swap "pro-ana" ruses with other disturbed members of their order. Abused children and spouses may be too terrified by the notion that who they live with abuse and undermine them, mistaking cruelty, manipulation, and exploitation for love, even if their blindness costs them their lives.

But it is not just confined to small dynamics. Those in bad working environments, oppressive regimes, and cults can easily delude themselves in a bid to pacify themselves that they are in a good position and they have control of the situation — all justified with an unreliable narrative. We can abuse ourselves and think we are looking after our best interests or we can let spouses, companies, religions, and even governments do the abusing for us.

To the extreme, terrorists, suicide bombers, and even victims of abduction and repeated sexual torture will not easily leave the sickness surrounding them even if they are given the opportunity for self-liberation. Do we strike down laws because these individuals think what they are doing is normal, and is a viable life choice?

Because their narrative sounds convincing enough?

Abuse and degradation are an integral part of any system of indoctrination from fraternities to the military. Priming and grooming victims to embrace abuse and then actively *seek* it ensures they see themselves as in control as they remain willing participants in their own exploitation — they don't see themselves as taking abuse because they are weak, but because they are strong. It's an age-old con game. Elites have indulged in the services of these servant enablers for thousands of years — it is not as if prostitutes are on the fringe of society as they prop up the very incompetent people who rule and control the lives of billions.

Instead, the press often gives the platform to explain away illusions and faulty logic, without challenging or deconstructing the sophistry.

Because the truth is that it is all too easy to champion your own exploitation. How could normal, everyday people get conned into thinking their torture is their triumph?

In 1971, a controversial experiment known as the Stanford Prison Experiment proved just how vulnerable the human mind is to the mere suggestion of confines, and how quickly attitude changes and habits can form. Psychologist Philip Zimbardo studied the relationship between prison guards and prisoners by way of a simulation: twenty-four male students were randomly assigned a role to play: guard or prisoner. The experiment took place in the basement in the psychology building at Stanford University.

The results? The experiment had to be terminated after only *six days* (though, the experiment was supposed to last two weeks) because of the very fact that subjects began to *internalize* their roles — with those who were assigned as prisoners suffering the most psychological trauma. Those who wore the paper crown of "guard" showed clear signs of *sadistic* behavior, even though they were *randomly* assigned a role and subjects had been deliberately screened so the experiment could use the psychologically *healthiest* of the pool. Subjects wore uniforms and carried role-appropriate props, but, otherwise, it was all make believe and no one was forced to stay.

Yet it took less than a week to alter the behavior of emotionally stable adults significantly (by the *second* day, the guards and prisoners had already begun to change their behaviors and attitudes). That means that people who are placed in a degrading situation will begin to feel helplessness and break by *the second day* of their situation. For the unreliable narrators of the world who have been thrust in their circumstances for nearly a decade, they cannot see who they have become or what they really are. We form habits that we take as natural and just, and then justify those actions with unfalsifiable faulty logic, even when the evidence shows us the error of our habits.

Normal, healthy people develop sadistic and defeatist tendencies after six days in a controlled environment. Journalism must be the discipline that understands this greatest of human folly and confront it at every turn. It is the only way that oppression, downturns, cruelty, and confinement are kept at bay from society. It is not a question of reporters being judgmental, but by being our constant reminder that all it takes is *two days* and we can veer individually or collectively into a debilitating vortex, from joining cults to embracing fascism, never to recover.

But there is another logical flaw we must factor in — our *innate* tendency to form non-existent groups, and retreat into these groups for protection. It is in the field of propaganda where this flaw has been scrutinized. In one 1984 experiment, two researchers (Susan Fiske and Shelley Taylor) took groups of randomly chosen subjects and told them that they were a "group", and then had them interact with other groups. People judged those in their in-group as being smarter, more attractive, and having better personalities than those in other groups and gave their groups more rewards than other groups. In a separate study, artificially contrived groups recalled more negative behaviors from subjects from outside their own group than people from within.

In those two studies, it did not take a mere two days to alter perceptions of one's self-identity and group affiliation —it took a mere couple of hours to accomplish, and hence, begin to form their own skewed narrative. Sometimes, it only takes a second for us to reach the wrong conclusion, but ramifications can last centuries.

Taken together, we have a very troubling view of human

nature: people are not the resilient individualistic comeback kids that they believe they are. While we can recover from traumatic events and even triumph, we can only do so when we rebel against our own innate tendencies, to enable our own delusions to see the subtle ways we are being manipulated.

Our job as news consumers *is* to pass judgment on bad arguments and twisted logic, especially when the news producers refused to do it first. Yet bad logic permeates in the journalistic product. *The Globe and Mail* fell into the trap as they gave the floor to Merge Gupta-Sunderji, described as "a speaker and author who has more than 17 years of experience as a front-line leader in Corporate Canada". She opined in an April 3, 2014 column in the Leadership Lab section of the paper called *Four things millennials hate about you*:

> ...millennials aren't thinking about a long and successful career with one organization; they expect and want to make "special appearances" at several. A new assignment once every two to three years? Are you kidding? Right or wrong, they expect to be CEO by then. "Paying your dues" is a mantra espoused by many a boomer, but the phrase simply isn't relevant to a millennial.

While the shallow assessment seems valid, it is wanting on numerous fronts: namely, that this chasm has been around for a very long time. No one starts their career out thinking they are going to give the next twenty years of their life working their way to the top. But when you are tied to your family and house, and repeatedly moving becomes a costly and exhausting proposition, your attitude shifts. Do most people think they are going to make middle management and live a quiet life in the suburbs — or do they naturally and secretly harbor fantasies of monster success and a jet-set life in the fast lane?

Youth in general don't think "dues" are relevant to them —

they watch enough movies and television shows to believe that their foolproof fast-track scheme is going to work, and work better than their parents' formula for a middle-class or working-class life. Except that it *does not* because the older crowd not only are wise to those schemes and know how to scuttle them, but they also all tried them in their youth and were burned, just as the new crop will be when reality rains on their fantasy parade. It is called life.

Most "groups" are defined by common self-interest, not any true important or salient innate differences. Divergent groups can see themselves as diametrically opposed, but flip the circumstances, and what defined them suddenly disappears.

During the Vietnam War in the 1960s, for example, anti-war activists were young while those who supported the government actions were older; giving a false impression that age had something to do with the difference. It was young men who were being drafted, not their fathers. Had the US decided that those young men still had not reproduced, and hence, were too valuable a commodity to be expendable, while those men who already performed their biological trick could afford to fight on the front lines — the doves would have been a little grayer, while the hawks would have had far fewer lines and wrinkles.

The divide between young and old is a matter of how much one side has to lose: the young still need to establish themselves and their lack of experience gives them the ability to push the boundaries while people with houses, stocks, and young children have a more delicate balancing act. Place a teenager in the same position as their parents, the behaviors and beliefs aren't all that different; yet the established narrative discourages that thinking in the first place.

We can look at the smoothness of the skin between two opposing groups and draw the wrong conclusions. Unless we dig, question, and test, we don't know if what we are seeing is the cause, the symptom, or merely the façade.

What it boils down to is this: journalists, producers, and editors should be applied experimental psychologists. They absolutely have to understand how easily the human mind can be deceived, so that they not only do not fall for other people's manipulations, but also expose those secret obstacles that impede the knowledge and understanding of their audiences — regardless of how educated and refined they delude themselves into thinking they are.

Our estimates of what we directly perceive, for example, can be influenced by a single *word* someone else utters while asking us a question (the classic experiment had two groups watch the same car accident, yet subjects who heard the word "collided" recalled slower speeds than those who heard the word "crashed" *after* watching the same video). We are vulnerable to suggestion, emotions, outside stimuli, illusions, and ignorance. As a species, we can have no virtuous airs — our brains fall to the same fallible methods of judgment and logic (called heuristics).

Reporters must understand how vulnerable they are to both the subliminal and the overt, in order to show how their subjects and audiences are also not immune to those same psychological traps.

Yet when we train ourselves to think critically and honestly, we can compensate and teach our minds to question our surroundings, and evaluate our information. For example, while we might become impressed with a magician's sleight of hand, once we learn the steps of trickery, we understand what we are *truly* witnessing. We may be vulnerable to our perceptions and biases, but once we compensate for those traps, we can see the big picture, and better evaluate the information we are getting.

Had the editors at the *Globe* been true critical thinkers, the column never would have run in its final form — instead, it would have been a more instructive piece about how we have failed to overcome the never-ending cycle of effectively cautioning younger generations from setting themselves up for failure, and what can be done to finally break the cycle. But then, an educated and truly savvy youth would be too clever to agree to be conned and exploited by their employers later on.

The simplest explanation is most likely to be correct. That is the heart of Occam's razor. The tangled web of lies and excuses serve to keep people from seeing that they are being scammed and exploited. By cutting away at the layers of protection provided by a false narrative, eventually no argument will be able to stand, because what is left are the raw facts.

However, that razor is created by using a series of the right questions. If the answer is simple, then the type of questions will cut away the layers of fat, and get to the heart of the issue. When done properly, the journalist's pen is mightier than the sword for that very reason. Journalists are professional question-askers, always cutting away at the layers of lies until they reach the truth and expose it.

But many people spend years building the walls to keep prying eyes away from the truth. They are not going to like someone questioning their well-rehearsed likely stories. They have a fake image to uphold, in order to grab the rewards and accolades they feel entitled to possess, even if it means destroying lives, businesses, and even countries to do it.

And there is no end to the ways they will spread their lies: they will falsify data, pad their résumés, lobby for changes to laws, threaten potential whistleblowers, slander and impugn the reputations of innocent people, shame those who question their dodgy games, spend millions of dollars on public relations, and build fortresses to hide how they are really comporting themselves, and all while they hide their secrets and spy on everyone else.

The only way to uncover their schemes is by using the right questions to reveal the vulnerabilities they are hiding. But good questions take solid critical thinking skills, and an open mind.

It is not about judging, but assessing. Logic requires examining facts individually before trying to understand how the facts fit together. It is about looking at alternative explanations, testing theories, and revising those theories before we decide what the real story is about.

Journalists on the whole have failed in this regard, because they use blunted logic to package a story. Far from asking questions as an outsider, they have formed their own groups with their own set of rules they have mistaken as normal and natural reality. Like Zimbardo's subjects, they have learned bad habits, and now cling on to those very practices and labels that impede their ability to report on the world around them. Like the subjects of Fiske and Taylor who suddenly viewed those grouped with them through the lens of superiority, reporters see themselves as a cut above those they are reporting to and reporting about, and the ramifications are troubling.

This is because a profession that relies on regularly exploiting unpaid labor will have no qualms with those who exploit individuals who can bolster unreliable narratives. If your in-group decrees exploitation the norm by words or by action, the flock will follow the script without question, distrusting outsiders who question their faulty logic.

Journalism is also the profession that has plenty of confines but few controls — you do not need a license or a degree to be in the discipline. It is the vocation where you are a journalist whether you are paid, work for free, or freelance, or work for a major publication or a local newsletter. There are no standards, just lines drawn in the sand declaring you a member of the in-group.

A profession that creates false groups and narratives prevents a naïve new generation from beginning their adult lives with the truth, and will encourage them to disconnect from others. This means that they will not learn the lessons of the past, because they are conned into believing they are *different* from their fellow human beings, when nothing could be further from the truth.

While our environments may differ, we still have the same core of agreement — we fall for the same ruses, hold on to our self-interests, and need the same sorts of reality checks to overcome our innate frailties.

In the news world, it is perfectly okay to do the wrong thing as long as you get the blessing of people you are abusing in the name of freedom, democracy, and the greater good, whether the abused are your young interns or the call girl you degraded after you couldn't stand up to your spouse at the breakfast table. The game can go on because both the people you are exploiting are abetting their abuser by thinking they are the ones who are the slier ones with street smarts.

The atmosphere of manipulations begins as soon as those in the news world walk into their place of occupation. The indoctrination is not deliberate — it is by the mere fact that these random individuals have formed a collective, and have become habituated to the unquestioned assumptions and structures around them. Of course, it is not just reporters who become corrupted in this manner — politicians, bureaucrats, and anyone else who sleepwalks on the job can find themselves impeded by the very structure that they take for granted.

Yet journalism is the profession of reporting the facts and disseminating them to the public, who will then clamor for new laws, regulations, and any other action that has significant long-term consequences. Dangers can be made to seem safe; sickness can be confused with health; and oppression can be made to seem like freedom. The seeds of our collective beliefs and illusions begin with the news and should reporters deify or vilify an individual, group, or cause, we can find ourselves supporting the very things that become our undoing. Finding the manipulative elements of a news story is imperative in order for society to right its wrongs to progress.

Chapter Seven

Lies and the lying liars who report them

Journalists have spent the last decade committing a peculiar argument fallacy in justifying their descent into madness. They have explained away the reasons for their problematic behavior, with the unintended result being exposing their darker motives for doing their jobs.

Alex Jones, the far right-wing radio host, writer, and power behind his alt news website InfoWars, made headlines when NBC's Megyn Kelly interviewed him for her program. Social media junkies threw their fits, fragile sponsors withdrew from the show, but it was Kelly's fellow journalists who turned on her the most, indignantly sniffing that to interview Jones would "normalize" him to the public.

Journalism is not meant to normalize people, beliefs, or actions. It is strictly to reflect reality as it is. With the Internet giving anyone with Internet access an instant audience, Jones did not need any mainstream media exposure to gain prominence. He already had it without them.

A journalist is supposed to expose news producers to reality, and like or not, Jones is controversial, a provocateur, a conspiracy theorist with clout who questioned, among other national traumas, whether the 2011 Sandy Hook Elementary School massacre was real. He has followers who will believe him, regardless if he sits down for a mainstream media interview or not. If he is a substantial influencer of a social climate or thought, whether it be positive or negative, he is fair game to be interviewed. If he is a mere fleeting distraction who relies on tricks, stunts, and canned events, then he should be ignored.

Yet the "normalizing" argument presented by US journalists should be troubling to anyone who cherishes free thought and democratic ideals. If reporters assume their job is to "normalize", that means they see themselves as social engineers, not detached chroniclers. That calls into question every interview any journalist ever conducted with a troubling malcontent. Journalists interviewed masterminds of murder and serial killers, such as Charles Manson, Ted Bundy, and Robert Chambers, to name three. Manson has been interviewed decades after his conviction, long after there was any justifiable reason to do so. Does that mean the press wanted to "normalize" killing? Journalists also interviewed dictators, war criminals, swindlers, drug kingpins, rapists, terrorists, and thieves. Were these interviews also used as a deliberate means to corrupt society?

While it is not likely, the "normalization" excuse adds an unsettling filter to the entire profession. Had journalists not made an issue of the Jones's interview, we could easily deduce that the press saw their job as one of reflection. Now, we cannot give them the benefit of the doubt. At worst, they fancy themselves as mass manipulators who are dealing with an audience whose intellect and will is far inferior to their own. The arrogance is inexcusable, and entirely unjustified.

Reporters are supposed to be the chroniclers of truth, and more importantly, reality, but if they cannot see their own reality, they cannot see the reality of others.

Susan B. Glasser's December 2, 2016 essay for the Brookings Institute began with the loftily confident headline, *"Journalism has never been better"*. Then it went on to ask why it seemed to lose its potency and relevance in society during the 2016 US presidential election (if it has never been better, why have its fortunes never been *worse?*). It also suggested that what they did tell them "did not seem to matter". In other words, the usual decrees were not being universally applauded or heeded, and Glasser's lengthy piece came to the conclusion it was the fault of a cruel "post-truth" world.

But how it got there Glasser never truly questioned; though, she did wonder why journalistic assaults (or stories) "that would have killed any other politician — truly worrisome revelations about everything from the federal taxes Trump dodged to the charitable donations he lied about, the women he insulted and allegedly assaulted, and the mob ties that have long dogged him—did not stop Trump from thriving in this election year". However, his rival, Clinton, was also equally dogged by many of the same accusations — as she stood by her man, who was an infamous womanizer and alleged assaulter. It was as if an angel had been thumped by the Devil himself in Glasser's worldview: these were two older candidates, and by the nature of living a long life, would have more mistakes and scandals to their name, meaning their dodgy lapses essentially cancelled each other out. It was not the same with Barack Obama — he was significantly younger when he ran in 2008, meaning he had a cleaner slate. It was not post-truth, but a lack of choice that made voters compare the two parity products on another level.

Clinton chose to chastise social media for the Trumpian victory, stating that, they "should rightfully be doing a lot of soul-searching about their role as the most efficient distribution network for conspiracy theories, hatred, and outright falsehoods ever invented".

It could not have possibly been that the traditional media had made so many errors that their own soul-searching would have not made it necessary for news consumers to look elsewhere for the truth of their reality. They had seen the failings of traditional outlets, and then went to those places that made them promises of picking up what the old guard abandoned long ago. People made their choices, yet the problems of news producing have gotten worse, not better.

Why?

It is a question of palatable illusions: we have the Post-Truth loophole, and we also have the Alternative Truth loophole. Both are, in essence, the same sort of double-edge denial: for believers that opinion is synonymous with truth, they can reject anything that falsifies their theory, while their detractors can use their own opinions to see the believers as completely wrong, evil, and proof that the other side's delusions are in fact truth. When the truth is inconvenient, many begin to replace a truth with more than just mere opinion: they substitute a lie to prevent others from seeing the true nature of reality.

The election showed just how out of touch journalists were to truth and reality, but more troubling is how unrepentantly unteachable the press has been since their shameful blindness to reality: when London faced yet another terrorist attack in early June 2017, President Trump responded in his typical hardline manner on Twitter, yet NBC Nightly News — a once venerable news outlet that had a pulse on global affairs — took to indulging in a petty jab in a tweet of their own: "We aren't relaying president's retweet, as the info is unconfirmed".

The unintended message was clear: NBC Nightly News — an outlet that should have known what hundreds of Londoners had just experienced and were very well aware of — had no idea what was going on in the world because they had been far too busy with composing snooty tweets in a vendetta with a man who had once had a television show on their own network.

How could journalists be completely unaware of violence on the streets or the sentiments of voters? As Media Sociologist Aeron Davis observes, "Journalists don't go out any more." They over rely on government and corporate interest as sources and their target demographic as they ignore the rest. They did not see the millions of discontent voters, who would cast their ballot in a way that challenged the journalistic narrative. Nor did they see a very complex, but effective strategy employed by Trump, whom they have repeatedly underestimated as he is someone who downplays his cunning. Trump did not break the rules of reality; he merely assessed the situation, saw a hostile press who were picking their pet candidates, and then carefully disarmed, bypassed, and then sucker punched them straight to the White House. Trump found a shortcut to bypass journalists, but as resourceful as he is, he merely picked a mundane weapon of choice to defeat his adversaries. After all, he may have used Twitter, but so do millions of other people who do not get the same results as he did, and that includes all those users who have the blue checkmark beside their name.

He deftly exploited the press, who were too busy recreating reality to fit their narratives, and used those lies as camouflage to make it to the White House without them entirely. While journalists used polls as proof that they had a pulse on the people, the results prove otherwise. It is not a post-fact worth; nor are there any alternative facts that can explain it away. The polls meant nothing, but a resonating message meant the difference between being a media curiosity to becoming the president.

The waves of protests after the election was a harsh reaction to more than just an unconventional and controversial winner. The press had done its best to present an alternative reality with their post-truths; one that assured Americans that Clinton would be the next president. It was in the bag and that was that. It was a cruel deception of the worst sort, and the press knew full well that the race was not a coronation. There is, as Aeron Davis cautions, a "huge vacuum" and, more worrying, "a death of public knowledge"; however, "journalists are in complete denial".

Yet they were still in denial as they lied to themselves how powerful of a social force they truly were: Trump could be mocked and scorned in the press, but he could take his case directly to intrigued voters by strategically conducting guerrilla warfare through social media. He saw truth. The press believed lies. They had no chance against him. As Ronald Brownstein mused in *The Atlantic:*

To the astonishment of old-school reporters, new-age data

journalists, pollsters in both parties, and to a large extent each campaign, Trump will take the oath next January. I count myself among those not smart enough to see this coming.

However, it was not as if the Clinton camp ran a flawless campaign. They did not. They were out of touch with a volatile core, who were persuaded by Trump's acknowledgment of their plight, and turned off by his rival's denial of its existence. She referred to his supporters as a "basket of deplorables", trying to qualify the jab by saying half were deplorable, the others were merely misguided, and it would be up to those potential voters to decide in what category she would place them. She did not campaign in Wisconsin at all, taking the state for granted, and they rewarded her assumption by breaking their habit and voting for the Republican nominee.

In an age where technology cannot override instinct, we are often not aware that the first message we hear is the one that we believe is truth. Yet with social media, the competition for our primary attention is fierce, and Trump beat reporters at their own game by typing short, simple, but easy to remember messages, while the press spent time chattering in their pieces. They had their articles outlining where they had caught Trump in a lie, yet they themselves had also been dishonest with the public — but mostly to themselves. It was a given to the press that Clinton would win, despite the fact that the Republicans were winning Senate races, House races, and even state races for governor.

The pack behavior of journalists amplifies the illusion of common knowledge. A news peg in journalism is defined as any person, event, or issue that is relevant — meaning other news outlets will find it relevant, as well. If a major outlet decrees a person to be seen as a hero, the others will follow its lead. But it goes deeper than that: how one outlet structures a story will inspire other outlets to follow the same script. Should the structure be fundamentally flawed, then the error replicates throughout the news world, sending silent signals to the news consumer that they are not getting trustworthy information. Many have caught on and tuned the press out.

Yet journalists, such as Glasser, are constantly reassuring the public that their profession has never been better, as did the Poynter Institute's Joe Grimm. Akshat Rathi had also declared in *Quartz* that there has never been a better time to trust journalism. David Plotz was certain that it was a Golden Age of journalism. Nevertheless, with readership declines and endless scandals, it seems as if problems are ignored as ego blinds those who do not see how badly their credibility has been damaged. Even a former Canadian prime minister — Kim Campbell — had decreed that journalism would "protect democracy" from "fake news", without thinking how much fake news had been disseminated by that very press.

For example, *60 Minutes'* Scott Pelley had done a piece on "fake news" on March 26, 2017, with the requisite media jab that President Trump used the phrase to "discredit reporting he doesn't like", yet when he interviewed one purported fake news producer and took him to task for falsely reporting that Hillary Clinton suffered from Parkinson's, Pelley was challenged by the interviewee who asked how Pelley knew that Clinton wasn't suffering from Parkinson's, to which the reporter replied, "the campaign told us".

Pelley had de facto admitted that national reporters blindly appealed to authority without question or further verification. Of course, a politician's "campaign" will downplay any negative information when the stakes are that high, and the Clinton family had proven in the past their denials cannot be blindly trusted, as they denied that Bill Clinton had an affair with White House intern Monica Lewinsky. A denial is meaningless unless supported by independent evidence. It is not to say she suffers from Parkinson's, but supposed "real news" journalists did not engage in any sort of real news activity, meaning the difference between real news and fake news has become nonexistent.

The desperate chorus of self-reassuring "we still matter" has become shriller as their circulation and viewership continues to plummet.

The dishonesty of their self-assessments would be devastating, but there were more problems tainting the profession, such as conflict of interest, where journalists did not disclose their close ties to their editors or the public. In 2012, for example, Steven Davidoff, otherwise known as *The New York Times'* "The Deal Professor", had written about a deal between Dell and Compellent Technologies without informing editors that he was paid as an expert for a subsequent trial when the deal turned sour. In the same year at the same paper, Jordan Flaherty, a freelance journalist who protested against five defendant police officers accused of shooting six unarmed citizens in the aftermath of Hurricane Katrina, turned around and wrote about the trial for the publication.

Then there had been the latent sexist and racist assumptions embedded in stories as the confines of the patriarchal structure of narrative. In one Women in Journalism study in 2012, 78% of front page stories in UK newspapers were written by men. Of all the women newsmakers to grace the front page, it was the Duchess of Cambridge and her sister who appeared the most, overshadowing female politicians, businesswomen, judges, or any woman whose decisions impacted society or daily life. In a non-scientific survey conducted by International Women's Media Foundation and the International News Safety Institute in 2014, 46% of female journalists who responded said they were sexually harassed on the job. In 2011, the International Woman's Media Foundation found that of 500 media companies around the world, only one third of news producers working there were women. A golden age of journalism, indeed.

The press have difficulties with self-assessment, often

framing it in such a way that they can condemn their rivals, while casting their own outlets as superior, or even above reproach: "We watched Fox News [Channel] from 6 a.m. until midnight on Thursday to see how its coverage varied from that of its rivals", proclaimed the March 26, 2017 piece from the *New York Times'* John Koblin and Nick Corasaniti, as if binge watching a television channel for a day were some sort of equivalent to investigative journalism. The meandering report from the *Times'* hall monitors was complete with a "fact-check" here of certain segments, and there (which would have been far better served if it had been used on their own former disgraced journalists Judith Miller and Jayson Blair, yet the *Times* has perpetual issues with their confirmation bias), yet the disturbed offered no true insight as to why the entire profession in the US has collapsed and devolved from the reportage of facts to the mudslinging of sophistry and insult.

The article went into detail, as if no one in the country had ever watched the top-rated FNC in its 20 year existence: "Still, while people who do not watch Fox News may think it presents a uniform voice from morning to night, the network's content varies plenty. It offers a heavy dose of opinionated fare...and has something closer to a more traditional news format for much of the afternoon."

When journalists acknowledge their sins, they still are oblivious to the extent of the problem. Paul Elie's March 10, 2017 piece for *Vanity Fair's* website is a prime example why journalism no longer has credibility, even when it looks openly at its transgressions. As he stated:

The surprise isn't that journalists are hard on journalists who fake it: that's right and just. The surprise is that the punishment is applied so consistently in a field where the practitioners agree on little else about how they do what they do.

Yet for journalists such as Margaret Wente and Fareed Zackaria (both caught in serial plagiarism transgressions and are, as of this writing, still gainfully employed as journalists, while others, such as Leslie Roberts, were hired elsewhere despite the misuse of their positions), it is curious that Elie did not see that far from being hard on their own, news producers have given publicity and interviewed the likes of both Jayson Blair and Stephen Glass, let alone those countless reporters who continually plagiarize from press releases, and face no consequences whatsoever.

Elie's rambling piece offered this logic as the reason for journalistic malfeasance: "As many people (including the hoaxers) have pointed out, there is really no clear and distinct idea of what journalism is", as if it was perfectly excusable for a profession whose very mandate is to be keenly aware of the workings of various institutions not to understand or define the most fundamental aspects of their own. Elie's apologist piece perfectly represents the absolute inability for realistic self-examination within the profession as the subtext of the piece laments that journalists should not be dismissed for deceiving the public. It is not enough to acknowledge that journalists lie nor offer tepid excuses for their deceptions: they must be completely transparent in where they truly get their information and stop employing feints and ruses to seem as if they investigated their pieces rather than merely cribbing from others, including from public relations firms.

The *Times* continued with their strategic campaign against their FNC antagonist Bill O'Reilly in an April 1, 2017, article outlining his chromic out-of-court settlement with female employees who accused him of sexual harassment. Sexual harassment is a serious problem in journalism, regardless if the venue is print or television, nor does political leaning serve as any sort of shield. Only when a media outlet can "other" a rival, do they expose the dark world of the business. It is nothing more than a feint that hinges on the confirmation bias: if we bring light to our rivals' sins, we will seem innocent of those same sins by default. Had the *Times* been truly concerned about the practice, they would have included more than merely the FNC.

In this case, victims of harassment become re-victimized by their purported saviors who use their cases to paint an incomplete and distorted narrative.

The spiral into oblivion is more than apparent in Frank Rich's March 20, 2017 piece in *New York* magazine "No Sympathy for the Hillbilly" — an article whose very title stoops to personal attack and suggests that not only his view of reality is superior to those who are in financial peril, but suggests that the act of pity is a sign of compassion and not abuse (replace the word "Hillbilly" with "African-American" or "LBGT", the bigotry of the mindset would be far more apparent). Rich could not contain his rage that Donald Trump won a presidency, despite reporters demands that he lose:

> There were, of course, many other culprits in the election's outcome. Comey, the Kremlin, the cable-news networks that beamed Trump 24/7, Jill Stein, a Clinton campaign that, among other blunders, ignored frantic on-the-ground pleas for help in Wisconsin and Michigan, and the candidate herself have all come in for deserved public flogging.

The paranoid finger-pointing shows that journalists have become so out-of-touch with the very reality they proclaim to be covering that their ideological arrogance blinds them to the most basic of facts.

Rich's tyranny is open and out of control: "the spectacle of liberals doting on a hostile Other can come off like self-righteous slumming. But for those of us who want to bring down the curtain on the Trump era as quickly as possible", as if journalists had the right to override election results. The antidemocratic rhetoric should be concerning for any citizen regardless of political leaning: it is not up to a sheltered wordsmith to decide how long a candidate they do approve of stays in office. He openly calls for intolerance and ideological bigotry as if that were a righteous and normal thing to do. The upper echelons of the profession are no longer rational or logical: they throw public temper tantrums as they make demands that the populace follow their self-serving decrees to the letter.

With all of the willful denials about the reality of the profession, it should come as little surprise that opinion and fact have been confused by the press so often that it seems one is interchangeable with the other. They are nothing alike, and understanding their difference can explain why journalism has lost its clarity of mandate as they veer into areas other than fact gathering.

The difference between a fact and an opinion is the same as the difference between a living person and her painted portrait. One is dynamically and firmly living in reality unedited and raw, while the other is a static and processed interpretation of the entity in a fixed moment in time according to the artist's ability, materials, knowledge of the subject, and understanding of it — as well as the artist's motives for creating the portrait in the way he or she chose. All of those factors are *constraints*. The painting is a stratified representation of the subject, but it can never *be* the subject whose image it represents, no matter how masterful or renowned the artist who drew it happens to be.

In other words, the portrait is an unreasonable facsimile of the person whose image was captured for posterity, just as opinion is an unreasonable facsimile of the fact. As the old song goes, "there ain't nothing like the real thing, baby."

However, eventually the portrait takes a life of its own, and becomes separate from the person it originally represented, but it can never be a complete and total representation of the object it depicts.

The process of news-gathering is very much the same as

the process of portrait-painting — a journalist may be smart, articulate, and capable, but is always constrained by the very definition of his job. Add to the mix that anyone — from veteran to amateur — face the very same obstacles when writing a story that is supposed to represent reality.

A reporter can get a story idea from any number of places — a source relays information that something is afoot either directly on the record, or leaks information off the record. The editor assigns the story, readers send in a tip, the reporter cribs the idea from another media outlet (this is not considered to be an act of plagiarism, and should not be confused as such; a popular or trending issue or newsmaker is referred to as a news peg), or the journalist comes up with the idea out of the blue, or has experienced the topic and now is inspired to write about it.

Sometimes where a story idea came from is pertinent in determining its truthfulness, but if all of these sources are honest and truthful, none of this truly matters. The journalist's window to the world can be big or small, but is still expected to report on what is seen through it.

The next step for the reporter is to hunt and gather, looking for facts that tell the story. A story needs voices and a face so the audience can *connect* to the issue. The journalist can interview a newsmaker, an expert, a victim, hero, villain, or eyewitnesses, who all give him information. Here, who the chronicler chooses to interview will influence and shape the story and can determine how the report will be presented.

Even if the reporter decides to interview "both sides" of an issue, not all members of each side are created equal. Someone can be a superb talker, who says absolutely nothing. Another person may be truthful, but be wordy, and have difficulty with names and dates. Still another can be controlling and manipulative as well as strident and biased, leaving a bad taste in the reporter's mouth.

Or, if the reporter is biased by nature, there could be the drive to seek poor representatives of the side the journalist wants to knock, while looking for the best representatives of the side the news producer wants to support.

Even if the journalist is objective, there may be time and space constraints that limit the ability to get *not the best representatives of a certain side, but the ones who most accurately reflect the truth of the side.* For example, perhaps there was a protest, where the police manhandled peaceful protestors, and the reporter now must interview some of the victimized protestors. Who does the reporter pick if only one side can be interviewed? The one who has the gift of the gab but was merely insulted by a frustrated police officer, or the inarticulate hothead who in this case did not provoke the assault, but is never going to win *any* sympathy contests? This is the judgment reporters, editors, and producers face every single day.

However, in this day and age of "social media" (a deceptive term if there ever was one), both those protestors are likely going to rant about it in their blogs, tweets, podcasts, YouTube productions, and Facebook statuses — unfiltered, unchallenged, and unquestioned. They may face public "blowback" or sympathy, but both can easily bypass professional information-gatherers — yet if one does submit to a reporter's interview, the nature of their stature will *change*. One vents as an outsider, the other has now been bestowed the psychological honor of credibility.

But journalists must gather more than mere words from frustrated people. The protestors were the faces plastered on the event. If the reporter finds a secret memo, recording or report that blesses and encourages unprovoked assaults on protestors, suddenly those protestors lose journalistic value. No longer are the protestors front and center. They were fleeting and disposable cannon fodder used to highlight the presence of a bigger villain, who is now the focus of the report.

There will be new people to interview — anonymous sources

who will whisper about a dysfunctional police culture, police spokesmen who deny the charges, prosecutors and politicians who mull inquiries, and finally, the ones who partook in the attacks.

Don't forget video and audio evidence, such as surveillance cameras and smartphone footage. With all that information, the reporter may still choose to interview experts in the field to give context, and then with all those threads of facts, the news producer weaves a single, coherent story.

However, there is something interesting happening between the hunting and gathering, and the newswriting: information-gathering is a strange and psychotic process. It is a fragmented world of taking disparate chords, and pulling them in to one single story. The reporter cannot interview everyone or possibly find every single fact — it will never make it into the final product. The news producer has to cherry-pick what goes in, knowing full well before constructing the story that the editor and producer are going to throw out a few more perfectly good cherries before the final product hits the stands or screens.

The reporter is making value judgments as to where to find the best and most accurate information — that may mean interviewing people who never met each other to discuss the same event. The journalist may have to look on seemingly irrelevant databases because it is deemed that this information to be vital to telling the story. The hunt requires a reporter to find fragments, and from those fragments, recreate the issue or event as accurately, truthfully, cohesively and honestly as possible. The goal is to paint a portrait with the information hunted and gathered to interpret a snapshot of reality.

It can never be the same reality as the one that the reporter is recounting to an audience; however, just as the painting begins to take a life of its own, so too does the news report. The portrait the reporter paints is a rough form of "connect the dots" — giving a map of the big picture to readers, with the most important and relevant points that seem to define the story.

There will be other storytelling elements to tell the tale — color, narrative, and opinion, for instance — but these elements are to enhance the most important element of all in any news report: the facts.

Once upon a time, the definition of a fact seemed simple and straightforward, and it was, mainly because there were so few people producing news. Thus, the definition perfectly described their mandates. When the gatekeepers lost their clout, and amateur news producers with little experience, training, or knowledge in the field began to wade into the game, the definition suddenly *seemed* wrong, or at the very least, became incomplete and wanting.

In a world that is still going through rapid ideological shifts and twists in news production, the understanding of what is a fact gets lost amid the white noise. While the definition may seem to be muddled and innately vague, the problem is that people who are not trained in the profession begin to bend the definition of what is considered a fact, by diluting what it means with faulty assumptions. Playing hard and fast with the definition may seem beneficial, but when the wrong elements are considered as equally valid and reliable as the right ones, disaster becomes inevitable.

Just as there are logical fallacies, there are factual fallacies, and not all facts are created equal. Taking an egalitarian view of defining facts is a perfect way to set yourself up as a patsy when a con artist or liar decides to slip in dubious facts, along with what has been proven right and true for thousands of years.

The person who makes a habit of slitting throats is not to be trusted. The cancer growing inside of you is not a good thing that will make you healthy, a better person, or keep you living much longer. A pyramid scheme is not going to make you rich, and no, you are not special enough to dodge bullets by standing in front of them.

If you wish to cleanse the gene pool by partaking in these foibles, don't let anyone stop you from doing your evolutionary duty. However, there are such things as consequences, and to the logically undeveloped, they seem like an inconvenience. Delusions that upset your parents may be self-indulgent fun for a while, but if you spend more money than you earn, ignore your health, and forget to tend to your future, you will end up not having a future, or fun, at all.

News is our collective daily to-do list. It is our checklist of problems in our everyday world that need our attention and tending in order to keep society *functional*. It is not enabling feel-good advertising patting ourselves on the back for being good mommies and daddies. It is not an exercise DVD, where the trainer assumes we are putting effort in the proper way, and encourages us with a perky "good job!" even if we are slumped on the couch eating junk food, and are watching just because we like to see buff people gyrating in skimpy clothing.

You are not always doing right. You are making mistakes, and holding toxic and incorrect knowledge in your head. You are rarely, if ever, trying your best, let alone are the best in anything. You are not always focused on your work, and it does not matter if you are flipping hamburgers or running the nation.

So long as we continue to lie to ourselves, we are setting ourselves up for others to be able to lie to us. Truth, fiction — they both become interchangeable commodities. Only after we get burned, do we angrily demand for the wrong to be righted… by someone else, who may repeat the same cycle that had harmed us before. There is no bigger chump than the one who refuses to face the truth.

Yet it is not a grim, inevitable conclusion. With the right facts, we can use the right logic to make the right decisions, while creating the right solutions for us that are not based in fantasy or wishful thinking.

Using jealousy, greed, anger, or fear as guiding principles, we are doomed to make the wrong decisions, while getting attracted to opinion and spin, and while becoming averse to facts, logic, and truth. The good news is we can avoid these pitfalls if we just stick to the facts first. But in order to do that, we need to know what constitutes a fact in the first place.

Those with poor logical abilities shun anecdotes; never realizing what they dismiss is not just the facts, but reality itself. An anecdote is a series of smaller facts that come together to form a larger, more meaningful fact. The smaller, supporting facts are evidence, while the larger, big picture fact is the story. Evidence is an auxiliary fact that is dry, and rarely comes with emotional baggage. The story, on the other hand, is a form of *emotional* fact. Where many people falter is they grasp one type of fact or another, but rarely can see both, let alone put the two together, as is essential when analyzing information.

Every report of rape begins as an anecdote a victim tells a police officer. Every report of illness begins as an anecdote a patient relays to a doctor. Every news story begins when an interviewee recounts an event to a journalist. The list goes on. Without anecdotes, there can be no facts and no logic, because *facts and logic need emotional context to be relevant.*

This statement seems counterintuitive, even absurd, but it is emotions, not facts, that drives human behavior individually and collectively. However, emotions can cloud our judgment and that is the reason many people fear anecdotes — because deep down, they know they are ill-equipped to determine whether the story is true or false. Instead, they assume all emotion taints facts, and thus can never be proven.

What the information-bunglers conveniently fail to grasp time and again is that anecdotes can be *verified* — but that verification process requires someone who isn't emotionally illiterate, mentally lazy, or work-averse.

The person who tells the police a story is recounting a series of facts that, taken together, shows the big picture. The person can provide evidence — the series of smaller facts — to prove what they say is true, but the police and their network of information gatherers and verifiers double- and triple-check those facts, until the anecdote is reinforced with a series of truths that when taken together, form a *bigger truth*. The doctor also verifies what the patient relays with a battery of tests until those tests verify what the patient has initially recounted to the doctor.

The journalist is no different than the police officer or doctor. They are all detectives who solve a certain type of mystery — hearing a story before finding the clues that reveal whether the subject is lying, exaggerating, or mistaken if the facts do not support the anecdote. A victim or patient may be upset, sobbing, and even in shock — but at no time do we assume that emotional automatically means irrational — *or wrong*. That emotional story is the call to arms for the professional information gatherer to start hunting down the facts one by one, until there are enough reliable and valid facts to tell them what the real story is.

Facts — whether they are rational or emotional — answer questions such as who, what, when, where, why, and how. They give information that helps us make a decisive, productive decision. Facts can support or challenge individual and collective opinions and assumptions, which are merely interpretations of what those facts mean.

Yet facts are not complicated beasts. They are incredibly simple atoms of reality. It is either snowing where you are right now, or it isn't. You are breathing without assistance, with a machine, or not at all (if the last option is true, you are no longer able to read this chapter and sincerest condolences to your loved ones).

However, for those who embrace truth, facts narrow the options to a few reliable and beneficial choices — often leaving only one logical, sensible, and appealing choice. To those who prefer lies and delusions, facts muddy the waters, providing too many bad choices, forcing the individual to dawdle, as none of the options are truly appealing. Right reveals itself with facts, yet wrong reveals itself with opinion.

Why? Because liars and manipulators must use misdirection and sleight of hand to make their odious offers to you seem palatable — and *more* desirable to the *right* option, and that is quite a feat. It is the way snake-oil salesmen take away your free will, confidence, and ultimately, your money. When you are armed with the facts, the ruse becomes transparent and laughable as you ignore the sophistry and come-ons, and pick the right choice without regret or hesitation. Worse, they will throw too few of the right facts and too many of the wrong ones to stall you, to buy themselves time. Manipulators can rush you while they steal *your* time.

When news reports are done right, the problems we face become clear to us — inflation will damper our future. Underemployment erodes the tax base, and our options for progression. Shoddy manufacturing drains the economy, and puts us in danger.

Yet those who make their living making all that damage are not going to want to change their ways. They want to brag about their mansions, as you are jealous and feel inadequate as a graduate student working part-time digging ditches. They don't want you to make them accountable for their toxic ways — hence, they will do all that they can to convince you that there is nothing wrong with what they are doing.

How do they do that? By micromanaging their message in public forums to gain consensus, even if it means shading facts, appealing to dubious authority, and any other down and dirty means. All may be fair in love and war, but the same logic holds true for shaping public opinion.

For example, in early 2014, director Woody Allen had made headlines with praise for his movie *Blue Jasmine*, which culminated with typical Hollywood honors from questionable award machines such as the Golden Globes (questionable, but a wonderful form of advertising and movie promotion courtesy of the equally questionable Hollywood Foreign Press Association).

The typical shallow fawning during the award season sparked a backlash from his estranged family: his son Ronan Farrow lobbed the opening salvo, reminding the public via Twitter that his father had been accused by his adopted daughter Dylan of molestation. Shortly after, Dylan Farrow penned an open letter to Allen in a blog on *The New York Times* website recounting her story, flaring tensions on whether or not Allen did, indeed, assault the young girl over twenty years before.

Allen was never convicted of the crime — mainly because the charges were not pursued or tested; however, he was denied custody of his children as he went off and married his former girlfriend Mia Farrow's adopted daughter, Soon Yi-Previn, with whom he began a relationship while she was still in her late teens.

The pro-Allen brigade dutifully did their best to smear the Farrows: according to the devoted, Dylan was either lying, mistaken, or was an automaton who was coached and brainwashed by her diabolical mother, Mia. Mia was also busy coordinating a vast grand conspiracy to help her lawyer and former Rhodes Scholar son Ronan launch a media career, apparently because the accomplished, attractive and above-average intelligent grown man with well-connected parents was incapable of doing it on his own. The only way to procure such employment was to drudge up an ugly episode in the family's past that would guarantee malicious and disturbing reprisals from Allen's enabling true believers. It was these same individuals who would angrily smear the Farrow name in public without a hint of remorse or mercy every chance they could for eternity. Some plan.

Yet Mia was portrayed as a horrible person, and a bad mother, with no redeeming qualities; despite the fact the actress adopted children (most of whom stand by her as they raise families of their own), including special needs children, or those in desperate circumstances. The devotees' underlying assumption that bad mothers could never have daughters who were molested was also equally curious.

Allen wrote his own open letter, and made accusations that his ex-girlfriend had questionable "integrity and honesty", as she hinted Ronan's paternity may be in question, and that she was in possession of something called a "shabby agenda". (However, having an affair with her teenage daughter behind her back apparently keeps *his* credibility and agenda perfectly pristine. Nevertheless, it was his *adopted daughter*, not his ex-partner, who made the initial allegations; hence, making the character bashing a predictable extraneous variable in the episode.)

So let us not become distracted by the shrill and discourteous manipulation, and focus on understanding facts instead.

First, the story began with an anecdote: in this case, a young child, who told her pediatrician that her adopted father handled her in certain, unsettling ways, in a potentially illegal manner. To have properly and accurately followed the story, a journalist would have had to use the anecdote as the foundation, and dig up information to see how solid the story was. That would have meant looking for both confirming and refuting evidence in all key areas of the story.

The fact that the accused is a famous movie director is immaterial; also irrelevant is that the mother of the accuser is a famous actress. Are we looking for salacious dirt, so we can pretend we are in the know? Do we handle the story with kid gloves on the off chance we will ever get a role in the accused's next movie? The anecdote was simple, and simple enough to verify; however, the story became contaminated with a glut of distorted filters.

Second, *the personal attacks on both sides were completely irrelevant to the debate*. Both Farrow and Allen could have been the *absolute worst people ever to walk the earth* — their personalities alone cannot confirm or refute such claims. Bad and good things happen to both bad and good people; ergo, there needs to be facts, not uninformed personality assessments. Ignoring the misdirection of the shrill and childish mudslinging, the question becomes simple: *how likely is it that the allegations are true?*

Can the pseudo-sophisticated ever refrain from proffering yet another preposterous conspiracy theory, or from vilifying a total stranger based on *no direct, first-hand proof or knowledge,* or will they have to find a new director to praise obnoxiously?

This chapter is not the forum to go into the details, but there is one point that does require special attention. During the custody battle between Farrow and Allen, there was a report written by alleged experts from the Yale-New Haven Hospital that stated it was unlikely Allen was guilty of the charges.

The report was cited by Allen and his attorneys, as well as his supporters and many lethargic scribes in the press, such as the *National Post*'s Jonathan Kay. Despite not spending a second researching his column with a single *primary* source, Kay decreed in his February 7, 2014 column with the subtitle "Who's the Real Monster?" that:

> My best hunch is that Allen didn't do it. A 1993 report from Yale-New Haven Investigators, based on extensive interviews with Dylan and others, concluded: "It is our expert opinion that Dylan was not sexually abused by Mr. Allen."

Does a columnist offer readers present and future a best *hunch* in a profession whose credibility and reason for existing rests *solely* on researching and verifying facts? Is that what news producers are supposed to do? Hunch with their best shot, with tenth-hand information they did not verify independently, or even bother to get *right* in the first place?

We can wave a report written by experts as some sort of proof, but few in the press actually chose to take apart the report and examine it *on their own*. It is important to note the report was *rejected* by the judge who oversaw the custody hearing. Furthermore, the so-called "expert" did not actually bother to interview either Dylan or her mother, Mia (among other troubling concerns). This made the report's value nonexistent and *unhelpful*. After all, how could anyone tell whether Dylan was lying, mistaken, or truthful if they ignored her?

There were other questions dogging the "report": Who are the experts? How did they gather information? What criteria did they use to confirm or reject the facts? How good have they been at predicting outcomes in the past? (The last question is crucial, as another example further in the chapter shows.)

We often rely on experts as we ignore mundane folk, yet oftentimes it is the everyday observer, not the expert, who actually has a clue of what is going on and what is the truth.

Around the same time in Canada, an inquiry into the death of a young boy, Jeffrey Baldwin, was wrapping up (an inquiry that was covered in graphic detail in the *National Post* by columnist Christie Blatchford). The boy was removed from his parents' custody, and placed in the care of his grandparents. Jeffrey was isolated, confined, tormented, beaten, starved, and finally died of septic shock in November 2002, all while under the watch of experts. Social workers at the Catholic Children's Aid Society (social workers, it should be noted, also had a significant hand in producing the Allen report), all who ignored the blaring signs of mortal danger, as well as the fact Jeffrey's grandparents were *convicted* of child abuse in the past.

The experts and their reports did nothing but condemn an innocent to an early grave. The same hard questions that applied to the Allen report are even more critical in the Baldwin case. In both circumstances, we have facts that are, in reality, evidence of something *else*. Namely, the arrogance and incompetence of those who wrap themselves in the label of "expert". Allen's experts declared that they absolved him from the allegation of abuse, but so what? Experts also gave the thumbs up to Jeffrey Baldwin's grandparents, who were directly responsible for the boy's slow and torturous death.

Journalists see unscrupulous, inept, and immoral experts every day in their line of work, and know it, yet they still rely on the bad experts as readily as the competent ones — more so if the competent expert is not a media-friendly package while the bad one will turn on the charisma and push for exposure. This is not to say experts have no place in the information pool, but turning off the critical thinking skills just because there is an expert in the room can lead to serious problems later on.

Manipulators shape the news, because they have figured out the media code, and have figured out how to work it in their favor. They shape what you think, and how to think about it, as they subtly goad you into stating a position in public. Their hope is that pride, shallowness, arrogance, and old-fashioned stupidity will keep you intellectually and morally stagnated, so that you never question yourself, or change your position to something reasonable and productive for you. They will pretend their made-up positions are cool, intelligent, rational, moral, natural, superior, and normal — whatever latent personal anxiety suckers you into their game — and then do their best to continue to frame the terms of debate as you alienate yourself from others whose life requirements differ from yours.

If you think that idea is far-fetched, think about what you ate today, what phrases you used, what TV shows you watched, what video you placed on your Facebook page — did you come up with any of that all by yourself? The posters — the ones with snarky and mawkish quotes in word bubbles of cartoon characters that you tweeted — where did they come from? Who created them and what was in it for them to do it? Was the nugget of your own making or did you find it on the ground and pop it into your mouth to swallow it whole without question?

From the links you share to the politics you believe, chances are, something out there in the marketplace of ideas seemed like a good idea at the time, but are you better off with it? Did that pithy quote make you richer? Healthier? More prosperous, powerful, compassionate, innovative, competent, or intelligent?

Facts are manipulated — propagandists often use outright deception, but it can also take facts to create a façade of credibility when none exists.

Journalists should be aware of the above quandaries, but so oblivious to their own hubris and sense of their mandate, the US press continues to justify irrational hatred and blatant propaganda in their own pages. They have replaced truth with vitriol with increasingly disturbing results. For example, the *Washington Post*'s resident apologist Margaret Sullivan leads the ideologue brigade at the paper, going so far as to decree it is moral to pollute a news product with open, unverified bias as she did in a June 11, 2017 piece:

Looked at through this lens, Trump's press coverage has been a political nightmare.

Isn't that terribly unfair?

Here's my carefully nuanced answer: Hell no.

That's because when we consider negative vs. positive coverage of an elected official, we're asking the wrong question.

The president's supporters often say his accomplishments get short shrift. But let's face it: Politicians have no right to expect equally balanced positive and negative coverage, or anything close to it. If a president is doing a rotten job, it's the duty of the press to report how and why he's doing a rotten job.

The idea of balance is suspect on its face. Should positive coverage be provided, as if it were a birthright, to a president who consistently lies, who has spilled classified information to an adversary, and who fired the FBI director who was investigating his administration?

Hatred can be justified with any sort of sophistry and Sullivan's piece is filled with it. Politicians have every right to expect the press to behave in a civilized and rational manner. Balance is absolutely critical to the job: denounce balance, and you have denounced factual information in lieu of propaganda. The US press threw their ongoing temper tantrum the day Trump did a good job of winning the presidential race. They could make no claims of fairness: they crafted their narrative long before he ever had a chance to prove whether or not he could be a good president.

If Sullivan hoped that she could fool all of the people all of the time, and believed that everyone had a short attention span, then she grossly overestimated her own cunning. Her piece suffered from a severe case of the confirmation bias. She conveniently ignored that the press had preset their narratives and ran with it. They ignored anything or anyone that disputed their deceptive and biased reportage. Sullivan is a veteran journalist, and she would know how dependent reporters are on canned events and public relations. That she omitted journalism's greatest deceit on the public speaks volumes to her own credibility.

The coverage of the US president abandoned any façade of normalcy or rationality from the moment Trump ran for president: it is shrill, contradictory, jealous, spiteful, delusional, childish, nonsensical, vulgar, unprofessional, deceitful, immoral, sick, and worst of all, unoriginal. A news peg is the unspoken agreement of those within the profession of what people or events will receive coverage, and how the topic will be covered. It is a children's game of Simon Says, and if one outlet decrees that a person is to be ridiculed and psychically stoned, the followers will dutifully follow orders without question.

In 2017, far from being free and independent thinkers, journalists have been reduced to parroting hateful rants, praying that their own nation falls apart to prove their paranoia and prejudice to be divine truth. The news peg the press has chosen to follow is the President is a monster who can do no right. Sullivan's words have condemned an entire profession, and irreparably tainted it. When journalism inevitably carries the same stigma as Nazism earned for itself, few will be surprised by its own suicidal demise.

Chapter Eight

The business of spin

The New York Times is a publication that liberally opts to use *The 36 Stratagems of War* as a guide to construct their news stories, rather than Walter Lippmann's *Public Opinion*. They are a newspaper that has gotten much mileage by merely picking fights on likely vulnerable targets, and then turning those targets into seemingly invincible enemies of their own manufactured war. They then transform those enemies into villains in their own contrived penny dreadfuls. It is a ruse not just used by the Leftist or by those in print; Fox News Channel's Bill O'Reilly also employed those identical techniques on his program *The O'Reilly Factor*. Just as a Venn Diagram maps out intersecting quantities, one of his regular on-going and mutually-beneficial feuds was with the *Times*. The rogue's gallery approach is not journalism; it is mere narrative propaganda. It is us versus them, and the *Times* has refined the act of propaganda to make it seem that the product they are producing is journalism, even when it is mere vindictive opinion.

Yet even veteran propagandists can make a slip here and there, though it is not difficult to spot the ruse if one remembers the adage that while a person can point a finger of blame, three fingers point back at them. For example, a *New York Times'* March 27, 2017 opinion by Jill Filipovic, entitled *All-Male Photo Op Isn't a Gaffe. It's a Strategy*, is a classic case of gendered ideological manipulation used to invoke fear over critical or scientific thinking. It was a talking points memo to panic the already frightened flock, instructing them that the monster known as Donald Trump was some sort of woman-hater who was giving a warning that the little ladies were in for a horrible time under his rule, as if women were damsels in distress incapable of objecting, negotiating, demanding, or retaliating in some significant way. The narrative of the piece was sexist in subtext, as it was demeaning to readers. Trump was so cunning, according to Filipovic, that he could stage a photo-op as a "strategy".

But perhaps he was even more clever than the author of the piece gave him credit for: perhaps he deliberately constructed such a scene to cause his critics to sanctimoniously condemn him, triggering others to compare both sides to see the glaring hypocrisy of the *Times.*

The above scenario is as paranoid and absurd as the *Times'* opinion piece, yet it is interesting to note their own executive committee has much the same problems as the infamous photograph. There are a mere three women in the lower levels of the executive of the *Times,* hardly reflecting the US reality that over 50 percent of the population is female — and of those women on the board, all are *white.* The company is hardly representative of the city, nation, or world they cover. Worse, the *Times* cannot decide whether the President is a brilliant strategist or a mindless buffoon. He cannot be both, yet few question the narrative inconsistencies of the paper of record.

Just because someone is pointing out someone else's sexism, that does not mean the individual actually has the right to point it out in the narrative framing of the critic's own choosing, and the *Times* did not have that right. They merely exploited someone's already controversial reputation, making the article pure propaganda. They attempted to emotionally exploit women in the bargain with a Trojan horse, in this case, a female author. The piece was pure manipulation of the most self-serving sort: a token here or there cannot be applauded, or seen as superior to someone accused of being less enlightened. The executives of the *Times* can have no airs in the matter, as their own make up of their ranks leaves much to be desired.

Their strategy of deflecting attention away from their own questionable practices cannot hide their reality or the truth. They cannot deal with it, and opted to condemn the reality and truth of another, greatly distorting the truth, hiding their own troubling practices, and hiding the true extent of sexism in the US, regardless of political leaning. Had the *Times* been truthful or honest, they would focus less on Trump, and more on making their executive completely in tune with the city they cover. They have not. The fateful picture was neither gaffe, nor strategy: it was a reflection of a Rightist US mindset, particularly as state politicians in the US have been even more extreme in their stances, yet the *Times* all but ignores the bigger pattern. To read more than what is there does not allow citizens to draw the correct conclusion, and hence, no true solution to their quandaries can ever be found. In this case, the *Times* repeatedly implies a Leftist victory comes with driving Trump out of the White House; however, as the Vice President, Senate, House, and the majority of governors and state politicians are on the Right, Trump is hardly worth their vitriolic obsession. The Left have far bigger problems than one man; in a single decade, they have alienated their own citizens on every level of governance. One finger may be pointed at Trump, but the hidden three digits tell a vastly different story.

But the *Times'* piece also exposed a troubling mindset of the news media. There are those who cannot deal with reality and truth on any level. If reality or truth does not align with their narratives and beliefs, then they deny its existence. They build fortresses of delusions with their chronicles and decrees, always looking to codify their shields, so they do not have to contemplate the possibility that there are those who have differing experiences or life requirements that would prove their beliefs are neither absolute nor realistic. It is a childish temper tantrum, but it is one that has done everything from sparking wars to enslaving people, and abusing others. Even indoctrinating them into believing an ideology that robs them of life, liberty, and opportunity at every turn. They keep rigging the outcome until the fortress finally collapses.

They deny the existence of facts. They claim it is a post-truth world.

Of course, facts exist. Truth exists, as does reality. You can bleed to death. That is a fact. That is truth. That is reality.

You can play mind games, spinning narratives with sophistry at length, telling anyone who will listen that there are no such things as facts, but keep on hemorrhaging as you play a contrarian know-it-all at your own peril.

Arguments do not reflect truth. Perceptions do not reflect reality. These are mutually exclusive quantities, yet there are those whose profession it is to enable illusions. They are in the business of spin: holding up veils to blind others. But should a kernel of reality or truth be exposed, they must come up with a plausible narrative that explains away the troubling piece that is the exception that tests the rule.

What journalism was supposed to be was more than a mere job, or profession: it was the *ideal*. It was to be, at the very least, a conduit, where citizens would receive pertinent information that affected their daily lives, so they could keep informed, and not be fooled or beguiled by those wishing to deceive or enslave them. No one's story would be taken at face value, as every stone would be unturned. There would be no benefit of the doubt: skepticism and critical thinking would ensure trust was earned, and people who consumed the news could be confident the information that they received was as accurate a reflection of reality as one could get.

But for a profession that proclaims truth and transparency, it is mired in unintentional opaqueness. Journalism was never intended to be an actual public service: it is a business, and as such, it is dependent on the marketplace. Good journalism requires quality researchers who have access to travel, technology, and legal resources. It must be profitable for those reasons, but profitability also is a barometer of an outlet's *health:*

if it cannot gain traction with an audience, it hints that it has no pulse on those whom they wish to inform. It is a delicate balancing act that the profession seems to have lost its feel for doing at a once unimaginable scale.

Because journalism is a business, it has its own set of variables to contend with: it must not pander to its audience, but it cannot be insensitive to their needs, either. It must connect with a base, without appeasing or flattering them; yet the business model of journalism has confined reporting. The partisan models of Rupert Murdoch made him the "unofficial Minister of Information": his media empire is a global one as he courts the Right with shameless abandon. With fewer media outlets, he gobbled up many of them, giving audiences fewer choices, with outfits that are centralized rather than localized in scope and mandate.

His tabloid newspapers in the UK enticed readers with naked women. His papers reveled in snark, gossip, and bitterness, as it made it seem a right-wing point of view was divine. The news value was nonexistent, and his greatest of triumphs was the creation of the US all-news network the Fox News Channel, where opinion was more important than actual news. The FNC broke no stories: it had no Watergate to call its own; yet it has made a niche out of exploiting male anger, assuring their flock they are not to blame for their miserable lot in life.

Murdoch's properties peddle in anger and fear, and it should come as no surprise it was his own newspaper properties in the UK that found trivial scoops by means of phone hacking. When exposed for their ways, Murdoch's News Corps merely scuttled one newspaper, and continued their patriarchal narratives, as they painted those who wished another route as laughable idiots. As snark and opinion require no research, it is a cagey way of keeping production costs down. Though Murdoch's empire is still a powerful one, it is not immune to the realities of an irrelevant press; particularly since partisan websites that are more extreme in tone, cost even less to operate than those who wish to find a fact or two on occasion.

Some other media barons have run their properties into the ground with their questionable ways as did Conrad Black and David Radler with their North American company Hollinger. Black was notorious for buying up newspapers, and then laying off staff to make a profit, until some of his antics landed both him and Radler in prison. Meanwhile journalists and editors, who worked for both men, seemed oblivious to his methods and had a major hard news story standing right in front of them, yet they were poorly equipped to take their masters on. Though, they were not the only ones who had let their guards down in such a spectacular manner.

The late and flamboyant Robert Maxwell, also a media baron who owned the Mirror Group Newspapers before Murdoch acquired the chain, had plundered millions of dollars from his company pension fund to prop up shares of his company. But it was not until after his 1991 death, when he fell overboard from his yacht, that his skulduggery had been exposed, causing the collapse of his once powerful publishing empire.

The consequences of those, and other, models of business has taken its toll on the profession. In the late 1990s and early 2000s, North American companies bought and sold newspaper companies at a dizzying rate. When the *National Post* made its debut in 1998, for instance, it did so by buying and selling other properties — including its flagship and crown jewel the *Hamilton Spectator*. The employees, including the editor, discovered the bombshell half an hour before it was announced. They also acquired the *Financial Post* from Sun Media (again without most who worked as reporters knowing what had transpired under their noses) in an effort for the *Post* to compete with rival paper *Globe and Mail*, whose Report on Business section was seen as its greatest journalistic asset. The *Post* was never a money-maker, and when Hollinger's fortunes plummeted, it found itself in other companies' hands.

While Canadian media concentration has always been a serious and perpetual cause for concern. In 1969, the Davey Report had expressed concern that the trend of fewer owners would continue; by 1981, the Kent Commission had determined the trend would be detrimental to citizens as major dailies such as the *Ottawa Journal* and the *Winnipeg Tribune* were scuttled. In June 2006, the Standing Senate Committee on Transport and Communications had determined that there were "some serious causes for concern" regarding high media concentration. Other countries have also experienced a shrinkage of owners, who prefer to harmonize and centralize their operations as local sentiment, sensibilities, and perspectives are removed from the final product. With circulations continuing to plunge, to the point of outlets closing their doors, the press has all but become an artifact of a bygone era.

As Daniel Hallin observed:

The traditional press appeals more to older audiences — part of those audiences — because those audiences grew up in an era when the political culture put a high value on being informed about public affairs, when there was a strong sense of a "public interest" that transcended individual interests.

However, even online publications such as *BuzzFeed* and the *Huffington Post* lose money, and finding a steady audience has become an elusive goal.

The reason it cannot find it is simple: it is a profession that has been overtaken by those who cannot see their own shortcomings. It allowed the Blacks and the Maxwells to own media outlets without challenge; hence, they could not prime themselves to see the dangers realistically. Even in 2017, *Vice Canada*, the Canadian-based online publication that smugly touts itself as having a street-smart alertness, was taken completely off guard when Slava Pastuk (the *nom de guerre* of Yaroslav Pastukhov) was accused of recruiting freelance journalists to smuggle drugs for him.

The facts of those games were in the newsrooms in black and white, but the press could not allow themselves to *see* it, let alone *expose* it. With sexual harassment claims that plagued News Corps, it cannot be the outlet that can truthfully expose such ploys of economic terrorism women in other industries face daily.

To justify the rot, reporters began to spin the facts to keep their façades in place. News Corps' various properties are driven by blonde, blue-eyed comely women reading the news — or posing nude on Page Three. To expose sexism in the workplace would require journalists to stand up to the sexism in their own workplace, and it is the reason News Corps has seen such societal ills with apathy.

Only when Fox News Channel's late Roger Ailes (who died May 18, 2017) was sued for harassment by a former employee, and removed, did the true and dark nature of the toxic workplace environment finally come to light. Ailes intimidated enemies, used smear campaigns to isolate and dismiss critics, gathered intelligence to leak to the press, including online publications, hired operatives and consultants to keep himself in power at the FNC, and had even reportedly gone so far as to use private investigators or surveillance to keep an eye on employees and detractors alike, even having his own "black room" where his campaigns of terror were executed, and by May 2017, federal prosecutors in Manhattan and the US Postal Inspection Service both opened investigations on the vixen network's questionable handling and settling of sexual harassment complaints.

Instead of using resources to find a real story, improve the journalistic product, or ensure that female employees could do their job without the threat of professional terrorism looming over their heads, Ailes had other ideas that strictly involved improving the power base of Roger Ailes as he strategically abused women and it worked its charm for decades.

Journalism is a profession plagued by its own inability to pull itself out of its own *infancy*. It is, despite its numerous shocking transgressions, forever seeing its members as heroic protagonists, rather than *narrators* and curators of reality. Like Superman — a journalist when he is in his civilian life, but a superhero when trouble calls — reporters often market themselves as *crusaders*. It means anyone who they decree as an enemy, whether it be a person, organization, or even nation, will be cast as a villain, and they will not stop until the threat is vanquished. It does not matter whether the transgression is serious, or merely trivial, journalists will be relentless in their attacks, yet claim their vitriol is fair and balanced.

Some presenters, such as the FNC's Bill O'Reilly, had taken it to a theatrical level, attacking certain newsmakers so often, it seemed as if he had a rogue's gallery to battle (though not part of his script, he has also battled several FNC employs by settling out of court after they filed suit claiming sexual harassment, eventually causing his employers to finally cut their losses and cancel his program. While the *Times* had claimed they had exposed his ways and stated, "inside the company, women expressed outrage and questioned whether top executives were serious about maintaining a culture based on 'trust and respect', as they had promised last summer when another sexual harassment scandal forced the ouster of Roger E. Ailes as chairman of Fox News" as if the allegations had never been exposed before and as if someone sexually harasses only a single person, yet news of O'Reilly's questionable behavior had been on public record for over a *decade*).

On the other hand, other programs, most notably *60 Minutes,* made it a habit for on-air talent to ambush their segment's designated antagonists, to show the journalist is not afraid of confronting the villain.

When journalists pick a specific target for their long-arc

coverage, they often see a spike in ratings or circulation, as the stories become a *soap opera*. It is fleeting, and temporary, and when the villain in question disappears from the narrative, the momentum plummets, and the outlets fail to retain their numbers as the penny dreadful has concluded. It is a dark morality play filled with gossip, not facts. These real-life characters will be relentlessly attacked, and often their privacy will be invaded for the most trivial of matters. Despite the fling reporters have with the public with such gambits, once the designated villain leaves, the romance abruptly ends. One would think journalists would steer away from this method of reportage that only serves as a short term *diversion*, as its liabilities far outstrip the temporary benefits.

Yet those in the profession seem to be unteachable. In Canada, former Toronto mayor Rob Ford's cringe-worthy antics were dutifully chronicled in the pages of the *Toronto Star*. The newspaper saw its circulation rise, until the carnival act was completed, and there was no retention of readers: furthermore, its mobile app *StarTouch* was a horrendous failure, and staff were let go.

When Donald Trump proved to be a viable presidential candidate, *The New York Times* followed a similar playbook to the *Star*, seeing a small lift in circulation that many observers believed was a faint sign that perhaps journalism would become relevant again without major overhauls. Their confirmation bias blinded them to the *Star's* attempt at the same smash-and-grab strategy. Should Trump's handlers clue in to how to subvert the journalistic narrative, or should he merely retreat from the spotlight, the papers' fortunes will follow the same path as the *Star's*.

While the *Times* has their regular email blasts drumming up more subscriptions (with the header: "Truth. It's hard to find. It has no alternative"), they have not expanded their coverage or mandate. Instead, they have hedged their bets on positioning themselves as the valiant heroes out to slay the monster known as Donald J. Trump. By the end of February 2017, fatigue of the coverage had already begun to creep in, and news consumers began to look for some other news other than what the *Times* had been pursuing obsessively. Leftist cable news saw an increase in ratings, appealing to an angry and puritanical fringe as the Fox News Channel did beginning in the 90s. Opinion replaced fact, yet it all hinges on sustaining a designated monster, regardless if the horror stories presented are true or not.

There is a difference between factual coverage and spin — and reporters often believe spin is a shortcut (or the modern term "hack") that will serve as a substitute. It does not. Spin requires no nuance in reporting. People are treated as binary units: all good — or all bad. While there are those who are prone to be evil, other times, it is a difference of opinion, and the individual has both good and bad sides to them. Yet reporters will downplay, ignore, or spin the faults of those newsmakers they like, while amplifying the real or perceived sins of those they despise.

Mayor Ford had been brought to task by the press for going off his diet; yet they did not see his drug use until the criminal element called them directly, and gave them the memo. But even then, his constituents stood by him as they recounted his direct involvement with their various problems; yet the press could only see the worst in him.

It was not as if they should have noted his serious transgression or explained them away. But the story of a troubled public servant, who had still done much for his riding and the city, required a more mature method of storytelling.

However, journalism relies on logical fallacies to tell their stories. They will appeal to authority. They will commit the confirmation bias. They will employ the strawman argument when their narrative is challenged, and they will use the sink or swim argument to force news consumers to agree with their assessments. If you do not resist their target of derision, then you must be collaborating with them.

Yet taking sides necessarily means there are at least two to choose from, meaning that to resist is to collaborate, and to collaborate is to resist — to resist one side requires you to collaborate with another. Besides, there are other options other than resistance or collaboration. With two warring factions (the standard narrative structure in Western politics), there is always another group vying for power who will deify itself while demonizing their rivals. Competing is favored over cooperation, never mind the long-term damage, ill-will, and waste of resources competition brings. There is always a third option that people will terrorize and shame others into not seeing because if they did, the ride on easy street comes crashing to a halt.

There are always more than two choices, and when both sides vying for control are badly mismanaged and corrupted, enabling one is just as bad as enabling the other. It's a rigged game: make this cabal powerful and wealthy as they ignore you — or make the other cabal powerful and wealthy as they ignore you. It is a forced choice no different than picking a card from a magician's deck — it does not matter which card is chosen, the outcome has already been determined. Now the façade of choice is the misdirection to give people the false sense that they had something to do with the card they picked. It's an illusion, and a scam.

It is a silly game that offers no third alternative that makes sense. Journalists use their stories as a three card monte racket, and news consumers are going to lose no matter how closely they keep their eyes on the shuffling. The guilting, shaming, and fear-mongering deflects attention away from the problem that the people have no real choice with allowing the status quo to stand. True solutions to problems are hidden with the narrative journalists continue to use — ones that imply the reporter knows who to root for, and the news consumer needs to come aboard — or else.

It has become a vicious cycle with more bureaucratic layers blurring the landscape. For example, CNN's Erin Burnett poorly played the game of spin on February 27, 2017, as recounted in the partisan *The American Mirror* (the *Mirror* is website cited by the partisan Left site the *Fake News Codex* as being "fake news". The *Codex* has no identifying factors of who runs the site, or the methodology of determining what is fake news or real. A Twitter account states that Chris Herbert, listed in his bio as a web designer, lays claim to it). Though, the footage of the actual interview with former Attorney General Michael Mukasey transpired precisely as the publication reported. The exchange was brazenly biased, and the anchor seemed incapable of understanding what the word "treason" actually meant.

The topic of the interview was about the Left's rumors regarding President Trump having discussions with "the Russians" during the presidential race, and whether or not those conversations amounted to treason. Note there was no confirmation of such talks, who the then candidate specifically spoke to, let alone the actual topic of conversation. The subject was a "what if" scenario.

Burnett had already decided that Trump had committed treason and tried to bait the veteran legal mind into a conniving game of smoke and mirrors. She asked Mukasey whether the current attorney general should step aside for a special prosecutor to open an investigation, to which Mukasey replied: "Special prosecutor of what? Where's the crime? We haven't even named the crime, let alone suggested that charges are going to be brought." She then parsed her words asking if he would be "fine with" Trump having such dialogues, to which he answered: "It's not a question of being fine with it because I'm not fine with it. There's a difference between treason and what I'm fine with or not. And saying you ought to get stuff on Hillary Clinton, believe it or not, is not a crime, even if you're saying it to the Russians." Burnett seemed disappointed that she could not do what Bob Woodward and Carl Bernstein did — take down a president she did not like, perhaps forgetting neither man preened in front of rolling cameras as they worked sources and followed leads for months on their own.

Yet the story was used by the relatively obscure website The *American Mirror* (a site operated by one Kyle Olson, whose credentials are never mentioned on his site — or elsewhere), and then posted prominently on the popular *Drudge Report*. The *Mirror* was deemed to be completely unreliable, by not just the amateur listing of *The Fake News Codex*, but also another group calling themselves *Media Bias/Fact Check*. It seems, like *Snopes*, to be an amateur/civic outfit (the owner of the site, a Dave Van Zandt, whose lone qualification is having a "Communications degree", without elaboration, though his skill set ends there). Both the self-proclaimed watchmen and the partisan propagandists are armchair critics, with no understanding of the actual dynamics of the profession. Yet now, thanks to the Internet, they can buy a web domain and "live out loud" their fantasies, gathering a flock who do not question how they come across their information — or why.

Like their online partisan counterparts, journalists pick sides in every issue. The concept of gathering facts and presenting them without latent or overt skewing eludes the profession. There are "good guys" and "bad guys": what the press lacks is merely presenting the positive, the negative, the neutral, and the unknown to the public, so they know where they stand, and what their options are at the moment. For example, a patient comes into a doctor's office for medical tests, and the doctor discovers the patient has cancer. The physician does not need to present the information in a narrative. The doctor must tell the patient of the illness, with what disease, at what stage it is, what can be expected, and treatment options, along with their side effects and chances of success. There is no need to demonize the patient's family for not dragging the patient in sooner, or lay blame on the patient for not taking better care of oneself. It is irrelevant to the current problem: what is needed is a reliable map of the landscape, and how best to get to the other side. Journalists need to see their profession in much the same way, and not pick favorites to fawn over, and targets to destroy.

The scorecard for the aforementioned example is chilling: CNN overtly engaged in a poor attempt at partisan propaganda — and this from the network that riveted the world during the first night of the US-led war against Iraq with The Boys of Baghdad (Bernard Shaw, Peter Arnett, and John Holliman) recounted the shocking turn of events as they groped in the dark, but kept a level — and objective — head. CNN can no longer keep their head high, but they were brought to task by a website that also engages in partisan propaganda. They, in turn, were brought to task by media watchers, who themselves were engaging in partisan propaganda. It is a vast sea of opinion, and in each case, no facts were ever given to the public. It was a chain of conjecture.

To keep up their destructive strategies, reporters will condemn those in the profession who do not agree with their every ideological decree. The in-fighting among reporters has begun to paint a disturbing picture of their ineptitude. On March 26, 2017 on *CBS Sunday Morning,* former ABC journalist and presenter Ted Koppel had taken Fox News Channel's Sean Hannity to task for "driving the country further and further apart", stating that "you have attracted people who are determined that ideology is more important than facts".

But Koppel is selective which anchors he defends and which he condemns: in an October 22, 2015 interview with *Time* magazine, he defended disgraced NBC anchor Brian Williams whose fabrications of his journalistic exploits during a war were exposed, Koppel defended his "old friend" and said that Williams "slipped and took the routine and did it on the air, and he has more than paid the price". According to Koppel's logic, it is perfectly normal to exploit a war with deceptive puffery; so long as it is done in private, as if deceivers have an off button when their methods push them to positions they are unqualified to handle or comprehend. Hannity's sophistry is bad for journalism, but Williams' exaggerations are not.

However, other reporters went on to praise Koppel, with wire services such as the *Associated Press* (printed in many publications, notably *USA Today*) using the word "calmly" to describe the way Koppel told Hannity he was "bad for America" (it was Hannity who used the phrase, and Koppel agreed with the assessment, meaning the headline itself was misleading), though *USA Today* was the one that allowed disgraced former journalist Jack Kelley to fabricate his international stories for years, especially in war zones and trouble spots, allowing his propaganda to alter public perceptions that would inevitably influence public policy, yet that was not considered "bad for journalism".

That the press has become openly partisan and propagandistic is not in question. It has become completely devoid of any informational value in North America, to the point that many news consumers must rely on UK publications to cover stories in their continents (such as *BBC America* and *The Guardian*).

But where traditional North American media outlets prove their greatest deceptions and manipulations is by carefully framing a narrative to pretend ideological reportage only comes from their rival ideological outlets. Fox News Channel will pretend they are above reproach, while *The New York Times* and CNN will pretend they have produced objective reportage free of personal feelings and agendas.

Perhaps the most disturbing and pathological sign that the press has fallen off the rails is their glee when their own nation suffers from serious problems, from a sluggish stock market to failed federal bills, as some sort of proof that whoever they deem an enemy is bad for the country.

That is not the function of journalism. That is the petty dysfunction of those who have lost their clout and standing due to their own machinations — screaming vindictive "I told you so", hoping that an apocalypse arrives as punishment for all those who no longer see them as deities, instead of focusing on being productive and useful to the society they are paid to observe and chronicle. The worst side effect is that the press sees allies as those who share the same ideological leanings, and do not see those who willfully deceive as their enemies — enemies whose untruths have sped up the profession's collapse.

The media watchdogs often have equal, if opposite agendas as the outlets they are chastising. They merely express opinion, with no facts backing up their claims, and have no training in spotting fraudulent information, or know how a media outlet operates, meaning that without a clear point of reference, they are working from their own untested theory, not fact, making them no more reliable, accurate, or truthful than those they criticize. The amateur status makes it easier for journalists to ignore their critics — blinding them to the fact that the growing chorus of discontent may be bleating out all the wrong notes and words, but are no longer silent or singing the press's praises for a reason.

The watchdogs make it easier for journalists to be in denial, while the critics are clueless to a reporter's reality, giving the impression that journalists must be right *by default*. It is a logical fallacy, but one that allows journalists to spin the truth of their own reality, to shield them from the collapse of their own profession. There has been a gap and an inability to connect to their core audience, making it easier for a chorus of people to speak out in public.

Journalists have become accustomed to spin — as they cover authority figures who stay in power knowing how to present themselves in the most favorable light. Reporters no longer speak to a broad audience; they speak to elites, hoping to curry favor with them, leaving a hole in the coverage of important issues from education to housing to workplace abuses. For example, Canadian news reports gloat about the "hot" real estate market and how the price of houses has increased. What they do not cover is the lack of affordable housing, the increase in rent for those who cannot afford to buy a home, or the crippling impact mortgage debt brings to those who buy a house in an inflated market. It is not reportage. It is spin. Yet the media watchdogs do little to challenge the holes. They merely express disdain for a political view that is not fully aligned with their own.

So unqualified and mired in the same problematic bias vortex, that those watchmen are no better, and in many cases, even more unreliable than the press they are chastising. They have not done a thing to improve the content and structure of journalism. They have no proposed workable and tested alternative methods of information gathering and dissemination, meaning the press can continue to ignore the signs that they no longer have a true cultural or social relevance to society.

It has become a vile and unfixable mess and the spin prevents reporters from seeing the extent of their fall from grace. As long as they are blinded by their own manipulative shading, they drift further away from the heart and soul of the very people they once valiantly vowed to protect with the truth.

(See the book *OutFoxed: Rupert Murdoch's War on Journalism.*)

Part Three

What Killed Journalism?

Chapter Nine

The miseducation of a profession

Reporters have traditionally been, in North America, at least, prone to hubris and pathological self-congratulation. The London Press Club had bucked the trend, and commissioned a study to determine what psychological strengths and weaknesses journalists tended to possess in 2017 (discovering that reporters tended to handle stress and their emotions poorly). However, the Canadian Journalism Foundation was busy spinning that same primal propagandistic screeching as a way to uncover truths. As one May 24 "J-talk": The Media as Opposition: Covering Trump in a Post-Truth Era decreed:

> In their first live joint appearance, these stellar journalists will discuss the need to apply constant, critical pressure on a US president who many feel threatens the fabric of democracy, journalism and civil society.

It did not concern the CJF that journalists were not elected by the people to be any official "opposition" to any regime: with declining circulation and ratings, citizens have voted out the press from such roles in the first place. Journalists are not in the business to be some sort of guerrilla opposition party: their mandate is to uncover and reflect reality and truth.

If an entire profession has no understanding of their own place in the world, how they conduct their jobs becomes a highly concerning and problematic dilemma. Journalists do not know what they are doing, and hence, future generations are doomed to fall into the same rabbit hole they are told is their Promised Land. With the obsession North American journalists had with Trump, the press has been ignoring truths as problems continue to go unnoticed, and hence unchallenged. The problem is that journalists have had no training that has clued them in that their blinders are only cementing their demise.

Training journalists should be an extremely complicated matter. First of all, there is the matter of understanding the greatest obstacles and enemies to the truth: lies and propaganda. After all, if you do not know what is real and what is not, then anything you report has the potential of making you a vector: a disease carrier who infects the information stream. The story becomes useless, harmful even, and can cost hundreds of people their freedoms or even their lives. The most important skill of becoming a human lie detector is essential for anyone in the information-dissemination business, especially those who have access to billions of people.

Journalism education was never so complicated, and the lax education has contributed to the profession's shocking decay and demise. If a degree or diploma cannot prepare you for the realities and obstacles facing the profession, then the degree itself has no utility, and hence no value, no matter the cost of the education, the credentials of those teaching, or the difficulty of obtaining the degree. These are all smoke-and-mirrors misdirection to hide the simple fact that new journalists, as well as veterans, have been helpless in saving the profession. Prestige and a journalism degree have become mutually exclusive concepts. Unlike other disciplines where educators understand their mandates as they intellectually equip their charges appropriately, journalism education has not helped the profession.

What is the difference between them? What students learn is craft. They learn how to put stories together, from how to interview to how to edit words and footage. There are classes on ethics and the law. There will be courses on covering the political and the arts.

What they don't learn are the critical aspects of questioning information they receive. There will not be courses on how media ownership will impact how they will do their jobs, let alone how to spot deception from those in high positions of power, who have veteran experience in intimidating and beguiling the curious. Psychology is an essential subject for any journalist to know; yet it is not taught in j-school. How does someone suffering from paranoia or depression misinterpret information?

J-schools do not consider the differences between reality and truth, or perception and reality, an ironic omission as it was journalist Walter Lippmann who brought attention to that very dilemma in his ground-breaking 1922 book *Public Opinion*, but it goes further than that. Truth is universal and absolute. Reality is relative, and can be altered. Perceptions and interpretations impede our grasp on both reality and truth, yet modern journalists and their educators have opted to ignore his warnings.

If journalism had a sturdier foundation, it requires a solid understanding of how people's habits and structures of thought guide them — and often, deceive them. Knowing how we make decisions and interpret (or misinterpret) reality is the most essential skill a journalist requires. It is not as if there is no body of work examining this kind of knowledge out there; in fact, psychology (from cognitive psychology to neuroscience) is filled with studies outlining how the disconnect from the visual and the audial can lead us to misinterpret what we hear. We talk about the troubles while implanting false memories. We know how our rule-of-thumb thinking can lead us to make logical errors. We know how people's responses are controlled by groupthink, and that artificially dividing people into random groups influences their perceptions of both those in their in-group — and those who an experimenter dubbed their out-group. We know people's behavior is influenced by authorities and by even the number of people in the same room, during an unexpected crisis. We know that a single word can influence how we perceive past events. We know all of those things as psychologists have discovered these patterns in human behavior for us for decades.

Yet j-schools offer no guidance in explaining to their students that there is more to journalism than conducting an interview, observing an event, or reading a database or court transcript. They do not warn them that interviewees could be appealing to an authority figure as they fall for a confirmation bias because they can be suffering from paranoid personality disorder (PPD), and are being heavily influenced by a trusted source who is feeding into their fears for personal gain. A source's understanding of the information may be distorted, but also may distrust journalists, and wishes to deceive. If a journalist takes the information at face value, there is a high risk of missing the motive for a potential deception, and hence, missing the real story. But even if the news producer verifies the information, the reporter still risks being influenced to misinterpret a situation if he or she does not question whether his source has skewed perceptions. The journalist must know how to formulate a theory, and then be able to test it before presenting the findings to the public.

How best to conduct an interview? Could questioning sources have long-term ramifications, especially if questions could taint eyewitnesses to a crime?

Psychologists have shown that, in fact, false and distorted memories can be planted by means of questions. For example, asking audiences whether they saw "the gun" will elicit more false positives than if they are asked if they saw "a gun".

Psychologists study how we think, feel, and interpret our surroundings, which is essential knowledge to all information-gatherers — not just to be aware how they can misinterpret information, but how they, too, can fall for the same self-deceptions to counter it. Journalism is, in essence, *applied psychology*. We seek journalism in order for us to understand how to navigate through the human psyche — individual as well as the collective.

For instance, many people are driven by their narrative confines: they always see themselves as saviors of those around them, when they are, in fact, meddlers. They may present themselves to the media as heroes, visionaries, or winners, and journalists are likely tempted to perpetrate the error in judgment. There is no school of thought in journalism. There are no studies or experiments that even entertain any notion of a source who may be inclined to see the world in a specific way.

There aren't scientific experiments conducted in journalism faculties. There are no clinical trials to determine how to spot a manipulator, or how to spot a false memory. When media companies look for salvation from declining circulation or ratings, they go to marketing companies and focus groups, often getting reports with flawed methodology. They do not look to academia to find out for them.

This demonstrates the shortcomings of j-school, and the impact of its lack of experimentation are apparent in the output of outlets.

We do not have to go farther than Columbia Journalism School, an institution that has been dubbed as "the thinking person's journalism school", and is one of the loftiest degrees someone in the field can earn, yet it has not led the way to reviving its profession's credibility or fortunes through innovation of theory and methods. Thousands of journalists have lost their jobs, publications have folded, and public trust has eroded.

Former dean Nicholas Lemann, who had been at the helm from 2003–2012, had been touted as a sterling example of a dean who helped transform the educational structure of the department. When he left, the university had boasted in a press release that one of his "major initiatives as dean was to ramp up the intellectual portion of the journalism school's offerings". Journalism's penchant for cultivating an elitist image was no problem, as he had been keen on it: "I have gone through life wishing I had three months to read Plato, Aristotle, Machiavelli and to discuss the master ideas that are most likely to be of use in journalism and then linking them to the practice of journalism."

Yet those "master ideas" Lemann wistfully discusses were white, male, and flawed. These ideas work only in a rigged system that hinges on encouraging the illusions of arbitrary confines that favor patriarchal and masculine thinking patterns of European males who existed in much simpler times. Once upon a time, the Great Man theory seemed to work — yet the profession perpetually marginalized and alienated those who were not part of the group of *master thinkers.* The Newspaper Association of America had, for instance, attempted to increase diversity in US newsrooms, yet never questioned whether or not the work structure or base assumptions of the profession secretly drove divergent voices away from it.

Had there been serious academic inquiry from places such as Columbia, there may have been an empirical way to confirm or refute the theory. Instead, students are trained to be more entertaining at posh cocktail parties during lags and awkward moments, rather than diligent experts at finding truth and reality in a vortex of delusions, lies, spin, propaganda, ignorance, narratives, or even chaos, anarchy, and madness. A journalist is not someone who is in love with his or her quality of thinking; the reporter is to be devoted to understanding the world, and push past the untested truisms and sanctioned insanity of the subjects and rigged surroundings.

Despite the incessant self-congratulations those in the field of journalism give themselves, Columbia has serious deficits in its approach to information verification. Instead of dead men who waxed philosophically, understanding the ways of scam artists and liars would be of more practical use for journalists, whose careers essentially boil down to listening and reading lies and propaganda from every direction every day, and finding the truths so many do their best to hide from the public.

In a profession where lawyers threaten and image consultants beguile, it is easy to lose sight of the truth, and begin to accept the base assumptions of those you cover as absolute truth and reality. Business reporters degrade themselves into becoming cheerleaders for robber barons. Journalists covering governmental affairs often choose to run for public office, particularly in Canada, where many make the switch, yet have no legacy or impact in their positions.

Some, such as former Canadian broadcasters Mike Duffy and Pamela Wallin, found themselves in legal trouble when their spending habits triggered suspicion and they were investigated. While they may have been cleared of illegal wrongdoing, their documented largesse caused a scandal, and made journalists as a whole seem obsessed with getting a patronage appointment. In turn, it brought into question how they used and misused their media job to snag a more lucrative political career.

There is no journalism school to guide students to understand the problems plaguing the profession, as those problems have increased over time, with no end in sight.

There has been speculation that of the top ten professions to attract psychopaths, two of the ten are in communications (media clocked in at number 3, while Journalist was number six, according to UK psychologist Kevin Dutton, though how Dutton came to the specific conclusion is not completely defined). There is much going for the theory that psychopathic thought is part of the professional fabric. Journalistic objectivity assumes emotions taint a story; hence, emotion must be entirely removed. However, the lack of emotions is the crux of psychopathic thinking. While it is true that emotional ignorance can taint our perceptions, we can first remove emotion and examine an issue logically, but then use emotion to understand the nuances better.

We need emotional intelligence and empathy, yet much of partisan journalism shuts out empathy entirely. Anyone with a different opinion, or even need, is to be demonized and seen as a villain. Journalism has gone from encouraging psychopathic thought in its very paradigms to taking sides without any regard as to how their coverage could potentially alter, or even destroy innocent lives.

But j-school will not be the place for future journalists to challenge the old structures, or learn how to find better ways of getting to the truth. They do not learn the art or science of understanding information, before letting others understand it, as well. After all, it is the discarded old guard who land on their feet in these academic halls and continue the cycle into oblivion, never questioning their old ways or considering the future.

Chapter Ten

Pseudo-journalism

The week of February 13, 2017 was an extraordinary one in US journalism. It had not been a full month of Donald J. Trump's tenure as President of the US, but the coverage had been relentless; so much so, that there were already news stories about "fatigue". The mass media hysteria had already almost seemed to reach its climax; yet there was more misery to come as the commander in chief set off more fireworks with contentious press conferences. Here, the insults would continue to be lobbed at the press, who, in turn, would return the favor in their coverage.

It was an unprecedented turn in the news world, and one that seemed a stark contrast to the press's love affair with Trump's charismatic and shrewd predecessor Barack Hussein Obama. By February 24, 2017, *The New York Times, Politico,* and CNN had been barred from a briefing by White House Press Secretary Sean Spicer, with the Associated Press and *Time* magazine refusing to attend in protest; however, partisan outfits such as the Fox News Channel and *Breitbart News* were both in attendance.

Some in the press conceded that their main target of consternation had managed to gain support with his words, as the *Washington Post*'s Ed Rogers admitted on February 17, 2017, calling the show "riveting", as he conceded: "I don't have the answer, but I have received dozens of tweets and messages from people applauding Trump's performance."

But for all the blustering and scathing tantrums against the president, what is important to note is the press had repeatedly covered a canned event — his press conferences. That was not original research. That was not active research. That was not investigative research. That was not research, at all.

Rogers had declared that Trump "had won the battle" in the

war with journalists. However, he did not question whether or not it was for the press to wage a "war" with *any* newsmaker. Theirs may be a war on lies, but when the press begins to target individuals, they are no longer soldiers making their way through reality. Instead, they are warmongers looking for a fight as they reward those who they see as allies willing to praise them — and punish those who see their own hypocrisy and flaws.

The media obsession with the puppet master who knows their ultimate folly and weaknesses could not be contained. *Vanity Fair* editor Graydon Carter — whose own defunct magazine *Spy* had not given Trump fawning coverage other outlets had shamelessly done in the 1980s — called the forty-fifth president's White House, "the gang who couldn't shoot straight". Yet despite the missteps, the press was incapable of finding any actual information happening inside the most powerful building in the US. None of the coverage was news; it was personal. That Trump had declared that the press, "is not my enemy, it is the enemy of the American People!" was not new. If it isn't his press conferences, the press report on the blustery musings of his Twitter feed, which anyone can do without the media. If it is not a tweet, it is one of his speeches to the public, which is also nothing more than a canned event.

The sum total of reportage for the entire week was nil. The press may not be the enemy of the public, but they long ago ceased to be its ally, let alone servant or guardian to the people.

Just as much of science and technology reporting is, in fact, advertorial (companies buying advertising in media outlets and are rewarded with legitimate positive coverage). Foreign journalism is often the result of countries hiring public relations firms to guide the slant, and contain any negative information from seeping into news stories. Edelman PR is as of this writing the "world's largest public relations firm". They were hired in 2016 by the Saudi government (a regime that has a long history of employing firms such as Hill+Knowlton to push their various interests) to combat the oil-rich nation's image of not being on the climate change train. As, too, were lobbyists The Podesta Group (founded by disturbing art enthusiast Anthony Podesta. Podesta's brother John was the former chairman of the 2016 Hillary Clinton presidential campaign in her failed presidential run. It was Anthony's invitation for his brother to attend a "spirit cooking" dinner from performance artist Marina Abramovic that was the subject of one WikiLeaks data dump during the 2016 US presidential election). Though Tony Podesta's affinity for disturbing artwork was proudly showcased in *Washington Life* magazine in 2015.

The use of public relations and lobbyists to shape press coverage is more than worth it. For example, in one January 30, 2017 amended filing with FARA (The Foreign Agents Registration Act), separate emails from Tara Chandra, vice president of the Podesta Group, and David Adams, principle of the same, that had included articles from Reuters, Bloomberg, and *Politico*. It also included a read-out from the White House of a phone conversation between President Trump and King Salman Abdulaziz Al-Saud of Saudi Arabia regarding Syria and Yemen. The coverage was lockstep with one another, and despite the fact federal and global beats are usually reserved for veteran journalists, they did not seem to stray from a lobbyist's choreographed script.

Public relations played a big part in shaping public perceptions in several high-profile global conflicts, such as Hill+Knowlton's infamous work with Kuwait during the first Gulf War, where their propaganda had citizens believe Iraqi soldiers had killed Kuwaiti newborns by taking them out of hospital incubators. Journalists had bought the coverage without reservation until *Harper's* magazine publisher John MacArthur had done what the press should have: his investigations found the story was a fraud. Even during the Civil War in the former Yugoslavia, firms such as Ruder Finn Global Public Affairs represented warring sides (the Republic of Croatia, as well as the Republic of Bosnia-Herzegovina). Later, one of its officials Jim Harff told French journalist Jacques Merlino in 1993 that his firm was not in the business to "verify information", but boasted that the firm had "managed to put Jewish opinion on our side. This was a sensitive matter, as the dossier was dangerous looked at from this angle". This is because then Croatian President Franjo Tudjman "was very careless in his book, *Wastelands of Historical Reality*. Reading his writings one could accuse him of anti-Semitism", as his book asserted that "only 900,000 Jews were killed in the Holocaust, not six million". Meanwhile in Bosnia, their leader "President Izetbegovic strongly supported the creation of a fundamentalist Islamic state in his book, *The Islamic Declaration*".

Harff went on to tell Merlino that "the Croatian and Bosnian past was marked by real and cruel anti-Semitism. Tens of thousands of Jews perished in Croatian camps...[o]ur challenge was to reverse this attitude and we succeeded masterfully". This was as they "outwitted three big Jewish organizations — the B'nai B'rith Anti-Defamation League, the American Jewish Committee, and the American Jewish Congress". He also went on to boast that:

> ...when the Jewish organizations entered the game on the side of the [Muslim] Bosnians, we could promptly equate the Serbs with the Nazis in the public mind. Nobody understood what was happening in Yugoslavia. The great majority of Americans were probably asking themselves in which African country Bosnia was situated.

He had assured Merlino that it was the first message that counted as denials and restrictions had no effect, meaning that:

> ...by a single move we were able to present a simple story of good guys and bad guys which would hereafter play itself. We

won by targeting the Jewish audience. Almost immediately there was a clear change of language in the press, with use of words with high emotional content such as ethnic cleansing, concentration camps, etc., which evoke images of Nazi Germany and the gas chamber of Auschwitz. No one could go against it without being accused of revisionism. We really batted a thousand.

There were many journalists during the coverage who feigned doing genuine and original investigation, yet it was no coincidence that every story they ever aired coincided perfectly with whatever press release those firms put out that day.

Every journalist that ever took the first packaged message they heard, regardless if it is a war story or a business one, is not a genuine news producer or even a reasonable facsimile or alternative, but a fraud.

It is not journalism, but *pseudo*-journalism. In a profession where transparency is not adhered to consistently, how a story is put together is not always obvious to those who have never worked in the profession. Often, a journalist is a passive and credulous conduit, who is used by an anonymous source who selectively leaks information as part of a bigger game: from removing an obstacle impeding their own political or financial well-being to merely wishing to seek retribution on a rival. Journalists skulk in front of rolling cameras in hot spots and war zones as if they were in hiding from snipers — yet the cameramen and the lighting crew would give their position away, especially at night — or a source being shown giving an anchor an interview on their laptop. However, it is more than obvious there is a cameraman in the room, meaning there is one superfluous recording device involved. These little tricks hint that there is far more dishonesty presented to viewers than news producers would admit. It is these inconsistencies that, on some unconscious level, tell news consumers there is filtering in their product, and when there is filtering, there is a question of accuracy.

The term bandied by both the US President and journalists was *fake news,* but for both, it had different meanings; namely, it was stories that went politically opposite to what the other side believed to be true. The facts may have been manufactured, but what made these stories *fake* had more to do with their underlying ideological assumptions than how accurate the 5Ws were in the piece.

However, it is not fake news that destroyed journalism so much as *pseudo-journalism* — a vastly different problem. Pseudo-journalism involves those in the news-producing business to go through the motions of putting together a story without actually doing the legwork. It mimics journalism in some ways on the surface, but on closer examination, there is nothing of value in a piece. Pseudo-journalism relies on easy methods of churning out a yarn: reliance on public relations, folksy logic, pandering to the partisan base by means of manipulation, and opining with color and logical fallacy instead of using logic — both intellectual and emotional — with facts.

When filler overtakes substance, disagreeing with a news story becomes a simple affair. Melodramatic music in a television story is a de facto dictate as to how the audience should be feeling: angry, frightened, or saddened. Few newsmagazines have resisted the use of music, just as newspapers have controlled the optics of photoshoots: victims always appeared doe-eyed and hunched, with a far-away stare. Having a mundane photograph of individuals is shunned in favor of one that pushes a narrative.

If there is one singular weakness that hounds the profession — it is that journalism is in its perpetual infancy. It is not a profession with a plan or set of methods and techniques. There is a decided lack of discipline, and it shows. Should a commodity, such as the enigmatic Trump, figure out how the press operates, journalists are helpless to deal with it, and instead, rely on tattling and tantrums, as they must play catch up to their puppet master. There is no war manual for the profession: there are only war stories — cheap anecdotes used to crow about successfully hunting a prey, but no viable system to find and properly interpret, analyze, and disseminate reality and truth.

Journalism has something in common with tattoos: a good tattoo isn't cheap, and a cheap tattoo isn't good. It is the same with news production: good journalism is expensive, yet news outlets cut corners in countless ways:

1. The press relies on press releases, video news releases, and press conferences instead of finding original information, primary research, and raw data. This is not to say reporters *never* use original research, but too many times, reporters attend briefings and other canned events instead of tracking down the raw and unprocessed information. Many hoaxes thrived on this journalistic weakness, from the Hitler diaries hoax to the Negativland hoax of the 1980s, where a musical group convinced countless journalists that they were wanted for questioning by the FBI. This was because they falsely claimed it was one of their songs that caused a teenaged boy to kill his family. Had the press tried to find the nonexistent FBI agent, they would have seen the ruse; instead, the band had to confess when they became bored with the publicity stunt.

2. There is no longer any discernible difference between soft newsmakers and hard newsmakers. Brad Pitt's love life carries equal weight to public policy in the eyes of the press. Celebrities have overtaken much of the local news, especially if the actor was once a local resident. Even local politicians may find it difficult to get press — good or bad. Voting records have given way to box office records — explaining the American — and Canadian — press's peculiar obsession with Trump at the expense

of overseeing what mayors, governors, senators, and congressmen have done since the 2016 US presidential election. Trump is a celebrity who catapulted himself into the sphere of hard news. While his political rival lived her adult life in the hard news sphere, he was unable to compete with someone whose advantage was previous publicity.

3. Using opinion over facts. It is the most troubling sign that pseudo-journalism has overtaken the genuine version of news production. How people should think and feel has supplanted what people must *know*. How they wish to use the facts given, should be up to the audience entirely. The Fox News Channel perfected the replacement of facts with knee-jerk opinion, particularly on *The O'Reilly Factor,* where former host, Bill O'Reilly, made it a habit of calling people with whom he disagrees with "pinheads" and "idiots". It is a given those individuals have no right to respect, let alone get a fair hearing in the court of public opinion. It is also a given that audiences need to be told who to like and trust, and who to hate. What isn't journalism is not difficult to discern; yet opinion has become so prevalent in news culture, that the mere presentation of factual information provided in an objective manner seems to pale in comparison.

4. There is the use of color as filler, padding out articles while reducing the factual information within articles. How a singer laughs in the dressing room is unimportant compared to whether the same singer uses the profession as a front for drug smuggling, yet print has made it a habit of providing extraneous details at the expense of the 5Ws.

5. Sophistry rules over logic and facts. When faulty arguments overshadow the evidence to back up those claims, it is no longer journalism. It is intellectual

directives disguised as news, telling news consumers to feel angry or afraid.

But most of all, it is the reliance on press releases, photo ops, and press conferences that is the biggest red flag that journalists are taking a passive approach at the news. Primary sources are ignored for processed information. Raw data is not linear; it is fragmented, and often contradictory, not unlike a civil trial which purpose is to determine percentage of blame for a misfortune between two or more parties. It is not to blame, judge, or condemn, but understand the reality of the situation, so a proper and effective solution can be found. A politician who reads a speechwriter's oration after practicing and testing it in rehearsals is not presenting real or primary information; yet journalists prefer the PR stunt over the truth.

As traditional journalism flounders, Internet barons are taking full advantage of the anarchistic void as they control the flow of information, with disturbing results. In February 2017, for instance, Facebook touted:

> ...a new program to establish stronger ties between Facebook and the news industry. We will be collaborating with news organizations to develop products, learning from journalists about ways we can be a better partner, and working with publishers and educators on how we can equip people with the knowledge they need to be informed readers in the digital age.

The impetus for the editorial hijacking had been simple: it was the 2016 US presidential election where Facebook's role as vector infecting the information stream made news. The explosion of unverified and bogus articles spread, as legitimate stories through individual feeds that had upset those whose presidential candidate had lost. How trustworthy was a site that had been short-sighted by allowing a live-feed to broadcast without vetting, leading to several suicides and murders to be broadcast live online, was anyone's guess. However, the company had decided it knew what it was doing, and was ready to impose its gullibility to billions of people.

Its online press release did not give a hint of the problems as it assured it would:

> ...help... with eyewitness media. Eyewitnesses who upload videos and images during breaking news events have become powerful and important sources for journalists. We are proud to be a member of the First Draft Partner Network, a coalition of platforms and 80+ publishers, that works together to provide practical and ethical guidance in how to find, verify and publish content sourced from the social web.

It continued to ignore its lack of credentials all the same:

> As we seek to support journalism, we will also be working on new ways to help give people information so they can make smart choices about the news they read — and have meaningful conversations about what they care about.

The Orwellian mindset is chilling hubris on multiple levels. It would decide what was newsworthy as it also decided that the gatekeepers would be the ones whose previous irresponsibility caused the problem in the first place:

> We will work with third-party organizations on how to better understand and to promote news literacy both on and off our platform to help people in our community have the information they need to make decisions about which sources to trust... and bring a consortium of experts together to help decide on what new research to conduct and projects to fund.

Journalists are accustomed to being gatekeepers, and they often do not see how entrenched the archaic mindset has become. The difference now is the media divide has pitted political factions against one another as they use their old mindsets against one another. On the Left, MSNBC's Mika Brzezinski had made a chilling slip on-air on February 22, 2017:

> Well, I think that the dangerous, you know, edges here are that [President Trump] is trying to undermine the media and trying to make up his own facts. And it could be that while unemployment and the economy worsens, he could have undermined the messaging so much that he can actually control exactly what people think. And that, that is our job.

While the right-wing partisan publications such as *The Daily Caller, Zero Hedge,* and *Breitbart* had covered her remarks with predictable consternation as the *Drudge Report* also picked up the story, the left-wing counterparts were deafeningly silent. (She had tried to justify her remark on her Twitter account, "Today I said it's the media's job to keep President Trump from making up his own facts, NOT that it's our job to control what people think"; though, her parapraxis implied something else entirely.)

The tag team of traditional media and social media has been a singularly destructive force in information gathering and dissemination, as the combination has been the place to incubate pseudo-journalism. This is because it eclipses the genuine article, and few know the difference. The rise and implosion of Milo Yiannopoulos — a controversial media figure whose guerrilla assaults on traditionally oppressed groups would be a non-news story, save for the fact he said them while being employed as senior technology editor for *Breitbart News* (and founder of *The Kernel,* an Internet tabloid dealing with technology). Had the press truly been dedicated to the gathering of facts over stunts and spectacles, pseudo-agitators such as Yiannopoulos would not be considered newsworthy, and would be ignored.

He is not a policy-maker who affects lives with his actions: he is an editor of a partisan website, who courted controversy by deliberately insulting identifiable groups with his sophistry. Once upon a time, he would have been an obscure fringe footnote on par with shock singer G. G. Allin. But as the press panicked at their decline, and looked for any figure to trigger responses from news consumers, they gave him attention he could not handle as he relied on tricks and stunts to keep himself a constant part of the news cycle. His opinions are not unique, nor are they substantial, yet the press has missed their gate-keeping mindset, and amplified his message. This gave him false legitimacy as he continued to push the envelope until his February 2017 comments on pedophilia cost him a $250,000 book deal, and he resigned from *Breitbart*. The left-wing publications had used the debacle to argue there were divides among their political rivals; the Right, on the other hand, had taken Brzezinski's slip of the tongue and attacked, deflecting attention away from the problematic Yiannopoulos. In both cases, it was ideological warfare driving both episodes, with very little news value to justify the coverage.

In a planet with well over 7.4 billion people, it is thanks to the press that public discourse has suddenly whittled down to gossiping about the Kardashian clan, Donald Trump, and Milo Yiannopoulos. Almost no one else matters. Instead of expanding our world and understanding of nuance, the press, and their intellectual inferior offspring social media, have grossly constricted it, and have proven themselves utterly incapable of fixing it. Monomania has been mistaken for tenacity, and paranoia has replaced investigation. In the US, the collective mental breakdown of the profession is unprecedented, and shows no signs of abating, especially as the North American press viciously attack those who dare question or critique them as they see themselves as superior to those they cover by methods of either fawning or bullying. Those who stand up to their tyranny often find themselves verbally assaulted with petty and personal swipes that imply they are completely defective and without merit by a group of people who cannot conceive that they are seriously flawed and destructive.

It took no less than journalistic maven Bob Woodward to warn the rest of his profession, that when it came to their vendetta with Trump they, "shouldn't whine, and if we sound like we are an interest group only concerned with ourselves, it does not work with the public. At the same time, we need to continue the in-depth inquiries, the investigations".

It is a very sorry state of affairs imploding as tunnel vision obscures the decay around us. And this, all while even those in the profession can no longer discern real journalism from pseudo-journalism, and for those who understand the profession, watching the crush of defeat has been a painful exercise to endure.

Chapter Eleven

The gullibility of the conniving

There is a difference between being cunning and being conniving: the former involves employing intellectual strategy to best an opponent with the future and goals in mind, while the latter involves being willing to deceive, scam, bully, or backstab someone without regard to long-term consequences of your actions. Connivers live in the now. The cunning always have an end goal in mind. The former group are simple and shallow with no understanding of nuance, while the latter are complex thinkers who see the big picture.

That makes connivers gullible by default. They have a narrative that blinds them to reality: that their actions bring vendettas and hard feelings, and that people who are wronged will not forget as others who witness the machinations stay away to protect themselves. There will always be those who believed they can out-connive the conniver, but alienation begins to mount until there are too many angry people and too few allies. These individuals will be left worrying whether or not they will be next on the conniver's hit list, but the conniver never sees the imminent fallout: only that he "won" another game against a decreed opponent.

In journalism, there are those who hunt and gather information with cunning, and those who do it through conniving means. How a journalist chooses to gather news determines the long-term viability of their careers.

John MacArthur provided history with one of the most stunning examples of cunning journalism in 1992: when the US decided to invade Iraq to liberate Kuwait, the government used the rallying cry of televised testimony of a 15-year-old girl named Nayirah, who tearfully recounted how Iraqi soldiers killed newborns at a hospital, where she volunteered while on vacation.

Smelling a ruse, he played a gambit to verify whether or not the gossip he heard was true: that Nayirah was a member of the Saudi royal family. He made a strategic phone call, congratulating the royal in question for her performance, and was told that he wasn't supposed to know that fact. The masterstroke was brilliant, elegant, and effective.

But true journalism absolutely requires employing techniques of uncovering truth hidden in spin and lies. People will not tell reporters they are embezzling from pensioners just because they asked nicely. Journalism is a never-ending campaign of truth-hiders trying to evade truth-seekers. Reporters have employed secret codes in war zones, getting explosive information past censors and enemy lines. They have disguised themselves, and gotten inside some of the world's most secretive and dangerous lairs. The world is much indebted to those reporters, who have put everything on the line for a single necessary truth to be freed.

Then there are those who are less concerned with truth, than they are with optics and competition. They are not concerned with uncovering facts, but humiliating people in public — if it can be done by exposing a truth that is fairly easy to uncover, they will do it, but if there is a shortcut, they will opt for the easiest method.

The classic conniver's scheme can be found when the *Toronto Star* followed then mayor Rob Ford to a Kentucky Fried Chicken to fink on him to their readers that he was not sticking to his diet (that his girth was not melting away would prove to be just as telling). It was not until *a drug dealer phoned a reporter directly* to inform her that the mayor was into drugs more than fast food, did the paper finally have its first substantial scoop.

A conniving reporter merely seeks to cause discomfort with minimum effort, but maximized results, with no regard to how their methods will impact on their future.

When the US government allowed reporters to "embed" with troops during the 2003 Iraq War, the deal seemed appealing: they would have protection, having riveting visuals of soldiers, and be given information directly from the government, removing the need for the labor in trying to find and verify information on their own. After all, many journalists had been accustomed to spoon-fed information during the civil war in the former Yugoslavia, where PR firms set up white tents to disseminate propaganda.

There would be drawbacks, however. The information was processed and skewed. Movements and routines of journalists would be confined. The army could easily expel any journalist who did not abide by their rules, and was no better than a white tent.

What is probably the most peculiar trait in media companies is their use of market research and focus groups. On the surface, a newspaper should be no different than a mechanic in terms of seeking outside consultants, yet journalists are in the business of having a pulse on their surroundings. They do not know their readers, viewers, or communities, and hence, must have others tell them instead.

Yet media outlets have also had to use outside consultants to tell them what went wrong internally, meaning they do not understand themselves or their newsroom. When *USA Today* finally clued in that their star reporter Jack Kelley made up his stories, they hired an outside private investigator to sort their mess out. When *Rolling Stone* was humiliated for publishing Sabrina Erdely's troubled rape campus story, they retained the Columbia School of Journalism to audit them. When the Canadian Broadcasting Corporation was hit by the scandalous claims of sexual harassment from their one-time radio presenter Jian Ghomeshi, they needed an outside consultant to investigate, even though women who went to their supervisors to report the abuse were told to, in essence, put up and shut up.

The implications are troubling. News producers do not have a read on their communities; they merely superimpose a preset narrative as they ignore contradictory evidence. The troubled ones do not have a read on their own failings. They look to experts to save their dying profession. In Canada, they have used inquiries and think tanks to push for more government intervention on their behalf to curb media concentration, or fund them when they no longer have audiences who will use their product.

There is a saying that journalists have a knowledge base 30-miles wide, but 1-inch deep, yet increasingly, it seems that, too, is shrinking. Their ground is eroding. While journalism is still viable in the UK, for instance, the rate of decay in the US is increasing, but it is Canada whose journalistic fortunes are in complete shambles with no relief in sight. *Maclean's* magazine, one of the country's oldest news publications with the highest circulation of the genre, not only received partial government funding, but its publishing frequency had gone from weekly to monthly by 2016.

Declining audiences mean journalism's ability to penetrate the public's awareness decreases over time as the habit of consuming news becomes lost; however, the Internet has not proven to be a reliable replacement to the profession, either.

The 2016 US presidential election was a turning point for more than just US politics: it was also a turning point for both social media and traditional media. Social media had ridden the same tide as traditional media: Hillary Clinton was going to win the election because she was the only sensible choice, and it was what all those hip kids wanted, anyway. *BuzzFeed* and the *Huffington Post* were enthusiastic supporters, while right-wing publications touted for Trump, though most reluctantly; yet their disdain for Clinton was severe.

Trump did not win the popular vote and became president just as Hillary Clinton did not receive the popular vote, when she snagged the Democratic nomination — it was *Bernie Sanders* who had more voters backing him, but the superdelegates pushed her over the limit. These two were not popular candidates, particularly in comparison with the far more charismatic Barack Obama or even Bill Clinton. (For those who follow US politics, the rule of thumb is simple, but reliable: whichever candidate looks like the one to be the life of the cocktail party will win the election.)

Trump's victory was the final nail in the coffin for modern journalism for many reasons: if one side places all of their firepower on a single target, it is a virtual given that they will take down that target, and in this case, on the surface, at least, the target was a 70-old political neophyte, whose modern claim to fame was being a presenter on a serialized game show.

But the press seriously underestimated the cunning of the one-man army known as Donald J. Trump. They failed to see that he was a veteran in exploiting them. He knew their old tricks, and used those tricks to gain lavish press for himself for decades.

They failed to see that publications such as *Spy* magazine had managed to do much to damage his public image; yet he was still standing and the elegantly witty satiric investigative magazine folded. They may have referred to him as a "short-fingered vulgarian", but he got the last laugh on them. They failed to see he was not afraid of taking calculated risks and hard work, or that he understood the public, and they did not.

With a Twitter account, Trump bypassed the media with short, simple tweets that were easy to understand and had messages that were memorable. While the long-winded journalists threw a meandering laundry list of his defects, his simple message stood out to voters: *Make America great again.*

As a slogan, it was one of the most effective ones in modern history, just as Barack Obama's *Yes we can* captured imaginations. Though, unlike Obama, Trump stuck with the single line, and managed to get his message past the fortress created by the press, who were no longer enamored with him. But most of all, they failed to see that he was a strategist without peer in the modern anarchy of communications.

To understand modern US politics, or why Trump bested journalists at their own game, one must understand the bane of the US Conservatives' existence — Saul Alinsky — an activist in large cities such as Chicago and Detroit, starting from the 1930s — is considered to be the father of community organizing as he fought for the rights of the poor, as well as for civil rights. His book *Rules for Radicals,* can be considered a modern war manual for the urban poor. His contribution to progressive ideology is profound and real, and much of minority and women's rise in US society can be directly connected to his keen sense of battling an Establishment that claims moral high ground, is wealthy — and has no desire to elevate the fortunes of those who are trapped in poverty and despair.

The Left used Alinsky's rules with slow but substantial success over the decades, and managed to create their own power base and moral code over time. This was much to the consternation of the Right, who lost the moral voice of the US to the Left over time. While Alinky's book was not without flaw, the Left honed in on several rules, managing to gain the upper hand in many Western beliefs, particularly normalizing feminism, gay rights, civil rights, interracial marriages, and, before the election, transgender rights. What would have been seen as scandalous even in the 1990s was now mundane. While there were many other activists who made significant contributions, Alinsky gave the Left their *method* of combat. (Someone such as Martin Luther King Jr. gave inspiration, for instance. Both men were pillars in their movements, but in vastly different ways.) The Right, try as they might, were losing ground, because Alinsky gave a simple, but effective way for the Left to challenge their confines and decrees.

Then came along former card-carrying Democrat turned Republican presidential candidate Donald J. Trump.

The Right did not like him, and many "star" conservatives from failed presidential candidates John McCain and Mitt Romney to House Speaker Paul Ryan would repeatedly denounce him. The Bush family endorsed Clinton; though, they no longer held any political title (their disdain for Trump had more to do with his spectacularly dashing former governor Jeb Bush's presidential aspirations).

Yet Trump won the Republican presidential nomination by ridiculing his rivals one by one before he won the highest office in the US. Not only did he not have the support of the Establishment Right, but he was also outnumbered by the Establishment Left. However, his victory was one even the Republican party could not help but appreciate, as it broke a barrier: he cracked Alinksy's code as he became impervious to its rules. For example, *Saturday Night Live* is not a comedy show, but it is an effective tool for the ideological Left, using Alinsky's rules with devastating precision at the expense of the Right.

US Conservatives have always had a profound fear of Alinsky, demonizing him, labelling him as evil. However, if their definition of evil is liberating people from a life of misery, oppression, and poverty, then they themselves have much iniquity to answer for.

While many on the Right have boasted they could overcome Alinsky's rules, they have not had much success with it. Many presidential victories merely reflected shifting sentiments: for the last thirty years, Americans have had a tendency to give one president from one side of the political spectrum two terms in office before giving the other side two terms afterwards.

However, it seemed that trend would alter in 2016. The press was absolutely certain Clinton would win, and all of the signs seem to point in that direction. Internet memes were clearly on the side of the former First Lady, as were the polls and press coverage. The skits of *Saturday Night Live* (SNL), were the loudest part of the chorus. SNL honed in Alinsky's fifth rule to perfection: "Ridicule is man's most potent weapon. It's hard to counterattack ridicule, and it infuriates the opposition, which then reacts to your advantage". It is this rule that has been the most problematic for the Right, and modern US political comedy has taken full advantage of it.

Ridicule is more than merely disrespectful: it establishes a pecking order where those who laugh position themselves as intellectually superior to those they are mocking, all as it hides under the guise of humor. Programs in the US such as *SNL, The Daily Show,* and the now defunct *Colbert Report* (though the host continues his antics on *Late Night with Stephen Colbert*) are all based in Alinsky's theories. While UK and Canadian broadcasters have their own satirical programs, they are not the same weapons.

Much of modern-day comedy has become propaganda with inherent assumptions built-in, or what Noam Chomsky would refer to as "internalized assumptions" — meaning comedy assumes their ideas of right and wrong are divine and absolute, regardless if they are or not, with the inherent assumption that we must isolate, mock, and ridicule those who do not think like us. This was not Alinsky's original intent, especially as it was to be a tool of the dispossessed; however, over time, those who rose to become powers of their own still continued to employ the rule, which had not been Alinsky's objective.

The power of satire is often greater than the power of the press. Sarah Palin is a case in point. To understand how powerful US satirists are in modern discourse, it is important to understand Palin's defeat. In a country where there have been very few female governors (the "liberal" states of New York and California have yet to have a single female governor, and neither Los Angeles nor New York City as of 2017 even had a single female *mayor*. To date, in the entire history of the US, only thirty-four women were governors, and as of April 2017, there were *five* currently in office, two Democratic, three Republican, and two — one Democratic and one Republican — recently resigned to take political positions elsewhere. Of those five, one had been appointed to take the place of scandal-plagued former Alabama governor Robert Bentley, who was forced to resign), Palin was a young, popular female governor of the rough and rugged state of Alaska, no small feat to accomplish. She was winsome, tough talking, attractive, and charismatic, while honing a folksy charm without seeming too perfect.

When then Republican presidential candidate and Arizona Senator John McCain was lagging behind in the polls against the charming and shrewd Barack Obama, it seemed as if his campaign was over; yet he chose Palin as his vice-presidential running mate, shocking everyone, and reinvigorating his campaign.

But Palin had done the unthinkable: she coopted the race and became the star, forming her own strategy — she was a soldier who could strategize, and took over the spotlight. By accounts, McCain was infuriated by the turn of events. She could best veterans in politics and forge ahead, seemingly unstoppable as she reignited the floundering campaign, while she somehow redefined it with her receiving top billing in the press.

What she could not best was Alinsky. *Saturday Night Live's* Tina Fey had done what an army of journalists could not, even then: turn a juggernaut into a joke with her eerily accurate impersonation of Palin with her now infamous one-liner: *I can see Russia from my house.* Palin never said those words (what she said, accurately, was, "You can actually see Russia from land here in Alaska"). Yet many people assumed it was Palin, not Fey who uttered the childish remark. Fey singlehandedly torpedoed Palin's aspirations with a single skit, while the press had endlessly written about her without the same result.

Though Barack Obama handily won the election, Palin's prospects after that considerably dimmed, while Fey's juggernaut merrily continued. It was that precision strike that turned a simple radical rule into a nuclear bomb. It then stood to reason that no one could survive such a psychic holocaust.

It was 2016, and Trump was giving Clinton a much harder time in the race than the pundits predicted. The political novice was proving to be a wily match to the political maven, despite the barrage of hostile missives from the press, talk show hosts, pundits, and satirists. It was an epically unequal match with Clinton's seasoned team of political operatives who knew what they were doing as it was all old hat to them.

Fey had a brainstorm, and suggested that her former fellow *30 Rock* costar Alec Baldwin go on *SNL* to play Trump, and many hoped he would do to Trump what Fey did to Palin: use Alinsky's fifth rule to ensure Clinton's victory. Like Fey, his appearance, voice, and mannerisms were eerily identical to the target to be ridiculed. The skits were iconic, memorable, accurate, sharp, and devastating to the target, even beyond what Fey's Palin had been. Most of all, they were genuinely funny, and some of the best writing the show had done in years, gaining notoriety and press attention without trying.

Yet none of it worked. Trump won, and Alinsky's fifth rule was revealed to have had flaws in it. It is not the scope of this book to outline where Trump managed to override it, but that he did override it by using another of Alinsky's tactic — igniting and channeling civil discontent — to do it, was even more devastating to Clinton's campaign, and ego.

The maneuver was more detrimental than it first appears, especially to those who are unaware of Alinsky, the Republican phobia of his theories, and the senior thesis of a young Hillary Clinton.

She interviewed Alinsky for her paper that Wellesley College in the late 60s released to the press in 2001. In it, she seemed to side with Alinsky's ideals — but she disagreed with his theory that civil disobedience was the way to do it, and she proffered an alternative that was more restrained and advocated working within a system to make change.

Clinton seemed to believe that Alinsky had it wrong — and that is in the precise place where Trump had proven her theory wrong in the real world. He had been the outsider marching in with the broken and fallen with the Rust Belt marching raucously behind him, propelling him to victory. His tactics were absolutely crushing to the insider Democrats as they no longer could count on their old war manual to foil the Republicans the way they did before, forgetting that Alinsky advocated modern guerrilla warfare that does not work if you are part of the Establishment. Despite the sophistication of technology, market research, marketing, focus groups, and all the other tools available to a veteran political team, their methods and ideas utterly failed them. It was a stunning blow that showed that the middleman's influence — the press — no longer existed, no matter how often they praised *SNL* for their weekly brilliance in mocking Trump. Neither the show nor the press corps had a chance.

Journalism, just like satire, had stooped to equally problematic gambits during the election. They, too, could not stop the results from going against their set narrative: that Clinton was the natural and logical choice for voters. Yet the myopic view was curious, given that in other elections, the Democrats were losing heavily to the Republicans, as the GOP retained control of the Senate, the House, and most of the governorships. The signs that the White House would also fall out of the Democrats' hands were more than obvious, and those in the press had paid scant attention to them in their stories. Even if Clinton won the election, voters had made it clear they were not going to give her the freedom to pursue her agenda. She would be tethered by two houses and at the state level.

It was these critical calculations that were entirely left out by all groupings of the media: traditional and online from those who claimed to be objective on both sides of the political spectrum that made no secret of their partisan leanings. Who controls the House and Senate are equally important to the outcome of an election, yet the press treated this warning signal as an annoying tidbit to be ignored.

The press's conniving ways had finally caught up with them, and they have not grasped their dilemma yet. Their tactics of strategically employing both flattery and mockery had failed them, just as it failed the satirists who used their finest techniques adeptly. Journalists did not see that their endorsements no longer meant anything, and they have been reeling from their gullibility. Their target Trump had played them for fools yet again by bypassing them completely, opting to use the brevity of Twitter for his short, simple, but easy to remember missives. The conniving had been taken by a single cunning man, making him the one-man army who used Alinsky's guerrilla tactics better than those who had decades to refine and perfect it.

While there are journalists who have confused being conniving with being a news producer, their slacking nature used to be hidden and propped up by those who were true news producers. Whenever there were criticisms about reporters' behavior, they could easily point to the ones who were producing investigative pieces.

The point is not whether or not good, even great, journalism still exists. It does. There are many reporters who still remember what a journalist is supposed to do, and have even given their lives and freedom to do it in an ultimate act of altruism. There are online equivalents in hacktivists who have gone even further to expose those corrupt in power. The soldiers to liberate truth from lies are in the war of their lives.

The problem is that *too much* bad journalism has taken over, and has infested the information stream beyond repair. The ratio of chaff to wheat has become such that it is not in a news consumer's best interests to bother finding the few grains in a mountain of chaff. The white noise has drowned out the warning sirens that there are too many problems mounting.

And the press has yet to concede to their sins of skulduggery, still pretending they have nothing to answer for, even as their castles have been neglected for so long, they crumbling to the ground, imprisoning them in the very evidence of every sin they ever committed.

Chapter Twelve

Sheltering the enabled

Fear is an exploitable emotion. Hatred and anger are others. War propaganda thrives in manipulating the fearful and the spiteful. Terror is a precious commodity that can be traded and invested, but for anyone foolish enough to believe it, they are perpetually at the mercy of those deceptive enough to control others through their emotions. The purpose of a journalist is not to install fear, anger, or hatred in its audience, but to inform them of their surroundings accurately, honestly, and realistically. How news consumers choose to react to the news is their own choice, but it is not the press's job to manipulate or rig an event to achieve a desired outcome, nor is it their job to protect or shelter an audience from the truth of a situation. In other words, the press is a living mirror, showing the world precisely what it is, good *and* bad, without hyperbole or treating the audience as children who need sheltering.

Yet depending on the country, sheltering is precisely what many news consumers get. North American journalism, which often feels it is on the vanguard of freedom and openness, rarely shows dead bodies on the evening news. Nudity is also frowned upon in newscasts; though, profanity is tolerated more on certain Canadian broadcasts than others. Self-censorship is heavily apparent. South American countries may oppress certain viewpoints, but their footage of devastation is more accurate and realistic.

Often, the trouble is the press are beholden to corporate and governmental interests, whether or not either group buy advertising or fund the outlet in question. Real estate companies frowned on Los Angeles' media outlets reporting on the high smog levels; hence, for years, they were not discussed. Publicists and public relations companies keep a tight rein on the coverage of their clients, and other times, the darker side of the wealthy is not fodder for mainstream news. Art collections of the rich and famous are seen as a status symbol, or a form of acquiring social gravitas, but to the criminal element, it is the secret currency that can be traded out in the open, but can be done so without overt detection. There will be far more news stories on the positive aspects of fine art than its darker side as a money laundering vehicle — never mind that Interpol as well as many national and international agencies have specialized divisions to combat the problem.

Criminal activity that is linked with a positive sign of upward mobility and culture is often kept out of news holes. It is one thing for celebrities and pseudo-celebrities to be brought to task for their antics and tantrums in the tabloids — these are individuals who can be dismissed as inane and ungrateful — but to question the entire collective of entertainers by means of an expose is another matter entirely. If, for instance, starlets enduring sexual harassment is expected in movie studios, the press will do little to expose it. If social media tycoons have become robber barons, revealing it may cause anger or despair with an audience who may believe the press is merely jealous or paranoid conspiracy theorists. However, refuting or confirming these issues is a simple affair as the numbers and/or eyewitnesses can easily reveal the extent of the systemic problem if it exists.

Yet when the press do bring up such scandals, often they are selective of whom they will expose as a rogue, just they themselves have been secretive, especially national broadcasters in the US who not only have their own publicists vet and attend interviews when their own anchors and reporters are on the other side of the microphone, let alone the nondisclosure agreements media outlets have their news producers sign. Some network executives issue directives, such as when former Bell Media president Kevin Crull had issued an order to CTV's head of news not to interview the head of the Canadian Radio and Television Commission, set to appear on the network's newscast in 2015, after the licensing commission had made an order Krull did not like.

The antics do not stop there. Left-wing publications will be careful to point out the skulduggery of their conservative enemies, while right-wing publications will return the favor to liberal enemies. There is an unspoken bible that dictates the profile of the targets: it must always be a businessman who tries to scam a customer for some outlets, or an unscrupulous government agency trying to harm a business for others. Roles in journalistic narratives have become caricatures: from love rats to monsters, there are parts to be cast and stereotypes to perpetrate, with no mitigating factors considered. When an individual is cast as a hero, any of the individual's vices will be ignored, downplayed, or explained away, sheltering the audiences from the truth about their chosen winner, implying he or she is absolutely perfect in every way; yet should the same person do something outside the accepted canon of what is perfect, the same variables will be plugged into a negative calculation.

Few people can recover: Angelina Jolie had been cast as a vixen by the press, yet had managed to rehabilitate her image for years — until she had been recast as a villain once again. She had been seen as untouchable as a good mother and humanitarian when she was romantically linked to Brad Pitt. However, when she filed for her divorce, she was accused of using her children and humanitarian work to generate good publicity for herself; though, the evidence to support the claims were not stated in any of the stories. A single individual who performs the same actions may often find those same actions interpreted in incongruous ways, depending on how benevolent the press feels at the moment. We do not always question journalists for it: if they knew seeming acts of benevolence were staged, then why did they keep silent? If those acts were benevolent, then why alter the narrative? At one point there was outright deception, and the explanations for the about-face are rarely, if ever, forthcoming.

Even when there is consistency, ideological divides can have the same schizophrenic effect: the narrative alters the interpretation of the facts depending on the side covering it. In the US, the Left have portrayed Trump as a mad monster, while the Right have portrayed him as a savior. In his first month in office alone, his press conferences were either seen as a deception and madness, or honesty and genius.

The same could have been said of his former presidential rival Hillary Clinton: when she had been fighting for the nomination, it was Bernie Sanders who had received lavish praise from the press, while *Harper's* magazine's November 2014 cover had the warning "Stop Hillary", imploring readers to prevent a "Clinton dynasty" (though there were outlets who were unabashed in their support. For example, *Time* magazine had already made up its mind long ago with its January 27, 2014 cover asking "Can Anyone Stop Hillary?", with a subtitle decreeing that her method was the way to scare off contenders "without even trying"). Once her nomination was secure, so too, was her positive press coverage. A difference in opinion is one thing, but the notion of balance has disappeared from the news entirely, and has been replaced with ideological memos and directives for the chosen flocks.

Partisan reportage and pandering to the disenfranchised has been journalism's current model for survival, and its slide into turning into a freak show has now been completed in North America. With partisan reporting comes the rise of the confirmation bias and other logical fallacies, such as the strawman argument, personal attack, and appeals to authority. The Fox News Channel ensured coverage was consistently tilted with Executive Editor and Executive VP of Fox News John Moody's daily memos to staff.

Partisan reporting necessarily means wars will either be seen as divinely justified, or barbaric undertakings. Certain groups will be embraced or reviled. Many countries who have been in the latter group have taken steps to rehabilitate their image to the American people by way of hiring public relations to fix the mess. (Since 1938, foreign entities who do so, must register with the US Department of Justice's Foreign Agents Registration Act, where www.fara.gov has its accessible database of current and former agreements. This means journalists are fully aware of such dealings, yet rarely disclose them to the public. In the UK, as Aeron Davis notes, such companies "can change their names. There is no transparency". Yet, he states media outlets are "highly dependent" on such firms for their reportage.) One would think such information would be critical in any coverage, but the belief that no such behind-the-scenes dealings exist is still perpetrated by the press.

Sometimes, the press cannot shield its chosen flock from a truth or reality they would despise. In the US, there is but a single event that has thrown the press into complete disarray, and even though President Trump had won the election months ago, the news media on the Left of the spectrum not only have not come to grips with it, but they also assume their flock cannot, either. Worse, their rabid behavior has forced many to justify to the public, as Bloomberg News did so with one January 2017 article: "How to stay sane in a world of crazy news". Their opinion of their audiences are so low, they assumed the public could not handle the raucous frenzy.

It is not only a despised campaign outcome journalists hide from the public: over a decade ago, it was the truly unstable state of their profession. For example, Canadian newspaper circulation had been in decline for decades: by the late 1990s, free newspapers (more specifically, newspapers sold for one cent) were included in circulation numbers, in order to keep advertisers from abandoning ship. These papers would be left in restaurants, universities, and even residential buildings, all in the hopes that the charade could continue, but as numbers tumbled downward, there was no hope of keeping advertisers from leaving.

How journalists hide inconvenient truths is simple: they overreport on celebrity news to drown out the economic woes that plague both them and their audiences. They over-elevate heroes and over-demonize villains. They pick a side and doggedly stick to it, even if there is enough blame to go around. The quest for truth is a tangled road, where it is easy to lose your way. What we *want* to be the truth and what *is* the truth can be two very different things. We want to think life grooves our way, but often, it has its own rhythm and will rock us right out of our senses.

Time magazine has had its share of scandals. When O.J. Simpson was arrested for the murder of his ex-wife and her friend in 1994, the publication deliberately darkened his skin on their cover, though then managing editor James R. Gaines denied race was a factor. They never considered that other publications would also have his picture on their covers, where a direct comparison would make their racist gambit glaringly obvious. The assumption that their readership themselves had certain expectations of those criminally charged with felony offences and would expect affirmation was chilling.

Journalism is the business of facts, yet it has once again become the business of opinion. However, when journalists are called on the carpet for their chronic dishonesty, they invoke scare tactics to deflect criticism.

When one of Trump's press conferences cumulated with his repeated accusations that the press was peddling in "fake news", NBC's *Meet the Press*'s moderator Chuck Todd had worried on Twitter that President Trump's attack on the press was reason to be concerned: *"This not a laughing matter. I'm sorry, delegitimizing the press is unAmerican"*. The manipulative shaming gambit was ineffective, as those who supported the president dismissed it.

Those who agreed had done so long ago, but Todd has every reason to be worried; though, it was not Trump who succeeded in delegitimizing the press: it was journalists who completed the job on their own with no outside help. They were the ones who, like Stephen Glass, Jayson Blair, and Janet Cooke, deliberately lied in their stories, or, like Lara Logan, Sabrina Erdely, or Dan Rather, spread lies by accident.

With the *Toronto Star* creating a laundry list of what they believed were the US president's lies and inaccuracies during one press conference, they had forgotten the number of their own deceptions they had spread to their own readers over the years. The press has repeatedly failed to grasp that their credibility has been destroyed, and without credibility, they will never recover from their destruction.

The press continues to shelter their readers or viewers, hoping they will not notice the truth of the state of journalism, and the press use a number of feints to do it.

There is nothing easier than constructing a valid sounding argument. We can find the logic and the facts to make our interpretation of reality seem right and infallible. We can drown out the chords of truth with our well researched arguments, and make it seem as if we know what is happening around us and what we need to do. The trouble is that history is littered with facts and logic that did not square with either reality or truth in the slightest.

Sophistry is the act where willful incompetence and sanctioned insanity are repeatedly justified. It is the place where the devil's advocates and spokesmen misuse arguments and logic to make toxic seem natural and healthy for physical, mental, spiritual, and emotional well-being. We are led to believe two wrongs make a divine right, and we should follow that questionable path. The news consumer is left with the task of thinking critically to determine whether the argument is objective, or secretly biased and manipulative.

The job of the news producer is not to sell sophistry to a public, yet those in the news-producing business make it a troubling habit to do so. Such was the case in the October 8, 2014 edition of the *Toronto Star,* when it decided that seemingly fragile Liberal leader Justin Trudeau had been damaged in the optics department by the ruling Conservative government: "By almost any standard, Justin Trudeau is the immediate political casualty of the war of words that attended the debate over Canada's role in the international coalition against the Islamic State".

How could Trudeau be construed as a "casualty" of political debate and natural philosophical individuality? He may be someone whose philosophy is different than those who are Conservative, but he is also a grown man, who knows full-well that his own father exploited controversy to gain attention and a devoted following who would be impressed by the Establishment playing rebel. (It is a reliable gambit that works for anyone, regardless of political stripe. For example, Fox News Channel's ex-host Bill O'Reilly made a career out of it.) Given that the younger Trudeau became Prime Minister with a comfortable majority government since the article was published, it is safe to say that he was not a casualty in any way. A false dilemma was manufactured, giving those who supported the Liberal leader concern over his political viability and well-being.

So why would a news producer try to invoke feelings of pity in the first place? Why do those who are in the information-gathering and dissemination business feel compelled to invoke manipulation at all?

For many, it is not enough to dryly give information to others: they must meddle to try to persuade people to draw a certain conclusion. Often, right and wrong seem interchangeable, and the slide into danger and dysfunction becomes undetectable.

We may believe our choice is the best one, even if every sign screams we are about to make a bad choice: we spin the negative to make it seem positive, or we incorrectly decide to compare our situation to people who have it worse, while ignoring those who had it better.

If you use folksy logic to assure yourself that everything is fine, you are making yourself vulnerable to con artists whose specialty is sophistry. A con artist is someone who has more experience in lying than most of us have experience in dealing with professional liars. It is an uneven fight.

Yet there are uneven fights in the news production industry. Public relations is a business that spins stories so they always seem positive, just as journalists and columnists are experienced in disseminating information with a specific slant, day in, day out. From crisis management firms to image consultants, there is no shortage of people whose job it is to spin, exaggerate, and produce propaganda. More troublesome, one side of an issue may have the resources and experience to put out their well-crafted lie, while the other side may not have the money or the experience to stand up to those untruths. Yet when we consume the news, that rarely is the thought that crosses our minds. Two sides may be given equal time, but they are not equal.

The news world is one that is rigged. Reporters promise to reflect reality as it is, but the truth is that what we see is not what is. Worse, still, as Aeron Davies notes: "as [newsroom] resources go down, the dependency on public relations goes up". The more the press relies on PR, the more likely those who can afford it, such as corporate and government officials, appear as sources, and "the more legitimate those sources appear", cautions Davies. His research had him interview over 60 UK politicians, and over 90% had media training on some level. The press has been, as he notes, "directed at the elite".

For anyone who has worked in the news business for even a short stint, two things become clear: one, that it is a messy profession that does not define its terms or use academia to refine its product, and two, it is an easy profession to exploit. When the wealthy powerbrokers invite journalists to their swanky galas, it is easy for the reporter to wish to become a member of the beautiful people, who talk about their Very Important Deals and Very Exciting Lives amid their fake laughter. The middle class and poor don't weave in journalists by courting them at all, let alone in a similar fashion. Not all journalists fall for such ruses, but enough do for it to be a problem.

The strategic wooing has a psychological function, but then those same groups have public relations firms and image consultants at their disposal. It is why journalists give too much coverage to the movie industry, that has almost no impact on our daily lives, and ignore the plight of the homeless or the disabled that can have a permanent and significant impact on our future.

When a profession cannot define its most basic of terms, anyone with an agenda can turn those fuzzy areas to their advantage. If journalists cannot define objectivity, for instance, someone can use sophistry to ensure that objectivity is defined by whatever spin flatters an individual the most.

Journalism departments at universities don't conduct experiments. They teach journalism students how to put together a story, without ever bothering to see if there are superior ways to put that story together. The oversight has had catastrophic consequences for the profession; yet few bother to ask why we don't have labs finding out how to do journalism in a precise and effective way.

What journalism suffers from is an acute case of willful incompetence: it is the refusal to question the most basic mechanisms and structures of the profession, even if it means journalism is reduced to being mindless and heartless propaganda.

Willful incompetence can take many forms in the news world. For example, a journalist who deliberately makes little or no effort in reporting all sides of a story is being willfully incompetent. A reporter may interview several sources for a story, but all those sources are clearly aligned with a single side of an issue, but then interview only one source from the opposite side, giving the false impression that one side has more support than another.

Willful incompetence has journalists forgetting how to see bigger issues. When there are people telling you where to look, it is often easy to be blinded to the real things happening around you. Such was the case in the January 16, 2016 edition of *The New York Times*:

> Yet some Democratic Party officials who remain uncommitted said that after nine months of running, Mrs. Clinton still had not found her voice when it came to inspiring people and making herself broadly likeable. While Mrs. Clinton is known for connecting well with people in small settings, she has not shown the same winning touch as consistently at rallies or in television interviews, they said.

The question to ask is why, despite the wealth of information in a literate society, do we have people, *educated* people, still vote based on traits that have absolutely *nothing* to do with the job? People look for charisma and inspiration, yet how does *either* quality fit into the job of running a nation?

In this article, for instance, the spotlight in this piece was about Hillary Clinton's deficiencies in her quest to secure the Democratic nomination for the US presidency. She missed the mark in 2008, losing to Barack Obama, and now she faced the same quagmire in 2016.

US politics is a peculiar game, where the candidate who looks likely to be the most fun at a cocktail party always wins the White House. The article does not question why people pick candidates based on completely irrelevant criteria. Do any know the *specific* plans and qualifications of the candidates? That means it does not matter how qualified presidential candidates happen to be, superficial criteria overshadow the deeper ones, and there is a serious flaw with the entire process, no matter who is running for the job.

Ignoring a troubling logical flaw among citizens as if there was nothing wrong, while second-guessing a single candidate misses the entire point: how we pick our leaders not only has much to be desired, but it also has long-term consequences as well. What is the point of working on your qualifications when you ought to focus on a winsome smile and empty catchphrases?

A good journalist is not a follower, but questions every part of the reality. *How* and *why* are the two most important questions to answer. The journalist cannot take anything for granted, nor does anyone get a free pass. The reporter questions everyone and everything. No one gets the benefit of the doubt. Why? The reason is simple: when you promise to give facts in a public forum, it is your duty to be absolutely certain that what you are presenting is a fact.

It is not sexism if a male reporter questions a woman. It is not racism and prejudice when journalists question those outside their in-group. It is not treacherous when journalists question those in their in-group. It is essential to the functioning of a society to question all assumptions to get to the truth.

A fragile society is one where asking hard questions is discouraged. Sometimes questions are drowned out because to answer them would reveal a sinister scheme.

Other times, we don't have a good answer but we simply don't want to admit to the collective delusion. Why do we light candles on a birthday cake? Why do we smoke cigarettes, pipes, and cigars? Why do we light fireworks? There are better uses for fire, yet all those activities are so ingrained, we accept those illogical actions, and may become *upset* when someone wonders aloud.

These are forms of *sanctioned insanity*, and while there is nothing troubling with those actions *per se,* they represent a side of human behavior we still don't quite understand. We don't question many forms of sanctioned insanity, and most times, it is not even necessary, but when a journalist covers events with elements of sanctioned insanity, often, finding the truth requires understanding that there are no sacred cows. A journalist must question by the nature of the job.

Some forms of sanctioned insanity form entire *professions*. Professional sports and acting — the two acceptable and revered industries — are, in a very real way, nothing more than a form of sanctioned insanity. There is *nothing* wrong with either profession, but both are peculiar in their dynamics that we take for granted, as many aspire to make a career in either or both.

Yet, we spend the majority of our finite existence arguing over whose make pretend was more convincing, watching people utter words they did not think as they go by false names, and move in the direction of another person. Nothing is natural or even logical about the process. Had professional make pretend been frowned upon by societies instead of embraced as a legitimate art form, thespianism could have very well been classified in the Diagnostic and Statistical Manual of Mental Disorders.

Sports as a collective entity is an equally peculiar form of acceptable behavior. People running in a field catching and chasing after a ball in uniforms, or hitting each other in a ring, has no utility. Strong men who use their strength to compete rather than use that same strength to build, fix, rescue, and create seems as if it is a gross misuse of power and talent. People watching the pointless expenditure of wasted power as they root for *their* team is equally silly. Do we as a species not know what to do with ourselves in a democracy? Or do we prefer to do everything and anything under the sun except the very things we need to do to confront our problems?

What is the point of either acting or sports? The entertainment value of either could all be obtained by more practical and logical means; however, history took a certain course, with particular individual or collective ideas becoming accepted and dominant. The consequence being that cultures, religions, and nations accept certain illogical behaviors as normal, while other equally singular ones are seen as strange, immoral, illogical, and blasphemous.

In other words, it is society's sanctioned insanity — bizarre and nonsensical behaviors — that we take for granted, and see as perfectly normal and natural. Like willful incompetence, we give these actions meaning *after the fact*, thinking up reasons why these unnatural actions are logical and necessary.

We do, in fact, have designated uses for both: acting is an art form that expresses thoughts and feelings and serves to bring people together across time and space. Sports has a similar function in a more aggressive and primal form. But out of the countless *other* ways to achieve both, over time, these evolved as the outlets we accepted without questioning them.

Both industries are not seen as being hard news items and their glamour is accepted, as their consequences are often ignored until it becomes a scandal. Bill Cosby was a revered figure and hero until one too many women accused him of being a sexual predator. Football players were seen as heroes who represented physical might until those who suffered debilitating concussions finally went public. Had journalists been vigilant and looked past the shallow glitter, they would have found a darker world with real casualties.

How do we know we are right when we have so few facts to go on? Often, it is by seeking others who think the same way. It is a form of confirmation bias. If 100 people think that X is wrong, then it must be. Facts and evidence are unimportant. Groups of everyday people become cults for the lost to find validation, even if it is sanctioned insanity.

Cultish thinking can lead to many forms of systemic dysfunction, from families who justify their abusiveness, to workplaces that justify endangering their employees, to political parties that justify discrimination, and religions that justify oppression. Hypothetical constructs are taken as real, and they are made legitimate by a collective's belief in them. Everyone is susceptible to groupthink. It is the reason women allow themselves to be subjugated by men in the name of piety, and why people feel emboldened to discriminate against those whose life requirements differ from the norm. When willful incompetence and sanctioned insanity collide, cultish thinking is allowed to go unchallenged. It is the way both functional and dysfunctional systems sustain themselves. We do not question the base of our group's structure, causing cracks and then crumbling later on.

Journalism is supposed to be our collective common sense and voice of reason. Without quality dissemination of information, we allow dysfunctional thinking to go unchecked. Journalism is not about being intolerant or judgmental, but it is about not letting any toxic ideas in the marketplace go unchallenged. Journalism questions ideas as it looks for quality evidence. It presents more than just a story, but a case as to why there is a problem festering in the collective and how it is impeding us.

Otherwise, bad information seems to support bad ideas.

When the news or social media users reproduce articles from other sources, they are, in fact, vectors who do not double-check the veracity of the facts in question.

We may be university educated atheists who think we can see the truth at first glance, but we may also be vulnerable to manipulations precisely because of our backgrounds. There is no reliable profile that will make anyone completely immune to falling for lies and manipulations. Your education does not make you invulnerable. Growing up on street corners and pool halls does not make you invulnerable. Being a con artist does not make you invulnerable, either.

You could be a criminal master mind with a PhD; you could not only fall for a scam, but a pathetic one played by someone younger and dumber than you.

How do people become inoculated by dissenting opinions

that can often reveal misinformation of the in-group? There are several ways:

1. They create an artificial pecking order: those who push a certain ideology are elevated, while those who question it are dismissed as being less intelligent, moral, or enlightened than others in the group.
2. Using in-group jargon, and mistaking the group-specific lexicon for security, correctness, or superiority. Not knowing Shibboleths does not necessarily reveal an outsider's intelligence or trustworthiness.
3. Disparaging those who do not share our beliefs that our ideology is flawless.
4. Justifying actions of individuals or collectives who partake in the actions we sanction.
5. Believing that accepting all ideologies and opinions without question is no better than rejecting all without hesitation, just as refusing to see negatives in a situation is no better than refusing to see any positives. There is no one all-encompassing method to protecting yourself from making mistakes or getting fooled.
6. Using accepted authorities as divine and unquestionable proxies for truth. Anyone who questions the authorities we accept is seen as ideological enemies. It should become clear that our yardsticks are highly inaccurate. We may do everything save the things we need to do to find the truth that terrifies us. When assessing a news report, it is imperative to see whether or not the story coasts on some sort of in-group shortcuts. Does it reject new ideas outright, or does it assume nothing from the past is worth considering? How much demonization and deification is going on? The Fox News Channel had perfected the divide of creating default heroes from the Right and automatic villains from the Left, but there are plenty of

other news outlets who do the reverse and see nothing wrong with the practice.

It is not the content of a thinking pattern that gets us in trouble, but the structure itself. If your tendency is to shame people who do not applaud your every idea, it does not matter if you shame people on the Left or the Right; you have a problem with the very structure of your thinking skills, as well as your emotional literacy. There are no loopholes that will save you, unless you can begin to be less judgmental as you accept that humans make mistakes, and that includes you. Scams come in two forms: the greed scam, and the pity scam. Each con hinges on the pigeon being led to believe they are *superior* to the con or a specific target. Victory over real and perceived rivals and enemies can be turned into reality if you take a certain gamble. In a greed scam, the gamble will prove you are a *winner.* In a pity scam, the gamble will prove you are a *hero.*

The yarn for either scam sells the pigeon a guaranteed victory, so long as the mark takes a gamble. The sucker must make a significant *investment,* and one that proves the worth of the individual. It is the narrative of the winner or hero that is the *lure,* but it is the confirmation bias that ensures the sucker is drawn onto the hamster wheel for life.

The individual has too much on the line and does not want the ego to be bruised by being exposed to reality. Anyone who merely questions the story will be automatically disbelieved, as the skepticism threatens to unravel the narrative. To protect the narrative, skeptics are demonized to be discredited and discounted. To discredit the ego's threat it is not enough to disagree with them on a single point or issue: *everything* they think, say, believe, or do is absolutely wrong, and nefariously so. But then anyone who agrees with or supports the detractor must be equally wrong, ignorant, insane, and evil. That means believing the opposite must be right by default. There is no slack:

it is all or none. Which brings us to narrative manipulation.

It is easier to believe those stories that dovetail with our beliefs than those that challenge them. Manipulators know human nature: they target their stories to specific audiences. If you believe throwing money at a problem without any emotional connection will work wonders, they will tailor their message to appeal to you. If you believe that you can save a romance by being your lover's perpetual rescuer, there are con artists who love you and your delusions. If you think everything is a competition, rest assured, there are liars actively looking for pigeons like you.

It is not the stories you disagree with that you need to worry about; it is the one you believe on first *reaction.* The woman who always defers to men and takes a man's side over a woman's because she sees herself as superior to everyone else belonging to her gender has a lot to worry about: any lie that supports her worldview will be believed.

When listening or reading information, it is equally important to question yourself: Why do you believe the things that you believe? Are you secure enough to admit there are exceptions to rules? That there are people who will lie about the things you hold dear? That ideological balance is essential to understanding reality? That you do not know everything about everything? It is all too easy to retreat into fantasy and extremism, but a willingness to reflect goes a long way to understanding and analyzing information. Otherwise, opinion seems like fact, and then our perceptions cannot reflect either reality or the truth.

Finding manipulations can be difficult if you cannot orient yourself. But if we know how we can be vulnerable to believing lies, the process becomes simpler. As the next section shows, the tools of factual manipulation are very simple, but easy to miss unless a news consumer is vigilant.

When societies are not taught to think critically, true skepticism flounders and people accept information at face value. Questioning information is mistaken for grouchiness or even jealousy. People trying to hide their incompetence, wrongdoing, or iniquity will do everything to ensure that prying eyes do not see the truth.

Adroit manipulators can do this in creative ways. They can make themselves seem wealthy when they are on the verge of bankruptcy. They make themselves look more desirable, successful, happy, functional, competent, and popular than what is the actual truth. It is not difficult to pay a group of people to cheer for an ordinary person. An audience can believe the person is special when the reality is that they are conniving enough to find those who can be easily bribed easily.

Most times, those who are adept at manipulating optics are smart enough to avoid detection. Other times, the manipulator has the right idea, but their execution leaves much to be desired.

For example, a manipulative politician will be savvy enough to ensure an entourage during a press conference reflects whatever demographic and/or psychographic they wish to court for votes. These are not random voters or audience members: each person standing behind the politician during a canned event such as a press conference has been vetted and instructed how to behave as the politician reads a script he or she did not likely actually author.

Other times, those not properly schooled in those machinations fall short, with seemingly knee-slapping results. But on closer inspection, the implications are anything but funny. Case in point: On January 5, 2016, Sue Stenhouse, the "executive director" of the Cranston Senior Enrichment Center in Rhode Island, gave a press conference where there were the stock human props standing around, including what at first appeared to be an elderly woman. The problem was that people recognized the elderly woman — as being a *male* bus driver from the Center wearing a wig, earrings, makeup, and a dress, complete with a tag declaring him to be a "Cranston Senior

Home Resident".

Was he having a gender awakening and was now identifying himself as a herself? Not a chance: the Trans Van bus driver apparently was asked to pass himself off as an older woman so that Stenhouse could "improve the visuals" at the press conference. Not surprisingly, former city councilwoman Stenhouse stepped down, and many were left wondering why the genuine Cranston Senior Home Residents were rejected: would they have brought those *oh so very important* visuals down?

The problem is, as of this writing, no adequate explanation has been presented as to why this trick was necessary to employ in the first place. The record is incomplete, but the outré nature of the story seems to have stifled journalists asking questions. But the gaffe drives home an important point: those courting the attention of news producers have masks and scripts they use to garner publicity.

The choreography of the media seekers has gone out of control: interviewees talk in banal and meaningless catchphrases, while they do not actually give any genuine factual information or evidence. The doublespeak is meant to sound learned, important, and optimistic, yet the white noise babbling offers nothing important to the news consumer. It is all distractions used to deflect attention away at the speaker's incompetence and inaction.

But optical manipulation is not confined to the attention-seeker: those in the news-producing business also liberally use optical manipulations to shade our perceptions of reality. It sounds strange, but that is the precise nature and dilemma confronting an information-gatherer. Reality and truth can seem synonymous, especially if they seem to align. But alignment still means there is a gap between two entities. They are not one and the same thing.

Let's take an example of a random unpaid intern who, as part of a course requirement, has to work for free at a television news program. You are watching the intern walking down stairs carrying papers in a random shot of the newsroom before the commercial break. What do you see? Someone hard at work. The intern is gathering news, taking papers from one place to another. These days, the person may be carrying a smartphone, texting the anchor some breaking news from a source.

Now, perhaps that is what the person usually does — but not at the moment you are watching. The intern may be on a break or she may just have come back from bringing everyone in the newsroom breakfast, or may just have been at the photocopier getting scripts ready. A cameraperson may just ask the intern to carry some papers for the camera, and the individual agrees because of a helpful nature, or an attention-seeking one, or perhaps the intern is studying a newsroom and is gathering information to understand how lies become news.

The intern may not run up those stairs at all as part of the job. She may merely have to give papers to people on the main floor. It does not matter. If you take cutaway shots for granted and assume you can take it all at face value, you are already vulnerable to being manipulated.

The fight to control one's image and ideology is strong, but for some people, it is an all-consuming *fixation*. These are the people whose every story paints them in the superlative flattering light, and they are *never* at fault. Their weapon of choice is the patriarchal narrative, where they spin a yarn how they are absolutely perfect and enviable, while any detractor is a vile, mean, and smelly villain. We all know people who feel compelled to find excuses, scapegoats, and positive spin for any fail that becomes public, yet hogging all of the glory for their real and imagined victories. We call these people narcissists, blowhards, braggarts, and cry-babies depending on whether they are recounting a success or a failure.

In our everyday lives, these people can cause us serious trouble if believed without question. They will demonize our allies, passing the blame on to the innocent as they distort our perceptions of friends. They will overstate their competence as we give them too much control of our finances, power, and destiny. They make lofty promises while they exploit our dreams. They will bankrupt multibillion-dollar companies, make healthy people sick or even kill them, and they will isolate their marks as they hold them back and keep them from reaching their full potential.

How do people manage to keep people under their spell? By spending so much time perfecting the narrative that shades reality, they enhance self-serving propaganda, or downplay the absolute *critical* information needed to see reality. Not all narratives allow for truth to be obscured or distorted, but the patriarchal narrative is a unique one that allows for such unimpeded information distortion.

In a patriarchal narrative, a single point of view is presented, usually by a protagonist, who is not only a hero, but also one who is contrasted with a villain. Moreover, the protagonist's narrative is usually taken at face value. In fiction, this is the standard way of constructing a story, whether the story is a novel, comic, movie, or television series.

Many patriarchal stories are easy to tell and understand, and are appealing to those reading or watching those tales. To be accepted as a hero who is not questioned and is beyond reproach seems to make the protagonist immune to criticism. The problem begins when people use the patriarchal template on nonfiction stories, and then expect news consumers to buy the story without asking the hard questions. When employed in the news product, the end result can be highly inaccurate and manipulative.

If a journalist does not verify an interviewee's narrative, it is a careless action, but when the journalist or columnist is the one spinning the narrative, it is an irresponsible one.

News reports aren't journal articles you find in academia —

the latter do not spin yarns, they lay out facts. While academic papers may have their own set of problems, spinning a dramatic yarn will rarely be one of them.

Journalism is a peculiar profession, where the reporter is a narrator of the nonfiction story, but it is presented in an informative rather than entertaining manner. With straight reportage, a journalist may become bored, or assume pure journalism is somehow beneath his or her abilities as a writer. While journalists are often eyewitnesses to world-altering events that are exciting, important, and historical, they are the observers who are not the center of focus.

To keep an arm's length from the story to see the big picture is a delicate balance. Often, reporters become too close to sources and issues. They begin to become persuaded by one message more than others. Make no mistake: journalists are being played and spun every waking moment of their lives. People want coverage. They want positive coverage. They work reporters, and many of these individuals are very persuasive, particularly those who run large companies: they are adept with advertising, and they are always selling, and sell to reporters in order to generate positive press that translates into free advertising. Journalists interact with crisis management companies and other public relations industries. They are courted and bribed in various ways: from getting graft at conventions to getting access to rich and famous beautiful people. A reporter who curries favor to government officials is more likely to get a government job should the reporting gig not work out much more than the reporter who exposes that same government's twisted practices.

It is easy for a journalist to get caught up in all the subliminal messages. Some may even try to compete with the wealthy newsmakers they cover, and then get themselves involved in dubious practices to keep up with the super-rich. While it is understandable, it is also inexcusable.

Someone in the information dissemination business is

obligated to leave the gullibility behind to focus on finding facts and evidence to get to the truth. But just because some journalists become corrupted by their jobs, it does not mean the news consumer is helpless. It is very simple to see through masks and scripts when you are aware that critical thinking can expose lies and spin if you make it a habit to question every fact presented to you.

Narrative manipulation requires both scripts and masks: in order to dress up a lie, props are needed to hide all the red flags that show us that reality is not what is being presented. The presenter filters information, and is very careful to hide facts that would allow the audience to make a better decision. When watching or listening to the news, there are several signs that serve as a reliable way of spotting manipulation:

1. The news producer or news source does not speak in an informative manner. They stoop to using posh and meaningless phrases. Whenever someone gives an interview, the question should always be: *What does that mean?* What does *we are taking steps to address the matter* really mean? What is defined as "taking steps"? What does it mean to "address"? What is defined as "the matter"? We often give a speaker the benefit of the doubt, but when the speaker is discussing a mass poisoning or scandal, chivalrous tendencies do not get us any tangible information.

2. The news producer or news source does not provide hard evidence to back up the proffered theory or statement. Taking the above example, no information is given by the phrase "We are taking steps to address the matter." For all we know, taking steps is defined by merely having a meeting, and engaging in undemocratic nepotistic practices. Any evidence of criminal negligence is destroyed, while the guilty party hires a crisis management

team to spin the press. Without the hard and *specific* facts, we do not know what someone else means.

3. The event in question is canned; in other words, contrived. Photo ops such as an opening of a new building is not newsworthy. A press conference is a canned event where the speaker has full control over that which reporters can attend, what they say, and who can ask questions, if anyone. Most political campaigns are, in fact, *staged* events. Visiting community centers and giving a speech of promises has no utility. Political debates are also meaningless. Uncovering embezzling or corruption is in fact newsworthy: there is a problem and the press gives the audience warning that it is happening. Explaining oppressive bills, and exposing gross government waste that can alter the fortunes of millions of people is news. A celebrity who pretends to be dating to boost publicity for their movie as they walk down a red carpet wearing clothes and jewelry that they do not in fact own is not newsworthy.

4. The story presented by the journalist or news source relies heavily on a patriarchal narrative. The divide between hero and villain is stark, yet there is scant evidence to support the linear divide. A hero, winner, or victim seems to be beyond reproach, while a villain is to be despised unconditionally. It is imperative to question the roles: it is important to see people as people, not fictional roles. There are times when a person is a villain, such as those who cause harm, from physical to financial or psychological. Yet even then, people are wrongfully convicted, and it is still prudent to verify the facts before we decide who we trust.

5. The presentation of information has a confirmation bias. Information that refutes a narrative theory is excluded, spun, or downplayed. Press coverage for comedian and

actor Bill Cosby was fawning for decades. Those who did not know him would be given the impression that he was a clean-cut man of integrity. He was deified at his height, but when he lost clout, the truth slowly began to slowly trickle in. But even then, it took another comedian's onstage rant before the collective was slapped out of its slumber.

When a news source relies on a mask or a script, it is a guarantee that those props are being used to hide unflattering and important information that would greatly alter the public's opinion of the individual or group. A news producer, by the very nature of the job, is obligated to look past the lies and spin to present information as it is. When we begin to question confined roles and demand to see people as complex human beings, it is only then that we can open our eyes and accept the troubles we face. We can then solve them before they grow out of control as we reward the very people who have no trouble destroying parts of society for personal gain, all while protecting audiences from the very truths they need to know to not just survive, but progress.

Chapter Thirteen

Trivial pursuits

For a profession that is supposed to be in the know and in the thick of things, they certainly were blindsided by the presidential victory of Donald J. Trump. The press has access to two important variables: the pulse of citizens, and the goings-on of those in power. Even in an age of social media, the press still has more experience and access to those things that elude most others. They are supposed to know things the average citizen does not, yet they did not see Trump coming.

It is a peculiar blindness that requires deeper analysis. When Trump announced his candidacy, the press was amused. When he won the nomination, they shrugged off his chances until it became evident he was gaining momentum. But then the traditional mainstream press turned on him, finding his every real and perceived flaw, to a point they lost every bit of their credibility. They did not see that his strategy would ensure victory over his opponent as he stumped and managed, despite lacking the popular vote, to nab enough electoral votes to gain a victory.

The howls from the press went beyond Election Night, but it was that day that showed that journalists no longer had clout, nor any ability to predict the pulse of the people. It saw the redundant votes going for Clinton, and did not bother to look at the finer grains to see a distinct and significant pattern arising. While Clinton's election team were equally obvious to the fact that they had their guards down and were about to suffer a humiliating and unprecedented knock-out punch, it was the press that lost far more that night as they proved themselves incapable of seeing reality as it is.

That is no minor deficiency. To be a journalist is to have a clear view of that reality, and react sensibly, rationally, and logically to it. They could not do so when it counted the most, and their gross collective ignorance spelled an end to an era.

How did it happen? How did the sky fall on their heads? The answer is that the sky did not fall on their heads, but the ground had eroded underneath them for years, and they were unaware of it until it was too late. For example, the *Hamilton Spectator*, a Canadian newspaper that has seen its glory days decades ago and has been reduced to a shadow of its former self, had tried to make itself relevant on May 5, 2017, with a large font message on its front sleeve: "JOURNALISM: MORE IMPORTANT THAN EVER". Unfortunately, by the time editors woke up, news consumers were no longer interested in the paper's ominous plea.

To work as a journalist is a curious job. You are surrounded by lies, spin, and feints at every turn. People put their best foot forward, and are on their guard in your presence, going so far as to take lessons from experts on how to behave and speak to you. You are expected to cover industries where people who excel at selling and persuasion are forever trying to manipulate you for their benefit. In a world where everything and everyone is touted as The Next Big Thing or Next Grand Visionary, separating fact from advertising becomes increasingly difficult, especially when those who seek attention know how to play you.

Unfortunately, at its prime, the press entered a troubling bargain with those with the flair of a flashy circus performer: they would pull stunts and spill all to the press, giving them spectacles to keep audiences coming back. Whether or not covering spectacles was in the reporter's job description was not considered. It kept the masses entertained, and it seemed like a fair trade.

But like opinion, spectacle has nothing to do with facts. They are amusements, not useable fodder. You will not prepare yourself for an economic downturn knowing the cup size of the latest starlet.

Yet reporters were the sullen children who began to frown at eating vegetables when there were people offering sweet candy free of charge. Those who sought media attention knew how to frame their pitches to lure the press into forgetting about covering a federal budget in lieu of attending a glamorous film festival: those stodgy power brokers were boring, and journalists should not be boring by association. If the reporter wished to be among the beautiful people, the price of admission was to give them fawning press, and plenty of it.

The press willingly obliged as it was cheap and easy. Hounding a prime minister is difficult, expensive, and stressful. Covering the love life of a celebrity lawyer's self-indulgent children who have no other claim to fame other than they are willing to do anything in front of a camera is the easiest and cheapest way to keep a publication afloat.

The Kardashian clan have been the recipients of the press's largesse since 2007, when second eldest daughter Kim's private sex tape was released. It put the family on the map of celebrity and, as of this writing, the news media's interest in them has not subsided.

Yet the Kardashians serve no purpose in public life. They are not scholars contributing to the marketplace of ideas. They are not artists who reinvented their profession or created a new system of expression, style, or genre. They are not activists or politicians. They were born to wealth and exploited themselves. It is a tried and true formula, and there have been other families with several female members who had already played the same tricks.

The Kardashian clan are, as comedian Rosie O'Donnell once mused, updated Gabors: Zsa Zsa, Eva, and Magda were known for their love lives. They used their fame to market beauty products, having a narcissistic obsession with themselves, and a connection to the Hilton family, while their mother, Kris, micromanaged them, long before reality television. It is the Kardashians who cribbed more than a few notes from the originals; though, none of the modern versions could ever get a genuine career in acting off the ground. And just as the foremothers of inflated socialites were truly unnewsworthy, so are the Kardashians.

They were both trivial pursuits, the difference being the former were mildly entertained in the press — always in the soft news and entertainment sections —while the latter make their way to more prominent real estate in the news.

The reason for the media divide is simple: with declining resources — despite modern technology, and a more liberal view of the press's role in modern life — the Kardashians are cheap news to fill airtime and news holes. The clan has publicists and is willing to strip naked as they discuss their intimate lives and marry men with wealth who live in the public eye. They do not play hard to get. Their wealth depends on them being in the news; hence, they court the press in any way they can.

The press needs constant fodder. It is a trade that benefits the Kardashians far more than those who indulge them: the Kardashians saw their fortunes inexplicably rise, while the press saw theirs plummet into oblivion, though it is the one that society requires to function properly.

Such an impact the Kardashians had on journalism, that even those who have real and serious careers have been relegated to the trivial, as high-profile human rights lawyer Amal Clooney found out the hard way when *Time* magazine and its online sister publication *Motto* (a site that is supposed to cater to millennial women) wrote:

The mom-to-be (who also happens to be married to George Clooney) stepped out outside the United Nations headquarters in New York City on Wednesday, showing off her baby bump in a dark gray pencil skirt and matching cropped blazer.

Unfortunately for Clooney, she spoke to the United Nations to outline human rights abuses by ISIS, imploring the Council not allow another genocide to happen, but her domestic affairs took precedence (*Time* is also the same serious "newsmagazine" whose May 5, 2014 issue had singer Beyoncé on its cover as one of the hundred most influential people — with her scantily dressed, unlike any of the male newsmakers it placed on its cover).

How did journalism reach the heights of Watergate to the lows of pseudo-celebrities and baby bumps in the first place? The erosion was slow, but there came a critical juncture that turned the press from purveyors of relevant information to gossip repackagers, slowly shifting their focus from hard news to soft news.

The 1990s saw the rise of the super-story in the US: the hybrid of hard news player caught up in a soap opera that played out in the span of months, or even years. The novel mix seemed perfect: there was a hook, a storyline with familiar characters, and the long-form saga was certain to keep news consumers interested. The players were already established in the press, and had not only had name recognition, but also public goodwill. There were twists and turns, along with villains and victims, and the press was justified in covering the stories, taking the role of serious chroniclers, even though it was not fact, but scandal and sensation they were reporting.

The love life of Princess Diana overshadowed her substantial and ground-breaking efforts in bringing attention to global plights from HIV to landmines. She was not merely a people's princess, but a political one. Though she fought for unglamorous causes, it was her marital woes that brought her the attention of the press, with publications such as *People* magazine speculating on her private life rather than its sister publication *Time* looking into her professional undertakings.

The O.J. Simpson murder trial also received the same singular obsession, with networks interrupting their programming to relay the latest trivialities of the case as if it were a world leader accused of killing the First Lady. The slow White Bronco police chase was deemed breaking news. While a popular former athlete's legal quagmire is newsworthy, it was inflated and elevated to shrill and overbearing levels.

The biggest super-story of all during the era was the impeachment trial of then US President Bill Clinton and his denial of his extramarital affair with White House intern Monica Lewinsky. It had just enough credibility to warrant coverage by investigative journalists; however, it was not the political that drove them to cover it.

Despite the insistence that the coverage was important, it was mere filler. CNN had devoted itself to cover every rumor and aspect of the melodrama as it unfolded; nevertheless, its fortunes still tumbled, and it has yet to recover. The gambit of overexposing and overreporting certain stories destroyed the industry's understanding of what makes news.

Journalists have forgotten what investigation means. In a January, 17, 2017 *National Post* article, "Has Lindsay Lohan converted to Islam? A National Post Investigation", writer Sadaf Ahsan speculated on the faded starlet's personal life, using merely what other media outlets had stated earlier, coming to the conclusion that perhaps Lohan did change religions; though she might not have converted, either. The same fodder also appeared online in celebrity-friendly fare such as *Us Weekly*, *Page Six*, and *Hollywood Life*, along with countless others after the actress deleted her social media accounts. That is not investigation by any definition of the word, and it certainly did not originate from the *Post*; yet the headline declared with gravitas that it did. No longer are the lines between hard news outlets and the advertorial publications and broadcaster clearly defined. Angelina Jolie's marital problems will be as prominently displayed in newsmagazines as it will be in a gossip tabloid.

The venerable US newsmagazine *60 Minutes* has also fallen

into an abyss. Once the program that made the ambush a staple of hard news programs, it now has interviewed the likes of Kim Kardashian, Hugh Jackman, Bruno Mars, Angelina Jolie, Bryan Cranston, and Taylor Swift. While there were profiles of entertainers from the beginning, the show once chose to interview only those in the arts who shaped their fields. Now, it is whoever is popular at the moment. By the late 90s, one study showed that 60% of *60 Minutes* segments were dedicated to soft news stories.

If *60 Minutes,* which is considered to be the best of its genre (in North America at least), relies far more on fluff than substance, then how much useable and critical information is being produced by news producers as a whole? The spurious intermingling of hard news with the soft to give the façade of gravitas has had its consequences: real scandals and dangers were left to simmer without opposition until they became a crisis.

For Americans, September 11, 2001 brought unprecedented carnage on their own soil in multiple areas. While the brunt of the blame rests on the terrorists who chose a destructive temper tantrum to take down unarmed civilians, one wonders how a sophisticated news media, trained and experienced in dealing with global affairs, did not see the writing on the wall earlier. There were many peculiar breakdowns, from lax airport security to mass funding, recruitment, precedence of malice, and simmering hatred. It is not to suggest that the media should have seen the event happen to stop it, but that it did not see that such a grand attack on their soil was more than probable.

Instead, some of the headlines of the *Los Angeles Times* on September 10, 2001 were of the banal sort: "Veterans Hope to Fund Bob Hope Monument", and "Sorority System In No Rush to Integrate". While this is a single snapshot of a single daily, it is an average broadsheet, and, like the others, it has, at most two hard news sections. It has an arts and entertainment section, sports, automotive, classified, and several sections that do not relate to important need-to-know information, but to mere want-to-know tidbits.

The press did not learn its lesson then, and it has yet to learn it now. It did not see the rise of Donald Trump. It could not, as they forgot to see the world realistically. They forgot his adroitness in snagging positive press, and that he knew how they thought and what they sought. From the 1970s, Trump first found himself praised prominently first in New York City media outlets before he captivated the country with his flamboyance and cocky demeanor.

They forgot they lost every battle they ever had with him. They forgot he was not as newsworthy as they made him out to be, and when he declared his presidency, they forgot who knew their weaknesses and vices, and how to use them to his advantage. It was Trump who made covering a glamorous lifestyle a viable option for journalists, and when he entered the political arena as a hard news commodity, the press, who were now out of practice, stood no chance with the puppet master.

Even on January 20, 2017, the day Trump was sworn in as the US's forty-fifth president, the press angrily howled and hurled insults at the one man who proved their inability to see reality. The once respected *New York Times* had its daily fit with Paul Krugman's opinion piece "Donald the Unready", yet was blind that it was Journalists the Unready who never saw the obvious before them. "It was obvious to anyone paying attention that the incoming administration would be blatantly corrupt. But would it at least be efficient in its corruption?" is a question better asked to news producers, as they had assured the public for decades that they were not corrupt, but efficient, moral, competent, and alert. Yet a single man took them down in a single breath-taking blow.

Instead of conducting a hard and realistic assessment of how they were the architects of their own downfall, the press decided it would be best to be shrill, attacking the man who proved their true value as a profession.

However, the press continued to fawn over the celebrities who threw fits that their decrees to the public to vote for Clinton were ignored. Madonna's opinion that the US went "as low as we could go" by voting for Trump was covered in *Time* magazine, while the *Times of Israel* got in on the act, as well. They were impressed that an anti-Trump rally included the likes of Alec Baldwin, Cher, and Robert De Niro. Many celebrities who are no longer on the A-list have been the most vocal, and prominent of pseudo-critics.

The media's addiction to celebrities who are used to throwing fits to get their own way did not abate; nor did they realize their bad habits arose from having a poor choice of role model. Journalists deferred to celebrities to tell them how to think, and those public figures were more than willing to get more coverage by throwing dramatic soliloquies in front of rolling cameras. They pulled more than Andy Warhol's fabled fifteen minutes of fame, ignoring the role the press played in its own crisis. Celebrities took full advantage of the press's dysfunction to gain free advertising for their mediocre and disposable vehicles. Those faded idols would hardly be the ones who would point out the problems to their own professional detriment.

It is that deceptive wallpapering over the decline of journalism that is the worse offence than the transgression it is covering. The press is not supposed to lie or sugarcoat reality, including its own. It is about honesty, even in the face of adversity, not feeding attention-starved trolls by giving them unquestioning coverage. While journalists have covered their declining fortunes, what they fail to disclose is their own role in their catastrophic fortunes, from spurious speculation without a single solid fact to fear-mongering and inciting frenzied fear among the populace. Journalists, particularly in North America, used sycophantic praise without regard whether or not the inflated superlatives will have repercussions to others later on.

That is the legacy of the press: glorifying starlets as they ignored the plight of their citizens, whose struggles were increasingly ignored, as they lacked the glitter of those who ply their trade on television and film. Worse, when those same dispossessed electorate voted for the lone candidate who promised to pull them out of their nightmare, the news media in the US dismissed those same voters as deplorable "populists" and even hinted they were fascists.

The press had not learned its lesson, instead they troll the Internet for the new breed of Kardashian. The so-called "Rich Kids of Instagram" are their latest muses as these "kids" would not be known unless the press paid attention to their antics.

Yet the struggles of the working class began to bore the media, and in the process, they lost their sense of direction, and stepped right into a trap of their own making. There is no simple solution to undo the damage; yet the first step is to turn their backs on the very glitter that blinded them in the first place.

Part Four

Unmasking the Imposters

Chapter Fourteen

Virtual, but not real

It was the 2017 Golden Globes when Meryl Streep accepted a lifetime achievement award. It was on the heels of the US's most shocking and once seemingly impossible presidential victory. She had used her airtime to outline her concerns about the incoming commander in chief when she said to her audience: "You and all of us in this room really belong to the most vilified segments in US society right now. Think about it: Hollywood, foreigners, and the press."

Streep is a wealthy mainstream actress who has benefitted from positive media coverage for the entirety of her career. She can ignore the fact that this is the same press that has perpetuated stereotypes, reported lies as news, as they deified abusers and sparked wars. Hollywood movies have also vilified foreigners and minorities with stereotypical performances, and a lack of recognition that culminated in an #OscarsSoWhite outrage on social media in 2016 when every nominee in every major category that year was white, just as it was in 2015. It would be same double standard as those who protested the fact that Trump lost the popular vote in the election, just as his rival Clinton had lost the popular vote during the Democratic primary to Vermont senator Bernie Sanders, but won with the support of superdelegates.

Streep seemed blithely blind to her own profession's identical transgressions; yet Hollywood's long history of sexism, workplace harassment, and pay inequity has been well documented. It is a business that had working women (namely, actresses) in a highly competitive profession of ambitious people portray women as submissive housewives, and incapable sex objects requiring perpetual saving. Hollywood held back society's natural progress for decades. Even now, popular programs such as the pseudo-reality franchise of *Real Housewives* showcase female vapidity, indulgences, shallowness, and dysfunction. However, even in the modern age, the "housewives" featured on these programs are financially enumerated for it. It is a job and these women are no housewives.

Women in both Hollywood and the press are still being paid far less than their male counterparts. Yet Streep's speech focuses only on a man who personifies all that is wrong with her own industry, and not the fact that those who claim allegiance to either side of the political spectrum function within the same kinds of confines that has held women back.

After all, Casey Affleck had won Best Actor at the Globes the same night as Streep's measured lecture — an actor who was sued for sexual harassment himself — yet she did not mention his scandal.

Hollywood and the press have much to answer for with their careless disregard to how their stories and fantasies impact reality. Women around the world have been exploited, sexually harassed at work, and forced into slavery, abusive marriages with no chance of liberation, and even into pornography and prostitution. Yet for Streep, she spoke without questioning her own profession's impact on the world. She was lauded for her stance by much of the traditional media, with only those who are ideologically opposed left questioning her motives.

In the same speech, Streep praised the press: "We need the principled press, to hold power to account, to call them on the carpet for every outrage; that's why our founders enshrine the press and its freedoms in our constitution... because we're gonna need them going forward, and they'll need us to safeguard the truth". She also said eloquently that "disrespect invites disrespect", and that "violence incites violence", without a hint of irony, as no one faction in the communications field has done more to glorify, normalize, and portray violence than the industry that cuts Streep's hefty paychecks.

The hypocrisy of Streep's speech had not been questioned as *The New York Times* called it "powerful", without reflection, or questioning whether the Golden Globes was a peculiar venue for a speech. Many movies such as *Rocky, Gladiator, Midnight Express, The Godfather, Spartacus, Saving Private Ryan, Chinatown, Bugsy,* and *Platoon* were all Globe winners for best drama, despite their own violent and troubling content.

The traditional press did not question the absurdity of giving a speech in a venue that was run by people who behaved in the same way. Many right-winged online outlets attacked Streep with the usual "she-is-a-limousine-liberal" narrative, just as many left-wing counterparts praised her as if she had delivered Trump a deathblow.

Whether or not Trump is a disrespectful bully is not the central issue here: it is that journalism has gotten into a habit of having a singular focus on the failings of a single individual, while ignoring others who have the same failings. Those individuals find other like-minded people, and they form collectives that are allowed to prosper as the press ignores their rise, causing greater problems later on. Terrorist groups, for instance, have recruited young men and women in Western countries; yet we do not know of their indoctrination until it is too late. Because of dwindling resources, many local media outlets do not know their surroundings, and instead rely on happy news, while shying away from hard news stories unfolding in their backyards and schoolyards.

In Canada, for instance, there is poverty in Aboriginal communities, resulting in the murders of a disturbing number of native women. Yet these debilitating societal conditions have not been the focus of either side of the current political spectrum until the body count had become staggering. It was not as if those there in the community, or even activists, were keeping this information to themselves: the press did not have

any interest until decades later. Journalists were too busy
reporting on Prime Minister Justin Trudeau's latest selfie — as
he is a highly accessible media commodity to go out and take a
look around their towns and cities — to stumble upon the silent
genocide themselves.

The medium is not the profession. It is merely the vehicle
to disseminate its message. It is a structure to present it to an
audience.

For those who lament the waning fortunes of print, radio, and
television miss the point: quality and useful information will be
valuable whether we hear it in person, read it in a newspaper,
hear it on the radio, watch it on television, find it online —
or receive it by some yet uninvented means. Truth is truth,
regardless how you deliver it.

Journalism is journalism regardless of the medium. In fact,
its greatest triumph was that it made a home in every medium
created. Communication outlets have always had a form of
information dissemination attached to it. An interest in our
surroundings is innate, as it is the best way for us to know the
people and problems that we deal with up close or far away. It
is more than curiosity that compels us to seek journalism — it
is a survival instinct. By all logic, the Internet should not have
devastated the profession, but enhanced it from the start.

Something peculiar happened when the extraordinary
Internet became a mundane part of daily life: journalism could
not keep up with technology. It has always viewed it with a
peculiar suspicion — as it does with any collective that threatens
the status quo it supports — and continues to do so. A March 2,
2017 *New York Times* op-ed piece from Thomas B. Edsall, entitled,
"How the Internet Threatens Democracy", complained that very
Internet, "disrupted and destroyed institutional constraints on
what can be said, when and where it can be said and who can
say it". It quoted an "upcoming paper" from Nathaniel Persily,
a law professor at Stanford University, who is bothered that

the "type of campaign is only successful in a context in which certain established institutions — particularly, the mainstream media and political party organizations — have lost most of their power, both in the US and around the world". That perhaps the mass dissatisfaction comes from unescapable poverty and incessant oppression imposed by the rigs of an Establishment does not seem to cross Edsall's mind. Every single one of his sources were skewed, as they were well-educated and well-heeled individuals, who do not have to bother themselves with The Great Unwashed, who now have a means to channel that anger toward those who seem oblivious and unresponsive to their screams. Edsall also seems unaware that democracy often has a bitter and violent means of expression, and it does not always reflect the theories of the minority, who preen and opine in their Ivory Towers.

That means that the Internet is not just another medium, as Barry Richards notes: "Many-to-many is very different from one-to-many...news organizations and professionals were unprepared for the impact of the Internet and digitization".

Journalism had been defined by the confines of its various media, as Marshall McLuhan had famously stated, and now a new medium had arrived that was more advanced than those who had not refined their profession's theories. News producers did not experiment with the medium, merely treating it as if it were a souped-up version of whatever medium they knew.

No one gave the new kids on the block the memo of how to do journalism. It was not rebellion that drove the neophytes to seemingly defy the conventions: it was pure fool's ignorance of the nuances of the profession. The difference would have a profound effect on how they would do their jobs.

For one, there were no gatekeepers telling the new breed what to do. Many had little or no journalism training or, more importantly, experience. They were young, and many had been shut out of jobs in traditional outlets. It no longer mattered: the new breed had options.

But what they did not have was an understanding of journalism. Snark — the attitude of both anger and arrogance — was the style of choice, with online publications such as *Gawker* thriving with it. The bored-with-it-all demeanor could not hide the fact those in the business had not *seen* it all. They would be doomed to make the same errors as the old guard, except more so. Sophistry, paranoia, and opinion replaced fact. A less disciplined approach was chosen — ignoring the fact that a lack of discipline was the reason traditional journalists were losing their clout and their jobs. Snark is what a modern person would refer to as a "hack": a shortcut to seeming competent in style without being it in substance. It also implies a certain worldliness on behalf of the journalist, without actually having the experience to see what exactly is the problem in a situation.

For another, there were no rules to follow. A new medium, by Marshall McLuhan's theory, would have new rules, and a new message. The ways and methods of the old guard would no longer apply, at least in theory. The rise of online journalism showed *promise:* without the traditional confines, there was no telling where it could go. Would it finally save the flagging profession that was averse to hiring younger reporters to cover hard news that spoke to those under thirty? Would it allow the once censored voices a platform to speak? What new kinds of journalistic models could we expect? The answer was to go back in time and pick up the bad habits of the past.

It was not supposed to happen. There was no reason for it. *Vice* marketed itself as a publication that had its writers walk in the shoes of the stories they covered — but forgot all about cognitive dissonance and the confirmation bias. This was because it forgot to keep a close watch on their watchmen to ensure none of them misused their position for illegal activities, as its former music editor Yaroslav Pastukhov did. He was not only accused of trying recruit reporters to serve as drug mules, but also of using his position to profile a musician. This musician was his roommate, and was arrested for attempting to smuggle cocaine on an airplane.

Slate, Salon, Huffington Post, and *Politico* became mouthpieces for the Left, while the *Daily Caller, RealClearPolitics*, and the *Blaze* did the same for the Right. *BuzzFeed* was an obnoxious, rude, and bawdy teenager who demands respect for his opinions while he disrespects those who do not applaud his every poorly-thought-out decree. *Heavy* is the slacker who thinks he can sound more learned than he is to keep up with the genuinely informed by reading someone's crib notes. The *Drudge Report* cherry-picked stories from other media outlets with a splash of explosive exclusives that eluded legacy media, but was not a news site with complete original reportage. With *Vox*, it was a throwback to the serious-sounding public service announcements with the same disregard to reality.

But journalism has lost its notions of curiosity or ideas of not having an opinion before doing a story. The old guard have their heroes and villains preset, and the notion of people being right on *some* points seems to be unimaginable. The new guard has their agendas preset. Both function on an all-or-none paradigm: an individual or an ideology is either all good, or all bad. The insensitivity of the life requirements of others took its toll, polarizing people rather than bringing them together.

The Internet's limitations, and errors often make it worse than the gold standard. Journalists have passively sat by and expected technology such as the iPad to revolutionize and rejuvenate the industry. However, the actual results have been wanting. Professional conspiracy theorists such as Alex Jones have devoted followers, who see his brand of opinion and narrative dissemination as news, just as the followers of *BuzzFeed* believe the opinion and narratives they read from there are also news as they dumpster dive the site for scraps of information. The two flocks could not be more different ideologically, but their structure of beliefs and thoughts are identical: they have found an outlet who is willing to indulge them and follow the indulger into the bunker fortress to reinforce their beliefs. The confirmation of their beliefs is virtual, but not real: hiding from reality and truth does not make either vanish. It is a default delusion: if a collective sees themselves as right and good, then anyone who opposes the group must be wrong and evil. Online publications with a deliberate penchant to commit the confirmation bias, to pander to, and appease, a willing audience, may gain the trust of a view, but is dismissed by the majority.

However, the new breed of partisan reportage continues. Publications such as *Vox* can boldly declare that misogyny, and not an inferior political campaign doomed Clinton from gaining the presidency. They can ignore that Clinton won the popular vote (and disregard that countries with far less progressive views of women have elected women as their presidents and prime ministers. These women were elected even if they did not have the same positive press, financial resources and connections as Clinton). The point of any competition is to test individuals to see who can overcome their obstacles to victory. There is misogyny in the world, and too much it, yet women around the world have led nations and won elections. These women overcame sexism, even in times and places far more archaic than the US.

But the neo-partisans could not entertain the notion: Clinton was either the devil incarnate and deserved to lose, according to the right-wing arm of the Internet, or she was a hapless victim who was owed a presidency, yet was cheated out of it, according to the left-wing arm of the Fourth Medium. Neither side could see her as a human being who lost because her campaign machine fell short of its mark.

And this is the reason online journalism has been a shockingly spectacular failure of the worst sort. Far from it bringing people together to understand reality, it has used argument fallacies, distortions, and outright propaganda and lies to separate people by drawing arbitrary — and often illogical — lines in the sand, while purporting to be the avatars of truth. There are no standards when working for an online publication. There are few standards when working for the more established press, as well. To keep up with the Fourth Medium, traditional journalism lowered their already untested standards, and became political propagandists, whipping fear, anger, hatred, and irrationality with their every story.

Once upon a time, a single election would be decided civilly; now, public temper tantrums of sore losers and even sorer winners litter the streets and social media sites as fewer people make plans, but are ready to make excuses why they will flounder for the next half-decade. If it is not excuses, it is the faint hope of schadenfreude.

For example, the *Washington Post*'s Josh Rogin had his January 26, 2017 headline decree that "The State Department's entire senior administrative team just resigned", implying that President Trump's presence alone was enough to get those in the public sector up and packing. However, the *Post* had placed this article in the Opinion section of their website, with Rogin noting that, "suddenly on Wednesday afternoon, Kennedy and three of his top officials resigned unexpectedly, four State Department officials confirmed". According to David Wade, former State Department chief of staff under Secretary of State John Kerry: "It's the single biggest simultaneous departure of institutional memory that anyone can remember, and that's incredibly difficult to replicate."

Vox was quick to counter the piece the next day, with their own headline decree that the *"viral Washington Post story about State Department resignations is very misleading"*. Writer Zack Beauchamp postulated that the standard changing of the guard was typical, and not a sign of the new president's influence, never mind that Trump had campaigned on ideological and political cleansing, and that, in fact, management had not resigned so much as they were fired. While many left, as a new regime wishes to install their own people in place, the State Department was a politically troublesome liability. State Department Under Secretary for Management Patrick Kennedy had been seen as then Secretary of State Hillary Clinton's *fixer* and protector, intervening on her behalf numerous times over her tenure.

Yet *Vox* has made more than its fair share of choreographed articles meant to be seen as thoughtful, while, in fact, logical fallacies dominate its product. Clinton did not lose because her campaign was out of touch with the reality of voters: it is *misogyny* that turned a contender of being a leader into a hapless victim, and if wasn't the misogynists, it was loose-lipped former FBI Director James Comey. Despite its arrogant authoritative headlines, *Vox* is short on facts: "Tax cuts undermine Trump's pledge that his Obamacare replacement will be 'great'", "Obama's best chance to influence the Israeli-Palestinian dispute will come after he leaves office", "Trump's coalition won the demographic battle. It'll still lose the war", and "6 reasons for the left to feel optimistic this election season", all hinting at an omniscient author. Its patronizing tone is a bluff and misdirection, though its feints and ruses become apparent over time.

For online journalism, they skirt and dodge as the traditional press has done, only more so. With fewer standards, they are free to go beyond partisan reporting, and they can fully engage in extremist propaganda. There is no center or balance of rationality — it is either the extreme Left or the extreme Right, meaning despite a new medium, there is no pushing beyond the confines to reach middle ground.

Sometimes the ideologues try to cannibalize their own political or ideological affiliations. The *Huffington Post* had one article declare that the "Bechdel Test Fails Feminism", without considering that a single observation (in this case, that Hollywood movies had an overzealous tendency to have female characters talk only about their sexual relationships with men without having any other topic of conversation to discuss) could possibly be all-encompassing to a single ideology — or that perhaps others may also actively expand from a crucial observation and standing point. However, traditional media such as *The Guardian* also seemed to think that one rule that explains everything was the only one that counted, and had also complained that the "Bechdel Test doesn't always work" (for the record, the observation was first published in a comic strip, not an academic journal).

Yet the ideologues who compete with one another to be the leader and most powerful of their ilk keep upping the ante. Steve Bannon, a radical right-wing player who was once "media executive" to *Breitbart News,* had successfully turned his position into a lofty patronage appointment as President Donald Trump's chief political strategist. By the tone of publications such as *BuzzFeed* and *Vox*, it sounds as if they are fuming about the way someone who placed all their chips on a sure thing, hedged their bets, and spectacularly lost would react. That online opinionists have received governmental patronage appointments speaks volumes, and hints at their true motives for their fanatical shilling. For example, former president Barack Obama's administration had been repeatedly brought to task for their own track record on press freedoms, yet as many journalists had found themselves landing patronage appointments within that administration, the criticism was muted.

For a new medium, suddenly the very old ways that impeded journalism in the first place have come back roaring from the grave to haunt the profession. Far from it progressing journalism, it has hastened its demise as a credible source of factual information that weaves society together. It has torn it apart with lies and deception, with no solution in sight.

Chapter Fifteen

The opinionists

The News Corps Phone Hacking scandal of 2011 was a peculiar, if telling chapter in the increasingly rapid decline of journalism: for the most part, when privacy was invaded by the *News of the World*, it was not in the public interest. For example, BBC presenter Jimmy Savile died only months after the scandal broke, yet despite the countless horrors he inflicted on the vulnerable over the decades, the tabloid had not found it necessary to hack *his* phone to discover his darkest sins. Most of the transgressions were of the milquetoast gossipy variety: no pedophile, rapist, murderer, gang leader, or drug lord ever had to worry that the paper's illegal methods would have interfered with their business.

It was easy to get away with it for as long as they did: the gossip was salacious enough to grab attention, but none of it threatened to topple a government, or spark a revolution. It was a dangerous gambit, but almost *safe* enough to continue without too much worry of an authority figure deciding to see how the paper was actually getting its scoops.

Much of what the *News of the World* had done was what groups such as WikiLeaks and Anonymous do as part of their routine: break, enter, and disseminate. Yet there is a difference: hacktivists go after those who have power and control over regular citizens, and, in essence, pick on people bigger than they are. News Corps went after those who had very little influence on public policy, laws, or even moral authority. There is another difference: hacktivists go after facts, while News Corps went after fodder to fill a narrative, and narrative, in turn, is driven by opinion.

US journalism is far less objective — and rational — in many regards, and in the early 2000s, facts have been replaced by the subjective. It is cheaper to produce than have an army of reporters turn over every rock as they face death threats and lawsuits. Present the opinion with authority and perhaps audiences will believe what they heard was deeply researched and vetted.

Much of US local newscasts litter the airwaves with the trivial. Anchors report what viewers opined on Twitter as if it were news. Facts have become a scarce commodity, even though they are the intellectual nutrient that gives individuals and society both health and strength. If you wish to be safe, you must be informed of the dangers around you. It is not enough for someone to wag a disapproving finger in front of a camera, and shout how governments are "soft on crime". What are the facts? What are the numbers supporting or refuting a theory that criminals are getting out of control?

We know less and less. Opinion is the fat and sugar of the news world: it is a hack, a cheat to stretching out a product with as much filler as possible. The fat and sugar is tasty and addictive, but as there is no nutritional value, news consumers are no better off than they were before they read or watched the news. Those uninitiated in the ways of news and even critical thinking prefer the misdirection over the substance: it is more assuring to be told that crime in their area is out of control than be given the actual figures to support the claim.

Another News Corps property, the Fox News Channel, is a case of an all-opinion channel being marketed as an all-news network. So entrenched in opinion that its influence on other media outlets to pursue the same feint is known as the Fox Effect. There are differences between opinion and fact, even if it is not always obvious. Opinion taints and devaluates the journalism product by eroding the public's knowledge base, and replacing it with a feeling of anger, hatred, fear, paranoia, or false confidence that is not aligned with the current state of reality.

How did opinion overtake the profession in the modern age? Instant analysis in television news has a definitive origin point: on June 2, 1957, CBS's *Face the Nation* had landed a controversial coup, and journalist Daniel Schorr interviewed Soviet president Nikita Khrushchev. However, the scoop was not considered good enough, as *The New York Times'* television critic Jack Gould had suggested the network should have given more challenging explanations to the audiences after the interview was over. According to William Rivers' *The Adversaries,* CBS took the advice, bringing the world instant on-air analysis. From there, the focus on opinion slowly began to take shape and impact how news producers saw their role in public life: not always as informers, but as thought-shapers.

Television was not the only one in the influence business. Newspapers and magazines had experience in the area, as it was there where the partisan era had originally flourished. Once editorials would weigh in on political matters, until opinion became personal and trivial. When 2017 Fashion Week rolled along in New York City, Trump's youngest daughter Tiffany who had attended was openly — and pointedly — ignored by fashions editors, who wished to register their displeasure over the election outcome by proxy. This resulted in their willful public humiliation of an innocent party, proving that fashion editors may have style, but not class. It was performance art disguised as a political protest, and the childish bullying of a young woman who had done nothing to warrant such psychologically manipulative groupthink could only be described as evil; yet editors thought they were justified.

Their opinion was their version of fact, and the open and relentless vendetta meant one thing: there was no search for the truth because the press had been too busy punishing anything named Trump, from children of his three marriages to the cards in the Tarot deck. Journalists gave up looking for truths or even taking a look around reality. The news media no longer reported, but punished. It may have been seen as shrill and even irrational, but it was a calculated gambit: they could not control or influence enough of an electorate, and then they had to redouble their efforts as they recruited soft news and hard news alike to make an impact, as their previous tricks had spectacularly failed them. It was a fight to the death, and it did not matter how they did it, the press was determined to overcome their Waterloo.

The denial that it was their opinions that brought them to their knees became visibly worse after the election, where it became normalized to speak in such openly hostile terms. Scott Pelley, a former CBS Evening News anchor and still contributor on *60 Minutes,* did not hide his partisanship on the February 14, 2017 edition of CBS News. He had smugly called Trump's counselor Kellyanne Conway a "fantastic fabulist", never mind the alarming number of lies once venerable CBS programs have perpetrated on the public over the years: whatever his feelings were for Conway — rightly or wrongly — it was not his place to opine them. Shortly after, Pelley lost the anchor seat.

If CBS News had concrete evidence that she deceived, all it would take would be to present those facts to speak for themselves without a roll through the gutter. Anything over and beyond implied that news producers either thought their audiences were too ignorant to know what they were being told — or those same news producers did not actually have any concrete information, and decided to prop up a shaky proclamation with hyperbole. The anchor once gave audiences perspective: now, they impose their thoughts on the public, thinking up the most pointed way to do it. The US press in particular can no longer feign honesty or rationality any more.

Nor do they try, and the slide had become a stark one: in 1972, Carl Bernstein, one half of the *Washington Post* investigative team that brought down a president, did so with facts and tireless research. By 2017, his son Jacob, a *New York Times* scribe, gossiped at a party that First Lady Melania Trump had originally made her living in an unsavory manner based on rumors, and had to be chastised for his sexist comments by a model on Twitter (the *Daily Mail* had published the same rumors and had been successfully sued by the First Lady for it). It was a clear devolution of a once noble and useful profession.

Journalism is an applied science in information dissemination, but it is also an applied art of nonfiction storytelling. There seems to be little room for opinion; after all, by the time a journalist finds and verifies all the facts, interviews all the pertinent players and experts, and then writes or broadcasts the final product complete with visuals, diagrams, and the like, theoretically, there should be no time left over to editorialize. Every day we are exposed to the ways of the cruel and corrupt, the selfish and the greedy, as well as the neglectful and oblivious, and we need our daily checklist of what needs minding and what needs correcting.

Yet opinion overshadows fact in almost every aspect of the news product. Narrative manipulation is at the heart of opinion: stories look for "heroes" as well as "villains" and "victims". Front page newspaper photographs show sullen and sad-looking people who have been wronged, rather than merely showing a neutral photograph of the same individual. It is the opening salvo, priming the audience to take the side of the designated victim, rather than merely outline the facts for the news consumer to find the bottom line for themselves.

It bears repeating, the difference between a fact and an opinion is the same as the difference between a living person and her painted portrait. One is dynamically and firmly living in reality, unedited and raw, while the other is a static and processed interpretation of the entity at a fixed moment in time according to the artist's ability, materials, motives, knowledge of the subject, and understanding of it. All of those factors are *constraints*. The painting is a stratified representation of the subject but it can never *be* the subject whose image it represents, no matter how masterful or renowned the artist who drew it happens to be.

In other words, the portrait is an unreasonable facsimile of the person whose image was captured for posterity, just as opinion is an unreasonable facsimile of the fact. Eventually the portrait takes a life of its own and becomes separate from the person it originally represented, but it can never be a complete and total representation of the object it depicts.

The process of news-gathering is very much the same as the process of portrait-painting — a journalist may be smart, articulate, and capable, but is always constrained by the very definition of the job. Add to the mix that anyone — from veteran to amateur — face the very same obstacles when writing a story that is supposed to represent reality.

Opinion is so prevalent, that reporters often don't question what they hear even in the most basic and unnewsworthy of reports. However, there is a simple reason why opinion dominates fact: it is cheaper and more provocative than the dry facts. It often takes months of hard labor to uncover important information, while opinion can be spewed off the top of someone's head without effort. Worse, all that hard research will not automatically translate to a bigger audience share, while opinion-spewers often find themselves with lucrative book deals. A columnist has a greater cache than a mere journalist, meaning the information gatherers get promoted if they show promise in presenting their opinions in such a way to become a headliner in their publication.

How that opinion is presented is overlooked: when opinion is staged as fact, the waters become murkier. Modern Western thought frowns on emotion as if it were a disease that infects knowledge; and hence, overthinking is used to compensate for the lack of emotional literacy. In other words, what is often presented as logical fact is the repackaging of manipulative opinion.

Sophistry is merely a ruse to sneak opinion in almost all

aspects of the news product, but other times, it is just a byproduct of a less discerning news producer. In either case, opinion is cheap and easy, and in a world of a never-ending news cycle, opinion seems to be a news outlet's best friend.

It is the news consumer who is left without the right information in the proper context. We often see newspaper commentaries parading opinions of those who are supposed to be experts in the field; even they rely more on opinion than the facts they supposedly know better than the common folk.

For example, the *Toronto Star* gave prime real estate in their pages to Anita Szigeti — described as "a criminal defence lawyer in Toronto and the Chair of the Criminal Lawyers Association Committee on Metal Health" — to write about the Canadian government's Bill C-14 (a bill dealing with mentally ill offenders) in the June 29, 2014 edition of the paper:

> One can imagine nods of grim satisfaction around the country last week as news broke that a recently convicted killer...had committed suicide in jail. Fear and retribution lie deeply embedded in the human psyche; these are emotions that generate primal responses...One less homicidal monster to emerge from prison some day and threaten public safety.

Not only was her opening highly emotionally manipulative, but it was also laced with absolutely no facts and plenty of shaming. It was a feeble attempt to make those who would disagree with her assessments seem heartless and even more sociopathic than someone who would slit the throat and then set their victim on fire. That is not the role of the journalist, but the propagandist.

Does everyone who wishes for true equality in dealing with the violent grin when a disturbed killer hangs himself in prison? How is the victim avenged when he or she is still dead? The strawman assumption is unwarranted; yet it did not stop the editors at the *Star* questioning the commentary and asking

Szigeti to justify her propagandistic diatribe with something other than making assumptions with blinders and melodrama. It is one thing to assert confidence in your argument, but quite another to try to rig the results by elevating your moral stance at the expense of others.

Journalism had for years painted itself in a corner with their ideas of *journalistic objectivity* (as opposed to scientific objectivity). Ideally, journalists should have been aware of their own personal biases, and then overcome them by challenging their own points of view. Once they jumped on the bandwagon, their detractors made them vulnerable. Saul Alinsky's *Rules for Radicals* explains their vulnerability the best:

> Rule 4: Make opponents live up to their own book of rules. You can kill them with this, for they can no more obey their own rules than the Christian church can live up to Christianity.

All opponents of journalism had to do is make reporters live up to that impossible ideal, and instead of clarifying their position with experimentation and research, many denied there was a problem, or fell into the other extreme of giving in to subjectivity, otherwise known as "immersion journalism". (It is not a scientific approach, where a researcher is aware of both internal and external biases, and challenges them to understand how a social structure works, including how the emotional interacts with the logical and instinctual.) Immersion journalism's fatal flaw is to give carte blanche for a journalist to behave as a pundit.

So which is the "right" way to report the facts? Is it by using objectivity or subjectivity? The answer is neither and both. Emotional literacy is the key to accurate and truthful reportage. It is not denying emotions that cut to the heart of the matter, but understanding *why* those feelings are there, and how they alter our interpretation of facts. Facts can be downplayed and twisted, just as emotions can be manipulated and enhanced.

The information chronicler cannot shut off feelings and pretend they have no role to play in a story just as one cannot shut off rationality and expect intuition to show the truth. It is a balance. However, there has yet to be a reliable and valid manual to guide a reporter in the right direction. Even in this day and age, journalism is at best, trying to feel one's way in the dark without trying to bring two seemingly incompatible realities — objectivity and subjectivity — together.

Those in the profession still don't see what the problem is, and have confused technology with salvation. As David Plotz opined in a May 27, 2014 commentary about what he called the "Golden Age of Journalism":

> Today, every single magazine and newspaper in the world is available to anyone with an Internet connection, instantaneously. A generation ago, the only people who could produce news were those millionaires who owned presses and TV and radio licenses. Today, anyone in the world can publish and broadcast.

But Plotz is grossly mistaken: just as story-selling is not to be confused with storytelling, the vehicle to deliver information cannot compensate or be confused with technique. We are not in a Golden Age of Journalism, but the Golden Age of Propagandistic Sophistry. The problem is precisely that anyone can disseminate anything, whether the information is accurate, distorted or a flat-out lie. Anyone can cyber-stone anyone else anonymously. Images can be as easily manipulated as facts, data, research, and eyewitness testimony. Do most people who tweet and blog understand the Sleeper Effect, the problems of using loaded language on memory, or how certain psychological disorders can taint a person's perception of events? And if they do, does it mean they try to ignore those pitfalls — or exploit them to push their own agendas?

While journalism has its fair share of problems, the trouble is that Internet journalism has all of the same issues, only *more* so. There are fewer checks and balances, more dependent on the honor system, and almost no controls for rogue propagandists who find their gullible flock of willing pigeons.

But that is the problem with opinion: any trouble spots can be glossed over with spin, and problems are allowed to fester as facts are ignored or twisted to suit one's own ends.

Just like news reports, opinion pieces rely on a form of telling (more accurately, *selling*) a story: there has to be a good guy, a bad guy, and a victim. The opinionist will most likely take the role of hero in one's own narrative. Anyone who disagrees with the opinionist is the villain, and the victim is either a specific person who is the subject of the piece, or, more likely, the reader.

At the most basic level, a right-wing pundit casts Liberals as the evil-doer, while a left-wing one will extend the same courtesy to the Conservatives. All refuting evidence will be ignored, and the piece will be filled with logical fallacies, from the confirmation bias to appeals to authority. While the opinionist may deny or spin the facts, what this means is the article will be framed in such a way that there can only be one logical and rational conclusion. With the lines in the sand based solely on narrative manipulation, the truth is obscured, and the news consumer is not getting the full picture of any given issue.

Many times, the gambit pays off, while other times, the ruse backfires on the opinionist, as it did on George Will when he opined on sexual assaults on university campuses in the *Washington Post* on June 6, 2014:

> Colleges and universities are being educated by Washington and are finding the experience excruciating. They are learning that when they say campus victimizations are ubiquitous ("micro-aggressions", often not discernible to the untutored eye, are everywhere), and that when they make victimhood

a coveted status that confers privileges, victims proliferate. Victimhood as a "coveted status" was a knee-slapper of an observation considering the difficult process of reporting a crime. Victims encounter hostile skepticism, spending months or years going through a court system. They are exposed to hostile questioning from police, and attorneys, with no guarantee the rapist will spend a day in prison, especially if alcohol was present. Inevitable questions of "What were you wearing?" "Did you give mixed signals?", "Are you sure it happened?", and "Do you want to ruin this person's life?" face the victim at every turn. The so-called coveted status is not one the Old Boys seem to want; besides, there is a difference in attending to someone who was wronged and harmed, and getting special attention you did not earn, but Will seems oblivious to it. In this case, the narrative was manipulated to paint anyone who reported a rape or sexual assault as potentially someone trying to get something for nothing, but the blowback was immediate.

The obnoxious primitivism does not end with the Right; it makes a beeline straight to the Left, as well. When the Canadian Minister of Justice and Attorney General was accused of saying to a group of lawyers that not enough women and minorities were applying to become a judge, especially women who did not want to be away from their children (a charge he later denied), Leah McLaren wrote "An open letter to Peter MacKay's wife" in the June 25, 2014 edition of *The Globe and Mail* to chastise Nazanin Afshin-Jam MacKay:

The last time we spoke — in an interview for your recently published book — you'd just married your husband, the Honorable Peter MacKay, then Minister of National Defence, now Minister of Justice and Attorney General, and in the words of this newspaper, Canada's "Minister of Wrong Again". As you may have heard, your life partner and baby daddy has managed to get himself in a bit of hot water where the women of Canada are concerned. And as I read about the fallout — from both his ill-judged comments about women in the judiciary and those very strange leaked Mother and Father's Day e-mails — I couldn't help but think of you.

Instead of using her column to conduct something that resembled genuine research (in fact, the *Globe* had to correct the article, as their scribe could not be bothered to get MacKay's correct cabinet position in 2012 right), McLaren took the coward's way by attacking him by proxy. She also chose to pepper her non-informational lecture with unhip slang, as she dragged in an irrelevant player into her web of manipulation — a politician's wife. She could have directly interviewed Peter MacKay, tried to track down a recording of the alleged exchange, or even questioned the motives and agendas of those who made the accusations. Yet to do all those things requires a work ethic as well as a moral compass, and in this case, the column was sorely lacking in either. Instead, it was filled with patronizing arrogance that not only gleefully veered into brazenly racist territory, but also went against every tenet of the profession. (It should be noted that the minister's wife replied in the *Globe* with a stinging rebuke.)

Opinion can be well thought out or a knee-jerk reaction; however, when it is used to persuade others through shaming, indignation, or simplistic and artificial framing of reality, it becomes nothing more than a tool in a propagandist's arsenal. Unless facts are used in the proper context, we cannot be certain whether or not a reporter or opinionist has an agenda that involves preventing others from questioning their work by shaming or horrifying us into submission.

We are now in the age where the press wishes to decree who is to be deified and who is to be demonized. No better example of such vulturesque practices occurred than in Erik Wemple's May 18, 2017 opinion piece in the once venerable *Washington*

Post the moment Fox News Channel's ouster patriarch Roger Ailes died as he decreed that Ailes' "programming sensibilities survive to this day on Fox News, a purveyor of conservative garbage information whose perverse impact on the country is becoming ever more clear under the Trump administration". The cannibalization within the profession was now complete: one ideologue shaming another the second he died as he could no longer contain himself.

The profession's problem is that fewer people are listening, or following their instructions.

Chapter Sixteen

The masters of delusion

Traditional media had been caught unaware when the extraordinary Fourth Medium first whispered, and then roared into mundane life. It was a peculiar blindness for the one profession that boasts of having an ear to the ground and knows what is happening anywhere in the world. Journalists, who are forever speculating about future events and interviewing people to speculate right along with them, were not speculating how losing their status of being the gatekeepers of publicity was going to affect their profession. Nor did they question how they ought to adjust to the radical new and rapidly evolving technology, but some saw it as a passing fad as they went along with the status quo.

In a February 26, 1995 *Newsweek* article, astronomer Clifford Stoll was certain that "no online database will replace your daily newspaper". Why? According to Stoll:

Your word gets out, leapfrogging editors and publishers. Every voice can be heard cheaply and instantly. The result? Every voice is heard. The cacophony more closely resembles citizens band radio, complete with handles, harassment, and anonymous threats. When most everyone shouts, few listen. ...Yet Nicholas Negroponte, director of the MIT Media Lab, predicts that we'll soon buy books and newspapers straight over the Inte[r]net. Uh, sure.

That may have been a turnoff to traditional journalists, but what journalists saw as a liability to their profession was what average citizens thought was a small price to pay in order for them to be heard.

While Stoll warned readers that:

> … what the Internet hucksters won't tell you is th[a]t the Internet is one big ocean of unedited data, without any pretense of completeness. Lacking editors, reviewers or critics, the Internet has become a wasteland of unfiltered data. You don't know what to ignore and what's worth reading.

While the article still amuses many people over two decades later, Stoll's sentiments were not unique at the time. (For example, as Edward Greenspon said in his Public Policy Forum paper *Shattered Mirror*: "Suggesting to my publisher at the height of the war with Conrad Black that perhaps we were being distracted from the true existential threat coming from the Internet. Several months later, he gave me the green light to create globeandmail. com".) He saw the future very clearly, but assumed that news consumers would turn up their noses at the chance to be known just because the variables were less ideal than the gold standard. There were people who *wanted* to water down the flow of information precisely because the knowledge of what was reality and what was truth would be inconvenient to their plans and ideology. Others wished to break the stranglehold journalism had on the public discourse. In any case, an alternate route proved too much to resist, and the flock decided to break ranks, and go up the new path without the news media.

Yet there are limits and serious ones that the alternative models have not seen solved. *Vice* relies on the Canadian government to fund it, though, as of this writing, the company was raising funds for a "possible IPO". *Huffington Post* has also hemorrhaged tens of millions of dollars in all its years of existence. *BuzzFeed*'s cheeky quizzes and other trivialities have brought in clicks, but they, too, have made job cuts as they discovered a news outfit cannot subsist on nonsense alone, despite how hard the publication tries to position itself as fun and hip. *Medium* is a DIY social media site that was something of a meta blog (allowing users to post their own articles in a single place with others), yet in January 2017, they were forced to lay off one third of its staff, as its founder claimed the digital advertising model was "broken".

These sites are not exceptions. *Gawker* was one of the stronger and more popular news sites until their prurient gossipy snark had resulted in two miffed subjects of their derision banding together and successfully suing them, forcing the site to fold.

Problems do not always have to be about the bottom line. *Snopes*, once considered the definitive website to verify if a story was true, hoax, or urban legend, was not all that it purported to be, either. Once run by the husband-and-wife team of David and Barbara Mikkelson, the site at first dealt with urban legends until it branched out into a fact-checking depot. It was the simplest way to determine whether an email making the rounds was real, or just an old wives' tale reborn.

When the Mikkelsons divorced (itself a salacious episode, with Barbara leaving the sites, while accusations betrayed the acrimonious nature of the split), the website's workings became better known. The investigative backgrounds of those looking into the claims were left wanting. No one at the site had formal training, or a background as a researcher or journalist. *Snopes*, like much of what it investigated, was not what it first appeared. While there are several websites that have similar functions (*FactCheck.org, TruthOrFiction.com*, and *The Straight Dope*), none have the mainstream profile as *Snopes*.

The technology is ahead of our understanding of it. Canadian communication theorist Marshall McLuhan may have asserted that the medium is the message, but what message the Internet has become hints that this medium is a two-part entity. One part of the message is the overt content. The other part is the unspoken structure of the message.

Journalism has always focused on content, but has never

grasped the importance of structure of a message. In traditional journalism, the "5Ws" (who, what, where, when, why — and how) are addressed in an inverted pyramid style, where the most important information goes first; so that editors can cut from the bottom should time or space be limited. There will be the use of quotes, and "color", to add interest and variety to a story.

Yet the structure of the narrative goes deeper than that. For example, a fictional story may have a single protagonist — the hero — who is more right, good, and just than those who stand in the way, or at least disagree with the designated hero. The patriarchal style is the only one used in journalism as well, making being labelled the hero by reporters a coveted position — and one worth hiring professional optics managers for, to ensure reportage goes on your side as the shading and divine assumptions work in their favor.

Online journalism is not produced in the same manner as traditional news, and its limitations show not only in some overt ways, but also subtler ones. There is a proliferation of so-called *think* pieces, relying on an academic study or two, and interviews with experts. *Aeon* is a good example of the slow news day reflection reads as the articles are not of pressing matters, from a discussion of logic to creating holograms of the deceased. *Buzzfeed*, on the other hand, is far more reactionary in purpose, as its frenetic and fragmented stories are not always verified. In both cases, slow or fast-paced, the rigors of information verification are not as rigorous as the ones in traditional media. Nor have most websites challenged the basic structure of telling narratives: it is good versus evil, with the same confining morality plays that have always been part of journalism. *The Smoking Gun,* on the other hand, puts raw data, such as court transcripts and police reports out in a public forum to tell a story, but it is an exception. There is still the assumption there are two sides to every story, but one side is absolutely right, while the other is always wrong.

This sort of structure can be used for single stories, or be the unspoken narrative with a collective of them, and when that is the case, the influence on thought can be far-reaching, encouraging readers to make questionable assumptions. We can take immigration, for instance: an aggregate site such as *MetaFilter* or *Boing Boing* can link stories that make the assumption that no immigrant has bad intentions or criminal inclinations, but there are other sites to assume the opposite — that all immigrants are potential criminals. By basic logic and experience, there are citizens in any given country who break the law, but far more are law-abiding, meaning, there will be a small percentage of immigrants who break the law, but more will follow the law of their new homeland. People are people regardless of where they come from. That is the logical middle ground. Yet with modern online journalism, that middle ground is annihilated: anyone pointing out this simple truth may be falsely accused of either racism or gullibility, depending on what faction hears the centrist argument.

The Trump Presidency turned into a watershed moment for the press, but not in a positive way. Some became his free image consultants, but others tore into him for every real or imagined transgression without a sense of direction. This ongoing vendetta-fuelled tirade has little resemblance to how the US media saw Trump when he came on the scene as a real estate magnate in the 1970s, they were in love with him, covering his every step as if it were newsworthy. By the 1980s, he had finessed millions of dollars in free publicity from every major New York City-based outfit, save for one, the now defunct *Spy* magazine.

Spy had not had the typical girlish crush on him: it had voiced its opinions in various ways, going so far as to refer to him as a "short-fingered vulgarian" — but it was not done obsessively. The magazine maintained its balance and was one of the lone voices that did not see his every action as newsworthy. If any one institution is responsible for a Trumpian victory, it is journalism that always had an unhealthy obsession with him. Whether it was driven by love or hate is irrelevant: his ways captured their imagination and took with it all common sense.

In the envy-fuelled drive to chronicle his every breath, many media outlets still tried to maintain a patina of credibility. Reuters, for example, tried to place a positive spin on the Trump monomania by putting out a January 31, 2017 press release of a staff memo from Reuters Editor-in-Chief Steve Adler entitled "Covering Trump the Reuters way". In the press release, Adler assured his shaken charges that everything would be all right in the world:

> It's not every day that a US president calls journalists "among the most dishonest human beings on earth" or that his chief strategist dubs the media "the opposition party". It's hardly surprising that the air is thick with questions and theories about how to cover the new Administration.

The delusion that it understood its function appeased those who already were equally obsessed with Trump, but for those who were not consumed by him, the strategic press release proved nothing, save that Reuters had learned nothing from the downfall of the US press. As usual, the blame is on the newsmaker, never the ones who created and enabled them all along.

Online journalism has also mastered presenting delusions and misconceptions as fact to take propaganda to its next level: aggravates are the modern-day gatekeepers who select certain stories that fit a specific narrative, making certain a particular ideology is the most logical and natural. The traditional gatekeepers have lost much of their power in this regard; yet their content still provides the modern aggregate the fodder to present reality selectively.

The Drudge Report is the most successful example of complexity made to seem simple. On the surface, it is a news aggregate site, culling stories from various reporters and columnists in a straightforward, almost *rustic* format. However, what it is, in fact, is *political performance art* that gave clout to theorists such as Alex Jones, and launched careers of some, while scuttling the ambitions of others with uncanny precision. Stories chosen tell a definitive, but subtextual *narrative* that hints at what is yet to come. Part seer, part stage magician, Matt Drudge tells the audience precisely what will be without having to flat out say it: on his website, his voice is a mosaic of seemingly random headlines. Donald Trump was dismissed by the overconfident, oblivious, and unteachable Left, who honestly thought they could vote-shame the entire electorate into voting for a female, yet the savvy insider Drudge had cast the faded 80s icon into the role of the inevitable future commander in chief, even as journalists such as the *Washington Post*'s Callum Borchers had dismissed Drudge, asking whether the Right's Internet Patriarch had "lost his grip on reality" in relation to a paternity story regarding former President Bill Clinton, but the implication was clear. However, as Trump eked out his victory, it was also clear that Drudge had a firm grip on reality, while Borchers was completely blind to it.

Even the perpetually clueless *Columbia Journalism Review* got into the wishful-thinking act, decreeing back in 2009 that "Drudge Has Lost His Touch". Considering his singular style of seeming to be able to read tea leaves through his choosing of journalism stories from around the world, his touch turns speculation into reality. There is no equivalent on the Left of the political spectrum, or even a reasonable facsimile of it. The Left seem to be stuck in a vortex, unable to see the *Drudge Report* is part narrative script, part hit list, and anyone who is a target of Drudge seems to lose their grip on power. They have repeatedly underestimated the influence of Drudge, to their perpetual folly, and have yet to respect the power his minimalist website has. Though he has other media platforms, it is the Drudge

Report that is his greatest strength, as it is its simplest. The quiet monochromatic elegance has played kingmaker and deal-breaker for countless battles, and has been the single greatest influence on American thought in modern times.

Of all of the digital news sites, only the *Drudge Report* has not only thrived, but has also defined itself from the rest of journalism — a peculiar feat given the site gets its contents from a decaying industry. It is a kingmaker and a history-shaper.

It is what journalism used to be; though in a vastly different form, as it is a partisan voice, yet one that can still create agendas and control public discourse in a cacophonic, fragmented, chaotic, anarchistic, disconnected, and schizophrenic era of fear anger, jealously, hatred, frustration, and jealousy. Its mastery of both simplicity and subtext make it a partisan force of unprecedented clout, yet finding a path for journalism to find its way is still uncertain.

Part Five

Resurrection

Chapter Seventeen

The school of experimental anarchy

Journalism is not the same as other information-gathering professions: it is made to be told to a general audience, meaning jargon, complex concepts, and proper context must be sacrificed for brevity of information that can be understood immediately. A journalist is usually interviewing and covering people who are richer, smarter, and more famous and important than the reporter, yet a reporter cannot try to compete or feel inferior to those experts and newsmakers he or she is covering. It is not a competition. It is a career that deals in facts, data, and evidence that reflects truth and reality.

It is a profession without any airs, and its greatest strength is to bring all events, people, and places — no matter how unique or extraordinary — into the realm of the mundane. It is an equalizer that is liberated from the confines that define other professions. Journalism is about egalitarianism, and accessibility of information, and it provides said facts to anyone who wishes to retrieve it, regardless of their motives or reasons for wanting it. Audiences do not require special training or a license to get it, making it one of the most extraordinary societal creations that ever existed. Until the rise of the Internet, journalism had been the sole keepers of mass knowledge. Yet journalists rarely see the blessings of their own profession.

Once guardians of the world, the press has confused their mandate, and become irksome *tattlers:* should a celebrity go off a diet, or a politician utter a crude drunken remark, journalists are there to scorn those missteps. It is no different than your younger sibling telling your parents you borrowed their wedding album without asking, yet the tattler having no clue that a prowler is casing the house. In the scheme of things, a minor infraction of no importance other than to irritate a newsmaker who journalists do not like, is no substitute for reporting on dangers around us. But often, all missteps are lumped in together and treated equally, trivializing severe transgressions in the bargain.

Routine is the journalist's enemy, as it creates false habits that chain them to expectations of what is and isn't reality. When attending press conferences of authority figures becomes a rote exercise that no one questions, the press becomes complicit in perpetuating the illusion that such canned events are normal, natural, and the best and only way to gain information. Order and predictability are natural enemies to the press: they mistake false patterns as divine law, not tools of convenience. From how journalists interview sources to how they present information on their various outlets, there is rarely any thought given as to whether the method is truly the best way to inform the public, or whether it is mere sanctioned insanity.

The press is in the business of asking questions — the 5Ws as well as the how, yet those are not the hard questions the press asks of their own profession. Who should be a journalist? What is the mandate? Where are we going wrong? When should we make changes? Why did we fail? How do we make the changes to thrive? With their perpetual defensive and indignant replies that their methods are not flawed, the fortresses of justification prevent those questions from entering their vortex. When the *Washington Post* decreed with their motto that "Democracy Dies in Darkness", it made no reference to how the profession's own negligence contributed to that darkness. It may have been the newspaper that had exposed the truth about Watergate, but it was also the paper that earned a Pulitzer for the fabricated "Jimmy's World", as well as re-imagining Private Jessica Lynch into a video-game hyper-action heroine. Not to mention that in a November 24, 2016 article it had accepted, without verification claims from a website called PropOrNot, that it had found "fake news" propaganda websites that were propaganda tools to ensure Donald Trump's presidential victory. When confronted with the truth that the site was not all that accurate or reliable, the *Post* somewhat backed off the claim with their mea culpa: "The *Post*, which did not name any of the sites, does not itself vouch for the validity of PropOrNot's findings regarding any individual media outlet, nor did the article purport to do so."

Since publication of the *Post*'s story, PropOrNot has removed some of those sites from its list, still leaving much to be desired. Other publications, such as *The New Yorker* and *The Intercept*, referred to the *Post* article as one that "smear[ed] dozens of US news sites" that are critical of US foreign policy as being "routine peddlers of Russian propaganda", and was "rife with obviously reckless and unproven allegations, and fundamentally shaped by shoddy, slothful journalistic tactics"; even *Rolling Stone* (which, despite their own scandal of *A Rape on Campus*, referred to the story as an "astonishingly lazy report") brought the paper to task for not bothering to verify *anything* the nebulous website claimed (from the content of the actual story, to their sources to even who ran the organization itself). If PropOrNot said it, it had to be true; after all, they presented themselves as "experts" and the *Post* legitimized their unproven claims.

The Right can have no virtuous airs, as dubious "experts" litter the media landscape on every corner of the political and ideological spectrum across all media, with the Fox News Channel having more than its fair share of them. While those who booked guests reported that the scheme was rigged to ensure better quality of right-winged guests than left-wing ones, often, the FNC is as lackadaisical as the Post when vetting credentials. In March 2002, the program *Fox Report with Shepard Smith* interviewed co-founder Ray Richmond from *Hollywood Pulse,* a satirical website, on the legal troubles of comedienne Paula Poundstone. What it did not realize was that the site's story "Poundstone Granted 'Supervised' Child Abuse" was a spoof. To his credit, Richmond gave a serious interview, but when the truth came out that the

FNC had made a serious error in judgment, instead of an honest apology, a spokesperson issued the statement that, "It's a well-known fact that Ray Richmond is a media whore", yet, the FNC apparently did not receive this "well-known fact" in time, and if they did know, more disturbing questions arise.

They learned nothing from the Richmond Gaffe, as February 2017 brought them another questionable expert guest: one Nils Bildt, according to *The O'Reilly Factor*, was a "Swedish defence and national security advisor", who discussed how immigrants in Sweden were, according to Bildt, not integrating into society, yet the Swedish press and government officials denied they had ever heard of him (Internet archives of articles and websites do confirm Bildt (né Tolling) founded CTSS Group/CTSS Japan, a global corporate strategic and security consultancy that had locations in Washington, Brussels, and Tokyo. It also confirmed that it gave interviews on the topic of Japanese security to the press prior to *The Factor* appearance, but was not an expert in the capacity of the topic at hand; nor do any book databases confirm he wrote any books, let alone the eight he claimed on his website that also touted that he was a "great geo-strategic and political foresight whom specializes in Intelligence, Information Aggregation and the FUSION and strategic meaning of disparate data".)

In the news world, credibility is the hook that draws audiences in, and when fake experts are paraded as real, audiences revolt at being played for fools. With every lie, slander, and hoax the press has perpetrated, the angrier the public becomes, and they begin to look for answers elsewhere. For every *BuzzFeed* and *Breitbart*, there were hundreds of media missteps that led to their creation: the press normalized trivialities in their reports, giving rise to obnoxious and worthless *BuzzFeed* quizzes that steal life with no reward. It normalized delusional opinion as a superior substitute for reality, giving rise to the toxic and bitter *Breitbart* that lead the fearful down the garden path. Whether it is the sophistry of *Vox*, or the defense mechanism of *Vice*, there is no shortage of inferior substitutes to the simple unit known as fact. We have moved so far away from the truth that most can no longer recognize it on first glance. Worse, fewer and fewer news producers can admit they have made an error in judgment, let alone are running on flawed ideology. It is a cancer spreading to news consumers who also do not believe they have deficits in their knowledge, or that they may harbor many erroneous ideas, opinions, knowledge, or beliefs.

How can the press undergo a desperately-needed revolution, when its keepers haughtily declare they are noble and infallible agents of truth, who happen to repeat blindly whatever others tell them without basic verification?

The soldiers who vowed to liberate truth from lies began to infect the information stream by spreading lies, and no longer see that they are an enemy to the people.

Trump understands the press better than most as he carefully cultivated them while they gave him fawning and unjustifiable media coverage, and then broke away when a viable alternative presented itself: he may be no better than his now sworn rivals, but they are not the saviors by default. The institution has become an enemy to the truth, and an enemy of the truth is an enemy of the people.

In a world where scripted and contrived programs of fake entertainment are labelled "reality shows", our sense for reality has diminished. The press has aided and abetted our blurred vision by treating pseudo-celebrities as newsmakers, and reported the prepackaged propaganda of corporations as original research. The system of dissemination has not changed, despite the fact that technology has brought a structural revolution of the Internet, where any citizen has access to the ideas of billions of people, just as billions of people have access to their idea. The traditional purpose of journalists has been obliterated, and reporters have not changed their ways to find a new purpose and method. Yet the stubborn refusal to embrace a revolutionary shift is choking the profession into irrelevance.

While the press had often playfully pulled pranks on the public on April's Fools Day (such as the celebrated "Swiss Spaghetti Tree" hoax the BBC's *Panorama* pulled flawlessly in 1957, aided with Richard Dimbleby's convincing authoritative narration), it is not the same as the level of deceit and gullibility that has plagued journalism in the decades since. The US press cannot have virtuous airs over Donald Trump when they presented men such as US comedian Bill Cosby, Canadian author Steven Galloway, or BBC presenter Jimmy Savile as clean-cut and brilliant men who could be left alone in the same room as your daughter. They assured the public that they dug deep, as they did far and wide, and did not use sources such as press releases and public relations firms to do the work for them. In fact, they did no original reporting themselves. With staged events being seen as spontaneous by the press, the crisis has shattered the profession. For every Glenn Greenwald (however, the Juan Thompson Affair casts a pall over his online publication *The Intercept*), or Nick Davies digging for truths, there are too many Stephen Glasses and Sabrina Erdelys burying them, making journalism an increasingly unreliable and unstable source for information.

Even if news producers are in denial that their credibility has vanished, those who see the gaps can easily take advantage of them. When Trump called the press "fake news", there will be millions who agree with the assessment, thereby making it a simple matter to inoculate followers from the media by merely pointing out that any facts that go against the speaker's narrative are calculated lies, spin, and propaganda. While those who point a finger of blame may have three fingers pointing back at them, the truth is the press fares no better in the credibility department, and hence, can be rightfully dismissed, and that still leaves a treacherous gap for the public.

Yet accessible and original reportage is absolutely required for a society to survive. Social media has replaced journalism in many ways, as they became the new gatekeepers, but spectacularly failed in significant ways: with websites such as *Reddit* being exposed in 2017 by *Forbes* for using paid individuals to game the comments, it is the same problems plaguing the Internet with even *fewer* checks and balances to stop it. There may be paid posters or even mule accounts used as stones in an online game of Go, where the point is to surround dissenting voices with personal attacks, bullying, or even demanding moderators take down or ban posters' alternate points of view, all while the scripted attacks seem natural.

Dissenting voices can be easily and effortlessly neutralized by paid posters (or a single poster with multiple accounts) choreographing ridicule and reporting posts to moderators, demanding they are removed with no one questioning the structure or practices of online discussions. There is no question that a system of information dissemination is absolutely essential for civilization to survive and prosper. The question is what can replace journalism as the means to do it.

Journalism does not have the monopoly on mundane research, as those posting live footage of breaking stories on their social media feed have proven. However, journalism is more than mere regurgitation of raw data. It is the hunting for sources and the gathering of facts from different and contradictory places. The purpose is to create a story that does not tell people what to think or feel, but to inform them of both reality and truth, so that they can make use of the information to guide their own lives in a way they want and need.

People have different realities and goals, and it is not up to journalists to dictate to them that they ought to support climate change or fear the demand for transgender rights: it is to tell them what is happening in the world that is problematic. What are the long-term employment prospects? How is the reigning regime spending tax dollars? Are teachers doing their jobs? Are minorities getting abused? How viable are the companies or functional the real estate market? How fair are the judges? Is everyone getting equal pay for equal work? How many spouses are getting beaten at home, and what are the police and courts doing about it? How safe is the drinking water? Or, How mentally stable is the investment banker?

Wherever there are problems festering, we need fact-gatherers to find out for us. This is not a desk job, where the gatherer sits at a desk and thinks up arguments that support a narrative; it is about chronicling the same world you live in actively, honestly, truthfully, and realistically.

But how this is done is only crudely known. Chemists are forever refining how they gather data — as do doctors, biologists, and other STEM-based researchers — but journalists have none of the same assessments and refinements required of any fact-gatherer discipline.

It is not as if there is no means to do this; there are many ways for reporters to develop a more scientific and disciplined approach to their jobs. Advertisers have found new ways of selling to audiences, yet journalists have taken nothing from that research to apply it benevolently to their own. How do people react to distressing information? What do they process? Is all information equally salient — or is some information more memorable than others? And if it is memorable — is it interpreted objectively, or misremembered and distorted? And if some items are not consciously remembered, is it possible we retain the information subconsciously, still influencing how we process and interpret information?

The press could answer none of those questions for you, even if psychologists and sociologists have much to offer on those topics. The research exists, but not in a manner that is usable for reporters.

Journalism has functioned under the assumption that the

world is ordered. It understands formats and formulas. It does not understand the frenetic, anarchistic, fragmented, and most importantly, *schizophrenic* nature of reality.

Journalists try to make sense of events, when they should be doing anything but.

The world is not ordered. It is chaotic patterns that intersect like Venn diagrams. Journalists must gather facts from these volatile areas and make *sense* of the patterns, not reimagine them to be something they are not. Predators thrive in chaos as they are aware of the reality of their surroundings. Yet journalists, who must be predators when looking for elusive truths, often stumble, as they are not aware of how to navigate and report on that reality. Editors have rewarded fabulists such as Patricia Smith and Stephen Glass, as both had understood how to present *order:* they gave editors a pleasing narrative and morality play that appealed to their supervisor's expectations.

Journalism is not about appeasement. It is about truth. And the truth is we live in anarchy that thrives in both physical and psychological war.

So how do we function in anarchy? That is the *first* question all journalists must answer to be credible chroniclers of reality. It is not to reassure a public that they are the heroes, and the villains will always be vanquished. Often, it is the audience who are the villains. Other times, the villain will triumph, or even be lauded. Journalism is not about normalizing villainy, or suggesting people should be resigned to injustice. However, it is the duty of journalists to expose the injustices in a way the audience can not only understand, but also make use of it properly. Only in its current form, the news media has become incapable of doing so. It balks at the methods of hacktivists, for instance. It prefers flowery sophistry and fake entertainment performers, otherwise known as reality show stars. It does not try to find or expose child sex rings, or catch an A-list celebrity abusing assistants. It does not question misogynistic assumptions in society, or latent racist ideology from those who purport to be progressive and egalitarian, yet still see the world as a White Man's Burden.

It no longer sees its role as liberator of truth, breaking the ideological shackles we mistake as unchanging and absolute truth — shackles that confine us and hold us back. It does not question its surroundings; ergo, it cannot reveal what it takes for granted.

It is a dead profession in need of a resurrection. But like the phoenix of lore, it cannot take the same form it had when it was felled: it must be reinvented in the present.

Why? For the simple reason there are too many new variables it must consider — variables it did not take into account when it began. There was no Internet or social media. Women and minorities were not seen as worthy to own property or have the right to vote. Homosexuality was seen as a mental defect.

The beliefs that propelled those confining thought patterns did not merely apply to one area of thinking: it applied to *every* facet of thought. Journalism cannot reflect reality, as it has always used a patriarchal mode of storytelling, where there is a single protagonist with a superior point of view, and opposition to the protagonist meant the opposite side was an antagonist — a villain — by default.

Its assumptions are patriarchal in nature, from the way it views objectivity to the way it presents information. Traditional media in the US has a difficult time reporting reality — for example, it sees its current president as an enemy to vanquish, not a person to understand. The press has become angry at his swipes, and has taken his insults personally — a ridiculous reaction given that reality is anarchy, and Trump thrives in anarchy, as he creates those favorable conditions in the minds of journalists who are stumbling in it. Had they understood the nature of reality, none of his taunts would bother them, as it distracts from their mandates of finding facts.

The press has long used an antagonistic approach to

newsmakers they do not like as they fail to grasp that there will always be a sizeable number of individuals who will not take sides — or will take the target's side.

To develop that level of intellectual maturity, the model of journalism as we know it must cease to exist in its current form for a new model to take its place. It is one that requires a new way of training reporters to understand and embrace the ways of reality and truth, as they become aware of how their own perceptions and misinterpretations of both shape how they see facts as well as find them.

Recreating journalism education requires more than using the latest technology. It needs a solid understanding of the Scientific Method, and an understanding that journalism is itself a school of experimental anarchy. It teaches audiences how to find facts in their own immediate surroundings, and how to analyze and interpret them, before disseminating those facts to others. Journalists must embrace that the Internet has made it possible for anyone to be a news producer. The problem is the amateurs have not been shown how to do it productively, as their current models for it have paid no mind to their own errors in judgment. Journalists are not in the business to compete with the public, but guide them, by not just finding their own facts, but also incorporating citizen fact-finding in innovative ways — although not by merely rehashing what they saw as they trolled the opinions on Twitter, YouTube, Instagram, and Facebook. For journalism to be reborn, it must start from scratch in its very education.

One of the problems tainting the journalistic product has been the confirmation bias. Reporters see fault with a designated villain, yet gloss over the same traits in their designated hero. The puerility is unacceptable on every level. It is not about taking sides: it is about thoroughness in research to find the facts that allow citizens to draw their own conclusions. This requires curiosity, and reining in the urge to meddle and tell audiences what their opinions ought to be — or keep professional propagandists and manipulators from doing the same by using the press as proxy.

How can this be done? The elements of the structure have already been available for over a century, as the methods of experimental psychology allow journalism to foster critical thinking. Journalists do not question the basic. They are obsessed with color, telling readers and viewers how a celebrity walks across the room, but they do not look in the person's house for the muted signs of trying to hide one's secret poverty, or abuse of narcotics or servants. Psychology has no shortage of studies examining the significance of micro expressions or how word usage slants memories. Journalists ask questions of eyewitnesses, yet the studies in cognitive psychology have long ago warned that a single word can permanently alter memories.

A new education is required, but one taught by those who actively conduct experiments in the field of information gathering, processing, and dissemination. It requires an understanding of anarchy, and how those who understand it take advantage of the chaos to manipulate and rig the outcome of their various games that are an illusion of order. Journalism must redefine its mandate: it is in the business of gathering facts and hunting down sources, and only quality facts and sources will do. It is not about impressing the young or the wealthy; it is not about racking up war stories; and it is not about becoming an icon or legend: it is about finding facts that are useful.

True information verification in a world of power, denial, fear, and deception is essential. Reporters cannot rely on reddit or Twitter to find them the reality of their surroundings. It is old-fashioned legwork that finds it as truth is often hidden under rocks lest someone finds it, and exposes individuals as exploiters.

But to do that, journalists must be trained to think like an experimental psychologist: learning to conduct impromptu experiments in order to test various hypotheses. Everything and everyone requires a comparison to see the similarities and differences. Is the situation better than before or worse? Psychologists often have more prepared answers than the press, who desperately need psychology training in order to understand interpersonal dynamics. If an individual who suffers from an anti-social personality disorder (ASPD) interprets the world differently than someone who is afflicted by depression, a journalist must be trained to spot it, and know how those individuals are interpreting their surroundings. Perhaps a situation calls for despair, but if someone is primed to see the darkness and ignore the light, a reporter must take that into the calculations. Currently, j-schools do not provide students with the tools to be able to do it.

The groupthink of the press has harmed its credibility. It requires journalists to be rebels. The US and Canadian press lauded Meryl Streep's Golden Globe speech, where she lamented those who use bullying tactics, for instance, yet no one in the press thought to ask her how the hostile climate of the acting profession mimicked the same bad behavior she found to be offensive.

Anarchy is an element that is well understood by psychologists, yet journalists are not fluent in its ways. A core of psychology would go a long way to rebuilding journalism, yet until reporters can see the problems that have eroded their discipline, nothing will change — and there will be no salvation from the Internet to bail them out.

Chapter Eighteen

The intellectual soldiers

A journalist is a soldier who liberates truth from lies. It is a simple mandate for news producers in the field. The execution of that mandate is difficult, complex, unpredictable, and often, even dangerous. Organized crime will not reveal their sins just because a journalist asks nicely. Nor will a warlord, dictator, terrorist, serial killer, or child pornographer. They need power and control from every possible source, and power comes from keeping secrets by creating a fortress made of lies.

The power of deception cannot be overstated. Sun Tzu's *The Art of War* went so far as to state that war is deception, but deception itself is more than just a war tactic: it is a hostile act, with an arrogant base assumption that the deceiver is more cunning and more intelligent than the audience the liar is deceiving. Deceit is the reporter's greatest enemy as well as obstacle, and the goal is to always to find the truth to reflect reality in a reliable and valid manner that has utility.

But in a world filled with manipulation, deceit, sophistry, propaganda, and ignorance, the battleground is a dark and fierce one. Reporters face lawsuits, threats, job losses, and in the case of Chauncey Bailey, Jill Dando, and Daniel Pearl, even death.

They face all of that with no thank you or acknowledgment from those who benefit from the warnings, and often those same audiences insult reporters and the gleeful call for their heads.

It often devastates those who begin idealistically, and honestly believe that they will expose the *bad guys* and the world will be cheerfully grateful as they learn the truth, and take the steps to rid their society of corruption and malice. Instead, they are attacked for their hard work, accused themselves of corruption, malice, and even insanity, and their findings are dismissed as the corruption is explained away, justified, denied, or even glorified.

So many in the profession give in or give up entirely. When the 2016 Chilcot Report outlined that multiple governments knew that there was no imminent threat to the West by Iran, so, too, did journalists, who played along all the same. That journalists did not question everything they were given by the government is not what one should expect from a profession that touts itself as the finders of truth. When lies are given by one institution, journalists are in the position to verify the information and expose the reality, not just when they ideologically disagree with a given regime, but especially when they are inclined to agree with them.

It is not as if the truth is always hard to find. Many times, it is a simple affair to do it, but the press often choose not to inform the public of what is really happening. In the US, for instance, any foreign country that hires a US public relations firm must register with the Justice Department, and that information is available to journalists. The name of the firm, the entity who hired them, the amount, and the reasons are there for any reporter to see, and, if they understand the reason for their employment, would relay the information to the audience to prepare them.

But journalists also see this information when press releases are disseminated to them. They know their former colleagues who once worked at their newspaper or television station, but have since gone to work for public relations companies. It is not as if PR can truly work in the shadows: they can only do so if journalists do not inform the public where they are really finding out what is going on. They know it, and are fully aware of it.

They may know it, but often choose to ignore it or explain it away. It is too easy to feign ignorance while taking credit for discovering a "fact". Many local television stations often rely exclusively on processed information for their content, from issuing statements from police and government officials, to the local county fair or singer who is performing. Many would consider such information irrelevant to the story; however, if the reporter has not independently verified the information given, then they have an obligation to reveal whether the source is a genuine one giving the raw, primary data, or an outfit hired to present information through a lens.

Journalists are supposed to be intellectual soldiers, fighting a battle against deceit and fantasy to find truth and reality so they can present it to their people. They are supposed to work for their audience, not against them. When they spread the lies and distortions instead of challenging them, they are no longer soldiers of the people, but their enemy complicit in harming them.

Toronto Star columnist and activist Catherine Porter is a case in point. Porter brought her 9-year-old daughter, Lyla, to a climate change protest. She thought she could present her narrative over a confrontation with fellow columnist Ezra Levant unchallenged in the July 6, 2015 edition of the *Toronto Star*, which accused Levant of "marching over" to her, browbeating her and her daughter by allegedly saying to Porter, "Did I own a car? Were my clothes made from synthetics? See, I was a hypocrite!" She then recounted how her daughter told Levant that he was "being mean to my mom", causing Levant to walk away.

But Ezra Levant had much to say about Porter's skewed account of events. In fact, his version was different in several significant ways, as he gave his rebuttal in the July 7, 2015 letters to the editor section of the *Star,* denying the events took place in the hostile way she described, and he had videotape evidence to support his side of the story.

With tangible evidence that Porter was deliberately engaging in distorting the narrative, regardless of the moral and professional consequences, Porter spun her non-mea culpa in the July 21, 2015 edition of the *Star,* claiming that she wrote the piece, "on my first day of vacation", and that she "was rushed".

With excuses, spinning, the only thing Porter managed to prove was that she was incapable of taking responsibility for her botched narrative as she continued to cast herself in the role of heroine victim, even though her actions were anything but. She admits to no wrongdoing or shading, despite evidence that her original account *contradicted* the video evidence. While the headline suggests she is about to admit she was wrong, her response does not, in fact, admit any fault on her part.

But what else can we take away from this incident?

1. Porter was a writer obsessed with a fairy-tale narrative. She spun every facet of the story, selling it as a good versus evil fable, where her daughter was the plucky and civic-minded heroine and Levant was the rude and obtuse egomaniac. With Levant an easy target, it seemed an easy story that would bypass scrutiny. She merely forgot that in a society obsessed with self-chronicling, there would very likely be evidence of what really transpired.

2. She used an easy-to-identify villain of the Canadian Left: Ezra Levant. She targeted him, sought him out specifically, set her young daughter to approach him in public, and then recounted it in her column as if it were legitimate news. It was a calculated move that had no news value. She pushed her 9-year-old daughter into this choreographed event, coaching her child what to say to him. A Big Right Bad Guy versus a little girl was over-the-top and staged overkill; though, what news value the melodrama had was not considered.

3. Porter later claimed activism, but what she delivered was narrative obsession. She framed the story by setting the stage, and then served as playwright and director. What she forgot in all her manipulative calculations was there had been a camera rolling, recording the director choreographing the dubious scene for a measly single

column of mediocre and forgettable fodder. She took the phrase Stage Mom to a new level, and it backfired, turning a news column into a self-serving spectacle. The gambit was more appropriate for a social media feed than a newspaper.

4. The actual event had *no news value in the first place.* It did become newsworthy when video evidence proved the original account was seriously wanting. Had the column been spiked for being a canned and contrived event, the ensuing controversy over a vanity column would not have been necessary. A poor news judgment led to an actual newsworthy event.

Worst of all, the *Star's* public editor Kathy English took the petty route on Friday, July 17, 2015, when she made strategic jabs deifying the one who mislead while belittling the target of the manipulative swipe, stating that:

> Porter, a National Newspaper Award-winning journalist, is a "social justice activist/columnist" for the *Star*. Levant, a well-known — and certainly controversial — former host with the now-defunct Sun News Network, describes himself as a "lawyer, author and all-round trouble-maker" who is now "rebel commander" of the *rebel media*, his start-up "news, opinion and activism" website.

Regardless of what you may think of the controversial Levant, or how superior a journalist or editor fancies themselves to be in the comparison, there is no question that what transpired was deceptive. If an award-winning writer stoops to such tactics, whatever awards or paper crowns the chronicler has amassed, it is no protection or excuse for deplorable manipulations.

News producers are only as good as their last story. Everything they have done before is meaningless. What makes this incident particularly heinous and more serious than it first appears is the fact that Levant was an easy target: Porter could have easily done the math and believed her award, and his history made her immune to questioning. It was a gross miscalculation that tarnished the *Star's* credibility as a news producer.

Not every journalist is of this ilk. Many have dedicated themselves to truthful and accurate investigative journalism, from Nick Davies (who began through the traditional route) to Glenn Greenwald (who began as an online reporter). This proves when journalists are focused, their work opens news consumers' eyes, forcing them to confront the demons of injustice and tyranny. Journalists are a priceless resource. They are the soldiers who fight corruption. They liberate nations when they dig for the truth with a seemingly contradictory balance of idealism, skepticism, bravery, and caution. It is by no means an easy or simple task: become too idealistic, and you become blind to the faults of those in harm's way. Become too skeptical, and you become too blind to the faults of those doing the harming. When you become too reckless, you begin to believe you are a character in the narrative, and too much caution prevents you from pushing forward to find the truth those in power do everything to hide.

But a journalist must always be truthful, honest, accurate, and realistic, and fanatically so. In the case of Porter, she was none of those things, and when the truth revealed that the exchange did not unfold in the way she described, she refused to come clean. She refused to acknowledge the facts, or, as it is now known, she provided her own *alternative facts* in a "post-truth" world.

The actual truth is that she deceived. She spun a narrative that cast herself in a positive light, but at the expense of another who served as an easy villain. She had forgotten that there are such things as cameras (Levant had a camerawoman filming the entire exchange), though Levant did not.

A journalist or columnist who forgets the nature of reality

cannot be relied on to describe it, and the reality is that journalists are there to report on the news, not inject themselves into it gratuitously, or use it as a way to settle scores. It is too easy to wish to be part of a narrative, but narratives are not facts, reality, or truth — just an interpretation of one.

Disgraced *New Republic* reporter Stephen Glass is the classic example of a journalist whose mandate was not to inform or liberate truth from the lies: he was the egotist who believed he bypassed truth to write uninformative fables of a freak show. He had always cast himself as the reporter who seemed to uncover selfish and uneducated yokels who did appalling things, thought despicable thoughts, and said obnoxiously outrageous things.

He was a man who had been willing to fake his notes in order to fool fact-checkers, who had assumed the materials he was giving them were genuine. He ingratiated himself to his supervisors, and for years, he kept his charade going. All this as his fortunes rose as a white-hot reporter who also wrote for *George* and *Harper's* magazines.

Glass had completely ignored reality to spin his peculiar and often covertly bigoted stories, but for Glass, it was easy to do so: facts are seen as boring, and those who present them are dismissed as being boring, stodgy, preachy know-it-alls and bring-downs. Who wishes to know that their favorite television presenter may be a child molester, or even spouse killer? Glass understood the fine line, and offered up a menagerie of phantasms, who were portrayed as poor, uneducated, and repulsive. These were non-threatening to the fantasies of the chosen demographic, and Glass had found his element. He was not a solider, but a saboteur of reality.

It is difficult to express the extent of damage Glass's deceptions caused to journalism. He wrote for intellectual and political magazines. It was supposed to be about things that mattered, but he was a distraction from the hard truths of political consequences. He ridiculed desperate and homely young women or taxi drivers with accents. He subtly presented stereotypes in hard news publications, tainting and reinforcing caricatures to those who fancy themselves as learned. The Sleeper Effect states that we begin to believe information we have read from sources we do not respect, as we forgot the source of the original data, but still recall the factoid in question. Glass's deceptions ensured those stereotypes lived on, even after his work was exposed as fraudulent.

Journalism is a profession that is idealistic in nature, but the element of corruption it must uncover and expose, forces those in it to be skeptical of information that they receive. When journalists corrupt their own idealism, as Glass did when he began to spin his first lie, they are of no use to the profession: they can only corrupt others as they feed audiences lies and distortions where they begin to forget how to tell a truth from a lie, and they begin to chart their lives on a faulty course.

While journalists must be skeptical when they hear information, society cannot function without journalistic idealism: reporters must believe in what they are doing. They must see the war against truth, and enlist themselves to liberate truth from lies. Breakdowns in society occur when too many citizens become resigned to the corruption and retreat.

Journalists are supposed to be the soldiers who stop those defeats by revealing where the troubles lie, who is causing them and why; so that society can begin to correct itself and heal its wounds.

If liberating the truth is the objective, then it is critical for journalists to train themselves to be able to see it, and know what is a truth and what is a lie; yet the field of psychology has no shortage of studies that show us how our basic perceptions deceive us.

For example, in one study, subjects were asked to adjust a colored square on a computer screen to match another colored square. If we all saw colors as they were, we would not expect any deviations in responses; however, there are great variations, meaning our perceptions are flawed, and vary from person to person.

We can implant memories in people, convincing them that a car crash happened at a greater speed than it did; that eyewitnesses recall seeing a weapon when there was none; and, most shockingly at all, that people remember significant events from their childhood that never happened.

From psychology, we also know that people with certain personality disorders have specific impairments in their perceptions and interpretations of events: those who are narcissistic see everything as part of their self-aggrandizing narrative, while those who are paranoid see everything as part of a dark conspiracy. Anxiety during stressful events alters memories in very specific and significant ways, and different drugs impair our memory formation as well. There is no shortage of blinders, filters, and lenses we unknowingly wear while we are processing information when we are relaxed and in mundane routines, let alone when we are under pressure when unexpected calamities occur. Low self-esteem causes impairments and distortions, just as a positive disposition can do the same in different ways: the former amplifies problems to make them seem overwhelming and unbeatable, while the latter leads people to gloss over or ignore problems that are more difficult to solve the longer they are left to grow.

It is a Tower of Babel that is a journalist's beat: a wealthy white male sees benefits to a new law, and cannot understand why the poor black woman is enraged at the same turn of events. The intellectually alert and emotionally nuanced reporter not only sees and understands the fragmentation so can also easily serve as translator to that fractured, but broad audience. This also explains why a newsworthy event benefits some, but puts others at a disadvantage, as it also explains why that divide will bring problems later on.

Reporters can no longer be mere chroniclers: they must be journalists, historians, psychologists, sociologists, anthropologists, experimenters, storytellers, and mediators all in one. They are the curators of a world that draws lines in the sand, with hypothetical constructs that form the backbone of the rituals of sanctioned insanity, and then treat those arbitrary lines as real, logical, moral, necessary, absolute, and sacrosanct. They must see the perceptions and misperceptions of others before they translate those interpretations to others, all while presenting facts to the audience. They have no need to take sides as perceptions are as tainted to one side as they are to the other.

The mandate of the intellectual soldier is simple: find lies, expose them, and then find and liberate the truth. Deceivers see the world as a game of Go, where the object of the game is to surround the truth with stones of lies, removing its liberties one by one, until the lies choke the truth, and hide it from the eyes of the public. Deceivers use sophistry liberally, deny the truth even exists, and use logical flaws to prop up ridiculous arguments. When all those gambits fail, the deceivers emotionally manipulate their targets by claiming to be misunderstood and wronged victims, who are condemned by the unenlightened.

Such was the case when Canadian author and UBC creative writing professor Steven Galloway had been fired from the university. They had investigated complaints that he had sexually harassed and assaulted students as he was abusive toward them, going so far as to slap one student in a bar. It was a shameful scandal in Canadian literature, but what should have ended with Galloway's apology ballooned into a scandal as dozens of well-known Canadian authors, Yann Martel, Joseph Boyden (an author who for years claimed to be of various Aboriginal ancestry who had been believed by the press, until one Aboriginal news outlet conducted its own investigation and discovered he was not Aboriginal; though, he had won awards and received grants based on his alleged heritage), and Margaret

Atwood signed an open letter decrying the university's decision to follow the law and instruct Galloway not to speak to the media during the investigation, and, by extension, defending a man in power who abused those under that power, causing an international backlash against the letter-writers who were not used to the bad publicity. They had turned Galloway's firing into a men's rights issue, claiming it was authority-figure Galloway who was victimized. He had slapped one of his students in front of witnesses at a bar. The press had lavished praise on these authors without second thought, particularly Galloway and Boyden, despite the fact that both men were both worthy of being the subject of a hard news investigation of their conduct and assertions whose behavior threatened the credibility of their own profession.

There are real victims and dispossessed ones; however, an Establishment professor and author is not one of them and to pretend otherwise is the reason journalism is desperately needed in the first place, but the Canadian news media do not take a critical lens to their icons, no matter the seriousness of the allegations lodged from credible sources. For many outlets, reportage is no different than any other advertorial: it is propaganda and advertising disguised as a news article, but news consumers often see through it, and begin to lose interest in patronizing an outlet that insults its audience.

If truth is important for journalists to find, then we would expect all journalists, regardless of their beat, to dedicate themselves to finding as much as possible. Yet some beats prove to be problematic, and often it is surprising which ones slack on the job. Science reporters are often guilty of serving as cheerleaders than investigative journalists who look with a critical eye on their beat. When *Time* magazine had Steve Jobs grace their cover with the latest iMac in January 2002, the story was a positive love letter to the device and its creator, not critical or at least factual. It was advertising that was any tech company's dream; yet with scientific fraud, medical incompetence, robber barons, and even systemic misogyny plaguing every facet of the profession, there is no shortage of hard news stories that these journalists could have chosen to cover. It is their reason for being; yet the idea of being an intellectual soldier repulses many in the profession, who prefer to cheerlead the easy stories, such as marveling over the latest trinket as they ignore the problems around them.

And when journalism lost its will to fight, it lost yet another battle until its lost the war, and no longer mattered to the public discourse.

Chapter Nineteen

The medium is not the profession

When the Internet began to become a mass medium in the 1990s, those in the journalism profession were not taking things seriously. Newspapers were still the dominant medium, surviving radio and television decades before. Those in the business did not see the radically changing landscape as a threat to their profession. Some saw it as a passing nuisance and fad, while others who believed they were future-thinking, honestly believed that the Internet was a souped-up version of their established medium.

Journalism is a profession that was not only defined by its confines of medium, but also the confines of gate-keeping. In a world of smartphones and the Internet, we can see footage of a terrorist attack or an assassination of a government official in real time from bystanders. Once upon a time, amateur footage was not available or rarely accessible. Now, we can see everyday people film riveting and shocking events, from tornadoes to police brutality. In the US within the last few years, several police shootings of unarmed African-American men were captured on camera not by vigilant reporters or their cameramen, but by average citizens. In the case of Philando Castile, his girlfriend, who was driving her vehicle while he was a passenger, and used her phone and Facebook account to show his senseless and baffling death at a traffic stop. Once broadcasting became accessible to audiences, journalists lost their exclusive rights to show the world how it was functioning.

None in the upper echelons of the industry saw the rise of social media, or that journalism was about to approach unprepared into a cataclysm. The concept of gate-keeping was about to be destroyed, as was the once elite club of people who had the sole keys to a public audience. Nothing would ever be the same again. An entire generation that had previously been ignored by journalists was about to be given free and complete access to WordPress, YouTube, podcasting, and Twitter, without an editor and publisher telling them what they were going to put out to a global audience did not fit or was too unprofessional for public consumption. Anarchy was on the horizon, but even in the chaos, there were patterns to be deciphered. Except that journalists — the very people who are supposed to go into chaotic war zones and disasters to see patterns and logic — could not see what was happening, and why they were about to become irrelevant.

They understood three media: print, radio, and television. But the Fourth Medium, the Internet, would become the enigma they could not solve. So blind were journalists that many of their trade publications such as *Presstime*, and *Editor and Publisher* ended their print runs, while the newsstand magazine *Brill's Content* shut down altogether. In other words, so badly would those in the profession misread the Internet that they could no longer understand the makings of the established media.

Marshall McLuhan had coined the phrase "the medium is the message", making the case that the medium alters the message: the same story covered in print will have a different meaning than if it were covered on radio or television. There is much going for the theory. Print may be a static medium, but a print reporter can cover more ground, giving more detail and allowing for more complexity. Television and radio must be bare bones and simpler: radio relies on sound and immediacy, while television relies on visuals to tell a narrative.

Yet so much of traditional journalism played up to nonessential parts of the story to fit their medium. Television newsmagazines often played music in the background to tell a story: victims of crime would be filmed walking to nowhere in particular as sad piano music underscored their status as the abused. Heroes got pulse-pounding brass music to enhance their image. Print had played the same games in a different sort of way: newspaper articles about the elderly who were scammed almost always had those seniors look like lost puppies in their photographs as they sat in their living rooms with big doe eyes and pouty faces. Children who were denied field trips or classroom candy would be posed in similar ways. Facts were seen as secondary to choreographed posing: it was never enough to outline that someone had been wronged — they had to look submissive enough to pass muster. The medium was the message, but, somehow, facts were given a secondary position to emotional filler.

That filler even has a name in the profession: color. Read a magazine profile and rarely does the opening go straight to fact: it is always an anecdote that was supposed to sum up the tone of the subject. Is the subject of the profile a hero, victim, or villain? The opening story will tell you what to think. When it is not fact, it is color.

In journalism, color takes many forms: from anecdotes to background music to cutaway shots, such as a politician sitting at his or her desk reading files and signing them. The medium is not quite the message, but it does dictate the sorts of colors journalists can use to make their point. For decades, the formula for each medium did not change.

Until the Internet came along and broke the rules. While it freed many from the shackles of the profession, it did nothing to provide a guide for disseminating facts to a mass audience, who need to be informed about the world around them. We still have media, but their confines have become confused with the essence of the message.

Separating journalism from the medium is absolutely essential to keep the profession relevant and viable. The shackles of the various media had many reporters believe their medium was journalism, not merely the convenient conduit for it.

The problem with social media as a conduit for information is the complete lack of checks and balances: liars can be the gatekeepers of their own deceptive narrative. No one is required to tell the truth on their Facebook page; yet we can believe we know a person as we scroll through their censored and dishonest life story. But the Fourth Medium has an illusion of being personal, omniscient, definitive, and private — even though it is absolutely none of those things. It is like phone sex with a stranger: they tell you everything you want to hear, and you don't even need to see how the person really looks or watch them get their paycheck or say the same lines to hundreds of other customers — so long as you are exposed to the parts that suit your delusions, and arouse you.

We do not, for example, have investigative social media journalists who look into random feeds and then prove the person is nothing but a lying braggart. On the other hand, we do have hacktivists who do a public service by exposing those people who think their lines in the sand are protection from people finding out who they really are. We get the raw and unfiltered facts; unfortunately, they are often found in places such as the dark Web where the uninitiated cannot easily get to them.

Publications not found on the deep Web (and its cousin dark Web) have not served as proper replacements of traditional media. As we have seen in previous chapters, these are purveyors of snarky and sophistry. We are left in a vacuum, and though we are living in the most literate era in the history of mankind, we are stuck in a vortex, where we know too much about the staged lives of pseudo-celebrities and nothing about the quality of the food we are eating. Food fraud, for example, is a growing global problem; yet we know the specifics of celebrity divorces.

If the medium is the message, then the message we are receiving is disheartening:

1   People were walking away from traditional media outlets in droves, especially newspapers. The trouble is television, magazine, and radio outlets are not as well-equipped with their apparatus, as were newspapers. Even online publications do not have it, and are, despite their cocky bravado, poor cousins to the height of the newspaper machine. For example, you will not get better quality or more information from television news than a newspaper, but most people are not aware of this wrinkle. Everyone watches television, but what a newspaper reporter can report is far more than the fleeting moments a TV reporter has, even for a newsmagazine. Take transcripts of television news reports, and then find the same news story in a newspaper, and compare. That means the erosion of newspapers means the erosion of news in general. That was the real reason people in the newspaper industry were so smug about the arrival of the Internet: they assumed they were safe, because they had the power, the experience, the knowledge, and the resources. They saw themselves as the favorite first-born, but reality would prove them mistaken. Yet they honestly thought they were just going to migrate online, and everything would be as it was before. They had no clue.

2   The publications that began online were oblivious to the news-gathering process — and still are. They are literally news-producing stupid, and are so far proving to be unteachable. Real journalism takes months or even years to produce, but publications such as *Vice*, the *Huffington Post*, *Vox*, and *BuzzFeed* are all about flash and being content feeders, not news producers. People see pundits on television spewing their ignorant opinions and sophistry and think it is easy. What it is, in fact, is cheap. Real news is about finding out whether or not the

school you are sending your child to is secretly housing some sort of child porn ring, or is structurally unsound. It is about uncovering corruption in government and business. It is about showing the seeds of terrorist cults before they have a chance to gain power and then slaughter in a mass mindless temper tantrum. Since 2005, we have been living in a news anarchy: we have plenty of poseurs, but no one is actually doing news or even knowing how to gather facts, or interview sources, or evaluate the quality of information received. The changes in media are happening so rapidly that people are too disoriented to get it — at least for now.

3   Social media has essentially hammered the final nail in journalism in multiple ways. It made propagandists and PR flacks able to bypass the press entirely to spew their advertising to the public who mindlessly post those lies and trivialities on their social media feeds, without thinking whether or not they are acting as vectors who are polluting the information stream. More importantly, people have now absolutely deluded themselves into thinking they are news producers themselves, when nothing can be further from the truth. They post videos, blog entries, and even podcasts, and now think they are contributing something. They interview no one, look at no database, make no freedom of information requests, or bother to do any original research. They read an article or social media post, and run with it as if it were fact. Do they interview all relevant parties? Of course, they don't: they are amateur pundits making kneejerk reactions based on a single say-so. They believe being confident is an equivalent to being right. That is not journalism. That is not even a reasonable facsimile of it.

Amateur videos of police shootings is one thing, as it is evidence of an action, but even then, you still need to be researching. Perhaps what we are seeing is a snippet, and there is more to the story to consider. Perhaps the police officer who shot someone has a history of violence, but the department has kept it hidden. We also do not know whether or not footage is misleading or even staged until we begin to square the facts to the actual video.

Second, people often confuse what is news. They mistake filler with information. People post all sorts of me-centered non-information on their feeds, such as taking photographs of their coffee, or vacation photos and have replaced the banalities of the bourgeois with actual newsworthiness. Posting unscientific quizzes as if they represented something takes precedence over whether or not there is toxic dumping in their neighborhood.

Finally, content has shifted and the new gatekeepers are those who run social-media sites. Filler sites such as *BuzzFeed* and *Cracked* get passed around even though they have nothing pressing to offer — just life-sink articles about popular culture. Yet we have many news stories not making it through because certain algorithms are preventing them from appearing. Censorship is a form of propaganda; yet few seem concerned that we are losing information diversity on the Web.

4   Journalism is not as simple as it appears, and nor is storytelling: it is innate, but it is a hunting-gathering activity: we hunt for knowledge as we gather grains of wisdom. It is not just technique, but learning to appeal to a broader audience takes practice. Large media outlets aren't in the business of giving a chance to untested commodities, regardless of how well they write. It is smaller local outlets that take most of the risk, and with fewer professional risk-taking outlets available, the finessing and refining for the next generation of writers to find their footing is lost.

The Internet is a medium that skips steps, and ill prepares writers to be more than filler, or a viral and fleeting distraction.

When you are one of a few, it is easier to matter to others as you develop a face and a voice they know. When you are one of many, you become an inconsequential grain: for those who seek immortality with writing, they must understand that expression is not enough — one must connect emotionally and genuinely, and offer something useful and different that touches the hearts and opens the minds of others.

Once upon a time, smaller publications were the refuge for the beginner: these outlets gave a platform and a genuine gateway to understanding how dangerous the industry was if you were too much of a fantasizer and not enough of a realist. The smaller venues helped the newbies cut their teeth as they could see how a real publication operated.

The problem is the local is the foundation that props up the national and the global: when we have no local venue, the larger venues begin to crumble. Then comes the black hole, where we have generations of content-producers with no common sense, savvy, or understanding of their profession, as they were led to believe the point is to make it big, not make it good, right, useful, or enduring.

And then the big players lose ground, as the writer has no place to move up anymore. Publications such as the *National Post* and the *Toronto Star* have pink-slipped veterans, and are not replacing them with younger models.

We have seen ratings and circulation declines, and sales for movies and music dwindle — yet the Internet equivalents have not made up for the deficits.

Where are the new movements? The new groups and schools of thought? We cannot have them if we do not start locally.

The current communications landscape is, in fact, a new

frontier, where we still need to find the various answers for the other steps of growing and fostering talent.

In Canada, the problem is particularly troubling, and the Internet has not been the solution. We have *BuzzFeed Canada*, *Huffington Post Canada*, and *SheKnows Canada*: hubs with foreign owners means that while there may be Canadian content, what there will not be is Canadian structure. Without experimenting with the structure, there is no innovation, and no growing or connecting with new audiences.

Many Canadian newspapers have been closing up shop in the last couple of years. The casualties include the *Guelph Mercury, Richmond Review, Lindsay Daily Post, Midland Free Press, Nanaimo Daily News*, and the *Kamloops Daily News*. This is not an exhaustive list. It does not cover publications that have amalgamated resources with other newspapers, or those whose newsroom jobs were severely slashed within the last year. The number of true venues dwindle, where a beginner can start to gain experience, refine the content, and reinvent the structure. It seems an odd dilemma in a world driven by the Fourth Medium; yet this is the precise problem writers now face. Some of these towns have weekend papers trying to make up for the slack by publishing thrice-weekly, but the number of jobs in the markets decline, as have the number of venues to take those first critical steps as a viable and competent writer who can make a genuine and sustainable living from writing. For many online publications, such as *BuzzFeed*, its fluffy life-sink quizzes and listicles offer nothing memorable, and as its fortunes continue to dwindle, the flash-in-the-pan style hints that legacy publications are hard to come by.

New publications are making the same errors traditional ones made, only more egregious. Newer publications often do not have those in charge who understand the nuances of creating a publication with roots that can last for more than a cycle or two. These global-reaching vehicles look to gain attention any way they can, even if it means pandering to the lowest common denominator, not realizing appealing to novelty and feel-good dreck alone is cheap and easy to do, but is not made to last. The point of writing is not to shock just to shock, but to stimulate and open new worlds to readers, who delude themselves into thinking they have seen it all, and know everything there is to know. In reality, they are ignoring the local, and assuming the global has every fact and answer, when nothing could be further from the truth.

Hard-hitting stories are ignored, and no-brainer dreck takes over, even though it is the former that brings in readers and generates buzz, while the latter artificially props up the Internet. This gives the false impression that there is actual content to be found. Real content takes months of research, hunting down sources, documents, and evidence; a sycophantic list of the best legacy superheroes takes zero effort, research, or talent to cough up. Without mentoring or having a genuine stage to practice, new writers are not challenged, and are allowed to replace thought with sophistry. When there were viable local publications, as much as new writers were encouraged to refine their talents and thinking, they were also humbled. They did not turn up their noses at local news. Now, when a global audience is instantaneous, it is too easy to think covering the local city-hall meeting is beneath one's talents, when anyone can wax nonsense over which world leader takes the best selfies.

There are many serious problems plaguing Western nations; yet despite having a vast machine we call the Internet, those issues aren't being addressed. Publications such as *Vice* and *Adbusters*, whose owners claim to be the next generation of information providers in various forms, aren't bothering themselves with the silent issues that are holding society back. No publication has provided a lens into these hidden worlds that only come into the spotlight once the problem has exploded.

Why? Because we don't have the local turning over every

rock, and thus, we've lost the pulse of our surroundings. There would be no ISIS, ISIL, or DAESH if the local outlets had an ear to the ground and noticed youth discontent in the local school halls years ago. We did not have local media, who went door to door on native reserves getting a pulse on the apathy and despair in these Third World regions in the West. This is the era where big stories got big just because the local outlets were scuttled and neutered.

Our current dilemma is that the local is shunned: why start with a seed, when you can explode on the global scene, grabbing a global audience at the get-go?

We have a generation who do not realize that they are blind to the subtle signs of a story, looking for exaggerated yarns because the sense to feel the silent current is beneath them. It is a smash-and-grab mentality, and when everything is viral, no one can hope to develop a legacy, let alone a magnum opus or tour de force.

They cannot tell a story with facts: they must opine, spin, mug, and pepper poorly-researched articles with sophistry and color. All those things are cheap filler with no utility, and hence, become forgettable. When writing becomes forgettable, we lose the ability to build careers for future authors.

It all starts with the local. It is the way to connect and develop a relationship with an audience. It is the way of learning literary intimacy, and learning to savor rather than mindlessly devour.

We may be the generation that is plugged into every device imaginable, but it is at the price of being completely tuned out.

We now no longer have any pulse on what a journalist is, and even those in the business for decades have no idea of what it is anymore, either. National columnists such as *The Globe and Mail*'s Margaret Wente can be a serial plagiarizer and keep her hold on her position. Her employers dismissed the fact they do not actually have a writer on their payroll. We are in an age where there is no real journalism; ergo, we can play make-believe and keep every liar, cheater, and thief on the payroll, because it does not actually matter. It is all for show, as "public editor" (read: apologist) Sylvia Stead proved in the newspaper's mea culpa: "It shouldn't have happened and the Opinion team will be working with Peggy to ensure this cannot happen again". Of course, it should not have happened, as it did four years prior and again now. The leadership, like their columnist, seems to be unteachable.

Let us take on another recent troubling episode in Canadian journalism — the 2016 suicide of *Toronto Star* reporter Raveena Aulakh, who, according to reports, had ended it all because she discovered her boss was having an affair with Aulakh's own married lover, who was an editor at the paper himself.

There is something troubling when a journalist is having an affair with someone in authority in the very place that she works. There is something troubling that she ended her life, at all. One troubling point is unrelated to the other; however, had Aulakh been exposed before her death, her journalistic credibility would have gone right out the window, as would two other players in this macabre melodrama. All parties involved in this fiasco were indulging in fireable offenses, including the unfortunately doomed Aulakh. It was not as if Aulakh was dating a fellow journalist; she was dating someone in a position of power where she worked and that act alone is fair game for any journalist to expose her. That the same philandering senior editor was also dating someone higher up at his place of work is no less egregious, and that would have also been fair game in a separate exposé. None of the players were young and foolish: they were all in positions of power, including Aulakh in her capacity of journalist, and each had been exploiting their position to use sex as a means to an end. Yet they are supposed to be exposing people like this. It strongly implies a casting couch at the *Star*, and that a fortysomething woman who, as a reporter, saw ugly realities, the double-cross of her already married boyfriend should have not triggered any sort of drastic action — unless, of course, there was far more to the story than a sketchy love affair ending in a foregone and entirely predictable conclusion.

Yet no one in the media — traditional and online — bothered to ask the true hard questions. The *Star* itself had kept the news of her death quiet until it leaked and they were forced to admit it. *Frank* magazine had all sorts of articles about the lurid and unprofessional work environment at the *Star*, but none had the courage to point out that all three of the participants had behaved not just unprofessionally, but also detrimentally to their very profession. The news filled up website pages, but that online writers did not pursue the deeper ramifications hinted at a dark reality: that online writers are passive. Theirs is not truly doing journalism in a new way; they merely scrape information from traditional media, and report what has already been reported. It is one of the reasons online journalism has never taken off: they have a symbiotic relationship with the crumbling old media, hitching their ride on a sinking ship, thinking once traditional media is dead, they will have the audience to themselves. They will not.

These may be just two examples in Canadian journalism, but I could cite hundreds more from all over the world. That is not the point. The point is we have news programs who start off their newscasts with reporters making faces while eating ice cream to tell viewers that it is a heat wave in July, while completely ignoring real scary things happening in the world.

And journalists seem utterly clueless as to their own surroundings.

Journalism has replaced so much of the substance with filler, but we still have information overload. It would be far better to present less information, but be careful what information is presented. Instead of reporting about the divorce of faded celebrities, we could easily ignore it, even if it means a shorter newscast.

What journalism needs is a more precise mission and mandate. What it needs to do is make the case, for not just reality, but also truth.

Journalism is about trust. That's it. With credibility, objectivity, skepticism, honesty, directness, completeness, reliability, utility, validity, accuracy, and thoroughness comes trust. The goal of journalists must be to earn trust. Their word must be their bond. If they declare that employment in a region is declining, they must prove it. There will always be those who are mistrusting, but if journalists have an eye on the big picture, they must always ensure that they can be trusted.

Then citizens will be able to make accurate plans: they will know whether or not that company can be trusted to employ them; they will know if that hospital will make them healthier going out than coming in; and, they will know if that government works toward a goal that will benefit them.

Much of journalism has become complicated, but it does not have to be so tangled. It is a question of trust and it is currently a commodity journalists have lost and have yet to find. It won't be easy as those with vested interests want to manipulate people to serve their own ends. They will also stop at nothing to make sure journalism stays dead so their brand of pseudo-information dissemination can be mistaken as a better version of it.

Journalists can regain their credibility to find their way, but only if they remember the goal, regardless if they work in print, radio, television, the Internet, or a new emerging platform. The medium is not the profession — it is the vehicle to get the job done, and the job is simple: find the truth amid the lies, and show them to the world, one truth at a time.

Good journalism is simplicity. It is the presentation of relevant, reliable, credible, useful, truth, and accurate facts. With solid facts, comes context. Why must we know these facts? How can we make use of them?

That is the sum total of a journalist's mandate. That's it: it is not about impressing people with frilly writing. It is not about manipulating people. It is a hunting and gathering process. Journalists are soldiers who fight lies to liberate truth. The mandate is simple, but the process is a messy affair.

However, the medium is the author, and it is independent of the confines of the vehicle. Truth is truth whether it is told in print, radio, television, the Internet, some unseen medium — or in person. Truth is the mandate of the journalist. So is reality. The journalist must prove that delusions and misinterpretations are no protection from the truth. And it is in this precise place where journalists must rebuild.

This is because there is no greater equalizer than truth. It applies to everyone equally. Lies and delusions are no defense. While there are those who believe there is such a thing as post-truth, they are mistaken. There is no post-truth about cancer. There is no post-truth about rape, poverty, injustice, war, or genocide.

There is no post-truth about drinking contaminated water, receiving fake treatment for deadly diseases, homelessness, or abuse. If we ignore smaller problems, they become catastrophes. Journalism is the business of showing us the problems and their current status. Is it getting out of hand? Are the right people doing the right thing to solve it? That is the journalist's message, and journalism is not about the medium: it is about truth and reality, and the facts that expose that truth and reality to us.

In the US, many journalists were in denial that the Clinton campaign was out-of-touch with the reality of poor Americans, who would go out and vote for change. They were out-of-touch with those Americans who would opine on their Facebook feeds with their DIY political propaganda posters, and assumed everyone else who saw it would go out and vote, and the poster could sit the election out without having to go to the trouble of marking a ballot.

The Internet had deceived the press, the same way it deceived those who thought Brexit in the UK would surely lose.

Or in Canada where Torontonians thought the urbane former provincial cabinet minister George Smitherman would become their mayor while the crack-smoking boor Rob Ford would go down in defeat. The medium had a message, but no facts to support it.

When journalists stop thinking about media and messages, and get back to facts, only then will news producing become viable once more They cannot compete with the reach of the Internet, but they must redefine their profession to take a more empirical approach.

Journalism is a profession that was once defined not only by the confines of its medium (print, radio, television), but also the confines of gate-keeping. In a world of smartphones and the Internet, we can see footage of a terrorist attack or an assassination of a government official in real-time from bystanders.

Once upon a time, amateur footage was not available or rarely accessible. When John F. Kennedy was assassinated on November 22, 1963, Abraham Zapruder's citizen footage immortalized him and assured his place in the history books. Now, we can see everyday people film riveting and shocking events, from tornadoes to police brutality, and most of us will never remember the names of those who filmed them. In the US within the last few years, several police shootings of unarmed African-American men were captured on camera not by vigilant reporters or their camera operators, but by average citizens. In the case of Castile, it was his girlfriend, not a muck-raking reporter or photojournalist, who recorded the shocking turn of events for the world to see and feel collective outrage.

Once broadcasting became accessible to audiences, journalists lost their exclusive rights to show the world how it was functioning. People already knew, as video footage came from every corner of the world: from the 2005 London terrorist bombings to DAESH beheading videos, but it did not end there. WikiLeaks and Anonymous could reach the entire world, as they obtained the kind of classified information that would have won many a reporter a Pulitzer once upon a time. The amateurs co-opted the sensational and the historic, while the hacktivists took over the muckraking, with journalists losing their purpose in the bargain, not to mention making them seem more timid than the brasher upstarts who had something to prove. The two extremes have taken control of journalism's two biggest assets, leaving it without direction or strategic advantage.

The woes for the press did not end there. Their measured opinion pieces were filler to hide dwindling resources, but many others saw the advantage, as they were not bound by the same protocols as the traditional press and too extremist opinions, gaining their flocks at the expense of the play-safe media. *American Spectator* is nowhere near as extreme in its views than *Breitbart News Network* or *InfoWars*, with the former not nearly generating as much interest than the latter. For spectacle, it is the ideologues who get more attention, without having to worry about allocating resources to research. In June, 2017, for instance, *Breitbart News* Editor Katie McHugh was fired for her spewing anti-Muslin tweets that proved very little save that she had no grasp of immigration policy, logical arguments, or the difference between race and nationality.

And when news producers do try to use the same methods as the others, the results can be disastrous. News Corps's phone hacking scandal in 2011 made international headlines and resulted in the arrest and convictions of those linked to the scandal. This sparked the unprecedented Leveson Inquiry, and resulted in the *News of the World* ceasing publication after 168 years, with its front page terse blaring in white capitals, *"THANK YOU & GOODBYE"*. The press may have tried the methods of the underground muckrakers, but their execution of it had set the profession back as it gave it yet another black eye. It seemed that if journalists were not breaking the law, they were reporting lies, giving positive coverage in lieu of compensation, or making stories up themselves.

The truth was not as horrendous as the optics, but perceptions guide the interpretation of reality, and the reality was that journalists were sullied — and badly — by their own sloppiness, archaic methods, and refusal to place the proper checks and balances in place to ensure their reputations were left unblemished.

Hacktivists were the outsiders who could get away with their rebellious ways; news audiences were enamored with the idea of expressing their own opinions and footage, and upstart publications may have lacked experience or even rudimentary understanding of journalistic standard and purpose. However, their clean slate allowed them to seem less corrupt or dirtied than the old guard. It boxed in reporters in many ways, not the least as they were the oldest ones on the communications block and seemed stodgy next to the younger generation, who grew up with the omniscient presence of the Internet.

It is this dilemma that is keeping the press in a vortex. If they are openly partisan, they alienate audiences, and lose their ability to inform to a wide audience. If they replace fact with opinion, they will be upstaged by extremists who will outdo them, as they are not tethered by any standards or professional confines. They can no longer lay claim to scoops or exclusives, as many newsmakers and eyewitnesses have their own social media accounts or blogs, where they can cut out the middleman and sell their message directly to the public. Like a game of Go, journalism has been surrounded by the changing social climate and technology, and have lost their liberties one by one.

Journalists cannot compete with the reach of the Internet, but they must redefine their profession to take a more empirical approach, but how to do it has been a difficult puzzle they have yet to answer.

While there have been arguments that the traditional media did not keep up with the times, there is more to their quagmire than lagging behind: it is the notion that journalists must scour social media to see what they should be discussing. As journalist Scott Bowles told *Harvard Political Review* in 2014:

> We were told to make stories shorter [and] pay attention to what is hot on social media… We were writing about Justin Bieber in a way we never were before. We were covering things that only kids cared about and that was now driving news.

New York magazine's Jonathan Chait expressed similar sentiments two years later:

> …social media was forcing our hand on all of these points at once, making journalists confront, out in the open, the possibility that their work might not be any of the things they imagined it was — objective, rigorous, informative. Instead, we found we often looked partisan, mendacious, lazy, sloppy, and shrill.

But even then, both men missed the point: they more than merely looked partisan, mendacious, lazy, sloppy, and shrill — they were, in fact, all of those things. Even when the obvious became apparent to average citizens on first glance, the press merely blamed social media and the changing times for their professional woes.

Many, including Chait, have proffered the theory that comedians, such as Jon Stewart when he held *The Daily Show,* were performing the task of informing the public of the latest news, but with comedy; however, the theory is left wanting. Comedians such as Stewart do not inform: they *persuade,* and persuasion is a form of manipulation. Comedians give us a lens to see the world in the way they wish, and then interpret that view for the audience. Mark Twain has written that "against the assault of laughter nothing can stand", meaning the role of laughter is often a tool to dismiss those who we view as an ideological inconvenience. Saul Alinsky took the concept one step farther in his book *Rules for Radicals,* when he wrote, "Ridicule is man's most potent weapon. There is no defence. It's irrational. It's infuriating. It also works as a key pressure point to force the enemy into concessions".

Is it the role of journalism to dictate thoughts to an audience in a democracy? Isn't comedy a mere offshoot of opinion? With countless snarky meme posters floating on the Internet for free, how profitable is it for journalism to follow the same path? Is it even their mandate to do so?

Those questions have yet to be answered adequately. Journalism's mandate is to inform. Ridicule and derision instructs the reader or viewer to *interpret* information in a certain way, and often, we can choose to engage in such tactics without justification — without needing facts. Is journalism the schoolyard bully or propagandist? Are news presenters supposed to behave the way Fox News Channel's former host Bill O'Reilly did, calling guests "pinheads" and "idiots", regardless of whether or not they are seeking to elicit laughs?

The profession may be rudderless, but it would be difficult to know by the confident comments news producers makes in public. *New York Times* editor Dean Baquet had called the modern era "the Golden Age of Journalism" in 2016, just as reporter David Plotz had loftily decreed the same before him in 2014 in the *National Post*. With the press's fortunes dwindling, along with their failures to see a Trump presidency, a Brexit vote come to fruition, along with many other public manifestations of frustration and discontent, the assertion is questionable at best.

Thousands of journalists have lost their jobs, as they seemingly were no longer required. Publications have been scuttled, as have television and radio news programs. Even Internet publications have not been immune to job cuts and losses: online publications such as *BuzzFeed* and the *Huffington Post* have failed to be sustainable profitable ventures, even if they are known "mainstream" commodities in the Fourth Medium. It is not as if journalism merely adjusted to another platform and continued its relevance in societies: it has lost its definition and clarity, as unreasonable facsimiles proclaim to be better journalists than the old guard. *BuzzFeed* published a salacious thirty-five paged document that its editors admitted they did not independently verify regarding Donald Trump's alleged ties with Russia. It was not as if the publication had a shortage of articles critical of the Republication candidate, and had a news hole to fill. Between the cat GIFs and callow click quizzes, the publication went out of its ways to make their disdain known, from their taking umbrage with the veracity of his statements, to his various platforms. The publication felt compelled to publish every over-the-top piece of dirt it could muster, mixing in lies with truth. This was an ironic strategy as they had repeatedly accused their prime target of being dishonest, making it easier for his supporters to ignore the rantings of a disreputable partisan publication that relied on "click-bait" tactics to draw in audiences.

With the wall of partisanship — whether it comes from the left-winged partisans of *BuzzFeed* or the *Huffington Post,* to the right-winged partisans of *Brietbart* or *Newsmax* — one thing is clear: online publications have devolved into baser creatures itching to smear and denigrate anyone whose philosophies differ from their own. So culturally ignorant *BuzzFeed*'s Stephanie McNeal's January 23, 2017 article about the alleged "sadness" of Melania Trump's expression on her husband's inauguration, the scribe failed to grasp one concept. That Trump's Eastern European upbringing (she is Slovenian born and raised) would be the reason she was not behaving as perkily, with an appeasing toothy grin, as is more common in the US. Eastern European women (and European women in general) have a distinctive culture from North American women, and would not have the compulsion to appear perpetually giddy. But to the neo-partisan press, culture — and facts — are irrelevant.

There have been many conceptual casualties in the world of online journalism, and objectivity is perhaps the greatest one. Current affairs are now marked by childish and manipulative games of destroying lives and reputations without consequence of what permanent damage will be inflicted. It is about irrational insults and smears used to panic a populace and keep them frozen, unable to use logic and knowledge to solve their problems maturely. It is not about making progress, but creating monsters who we can blame for our own personal failures.

But *BuzzFeed* is perhaps the best example of producing an ersatz journalistic publication: the aforementioned McNeal is labelled a "social news editor for *BuzzFeed* News", yet her list of articles do not have newsworthy information, or original research. "People Are In Love With This Dog's Reaction To Seeing His Family On Facetime", "15 Of The Most Relatable Tweets About Michelle Obama's Reaction To The Inauguration", and "This Teen Shared Adorable Pics Of Her "Aggressive" Dog And It's Too Cute", is a small sampling of the kinds of stories *BuzzFeed* considers *news*. It is anything but. It is scraping, and at the very least, trolling social media to find some innocuous gossip to prattle about as one pretends to be living something that resembles a life. There are no standards; merely digging the bottom of a barrel to have some sort of watercooler talk. These are talking points of the most peculiar sort: looking at what is trending on social media, and then giving an audience the crib notes so they will seem in the know and have enough free time to scour the Internet properly.

Strangely enough, *BuzzFeed* is considered a *news* source, just as any traditional media outlet. In fact, traditional media often quote *BuzzFeed* as a source, despite their aversion to fact checking or finding something that did not originate from a teenager's Instagram feed. This is a publication that had no qualms openly musing the assassination of President Trump amongst themselves, revealing the extent of both their ignorance of what a news outlet is supposed to be and their obliviousness of professional decorum — yet traditional outlets such as *Newsweek* went out of their way to serve as their enablers and apologists. In a May 4, 2017 piece, Alexander Nazaryan went out of his way to frame the disturbing scandal as something normal as he warned readers to dismiss *BuzzFeed*'s organizational sickness. It is no wonder *BuzzFeed* has grossly failed as a news outlet.

The definition of what is considered journalism has radically changed and become unstable, as the ratio of filler to facts has changed dramatically. No longer is the line between soft and hard news evaporated: the line between opinion and facts has disappeared — as well as the line between diversion and information. Gossip and games have now been woven into the news product without any regard to what the sloppiness will bring to the profession in the long-term.

And what it brought was the destruction of journalism.

It has brought us publications, such as *BuzzFeed*, which refuse to verify the information that it prints. Its website encourages readers to sign up for their alerts because, "News moves fast". But taking the time to verify the veracity of claims is a slow process, and one that cannot be sped up by technology.

While the collapse of the profession can be attributed to the rise of social media, it is not the only reason — nor is it a foregone conclusion that a medium such as the Internet would necessarily bring its demise. For one, journalism survived the advent of both radio and television, finding viable ways of producing and disseminating information. By all logic, the Fourth Medium should enhance and strengthen journalism, not destroy it. But the blows have been so severe and prolonged that journalism has crumpled. When publications openly deify and demonize others as they openly boast about not using standards of determining a lie from a truth or a fact from an opinion, there is no journalism being produced. Trivialities are given the same weight as critical information.

But journalism is not about print, radio, television, the Internet, or any other technology. Those are the mere conduits to disseminate information. The press has suffered losses unseen in the profession within the last twenty years. Even as the news media tries to use social media with their partnerships using platforms such as Twitter, Snapchat, and Facebook, the results have been unprofitable. Both *The New York Times* and the *Toronto Star*, for instance, spent millions on promoting their apps meant to attract younger readers and expand their audience base, yet their ventures had been failures. If the medium is not the profession, then why has journalism imploded by the arrival of the most sophisticated medium ever created?

Those who understood journalism in its old form did not understand the nuances of the Internet, while those who understood the potential of the Internet did not understand the nuances of journalism.

Because journalism was ill-defined in many regards, it was difficult to see its strengths and mandates clearly. A sensational story could bring in a large audience — both the traditional media and the new media saw that much. But journalism is more than whipping people into a frenzy: it is about giving facts to explain why a certain cluster of facts are important. The power of mass persuasion was intoxicating, but there was far more to it than mere strategic superiority a news producer had over consumers. If the medium is not the profession, what is journalism?

It is the gathering, verification, analysis, processing, and dissemination of relevant facts that are valid, relevant, reliable, and useful to a general or targeted audience. Out of all of those functions, the medium is pertinent only to the dissemination of facts. The medium is the *final* link in the chain, and that the Internet has taken a strong profession and weakened it by disseminating lies, propaganda, trivia, and opinion gives us much to worry about. When someone is given the label of "reporter", and then writes about "Teens Are Going Nuts Over This Meme That Claims To Teach You To Break Your Thumb", we have lost all sensibility, credibility, self-respect, standards, or grasp of reality. Journalism is a difficult profession, yet its definition is simplicity itself. Find facts that matter. Find information that makes a difference in a personal and collective outcome. Is war coming? Will the economy flounder? How well will you be paid? What new law will alter the course of your life?

It does not matter how you get the information, but if it is buried amid the scandals of game show contestants and cat memes, its effect is lost. We have rambling sophistry posing as news. We have rabid and uninformed hysteria posing as news. We have gossip posing as news. We can no longer tell what is truth or facts, and journalists have paid the price for their insistence of keeping the rigors and discipline of academia out of their work.

Instead, a new breed of content producer infected the information stream, and many have taken advantage of the ignorance, launching their careers with destructive vitriol that is believed by millions.

Journalists have much to answer for the rise of the charlatan. Once, they would have exposed the robber barons. Now, they aid and abet them with their lax methods, hoping for a patronage reward. Until journalists take a hard stand on what is considered news, the slide will only get worse.

Chapter Twenty

The battle for truth

Getting past spin and propaganda is difficult in an era where public relations and focus groups are involved in every aspect of public life and have rapidly evolved over the decades. The latter two have used scientific and psychological research to refine their craft for decades, while journalism has not.

It is akin to androids taking on Neanderthals, meaning reporters are woefully unprepared to an intellectual onslaught. The army of manipulation is fully armed, while the army of truth is in disarray, with archaic and broken weaponry, and no strategy, game plan, map, or compass. There are global child porn rings, organized criminals paying one another using stolen paintings as currency, formerly legitimate companies turning into fronts for illegal activities, dangerous medications whose researchers rig and misreport the results in the name of profits, and other toxic and oppressive practices. Yet reporters have been reduced to reporting about the backsides of Kardashians, who have zero newsworthiness and make no world-altering decisions.

Confront news producers with their acts of laziness and propaganda, and they twist sophistry to deflect attention away from their sins. CNN host Chris Cuomo's response to Trump's accusation of the traditional press becoming "fake news", Cuomo, outrageously retorted on one February 9, 2017 broadcast that the accusation was akin to a racial slur. Cuomo was also the one who erroneously told viewers on an October 16, 2016 broadcast that it was illegal to look at WikiLeaks's website during the US presidential election when the group leaked hacked emails from Clinton's campaign managers.

Not everyone uses those ruses. WikiLeaks and Anonymous

have been the Internet's sole investigative muckrakers, as has much of the dark Web, but in the narrative of the traditional media, they are villains. The aforementioned Cuomo going as far as claiming it was against the law to read WikiLeaks's document haul. These groups provide the raw data, but rarely context with interviews, corroborating sources, and a story that weaves it altogether, connecting the dots and drawing audiences in.

But as they compete with traditional media, they have been cast as evil villains who hold a partisan agenda. The press then insist they are the heroes who have no partisan agenda. The narrative of this forced dichotomy is questionable. *The New York Times*, for instance, has the motto "all the news that's fit to print", but now has been reduced to stating in their email blasts that readers should "put independent journalism first", and that "real news deserves real journalism". However, in so doing what they imply is that theirs is the vehicle to find, without stating it outright. The Fox News Channel, despite its overtly and unashamed right-wing agenda, always, until June 2017, insisted by their motto that they are "fair and balanced".

The history of partisan reporting is a long one. Before the 1830s and the Penny Press Era in the US, newspapers were openly biased, cheering one side of the political spectrum while vilifying another. This was done mostly in the hopes the editor, publisher, and journalist could snag a patronage appointment from a government official that was far more lucrative than toiling in the news-production business. The notion that one side had a different idea than the other was never entertained: it was always one side was infinitely better, while the other side was detrimental to the functioning of society. Readers picked sides, and followed the decrees dutifully.

Wire services greatly altered the professional mindset, as they soon discovered neutrality ensured more newspapers would purchase their copy. Newspapers also discovered that leaving out the calculated cheerleading also meant more people were going to buy their product. It was capitalistic tour de force, and the press began its rise to becoming a powerful collective power.

It also marked the era when truth and reality were to be embraced: with partisan reportage, there can be no truth or reality — merely a skewed misinterpretation of it. Narratives are an unreasonable facsimile to what is really happening, as it is impossible for one side to be perfectly right and, just while others are always wrong and evil. Reportage, once being marked by being a never-ending gladiatorial battle, settled down to be a more functional and useful enterprise. Personal attacks seemed to fall out of favor. Instead, the mandate was to gather information to keep news consumers informed.

However, while editors and journalists became focused on the art and craft of information gathering and dissemination, what they rejected was codifying their methods in an empirical fashion, finding ways to improve researching and interviewing techniques, for instance. There was an unspoken fear, however, that a more academic approach would alienate a general audience; thus, the rigors expected of scientists was not passed on to journalists.

The difference between the two groups of researchers is important to note: the concepts of objectivity, for instance, are very different. Scientists study it, research it, debate it, and continually refine it. They can better define objectivity than a journalist can. In 1976, for instance, psychologist Robert V. Guthrie wrote the groundbreaking book *Even the Rat Was White,* serving as a reminder of the importance of confronting latent and overt racist assumptions in fact-gathering professions, such as his own. While journalists wrote books about their profession, these, for the most part, did not consider how their lack of professional discipline would cause problems later on.

At first, the indifference did not seem to matter. For decades, the model functioned well in the West. The emphasis was on hard news, such as politics, economics, global affairs, and the like. In the 1960s, political scandals in the UK, such as the Profumo Affair, and the 1970s Watergate in the US, had shown precisely how powerful a determined and focused media could be. Leaders of powerful nations were forced to resign. New titans of industry were incubated and blossomed after positive press coverage: it was the way Richard Branson, Steve Jobs, Bill Gates, Harvey Weinstein, Oprah Winfrey, Mark Zuckerberg, Jeff Bezos, Martha Stewart, Elon Musk, Victoria Beckham, and even Donald Trump became synonymous with industrial success. These individuals were the face of their enterprises, and the press gave their seal of approval, giving them legitimacy.

While these players are legitimate successes, the press had also given their seal to fraudsters such as Bernie Ebbers, Tomo Razmilovic, and Kenneth Lay. The press had been as fawning in their coverage as they had with bona fide successes. It was a sign that their assessments perhaps had less to do with finding facts, but instead, allowing partisan reportage to creep back into their product.

How so? By allowing opinion to replace facts. Once it became acceptable to praise rather than report, the nature of the industry began to change.

Partisan reporting has corrupted journalism beyond repair: left-winged reporters demonize the right's actions, while justifying their own, while right-winged reporters demonize the left's actions, while justifying their own. The content of thought may differ, but the structure of thought is the same. Both cling to partisan reporting, while maintaining they are objective, despite the shaky definition of it making such an assessment impossible. If what modern journalists consider objectivity is such, audiences must ignore truth and reality, and brainlessly take a position and stick with it, as refuting evidence is dismissed.

There are no infallible political systems: every ideology has not only its strengths, but also weaknesses. Circumstances evolve, bringing new variables the old model could not foresee. It is the reason why journalism is necessary: there must be some way for citizens to know of those variables, and how well the current system deals with them. When journalists begin to justify and excuse a political party or candidate, they are hiding the truth from an audience who are deceived into thinking everything is all right, and are not allocating their resources in the most critical or effective place, all as problems continue to mount and ultimately worsen. There are real consequences to journalistic cheerleading, as groups do not mobilize where they must; nor do they see where their theories and strategies are left wanting. Intellectual evolution is stymied as perceptions are misaligned with reality, and anger and frustrations simmer.

Social media, which seems ideal to rebuild journalism, has made several high-profile messes as it blurs the line between sophistry and reportage. Facebook's controversies in 2016 meant bogus news articles were allowed to go viral in a heartbeat, and the company's decision to use computer algorithms instead of human editors resulted in trivial stories (such as celebrity birthdays) gaining more precedence as hard news stories were routinely ignored. Moreover, with Facebook's Nicola Mendelsohn declaring that the written word will be obsolete, even though it is essential for communication, the company's dedication to disseminating information while spreading cat memes is questionable at best. Not all information can be processed by images alone, but that seems to be of little interest to Facebook. After all, video and verbal processing require two separate parts of the brain. Moving images stimulate different parts of the brain than the written message.

Moreover, people have been using symbols since the beginning of time for a reason: it is the way to communicate in a different way other than verbal. We have had video for certain information, but it cannot replace the kinds of information we process through the written word. Video is in the realm of reaction and the passive, but the written word is the realm of *reflection* and the active. Video requires less imagination than reconstructing images from words. While it may seem more cumbersome to imagine scenarios from words, video has never been a panacea, and can often do a great and unintentional disservice to ideas.

There might be two media, one concept, but the divergent paths are striking. Video can be complicated to produce, but the message must be simple. On the other hand, the written word can be very simple to produce, but the message can be extraordinarily *complex*.

Video must be simple because its impact is shockingly *fleeting*. In one study, the majority of people who watched a thirty-minute newscast could not recall a single story they viewed.

And we cannot find truth if we are actively shedding the very tools that are essential in finding it. When gatekeepers, such as Facebook, openly muse about the destruction of one of the most important tools we have, we must question why.

Journalists have forgotten to observe their surroundings and question them. While social media and smartphones make citizens chronicling events straightforward and simple, journalists never bothered to up their game, going further and deeper than what an average citizen can do. Journalists have access to more than a celebrity's Twitter account: they have the resources to probe into matters that can impact the lives of millions.

The first Gulf War is a case in point: a 15-year-old Kuwait female testified in front of US politicians that she witnessed Iraqi soldiers storm the hospital where she was a vacationing volunteer, remove infants out of incubators, placed the babies on the floor, and then take the incubators with them, causing the children to perish. This was the rallying point resulting in the US going to war to liberate Kuwait from Iraq.

Journalists reported the story as fact, when there were many unanswered questions: Who was the teenager? Why did not soldiers kill the adults in the hospital? Why would they take incubators and not more vital equipment? Why did not the staff pick up the infants to save them? Why was this young woman testifying in this forum? What kind of forum was it? Who gave journalists the information about the episode in the first place?

Had journalists chosen truth over sensationalism, they would have discovered the forum was not a formal hearing. The girl was a member of the Kuwaiti royal family. No one could verify her story. There was no evidence of the episode. The footage of her "testimony" came from a public relations firm hired by Kuwait. It took one editor to discover the truth — but when it was revealed, the damage had long been done.

The truth was the story was vintage propaganda, yet audiences would not know until long after the war was over; that is, when it was no longer critical to know it in order to make a better decision.

Hacktivist groups have exposed information, and had a better record of delivering it sooner than the traditional press, but they lack context, perspective, emotional connection, narrative, and a face to personalize the data. They are competition to other media forms, and hence, are viewed with disdain and fear. Both forms of information gatherers have their own set of confines and problems, yet despite all that has been said about WikiLeaks (it is a rogue outfit, it is a pawn of various nations, its leader Julian Assange has personality flaws, etc.), what it has disseminated to the public has not been untruthful. With the personal attacks mounting, the quality of information has, as of this writing, not been disputed. So far, they have been on solid ground.

They have given us facts. What those facts mean is another story, but we have important information that those in power wish to keep hidden from their citizens. Once upon a time, that would have been the reporter's reason for existing. Now, that journalists are being challenged, they have not gone into a competition to find more important information to prove they are superior to fact-finding than the upstarts. Instead, they have chosen to trash talk their rivals, making accusations without proof, preferring to rely instead on authorities to tell them these groups — who threaten both — are the ones in the wrong.

They have lost interest in the quest for truth. Hacktivists have not sparked journalists into standing up to all authorities equally. If a group of reporters stands up to a left-wing leader, they will defer to a ring-wing one, and vice versa. The partisan press has returned with a vengeance, and truth has been pushed aside in the bargain.

Had the US press been more aware of the truth around them, they would have seen the Trump presidency was imminent. The press did not dig: it followed. They arrived at canned events, heard prepared speeches, documented routine photo ops, and assumed what those in authority told them was truth: that Clinton would win the presidency. The reality screamed otherwise for years: in eight years, the Democrats were losing governors, House seats, and Senate seats as they lost control of both Houses. The chances were great that they would ultimately lose the White House to Republicans.

They had failed to cultivate sources from all sides of the political spectrum, and in the process, lost valuable clues to the changing tides slowly drowning them. The ramifications of their cluelessness would be devastating: if reporters cannot see the reality of the future, they cannot be relied on to arm people properly with the information they need to plan their futures.

It was not just Trump's controversial rhetoric that had angered millions of voters: they were meticulously primed to expect one outcome, but the press had failed to prepare them to truth and reality. The marches on the street did nothing to change that truth and reality; yet it was the media who were responsible for the backlash and devolution of rationality. All it took was for the press to report reality truthfully without speculation or opinion.

All it took was to ask the right questions and not appeal to authorities who had a vested interest in preserving an illusion as a gambit to maintain the last fortress where they had power.

The press needed to ask questions to observe their surroundings empirically to see reality. It is the best way to liberate truth from lies; however, the track record of asking those questions has been poor. The results often end in bloodshed, the senseless destruction of innocents, and setting human rights back decades.

Many see the problems traditional media have made and try to provide alternate outlets. These, too, have been left wanting, returning to the partisan ways of the pre-Penny Press Era. What are the standards of research? How well trained are the interviewers? Where are they getting their information? How well are they schooled in critical thinking? How much psychology do they know?

There are many online publications, yet none have better standards of information-gathering than the problematic traditional press.

We cannot make arguments without facts. We cannot have facts without understanding the nature of reality. We cannot see reality if we deny the truth.

For all its egalitarian and liberating qualities, the Internet has distorted our perceptions of what is truth and facts. Many defenders of unvetted information even go so far as to make the claim that truth and facts do not exist, especially when those facts prove their own theories wrong. The Internet has failed in the quest for truth for the simple reason there are no gatekeepers or standards for information-gathering. Many merely cribbed from the previous gatherers of the present, or lapsed into the ways of the old partisan press. No one needs to get training or a license in fact-finding or analysis to be a journalist for a newspaper or online publication.

That is the root of the problem that has destroyed journalism: there are no standards in finding truths, and that is the problem of perception, sophistry, and limited experience. We have gatherers who are not trained to see every grain and know its quality. A charismatic speaker may elevate our spirits, but journalists cannot be beguiled by flowery words or a pretty face. They cannot be beguiled by tears or shaming. They must research. They must ask questions. They must doubt without losing their idealism. To gain credibility and utility, journalists must define their terms and mandates clearly, then find ways to see their jobs through, always refining their methods to keep up with the changing world.

Journalists must vet who they allow to be considered one of their number. Of course, anyone, regardless of what they actually know or understand, can post whatever they wish. Freedom of speech is necessary in a civilized world. But journalism is more than just the right to freedom of expression — it is also a duty to express reality and truth. That is what separates a journalist from a regular citizen. Reporters inform, so as many people as possible are aware of all realities affecting their lives and well-being. You cannot base a plan on a lie and then expect the plan to work. Journalists open worlds of truth to us, but when they close their eyes to reality, they provide us nothing.

And opinion and partisan reportage will not make up the severe truth deficiency we have at the moment.

Chapter Twenty-One

Creating a science of journalism

Discipline was never journalism's strong point. Objectivity was always poorly defined, unlike scientific objectivity that had been debated, tested, and refined over the decades. Journalism is the only information-gathering profession that does not have rigorous or academic roots, and it is meant to be consumed by any audience, regardless of their knowledge, academic background, or expertise.

Because those definitions were never quantified or defined, it has become easy for the peddlers of sophistry to misuse the title for any and all purposes. The *Toronto Star* has seen its share of "activist" columnists who have muddied the waters — Catherine Porter tried to manipulate the optics to make an ideological rival look bad and it backfired publicly, but it did not stop another *Star* columnist Desmond Cole from mistaking the role of news producer with a soapbox. When he was brought to task, he quit his position, and seemed to massage the optics to seem as if his editors had given him an ultimatum. Many of those who never understood the role of journalist could not understand the depth of his transgression, but a journalist has a single mandate: to accurately and truthfully report reality. It is not a venue for activism: it is the gathering of facts, evidence, and data for a general audience to consume and then make use of those facts the way they want and need. It is not a venue to meddle, talk down, and manipulate an audience for them to interpret the world the same way as the news producer. Otherwise, what the journalist becomes is a propagandist.

It is not just Canadian journalists who have lost their way. Even after months after Trump's shocking victory, the US press was as tone deaf as ever, obsessing over his win, yet not grasping why they had no clue about the reality they are supposed to cover. In its May/June 2017 "media edition", *Politico's* article entitled "What the press still doesn't get about Trump", itself proved the press did not get what it did not get: they covered old ground about the press's obsession with faulty polls and their own wanting narratives that have yet to align with reality. What they failed to realize is their own methods for observing reality to find the truth are useless. Worse, in an April 28, 2017 *New York* piece, Andrew Sullivan had revealed he had been afraid of a Trump presidency, but had forgotten that the system had checks and balances and was not as afraid of the bogeyman as before. With a headline, "Maybe America Wasn't Crazy to Elect Donald Trump", one wonders how irrational an entire profession has become as it fell head-first into the rabbit hole. The US media's sore loser attitude post-election has been shocking: how could *any* citizen trust the judgment of hateful, vindictive, and malicious gossip-mongers who are blind to their own dysfunctional mindsets as they throw a months-long temper tantrum for the simple reason that the candidate they backed did not win an election?

With its increasing irrelevancy, the news media is at a crossroads. The old routine of controlling the terms of debate and gate-keeping was been deeply entrenched in the profession, but the Internet has changed the environment permanently. News producers are still fighting an internal war, refusing to see the new reality has yet to be accepted and integrated in the profession. Even with online publications, how journalists see and process their product and profession is dangerously wanting. For every Glenn Greenwald, who took on and exposed the shadowy workings of the NSA as he openly criticized his fellow journalists for their various appeals to authority, there are countless others who write articles on the positives of belly-button lint, but then demand the same level of respect, and to be referred to as journalists.

For example, on December 27, 2016, Buffalo, New York media reacted strongly to Buffalo Bills' coach Rex Ryan's firing, devoting extensive television coverage to it. One station that had one-third of its broadcast exclusively reporting this story; yet, there were few facts offered in the extended coverage. Of that coverage, WGRZ-TV contented themselves with man-onthe-street interviews, Twitter reactions, and a retrospective of previous Bills' coaches. Its rival station, WIVB-TV's coverage, did not deviate from this formula, either.

Almost none of the coverage was factual in nature, nor was it useful, but most importantly of all, it was unimportant opinion that was easily accessible on Twitter and Facebook. A sports team coach being fired is fodder for the sports section, but how average citizens react rarely warrants precious minutes on a newscast. They were not picketing or dancing in the streets. Once upon a time, reporters would be asking citizens their views on politics, civil rights, and war. Now, it is whether they are surprised that a high-profile job with a high turnover continues the tradition.

Newscasts in North America have their scripts and stick to them, regardless if reality no longer applies to the format. In Canada, retail sales have declined. However, television reporters marched to the malls come Christmas season, and reported that the shopping outlets "were busy", despite the fact their visuals clearly showed sparseness that would worry any economist, contradicting the yearly stereotypical report. It does not matter that the way people shop and when has radically changed in twenty years; what matters is every year reporters air stories about shoppers packing the malls, keeping the tradition going. There is no comparison with past footage to notice shifts and trends. There is no observing reality. There is no context. There is no science, and it shows.

But it is not just television news or soft news stories used to stretch out a newscast. It is also national hard news stories of global consequences that follow the same archaic formulas.

The victory of Donald Trump's presidential bid was a watershed moment in North American journalism that will have ramifications for the profession decades from now. It was the moment where the US model of reportage was exposed for being dysfunctional, manipulative, and ineffective, shattering the once invincible façade of being the one institutionalized power that could destroy any corruption and stop tyranny dead in its tracks. The profession saw itself as a superhero, but when its self-appointed villain bested their damsel in distress Clinton, its narrative proved untrue, and reporters are left wondering where it all went wrong. The answers to that question is simple: journalists neglected the scientific for far too long, and lost valuable power and resources as a result.

Trump had been a puppet master of the US news media for decades: he once had the unique gift of generating positive press, and the press had knowingly and actively played along on his terms all along. Media critic Howard Kurtz had outlined Trump's first open musing about running for US president — for the Democratic ticket — in 1989. The book, *Media Circus*, was published in 1994, where the first chapter, entitled "Trump: The Decade", made it clear that journalists were by then completely open about their knowledge about Trump using the press as a tool to further his own agenda. They gave him their willing compliance without reservation.

When he announced his candidacy in 2015, he did so as a Republican contender.

But when he campaigned, the press had been completely bypassed — an unprecedented step for any legitimate contender. That Trump chose to be the first was shocking on many levels. The press took the calculated slight personally, and were relentless in their attacks on him.

If Trump was successful in his media bypass gambit, the consequences of their defeat could permanently hobble their profession. This election was more than just a battle between Trump and Clinton: it was a war for journalistic survival and relevance. Should they lose, the message was clear: no one with power need worry about a media strategy.

Yet when the worst happened, their power was neutralized in a single breath-taking election. Once upon a time, Democratic contender Gary Hart had his presidential ambitions halted when his affair with Donna Rice was leaked to the press. A single photograph of him with his arm around a woman sitting on his lap buried him. By the time the enigmatic Trump came to run for president, the balance of power had shifted away from the press, and toward those who understood selling a message to a mass audience and could entirely bypass them through social media. While his rival Clinton went after popular votes that turned out to be redundant ones (once a candidate wins a state, only a fixed number of votes are given no matter if the candidate wins by a single vote or a landslide), he courted strategic ones and managed, despite the press's best efforts, to win the election.

The collective of journalists proved to be no match for him, his team, or his brand.

Yet there is an interesting aspect to examine: journalism lost its clout, in part, because it became adversarial in its mandate, rather than finding facts and reporting them. It ceased to be a legitimate industry when it decided to choose sides instead of finding data and reporting it. It trusted their audiences would have the intelligence to interpret the data in the way they wanted and needed, because they were shallow observers who did not think they needed to do what journalists have had to do from the beginning: dig the dirtiest and toughest of grounds, and dig it deep.

News producers became increasingly desperate as they saw their fortunes slip away from them, and in the US, the 2016 election became their last stand, with disastrous results.

Why does the profession need to start from scratch instead

of merely allowing the chips to fall where they may? Because it provides necessity: verified information with context. It takes no standards, license, or expertise to post information on a social media site or a personal web page, just as people could put out their own ephemera before the invention of the Internet.

The difference between the two then — and even now — is that one source has not been independently verified, while the other has relied on multiple sources that have all been double-checked for accuracy. Journalism is supposed to be the source of information that has been thoroughly inspected. The problem has become that journalists have not done their due diligence as others have picked up the slack, eroding their base. When First Nations researchers and APTN's (Aboriginal Peoples Television Network) Jorge Barrera did their job with their Twitter account @IndigenousXca, they showed that Canadian novelist Joseph Boyden, who claimed to be of First Nations ancestry, was not. Traditional media outlets had never questioned his ethnic roots, even though he gave conflicting information about which tribe he came from, and it was easy to do a basic online search to see his stories were repeatedly shifting. As Boyden had taken thousands of dollars in grant money earmarked specifically for natives, written books that stereotyped the very people he claimed to be a member of, and usurped media attention on issues he was not knowledgeable about. He did this at the expense of Aboriginal Canadians, who were the real experts. The effects of his offensive charade were damaging and horrendous, as the mainstream Canadian press had repeatedly declared him to be a competent author worthy of attention and praise. Canadian reporters pushed a narrative, and did not critically search for the truth. It was up to those in non-traditional outlets to set the record straight.

Many reporters wonder aloud about what would happen to democracy if journalism ceased to exist, but the better question would be what happened to democracy as a result of bad journalism? Well, many bad things happened to democracies thanks to irresponsible journalism: wars started, corporations were run by con artists, innocent people were maligned as they were convicted of crimes they did not commit, liars became lionized as they distorted the public record with lies, and voices became lost as their warnings of danger were cruelly ignored. Journalists turned their backs on the homeless as they wasted airtime and copy inches speculating on Kardashian backsides, the fluctuating mental state of Charlie Sheen, and the latest manufactured gossip over Angelina Jolie's married life as they ruthlessly speculated what Jennifer Aniston may have thought about it.

The current model of journalism has made it irrelevant in a modern age, and for it to find its place in the world, news producers cannot stick to those ways of seeing themselves as infallible and omniscient. There have been too many missteps and scandals within the profession to deny they are functional and have no need to change. In a world where those in the optics manipulation industries have a global reach from their smartphones and have the science to maximize their trade, journalists can no longer continue with their non-scientific methods. Punditry and opinion are cheap qualities that are easily mimicked and disseminated by an amateur audience, who prefer to indulge in their own amateur opinions than the professional opinions of strangers. The color of opinion and sass of partisanship gave news producers the spectacle that gave a short ratings reprieve as the industry reinvented itself on a budget, but when social media equalized citizens and journalists alike, the latter found themselves redundant.

Yet journalism is not redundant: it is an essential service to the progress and survival of a functional society. It needs to redefine itself, but in a way that justifies its existence, and lives up to its mandate to inform the public. However, as journalists are the middlemen who can be bypassed thanks to social media, how they redefine themselves is critical to their future survival.

When police, governments, corporations, celebrities, and citizens can disseminate information to a global audience with their mobiles in a matter of seconds, that sort of advantage is not one reporters can compete with on a serious level. The fact that many media outlets stoop to reporting on things they have seen on Facebook and Twitter is a sign that the profession has lost its way — and common sense.

It takes no effort or resources to troll Twitter accounts of celebrities who hired assistants to compose their tweets for them. By the time they report it, news consumers who have a Twitter account have already read them and retweeted them on their own feeds.

On the other extreme, the hard news has been redefined by hacktivist groups who have broken every barrier to release information that shows the darker nature of corporate industries and governmental institutions. WikiLeaks became a serious player in the 2016 US presidential election by showing the mindset of the Clinton campaign; however, American journalists chose to distort the narrative by casting the renegade messengers as untrustworthy. (This was an ironic choice to say the least: when former FBI Director James Comey temporarily decreed that Clinton's email scandal required further scrutiny in the final days of the campaign, the press entirely dismissed Comey. But when the CIA decreed the Russians had a role in the hacking and influenced the outcome of the election, the press decided to use the latter's word as gospel. Never mind that it was equally likely that other nations were also hacking into the emails and servers of both sides. Espionage is par for the course for regimes and corporations alike. The content and veracity of those emails was never disputed; nor could anyone prove those emails had any role in voters choosing Trump over Clinton, or that they would have voted differently.) Instead of realizing hacktivist groups are actively supplanting journalists as muckrakers, making the media increasingly marginalized and unnecessary, the press decided to portray their competition as villains to be ignored. The media continued to choose to report on trivialities and press releases as if they were worthy of attention. Even if WikiLeaks ceased to exist, there are other groups who can easily supplant them, and the threat of a superior model of information-gathering remains. Professional jealousy is impeding journalism, and is not helping the industry.

The Fourth Medium has torn traditional journalism from both sides: the trivial and the substantial have been co-opted by various factions, yet news producers have done absolutely nothing to redefine their mandates. Twitter feeds and Facebook posts are DIY press releases, where people merely put their best foot forward. Hacktivists provide no context. Neither side understands reality, truth, or the function of factual data and practical nonfiction stories. Journalism is a form of applied psychology and is the science of facts; yet news producers have not bothered to examine their profession from a different angle to modernize it in order to make it relevant. They cannot compete with social media or Hacktivists, but they can carve a niche where they can be relevant and provide something others do not: a scientific approach to information dissemination for general audiences where they have access to non-partisan facts that they can make use of that is straightforward, and free of sophistry and propaganda.

Do you need to know how many people in your neighborhood reported being robbed or assaulted? Journalists can do more than just produce maps marking every street: they can obtain reports, and transcripts, and interview witnesses and victims to provide context and find patterns.

Do you need to know how many university students have been caught in acts of academic dishonesty by faculty? How many child molesters have been convicted and their sentences commuted by the presiding judge? How many women have been turned down for a business loan in comparison to men? How well do refugees integrate in various cities within the first year? How many businesses file for bankruptcy based on CEO salaries?

If we discover that mid-sized cities are the best chance for refugees to find their footing and contribute to both the economy and society, but that big cities are causing problems, conflict, and resentment, then public policy can shift without animosity for either new citizens or established ones. From under-employment to pyramid schemes, journalists can provide the essential information society needs to know its functionality and health. Can a university graduate find decent employment in a chosen field of study? Can an artist work in a chosen trade without government grants? Can a working-class family pay their utilities and mortgage with disposable income at the end of the month? Does a teenager have effective recourse if someone stalks and intimidates them online? What laws and regulations are available to average citizens — or are there any laws or regulations at all?

While there are countless people who post their grievances and tribulations on their blogs and social media feeds, we do not always have context or a sense of the veracity, or the extent of the problem. Often, these complaints are shackled by a personal narrative, and there is far more to the story than a *Davy and Goliath* story. An average citizen sees the problem as it affects them; a journalist can explore the problem from a more practical perspective.

In other words, journalism must embrace science to become a different thing.

It must be more than what it has been in the past: it must provide facts in a personalized manner. It must allow for proper comparisons. Why is there a difference one way or another? Are some citizens safer than others? How well does a gold-standard drug do in comparison with a new drug? Are they both equally accessible to citizens? This information is essential for any citizen to make informed decisions, but it is not accessible to people in a non-academic setting. However, even if someone can read an academic journal, those monographs are not personal in presentation: there are clues in personalized stories that can inform us of signs of problems we can make use of.

In the January 1, 2017 edition of *60 Minutes*, the discussion of the Cuban rum wars was filled with theatrics of the journalist smoking a cigar and drinking Havana Club, but it was short on practical specifics. It was a subpar and unfocused story with no sense of purpose, other than there is a dispute with two large distilleries fighting over ownership of a single brand of rum.

It is time to embrace the kind of practical science that provides the facts of both truth and reality. Journalism needs a shift in focus, mandate, and methods to revive its relevancy. But it cannot come overnight, even though the profession has no time to waste. Time is of the essence, yet news producers are still in denial how irrelevant they have become.

Teaching a more scientific journalism is critical for the professions survival. As it stands, journalism is, at most, half explored. We do not have different forms of journalism. The structures and methods have not changed. We do not have professors at j-schools conducting empirical research in how to improve the techniques of information gathering and dissemination. How should reporters interview different sources? How should they use undercover techniques? Police officers have textbooks and standards when they engage in undercover work, yet journalists have no comparable guides. How to employ control groups and double-blind techniques are standard in teaching scientists and psychologists, but journalism students may graduate without ever hearing either term if their electives strictly veer into the humanities, for instance. Yet no competent information-gatherer can function without knowing the tenets of the scientific method.

It is time for journalism to wake up from its slumber of denial, to face both truth and reality in order to embrace it. There is much to celebrate: journalism is needed. Journalism is a beautiful and noble calling with both idealism and purpose, and it can be achieved if those in the profession open their hearts and minds to a more scientific approach to their profession by taking the following into consideration:

The confirmation bias is a reporter's greatest enemy. When we form a hypothesis, we tend to look for evidence to prove us right, and ignore the facts that weaken our theory. In modern journalism, the confirmation bias has infested every facet of the collective mindset, reducing the profession into a silly caricature of itself. Journalists, particularly American and Canadian, became openly partisan cheerleaders, with one group of conservative proxies shilling on the Fox News Channel, while liberal proxies found other traditional outlets to push a different agenda. Neither group make it a habit to question their truisms, and the willful blindness has its consequences: for those who have been harmed inside that blindness, they become enraged that those proclaiming to be fair and balanced are pretending the victim does not exist. The Fox News Channel pushed the second Gulf War, portraying a simple victory with minimal casualties in a war that was completely justified. Evidence that the war was anything but simple and straightforward was suppressed. For those who witnessed the messes, they could not trust the news channel for information. After Larry Johnson, a paid contributor and expert on security, who worked in both the CIA and the US counter-terrorism department in the State Department told one FNC host that the US could sustain wars in both Iraq and Afghanistan in November 2003. Johnson soon found himself no longer contributing to any FNC program. He told the truth from his experience and knowledge; yet as it did not conform to the network's established narrative, he was exiled. He provided evidence that refuted that narrative, and for all those who also know that reality, they lose faith in the very institutions that ignore that reality for a fairy tale. Journalism's credibility hinges on an egalitarian understanding of truth: it applies equally to everyone. Wars are messy affairs that do not end even after a surrender, and journalists are mandated to report an accurate picture without a sunny or melodramatically negative spin. What is working? What is not? The fuller and more accurate picture we are given, the better we can understand a problem, and the more realistic and effective solution. We can demand a solution — or implement one ourselves. We may not have expertise or knowledge to read a densely-worded formal report, but journalists can provide news consumers with an alternative text, so that we can constructively contribute to society with effective actions. When reporters fall for the confirmation bias, they restrict and reduce the number of solutions available to us, and no one has the right to keep others in such a holding pattern.

It can be a story, but never a narrative. There are differences between a story and a narrative: a story explains, but a narrative justifies. Reporters are in the business to explain, but often cross a line to justify anything from wars to corporate greed. Many reporters understand the difference as they respect their audiences, but then many others pushed the boundaries, assuming news consumers are not smart enough and cannot draw sensible conclusions without the journalist's meddling. The dim view of human intelligence has resulted in the declines in both circulation and ratings.

A story draws in viewers, but narratives risk pushing them away if that narrative seems contrived, deceptive, or manipulative. When someone tries to sell a story, they will often force facts into fitting their narrative, and it is here where many journalists are led astray. Many hoaxes made the news as fact because the narrative appealed to certain stereotypes and beliefs. If journalists focus on facts over narrative, it is more likely they will discover a ruse. The world does not need another narrative, but they will always need more facts as they become available. Making those facts accessible should be the journalist's primary focus: facts that are truthful, accurate, honest, relevant, reliable, valid, and useful, that have been verified and placed in the proper context. But the allure of narratives is too much for many news producers to resist.

We often see this game in amateur sports stories: a young person comes from poverty or is a refugee and they make it to the Olympics to win a medal. Then, facts are simple: a person came from behind, but had a talent, perseverance, and luck to find people to cultivate that talent to a public forum, where they best all or most of the other competitors. There is nothing wrong with this soft news story, but when it overshadows facts, that is when news becomes advertising. That is no longer a story, but a narrative.

Journalists often do not know where to draw the line between a factual story and opinionated narrative. They err on the side of a feel-good dreck that serves no purpose and has no utility. The gambit has often backfired at the expense of journalistic credibility. When the *Washington Post* allegedly chronicled the rescue of Private Jessica Lynch, they spun a war-hero yarn; however, the story was far different from what had been presented to readers. There was no shame in her ordeal, and it did not require remaking her narrative. And even if someone's story does carry with it elements of shame, it is one we have to deal with truthfully and honestly. We cannot hold back accurate assessments.

A neglectful parent whose apathy caused harm to their child cannot be given a sympathetic narrative, as it serves to justify others who will also employ the same narrative, causing more children grief. If journalists veer into a narrative that demonizes those parents, they risk tainting the information pool with other problematic elements. If reporters rely on facts to guide the story, we can see how mistakes were made, what happened, and then begin to find solutions to prevent neglect from harming other children. It is tempting to enhance certain aspects and downplay others in order to gain attention, but when the picture painted becomes exaggerated, we are not working with a reliable map, but one that emphasizes the wrong things, suggesting that certain remedies will work better than they actually do. Journalists cannot misrepresent the truth or shade reality to suit an agenda. They find, verify, and present facts. It is a simple mandate that is harder to execute than what most people realize.

Perceptions are not reality. We have studies that show our perceptions vary depending on numerous factors, such as our emotional state, outside influences, previous experiences, and even biological variances. We do not perceive sound as it is: our minds must deceive us into thinking sound is a smooth entity, and does not bounce off surfaces as it echoes with extraneous noises. We process the unity, but should our ears be covered long enough for our brains to forget, we will experience the true cacophony until it remembers and sound turns smooth once again. Yet all of our perceptions can and do deceive us in different ways, and journalists must be the ones aware that perceptions are a valuable commodity that is vulnerable to manipulations.

The singers of the 1960s had throngs of seemingly screaming female fans, that were paid to do so, causing future fans to scream in genuine affection. This is the same as the throngs of social media fans supposedly following the latest white hot singer, often being fake accounts created for the express purpose of padding a celebrity's worth.

There are too many stunts and tricks used to enhance reality; yet we do not have journalists whose beat it is to expose and cover how modern propagandists manipulate optics. Journalists must redesign how they cover the world as they redefine what issues they cover. In a world where we blithely take our perceptions as absolute truths and unfiltered reality, journalists must show how vulnerable our interpretations of reality can be.

344

If we can easily grasp that movies use technology to deceive our perceptions, as do magicians and artists, then it is no stretch to make the leap that public relations firms use the same methods, and do the same, but for darker purposes.

Opinion is not fact. This truth is difficult to grasp. You may think it is stupid for adults to fool around with coloring books, but to those who partake in the vice, they find relief and even therapeutic release. Perhaps collecting comic books is childish, or just fun. It is not up to you pass judgment on yoga, watching old B-movies, or collecting stamps from Latvia and Serbia only. We all have our quirks; as long as there is no permanent damage to ourselves or others. But opinion and logical conclusions are often confused with one another, and journalists have forgotten which is which.

A government spending more money than it can ever repay will be at the mercy of creditors, and will have more serious problems if an economic downturn or other unforeseen catastrophe hits. That is not opinion: that is an educated guess based on history, and is a logical conclusion. Now, whether catastrophe does hits is another matter. How credit ratings will be employed against a free-spending regime is also debatable, but it is not a ridiculous scenario to dismiss automatically. It must be taken into account as journalists find the facts to confirm or refute the theory, and if it is confirmed, determine how likely or severe the potential will be, and when. Journalism is about investigating events, people, and places, finding facts that both support a theory and refute it, before balancing those facts to see how likely trouble will harm society. Opinion is an unnecessary tool in the profession. Perhaps a certain mayor is incompetent, but there are ways to prove the politician is not fit for office or to disprove it. It is not a reporter's job to stalk and malign public officials in order to stress them into looking bad in public and then make missteps as a result. If journalists know facts, they must disclose them to the public. Making broad and ominous hints is not journalism. Using strong opinions in a column is not journalism. Presenting facts is journalism, as is allowing news consumers to draw their own logical conclusions.

There is no such thing as post-truth; only lies, sophistry, and delusions. Reality can be a cruel monster. It is not Santa Claus or a fairy godmother who bends to your narrative that you are a great mom or a cool dad and will reward you with a happy life. Many wonderful parents have become homeless, lost a child to illness or a predator, or had some other horrifying turn of events befall them. That is the truth. Reality cannot improve if we do face the most frightening aspects of truth. You cannot rise above truth: it is not only up in the air with you, but your every grain was created by truth, and is made of nothing but truth.

The truth is not some sort of authority figure whose nose you can tweak by denying its existence, or that you can proclaim you are superior to it. Cancers spread and kill, as do psychopaths who are left unfettered and unchallenged. Shoddily constructed buildings will collapse and destroy lives in the blink of an eye. Wars will cause decades of ruin, trauma, and hard feelings.

Humans cannot pretend they have reached a level of post-truth when they have yet to deal directly with the most basic of truths. Covering up truths with lies, excuses, denials, temper tantrums, defense mechanisms, delusions, apathy, and sophistry is not post-truth: it is malicious cowardice. Journalists see the fallout of unacknowledged truths and realities every day: they see the mangled bodies of victims of violence, neglect, tyranny, and poverty.

For journalists to regain credibility, they must do what others are too fearful to do: face truths and report them without spinning the optics or enabling the delusions of the irresponsible. The truth is the greatest of equalizers, as it applies to everyone equally. Reporters need to take advantage of this first truth as they show the power of understanding truth, rather than denying it or thinking it is some sort of enemy to defeat or outwit. It is the best way of altering reality, to be better than the one we currently face.

There is such a thing as a fact. Just because the fact disproves your theory, narrative, or beliefs, it does not mean their inconvenience to your ideas make them non-existent entities. If a factory in town closes, there will be financial loss. Jobs will be lost. Companies that supplied materials to the factory may also close as their bottom lines shrink. There will be less disposable income. That is a fact. If a new company opens up shop and hires once again, the chances are slim that people will regain jobs at the same wages. Nor will those who had positions of seniority at the previous factory have the same with the new one, meaning they will be earning less. They may even have debts they must pay off, as they had less funds while they were unemployed. That is a theory, but it is verifiable: we can look at various figures and conduct interviews, to see which parts of the theory hold up, and which do not. Data exists, but it is only as good as those who find them and measure them.

Some people are sloppy, while others are fastidious. But if you lose your job in a place where jobs are scarce, your facts will be different than those who have job security, or those who live in an area where there are other comparable positions available. Journalists often have no clue what are facts, and are perpetually surprised by economic data in their area. Journalists must always look for facts and verify them. Even looking at their surroundings can be hint enough to call companies to see what their hiring plans are for the foreseeable future, as well as other institutions to find out what is happening in a given area. Yet a peculiar chill has gripped journalism: the self-doubt that makes it seem as if facts do not exist. If there are people being mugged, the fact is there is crime. If people are dying of food poisoning after buying the same food from the same company, the fact is there is negligence and illness. There is no question the facts show serious problems afoot.

Many wrongdoers have muddied the journalistic filters by manipulating optics, and using excuses and sophistry as a misdirection to absolve themselves of their toxic actions, but what they cannot muddy is the nature of reality and the truths rising from the reality. Journalists must be braver and make bolder attempts to re-engage with the concept of facts to find them and report them as they are.

There is such a thing as truth. When opinion and truth are confused, it is easy to pretend that truth is relative. For example, it may be your opinion that women do not deserve the same rights and freedoms as men. That is not truth. What is truth is that when people are artificially held back and denied opportunity, their behaviors change in a certain way, becoming increasingly angrier and toxic. When people are poor and cannot find legal work, they still need to eat, and they will turn to illegal activities. It is a theory, but we can find facts to see. Both the reality, and then the truth.

Reality is that poverty brings certain constraints that, in turn, bring certain thought patterns and behaviors that we do see when an area is economically healthy. The truth is that people rebel against confines imposed by other people. When we look at larger patterns of behaviors, which is the way a sociologist, criminologist, or historian does, we can see that certain behaviors are triggered by certain events. Journalists have the luxury of seeing the world in its natural setting, and can see patterns, shifts, and movements in real time. They have the ultimate laboratory, and the largest one in the solar system; yet they do not take advantage of their playground, because they do not see what they do is scientific, or even academic in nature. Scientists look for truths as part of their work, and when journalists adopt the science into their craft, they can feel more secure looking for truths in more rigorous ways.

Emotionality is not irrationality. The lack of emotions, however, is the defining trait of someone who has an anti-social personality disorder. There is no "safe" rule that gives anyone a free pass from critically and actively thinking. Emotional people may have a perfectly justified reason for being distressed or angry; after all, our emotions are our internal barometer to give us signs of our external environment. Emotionality cannot be automatically dismissed: journalists must investigate claims of the emotional before deciding if the emotions are tainting the interpretations, or are the reason why problems could finally be seen and exposed. The lack of affect is not always a sign of logic; there are often signs of other problems at play, from apathy to resignation to even deception. Every source must be judged on his or her own merits. Angry protestors cannot be dismissed as being overly emotional, and hence, unreliably irrational. Their grievances must be examined. Perhaps they are wrong in their claims, but it is up to journalists to verify the information, not make value judgments on those they cover.

It is not about fluff. Soft news, fake entertainment labeled a "reality show", and celebrity reporting are all cheap filler. You can make very little use of knowing the latest pop singer's tattoo. It is none of your business, but if there are no regulations governing the tattoo parlor you frequent, where you risk getting hepatitis as a result, that is absolutely your business. The news media does not take their mandates seriously and feel it is all right to dilute their product with inanity. But if they saw themselves as scientifically oriented, they would be less likely to look for quick fixes to boost ratings and circulation.

A paper crown is not the same as an accomplishment. Journalists rely heavily on experts for their stories: the problem is many so-called experts are merely uninformed people with lofty-sounding titles who do not actually know what they are doing. Paper crowns mean very little. Journalists must be more discerning as they no longer appeal to authority. They should scrutinize those with titles by seeing whether titles reflect real, tangible accomplishments that result in real progress or padding of a résumé.

Do not spin an ugly reality. This problem is more evident in Canadian journalism, rather than US or UK reportage, where both countries focus on darker aspects of human behavior without the compulsion to soften the blow. But when journalists excuse destructive behavior, spin bad news, or gloss over facts that challenge their narrative, they are adding deceptions to their stories, and the practice has hobbled the profession. If there are problems, they should be stated as they are — not exaggerated or downplayed for ratings.

The science of questions must be fully explored. Journalism does not reflect on their methods, and nowhere is the neglect more evident than in the way reporters ask questions. Yet psychologists have spent significant time studying the dynamics of questions and their consequences. We know asking loaded questions alters memories, yet journalists are not formally trained to ask them. False memories can be planted, such as witnesses misremembering seeing a weapon or a person who was not present during a stressful event, such as a robbery or hostage-taking. Journalism professors have an obligation to study the science of questions more thoroughly to improve the quality of answers received.

It is not personal. US journalists became blinded in the coverage of Trump, to the point of becoming irrational in their narratives. It would have been a far more productive enterprise to focus on finding facts regarding both presidential candidates, and to do a direct comparison: Who were their biggest donors? What were their platforms on various issues? What were their success rates in their various enterprises? How did they think? What were their base assumptions about life? Had they focused on finding relevant information, it would not matter who won: what would matter is whether or not audiences used that information to make an informed decision.

A journalist has to stop trying to please or to be liked. Popular kids in high school were never liked: they were exploitable units who drove others in their car, let them swim in their pools, or had parents who hired teens for summer jobs. Once high school was over, these same students floundered, oblivious that their "likability" was in fact "exploitability". Journalists were once the adult world's popular kids, as they were also exploitable units who gave scoundrels a vehicle to shill their lies, and a large pool of news consumers to abuse with manipulations. They launched careers by wasting copy inches and air time writing about their padded achievements. Those who chose to be muckrakers got grief from those they exposed, and news consumers whose beliefs were challenged by the truth. They are held as possible as police who must inform loved ones that tragedy has struck down one of their own, or the doctor who informs a patient that the individual is terminally ill.

With the rise of social media, the popular kids lost their cache, and players such as Trump snubbed them entirely. The shock was a deep and unsettling one for journalists, but the election offered a new opportunity for those in the news-producing industries: it is not about popularity, being liked, or being exploitable. Journalists must find information and become the warehouse of useful truths, regardless of whether or not they are patted on the head or insulted by those who are averse to truths. It is respect and credibility journalists need, not likability.

Not all minds are functional on an equal level. There is no prejudice with this statement; though, there is anxiety when people believe or realize they are the ones who are falling behind because there is a filter or blinder that is impeding their progress. Sometimes the impaired functioning is organic in nature, but often, it is a willful choice to be distracted by trivialities, such as greed, narcissism, jealousy, self-loathing, bigotry, pettiness, fear, self-pity, anger, lust, selfishness, or any other emotional over-indulgence. Journalists cannot play egalitarians by pretending cognitive illusions, or even deficits, do not exist. Judgmental assessments that bring shame and stigma to others are not desirable. However, when glossing over psychopathic tendencies leads to thousands of people getting poisoned, impoverished, or killed because those dysfunctional traits were ignored or even glorified, then it is time to realize that the other extreme is equally toxic to individuals and collectives alike. Journalists cannot indulge narratives, as they are hypothetical constructs of convenience. They are purveyors of facts, meaning they must navigate through human psyches, understanding how various mental blocks and filters affect perceptions of reality, and then make allowances for them. That does not mean information is dismissed because someone suffers from depression. However, journalists must compare viewpoints and perspectives, as they understand that perceptions are not reality.

There is no us versus them. It is an illusion; though; journalists have been taught to get "both sides" of a story. Linear divides are lines in the sand, yet are seen as real entities. Studies in propaganda have shown that people randomly divided into one of two groups suddenly rated themselves being smarter and more attractive than those in the other randomly assigned group. The lesson is clear: people use after-the-fact reasoning to justify the perpetuation of being a member of a group. However, the creation of such groups is to obtain some sort of advantage at the expense of another group. The consequences of feuds are real, but often mediation and balance with truth and objectivity can solve many impasses. Other times, it is a strategic move for one side to grab the spoils of a conflict all to themselves. The point is not to accept conflict at face value, but to see the deeper dynamics of the conflict, and see the economic benefits of keeping it going.

Journalists must not take sides, as it is too easy to use the same after-the-fact justification why group A is right and group B is wrong. As previous chapters have shown, conflicting groups use identical strategies, ruses, manipulations, and structures of control to keep their members in place, accusing the other side of doing the same things they do to others. The press cannot allow themselves to get sucked into a rigged game, but instead find facts that explain the reasons behind the dysfunction in order for it to be resolved.

A pecking order is a misdirection. Journalists cannot be intimidated by those with more wealth and power. They are people, and people are flawed and can misperceive, as they make mistakes. Reporters can neither defer to power nor feel inferior to them. Respect for others applies to the poorest citizens, as it does with the richest, but each person must be examined with a scientist's eye. There are truths to find, and it is up to the reporter to find them.

A patriarchal story structure confines our understanding of the truth. There is not only content of thought, but also structure of thought. We often see two groups with conflicting contents of beliefs clash and fight for ideological supremacy. When their structure of beliefs is closely examined, they are no different, with their collective narrative being patriarchal in nature. For example, a liberal-oriented ideology and a conservative-oriented one are different in content: one may advocate greater personal and social freedom and choice for groups of individuals, while the other may advocate greater financial freedom from social obligations for other select groups. However, both may employ the same strawman arguments to discredit opponents, employ personal attacks and shaming of those who critically examine their policies, and encourage members to appeal to select authorities, as they also encourage a confirmation bias. Both may also set up the same patriarchal narrative to their members: we are the heroes of this story. Those who disagree with us are villains, who are monsters with no redeeming qualities. We must defeat these antagonists as we celebrate their humiliation as some form of divine justice, as there can be no cooperation or negotiation, let alone any form of acknowledgment that different people have different life requirements.

Journalists repeatedly use patriarchal structures in the stories they write, meaning their very templates perpetuate a stratified view of reality that distorts the truth. In a world where anything disseminated through the Internet has a potential global reach by default, reporters must rethink their old methods. It is imperative that journalists expand their mandates with alternative structures that give a truly balanced view of reality: there must be balance. We cannot allow one side of an issue to dominate all other sides with rhetoric or a self-serving narrative that hinges on ignoring facts, or hiding the deceptive use of argument fallacies. Reporters must deconstruct traditional story paradigms, and expose their use by manipulative groups and people. Many hoaxes and scams that made the news did so because someone exploited the narrative, and because the news media accepted their story without question. Reporters must question structures of thought as much as the content.

There is no journalism without experimentation. We need proper comparisons in order to know our social and economic health. The shocking lack of basic self-awareness seems peculiar; yet their ignorance stems from the press not making their realities clear in their stories. Journalists deal with reality, from its most mundane aspects to the most extraordinary, and they must show reality with absolute clarity and unambiguity. For example, journalists could run a simple experiment by having groups of reporters making do for three months on various wages in certain cities, to see where a comfort level resides. A direct comparison gives context that allows news consumers to understand their own realities more truthfully. News consumers know how much they earn, and if they can see the scale of access and opportunity they are being denied, they will begin to see their own world with an unfiltered lens as they let go of their delusions.

There is no journalism without psychology. Understanding

people's thought processes is essential to the profession. Journalism is the study of human behavior and the consequences of their thoughts, feelings, and actions. We are not taught to distinguish between the various forms of intelligence. Memorization, mimicry, and modelling is rote learning, not intelligence, for instance; yet those who crib and follow are often seen as bright. Some forms of intelligence are myopic in nature: some people can come up with short-term fixes, but they lack the foresight to see the consequences of their actions. Logic is important. Emotional intelligence is also important. Journalists conduct many interviews for profiles of newsmakers, but only scratch the surface: they may merely buy a manipulator's well-choreographed narrative, but the true portrait eludes them.

Journalism and psychology go hand in hand: in order to determine the viability of a prime minister or president, we must see their thought processes and how they handle themselves when there are obstacles. We cannot go up to these candidates to watch them up close as we ask them hard questions, but we can have reporters interview them for us, and then give us a reliable and valid guide to seeing both the positive and the negative of the individual. Is this candidate a visionary? What is the plan? What is Plan B should the original plan not be executed? Journalism has too often veered into hero worship as it ascribed to The Great Man Theory, but fanboy journalism is advertising, and it has serious repercussions. Bernie Ebbers and Kenneth Lay ran corporations into the ground, because they were aided and abetted by a credulous press who lionized them in profiles instead of questioning their narratives. Tomo Razmilovic, a man who fled the US after it was discovered he has swindled investors through a technology company in the late 1990s and early 2000s. Yet he was given softball questions by *The New York Times* on May 19, 1996 when he was promoted to president and chief operating officer of Symbol Technologies Inc. in 1996. The piece read like an advertorial, asking him about the benefits of his technology rather than more probing ones that would put him on notice that the press would bother to keep a watch on him. Even as late as March 2001, with his house of cards edging closer to collapse, one brief article in the *Times* had dutifully reported that while other companies were struggling, "President Tomo Razmilovic noted increased revenues for the year and quarter, and said he saw no softening underway". They had left out that he was in the middle of a shocking $200 million accounting fraud.

He left the company in 2002 and had fled the US for Sweden when he was indicted in 2004, yet it was not journalists who had an inkling who the man had truly been. But nowhere had fan fiction disguised as serious journalism be more present than in the case of Tyler Cassity, one member of a family who were the architects of $450 million Ponzi scheme through prepaid funerals.

Yet the press could not stop fawning over Cassity in their poorly-researched stories (considering what the clan had gotten away with under reporters' noses, any argument that anything resembling research occurred cannot be convincingly made). *The New Yorker* drooled over him in an August 29, 2005 story, decreeing that at "35, Cassity is already renowned in the world of 'death care.' Cassity's most influential invention so far has been "LifeStories", video biographies of the deceased that are shown at memorial services". The *Los Angeles Times* was equally fawning in more than one article: one article decided that he was "movie-star handsome", while another reporter quoted a rabbi who gushed, "He's hip and he's visionary". What he was really was nowhere found in any article. There was no investigation: there was a cover made where conmen could fleece without suspicion.

The world can no longer afford to enable or indulge the fantasies of narcissistic grifters — nor ever could: it must be made aware of the dangers of shutting out truth and reality.

Journalists can be equipped for a mandate with clarity, in order to give accurate portraits of those who seek power and control.

Journalism faculties must bring in empirical research now. From how to do better journalism to their research methods to their actual product, journalism has shied away from the science for far too long. They need science along with the journalism. From real-world experiments to more precise interviewing techniques to using artificial intelligence and the Internet in innovative ways to disseminate information, the profession needs a complete revamp that embraces the very things it has feared the most.

The medium is the conduit, never the profession itself. Journalism is not print. It is not radio. It is not television. It is not the Internet. It is gathering, verifying, processing, analyzing, and disseminating facts. The vehicle used to disseminate those facts is a mere tool of convenience. The press must break away from the shackles of the medium, and focus on its purpose instead, always improving a pod refining its mandate, tools, theories, and methods.

To be a competent and effective reporter, the individual must take from other disciplines. A good journalist understands human behavior, meaning a background in psychology is essential; yet reporters are not taught it. It also requires an understanding of conflict and power struggles, based partly on gut, and partly on knowledge, but not based on folksy logic. Knowing military strategy is an asset, as is criminology, history, anthropology, economics, sociology, political science, and other areas. Education must focus on giving journalists a background in understanding human behavior as individuals and collectives, instead of the mere craft of putting a story together.

Journalism compares worlds in both time and space. It is the way we can tell if we are stagnate, regressing, or progressing. Reporters require a good memory, or at least the foresight to look into the past of the people, places, events, and companies it is examining. It must never forget the past, or that people are people regardless of their accomplishments and history. There is always a lesson, and one of the biggest is that anything can happen to anyone at any time. Those who think conflicts and catastrophes cannot happen to them are being both arrogant and bigoted, and reporters must show them how people are more alike than not. They must open the eyes of those blinded by fear, hatred, and hubris with their every story. They must make the case that we are all flawed and vulnerable, making us potential victims of scams and campaigns.

Journalists cannot be partisan or biased. Appeasing ideologues is a quick fix. Ideologies change, and the flock will abandon the ideology the moment it proves not to be the panacea the ideologues once promised. There is no point in taking sides and alienating those by ignoring their life requirements and experiences. We have different realities, but share the same truths. Journalists use facts to show those various realities as they reveal universal truths, bridging factions together.

Journalists cannot be psychopaths, either. There is no truth without emotional intelligence and sensitivity. Blaming the homeless for their plight is psychopathic — and ignorant of their reality. We need facts, and psychopaths making erroneous judgments have no place in the public discourse. Journalists must stop trying to emulate psychopaths in the false belief that it is the right way to seem learned and logical. Facts will tell us how people became destitute. It will also tell us how to prevent it from happening in the future, as well.

Denial is one of the toughest fortresses to break open. The truth hurts, and for many people dealing with an ugly truth, they begin to justify it, and then try to force others to, not just accept it, but also live it. They portray themselves as superior and more enlightened; yet their problems pile up and become unmanageable; just the same as they blame others for their negligence. A journalist's job is not to enable delusions. It is not to pretend it is normal for a CEO to make over 200 times more than the lowest paid employee as the company loses profits and momentum.

There is a difference between overcoming an obstacle and believing the obstacle is a sign of health and righteousness, and no narrative or argument will mask the stench of truth. There is no shame or stigma in admitting that we have a problem or have deficits: some people are gifted artists with an appalling grasp of mathematics, and there are physicists who excel at their jobs, but have no social skills at all. We must face the reality of deficits: a poor person may begin to spin a narrative of the benefits of abject poverty; a rapist may begin to claim he merely is aroused by an unwilling partner, and should not be judged as evil; a person who is serving a long sentence in prison is not blessed to be confined; and a cancer patient is not lucky to be sick. These are not facts, but defense mechanisms used to cope with trauma beyond our ability to overcome without consequences.

Psychologists talk of cognitive dissonance: it is the way people begin to justify incongruous beliefs and actions. We can explain away just about any trauma or evil, but the long-term damage and consequences are immune to our excuses. However, cognitive dissonance is the way cults gain loyalty from recruits, and victims of domestic violence stay in abusive relationships that can — and often do — lead to their murders. But these chronic problems are kept alive with denial that must be challenged on every level.

Journalists are not in the apologist or hand-holding business. They must challenge the lies the corrupt use, in order to keep rot that benefits them from being removed. Finding truths requires a firm and clear understanding of not just reality, but also how our perceptions deceive us. It is not a journalist's place to infect the information stream with the sophistry of denial.

Those suffering from anorexia will delude themselves into believing they have the intellectual superiority and cunning to be able to hide their illness that, if left unchecked, will kill them by degrees, never mind their emaciated frame is in full view of anyone with vision. Anorexia is a mental illness. It is not a lifestyle choice. If prisoners of war were starved the way anorexics harm themselves, there would be more than an uproar: there would be many people making a one-way trip to the Hague. If their captors had websites telling one another how to starve their prisoners the way pro-anas give each other tips to continue their personal destruction, it would be viewed as a modern-day *Mein Kampf*. But when the captor and the prisoner are one and the same individual, we must not only show compassion, but we must be firm with our reality, and deal with it for the tragedy and dysfunction that it truly is.

Self-harm increases the chances of death — the very definition of mental illness. Whether it is a disease or injury or corruption, journalists must come to grips with the fact that nothing changes until a problem is truthfully and accurately acknowledged. We can understand destructive behaviors, but it does not excuse those engaging in it. They must be held accountable in a way that benefits and liberates all who are harmed. That may mean re-examining past remedies: perhaps prisons are too archaic and we need an alternative system to fix our problems, for instance. But we cannot ignore problems hoping they will go away and resolve themselves. The greatest service a journalist can do is to expose reality as it is, not just for individuals, but also the whole of society. We cannot allow stigmatization to infest the information stream, but justifying dysfunctional systems is equally harmful. Reporters cannot be apologists for those draining society of resources and energy.

There are differences between idealism and romanticism, and journalists must know them. Journalism is the science of realism. Idealism motivates and inspires to improve a status quo, but romanticism masks the negatives to focus on the positive. When romanticism masks every negative element, it becomes a propagandistic tool to push an ideology or agenda to recruit idealists or keep the disillusioned in place as it falsely paints critics as villains to be dismissed and seen as intellectually or morally inferior.

When journalists look at a single side of an issue and apply pure romanticism, the truth becomes distorted. For example, on the January 1, 2017 edition of the US program *Face the Nation*, the panel discussion was on the topic of the immigrant experience in modern day US; yet the discussion veered into a one-sided us versus them that gave no insight to integration or mediation of two groups: people who had seniority in a country with those starting from the beginning. It was a romanticized view of immigrants, painting an entire group as near-victims, without contemplating whether immigrants were impeded by their misunderstandings of their new homeland, or questioning where those misconceptions came from in the first place, causing friction and misunderstanding. There was also a clear confirmation bias in the discussion: looking at anecdotes that confirmed a theory rather than also considering evidence that challenged those assumptions. However, conflicts between established groups with new members is a universal concern as studies from evolutionary psychology have shown. We know that dynamic happens everywhere, from the plight of refugees to the plight of employees of a smaller school being merged into a larger one. This is not always bigotry at play, but a hard-wired one that takes over when a clear integration policy is not in place. A more helpful discussion rather than the stereotypical and flawed narrative would have been how to ensure a public policy that does not sacrifice one group with another, or weaves new members to an established group so that all sides prosper. Proper journalism must be driven by idealism, as it respects the idealism of others. But when romanticism is left unchallenged, it entrenches an unhelpful narrative that prevents solutions from ever seeing the light of day. One collective is not superior to another, and journalists must take care to understand that truth to report on reality accurately.

Narratives blind us to both truth and reality. Partisan Democratic paradigms have become the Establishment ideology in Western culture; yet many in the press seem to be oblivious that the Left are no longer the rebels or outsiders, but the rule-makers. These are journalists who can no longer do their jobs clearly, as they are stuck in the past and do not see the reality that the world has adopted liberal platforms, but the Promised Land is still nowhere in sight.

When Trump won the US presidency, he did so because he understood what journalists did not: people wished to rebel against an Establishment that was not helping their lives. Journalists assumed it was a case of reactionary nostalgia driving those voters. It was not. It was pure desperation of a decaying life, as the Establishment was deliberately blind to their plight. With rampant poverty ravaging much of the once prosperous working class, the Establishment Democrats seemed apathetic. This implied that those who lost their jobs and went from owning their own houses to living in tent cities should just suck it up and be resigned to be dispossessed for the rest of their lives.

The motto "Make America Great Again" was an economic trigger, not a social one, yet journalists could not understand that difference, and refused to acknowledge that not everyone was doing well financially in their own country, or that over ninety million Americans were unemployed at the time of their election. Liberal ideology was not kind to the poor. The poor supported Trump, while the wealthy preferred Clinton.

On a different segment of the January 1, 2017 edition of *Face the Nation*, panelist Michele Norris bristled at the Trump victory, stating that those on the Left did not want to go back to a more oppressed era. Norris ignored the fact it was economics driving droves of voters to Trump, not racism. She then lamented his victory as she said that "fear was not our brand". Her narrative was entrenched on the misconception that Trump voters were nationalistic haters of progress. "Fear is not our brand" was itself a nationalistic and arrogant declaration: no nation or group would claim to be a fearful one — Russians, too, would also declare that fear was not their brand, and so would ISIL. Rehearsed phrases are meaningless, and usually the sign of deception.

The lesson from the outcome of the election was simple: progress and prosperity should not be at the expense of any group, but should benefit the collective. The panel missed the point: the US has serious problems the Left has not even acknowledged, let alone offered or implemented a plan to solve. To further their narrative of liberal superiority, many in the media have forgotten about the poor or their growing ranks and choosing instead to focus on their shallow successes over their shocking failures. The path to Trump's victory may have brought down US journalism, but the rise of the former and downfall of the latter was cultivated by the very press that was oblivious to their surroundings, and did not see the obvious cataclysm that was approaching. The election was a revolt to journalistic romanticism, that was masking serious problems, and that was tearing down a nation.

A journalist who cannot read reality is a fraud, and partisan reportage is in itself an oxymoron. That US journalists were still trying to demonize those who registered their desperation the only way they could as they deified their own actions made their profession irrelevant to the discourse of public life. The panel discussion only hinted that journalists in the US do not care one jot about the state of their country, but the power they irresponsibly hoarded, abused, yielded, and then ultimately lost. When reporters engage in any form of partisan reporting, they are no longer reporters. They are propagandists. The line is fine, but a definite one that once crossed, destroys the fragile deal journalists have with the public: we give you facts that you can believe without reservation that will keep harm away from you. It is the reason fear-mongering, distortions, and lies are toxic to the profession: when journalists lose credibility, they lose everything. If journalism is the science of facts, then there is no role for partisan reporting.

It is not about looking down on people whose life requirements are not the same as yours. The terms "limousine liberal" and "champagne socialist" are ones that come from frustration, yet dismissive labels often marginalize people as we shut out understanding and knowledge for the reason that their grievances are inconvenient to our own beliefs. Journalism has often given in to labelling people, depersonalizing, from "long-haired weirdoes" to the Great Unwashed. Journalists can get into a toxic vortex, as their profession made them something of an authority figures, and the arrogance sets in. Humility prevents judgmental labels, as the reporter knows everyone has information and stories that others need to know to properly navigate through the world.

Undercover journalism must be scientific. Undercover investigations were once a critical staple of journalism. American journalist Nellie Bly used it to expose the horrifying conditions of asylums, but over time, undercover work has been watered down and used less effectively. Yet there is much value in long-form undercover work, especially if a more scientific approach is used. Having journalists gain employment in places in order to find information has enormous advantages. Having two journalists gain access to compare their experiences — a white reporter and a black one to see how they are treated — can shed a light on racism in an entirely new way. A male and female reporter could also be used to see how their experiences will vary. Real social experimentations through journalism would transform the profession, yet we do not have it.

It is about benevolence and idealism through realism.

Journalism is a peculiar profession in that it requires realists to face ugly truths in order for society to progress and improve. It is about ending corruption, exposing lies, and standing up to tyranny. It is not about hobnobbing with the beautiful people, or showing up the boy in grade school who said you were ugly by being a well-known journalist. When journalists retain their savvy, curiosity, and, most importantly of all, their idealism, they become a force to be reckoned with, but if they are conniving, gullible, and jaded, they begin to veer into troubled mindsets that have already destroyed much of their profession.

It is not about holding the hands of the deluded and perpetually offended. It is easy to appease by spinning and distorting information. Anti-vaccination advocates often complain they are ridiculed in the press, but while their detractors do stoop to personal attacks, what is more important is the evidence about the benefits of vaccinations versus the problems associated with not having them. We can find data without insulting those whose opinion about vaccinations differs from the evidence. However, we cannot ignore the evidence just because the facts are unpopular with those who do not like the nature of reality. It also helps when journalists spare no one: if everyone's delusions and wishful thinking is challenged, then accusations of bias are lessened. After all, if the press scrutinize those on the Left and Right, then everyone knows journalists are after the truth, not convenience. Journalists are not in the business of assuring the public. They are in the business of informing, giving people the information they need to solve their own problems and assure themselves.

Journalism is not about being all things to all people. It is about facts. The mandate could not be simpler. Find facts. Verify facts. Disseminate facts in an accessible and easy-to-understand way. It is not about appeasing people. They may not like that their neighborhood is filled with criminal activity as they complain the re-sale values of their homes will be affected by the negative publicity. But if it is a fact, then journalists are obligated to report that fact as it is. That's life. But citizens would be better served if their complaints to the police were heard and then exposed, so that there is no longer neglect of their neighborhood, or that the criminals who have targeted them are thwarted. Censorship harms the profession, but self-censorship caused by fear is what helped bury the industry. If journalists pull their punches, they distort reality, and nullify their reason for existing.

Profitability models must change. Universities rely on donations, tuition, and research funding to sustain themselves, but media outlets usually rely on advertisers and subscribers to sustain their product. With the rise of the Internet, subscribers preferred the free model of getting informed, while advertisers left when audiences shrunk. To thrive, news outlets need to rethink their models, but they are at an advantage: they have the ability to find factual information.

Some magazines used similar models when publishing yearly national university rankings, but it can go further than that. Reports can be relevant to news consumers in a variety of ways. From industry strength to trends in government corruption, the profession can repurpose their factual mandate to present information in a more accessible way. From profiles of areas that are plagued by different crimes or illnesses, journalism can give snapshots that news producers can make real use of, making the most of both the profession and the current structure of the Internet.

Journalists must create building blocks over time to paint a larger picture. How many people voted in the last election? How does it compare in relation with other elections? Why have there been increases or decreases? We can have stories of reaction before building on those of reflection. We can make comparisons to get a clearer view of how healthy society is at any current time. But it takes a more visionary mindset and a more focused mandate.

Journalism should give clear facts about any aspect of society at any given time. How many specialists does the best hospital have? How many does the worst? Where are these hospitals located? What differentiates them? Facts should interconnect so we know as much as we can, and so each one gives us information on multiple levels. We can find the answers we need based on the combination of facts we have: What effect does poverty have on obesity? What effect does education have on marital rates? While social sciences often study these very issues, they do not do it in a practical way that average citizens can make use of. Journalists are in the business of giving information to non-academics, but they can refocus journalism to be applied *science* (not a social science) for people wondering why they suddenly lack disposable income, so that they know where to concentrate their efforts to improve their lives.

A viable media outlet does not need outside focus groups or market research companies to tell it what audiences want and need. It already knows because it has journalists examining those people and finding truths about their reality. When media companies have to hire outsiders tell them what people are looking for, they have no pulse on or understanding of their profession.

Journalism is a school where teachers keep learning as they teach their students. No one knows everything; nor should reporters compete with deities. They must learn something new themselves before sharing what they learned to others. Journalism is the school for everyone and the subject is life, told with facts that become stories. Facts are found through research, interviews, experiments, and curiosity. Facts bring knowledge. The stories bring wisdom. Journalism thrives in simplicity, and weaving facts to bring compelling stories that audiences can make use of in meaningful and significant ways.

Journalists cannot compete with social media — nor should they try. Social media has co-opted the worst parts of journalism:

the empty opinion, the lists, the soft news, the advertorials, and the disposable pseudo-celebrity gossip, all the very things that sent it to its demise. What social media has not done is find facts, verify them, create experiments to find new information that the public can use, or find new angles. The press has a role to play in everyday life, and it can do it in innovative new ways.

Journalists cannot compete with Hacktivists — but they ought to learn from them, rather than condemn them or dismiss their purpose in the information stream: to uncover the tricks and feints of those whose decision determines the fates of billion of people. Journalistic paranoia and jealousy has made the industry ignore that outfits such as WikiLeaks are the modern muckrakers. They are the ones finding information that exposes those in power. What hacktivists failed to do is tell stories or provide context, making much of what they are doing hard for a general audience to digest or remember, let alone apply it to improve and secure their well-being. Reporters should not ignore these groups, but learn and improve on their mandates, intents, and dissemination.

Journalism used to be a thing once upon a time. We made news a habit in our lives. We watched events unfold and were riveted by it, from the death of Princess Diana to the terrorism attack on the US on 9/11. From the rise of riots to the fall of dictators, we relied on journalists to not just bring events of the world to us, but also to give us meaning of what those events would mean to our flow of life. However, somewhere along the way, journalists began to look less as they opined more, leaving others to give them press releases from pseudo-celebrities to corporations hiding their misdeeds, by distracting the media with slick social media campaigns that exploit those being harmed by them. The media believed the liars and the thieves, glorifying the robber barons and the grifters who plundered as they strutted their way to the covers of magazines and gossip columns. We believed there were weapons of mass destruction.

We believed people who harmed others were to be cheered. We felt relief when the wrongly accused were sentenced and went to prison for crimes they did not commit. We felt awe and envy when the fraudulent proclaimed to be titans of industry.

Why did we believe? Because we believed the journalists who told us what we saw was reality and truth.

But they were wrong. They did not always present reality or truth. They did not always present facts. They presented lies, hoaxes, opinion, propaganda, delusions, and beliefs to us, but then muddied our filters, as many came to believe that facts, truth, and reality did not exist. But they do exist, and if we do not see them, face them, and understand them, our ignorance slowly leads to our ruin.

The sky may not fall, but the ground will erode. Journalism is the science of facts, in order to measure that ground, to see both the extraordinary and the mundane problems that threaten our every step. It is not a safe world with countless dangers simmering all around us at any minute.

Yet if we find the facts that tell us the truth about our reality, we can keep those dangers under control. Safety comes from embracing facts, not denying their existence. Progress comes when we improve our reality. Innovation comes when we grasp what a truth means. Genius is the discovery of a truth we have not known before. As Barry Richards notes it can be done, "open-minded, curious, thoughtful, fact-based journalism, steering between gullibility and idealization on the one side and disrespect and cynicism on the other. Hopefully enough of the public do ultimately value that".

It can all be ours if we find the facts that show us where those new truths are slumbering, and journalism can be the very thing to show us the way.

But not the current model that has not lived up to its promises. To be reborn, journalism must change, and radically so. It cannot be acceptable to regurgitate press releases from government sources without question. It cannot be acceptable to lead a newscast with the anchor whining about how hot or cold the weather is when we have homeless children on the streets who are suffering and exposed to death. We cannot allow starlets unfettered access to news stories when there are arms smugglers and exploiters of refugees infesting our cities. We must rebel against reporting on days-old viral YouTube videos of a cat chasing yarn when there is food fraud, stolen art used as criminal currency, cult and terrorism recruitment in universities, domestic violence, dangerous workplaces, and elderly being fleeced of their life savings.

We can no longer afford to allow journalism to be a warehouse of trivial distractions and lies. Because news consumers deserve more than just wasting their lives on lies. Because true news producers deserve more than just wasting their talents on lies.

And it is time to find the courage to rise confidently above those lies to find truths to change our lives for the better by creating a better journalism that has the mandate, tools, skills, and drives to find what we are forever seeking, but do not always know when we have found it.

Chapter Twenty-Two

The keys to a better world

Journalism is a profession that lost its way, place, respect, and perspective. It is a profession that proclaims to see the state of the world, but has yet to see the collapse of its own state. It is a collective that makes bold statements, that hardly line up to its own reality. For example, *Variety* magazine relayed the news that: "CNN said it intends to continue flouting the typical conventions of TV's morning-news programs with its 'New Day', a show executives said Thursday morning is built to hold newsmakers accountable rather than ease viewers into the AM with soothing tones and cross-staff chatter".

The *Toronto Star* was equally oblivious in a June 16, 2017 self-love letter disguised as an article, informing the reader how its reporter Daniel Dale "fact-checked" the US president the same way he did with the late Toronto mayor Rob Ford. The piece may have been short on facts, but was filled with an inflated sense of self-importance. Dale may have been covering the antics of Ford, but it was the city's criminals who finally had to call the *Star*, and do their work for them. This is the same newspaper that, in 1996, had perpetrated a hoax on the city in a story about a dying and anonymous mother who was mugged of her purse, bus ticket, and medication. Instead of finding out the story's veracity, they printed her maudlin narrative without question, but had to be corrected by its own readers that the woman was a con artist. She was not dying, but had an addiction to painkillers and lied about the mugging to get another prescription, using a gullible media as means to an end. The paper takes the claim and the glory for legwork others do for them. The *Star*, like the others, are covering the world without reflecting on their own shocking professional deficits.

The news media is trying to position itself as avatars of truth by using every lie and deceit to do it. With no independent governing body, licensing, gold standard, empirical training, or any vigorous academic research, how exactly could the press be qualified to hold any person, group, or institution in account when they are in greater strategic disarray than those they criticize? The truth has always been journalism veered into amateur territory without ever considering how damaging their ways would be to society. They cribbed from press releases, deceived news consumers, or, liberally allowed others to deceive them by proxy. *New Day* is the same show where presenter Chris Cuomo untruthfully told viewers it was illegal to look at WikiLeaks's findings, and decreed calling journalists to task for disseminating untruths was tantamount to using a racial slur.

There are no reliable or valid journalistic standards to determine if a source is lying, manipulating, or distorting. There are no studies to give reporters a clue how to think in terms of finding truth amid the sea of lies. There is no manual in the profession the way psychology has the *Diagnostic and Statistical Manual of Mental Disorders* or police have the, albeit flawed, *Crime Classification Manual. The Reporter's Handbook,* for example, does not cover how to determine a source's truthfulness, validity, utility, or reliability. While psychology has made serious efforts to be credible and consistent, journalists never have, and their perpetual puffery shows in their output. Their shouts of being crucial to society is a mere misdirection for the simple fact that journalists in North America have ceased to be journalists.

They now incite hatred, fear, and anger as if it were normal, but then blame others for bringing unease in civilized societies. When a gunman went on a rampage on June 14, 2017, Rep. Steve Scalise had been one of the seriously wounded. Instead of questioning the complex reasons why there was increasing outrage and instability in their own country, *The New York Times* had opined a very simple and childish answer in a June

14, 2017 editorial that: "Sarah Palin's political action committee circulated a map of targeted electoral districts that put [Rep. Gabby] Giffords and 19 other Democrats under stylized cross hairs", linking Palin to the 2011 shooting of Giffords, and thereby implying Palin's mere presence caused adults to commit homicidal acts against politicians. The outcry compelled the newspaper of record retreat, and then reword their ignorant and simplistic editorial, but they learned nothing from the backlash. Not once did the newspaper consider whether its own manipulative games were to blame for awakening of frenzied hate.

But citizens do not have to endure any of it. They do not need to "take sides" in the ugly partisan war where lines are drawn in the sand on a whim. They need to reject the onslaught of desperate and calculated manipulations, and make demands for journalism to completely overhaul itself. People need facts, not fear. People need to jump out of the loop created by journalists, to see the big picture. There are false divides constructed through logical fallacy that blind citizens to both reality and truth. The use of cold terror and a false need to react to information rather than reflect is not helping society. Journalists create targets like Trump by first lionizing the newsmakers, before demonizing them. Journalists them relentlessly scream and make any accusation, hoping something would stick, while ignoring the fact if it weren't for the press creating the newsmaker, he or she would have never been in a position of power in the first place. Force accountability with the press, and the reality finally emerges.

The news media in the US has sunk to pathetic levels where mainstream journalists such as Megyn Kelly must rely on media manipulators, such as *Infowars*'s Alex Jones to gain attention and seem as if serious journalism was a factor in creating the news. Kelly not only failed to gain traction with her fledgling NBC program, but also ratings, and gravitas.

Adding to Kelly's gratuitous humiliation, Jones had secretly recorded his conversations with her, revealing she had praised him in an apparent bid to snag him as an interview. She seemed completely unprepared in dealing with someone as cagey as Jones and he had fodder for his own program as he completely controlled the media narrative. Kelly could not have sunk lower: while Jones may have been fair game for an interview, she grossly underestimated his cunning as she did with her premier interview with Vladimir Putin.

Yet news producers remained proudly unteachable. *BuzzFeed* added nothing of importance in a June 16, 2017 article: "The media got owned yet again, underscoring what's becoming a universal truth of the Trump era: the old media is not prepared for the new trolls". Neither is *BuzzFeed* who were too busy lecturing Kelly and churning out rubbish quizzes than concentrate on producing quality information. *BuzzFeed* are the trolls they warned Kelly about. The Kelly-Jones fiasco became yet another disposable media obsession. *The New York Times'* spewed sophistry about the interview before the episode aired and *Slate* even speculated about it without viewing it. It was cheaper and safer to talk about the latest dysfunctional journalistic soap opera rather than wonder how many homeless children were on the streets without a single person worrying whether they would vanish in the night.

Journalism used to be a thing. It used to be an important thing, a necessary thing, a thriving thing, and, long ago, it had its moments of being a beautiful thing. Now, it is none of those things. It has turned bitter, ugly, destructive, petty, deceitful, manipulative, shrill, cruel, and most of all, unimportant.

The keys to a better world will not be found in a current newspaper, magazine, website, or broadcast in their current state. There is too much fragmented, frenzied hate and desperation simmering in newsrooms as their fortunes continue to plummet. It will take humility, honesty, idealism, and most of all, bravery to make the bold revolutionary changes. From the way the profession views itself, to how it trains the chroniclers of tomorrow, this is a world full of upheaval and uncertainty. Journalists once opened the eyes of its citizens by presenting facts without snark or derision. It has forgotten its beauty, grace, and stoicism, replacing goodness with narcissism, and hard work with mendacious indolence. It is time citizens take control of their world by looking for truths in reality.

Journalism can be rebuilt. It can become the ideal. It can be a powerful force that respects news consumers. It can be a powerful thing once again, but it won't be until the first steps are taken, and the reality of the world, and human nature is confronted. There can be no solution or peace without facts, but there will be chaos and problems so long as opinion and sophistry are confused for evidence. Journalism locks its citizens into psychic dungeons, forever terrorizing them with deceptions and fearmongering. It is a game no one can win. In the battle for ratings and readership, news producers forgot that it is the battle for truth that counts the most, and without truth, reality has no context, and no solution can ever be reached.

It is time to see the world's biggest truth: that is short on facts, bringing frustration and discontent. Journalism can help the world find its footing, but it has to face its own ugly truths before it can rise and be of service to the world once again.

Glossary of Terms

Advertorial: A paid advertising made to mimic a news article or news report.

Color: Unimportant information print reporters give to personalize a story, such as how a celebrity laughs or an anecdote that sets the tone for a story.

Fake news: A propagandistic term used by partisans on the Left and Right to dismiss information that does not fall into their accepted ideological narrative. Not to be confused with pseudo-journalism.

Hard news: News of an individual, group, or event that has a direct and significant impact on daily life: such as terrorist attacks, new laws, and employment rates.

Lead: Information or facts that come first in a news report.

News hole: The amount of free print space for news stories after advertising is laid out.

News peg: A newsmaker or event of significance at a given time and/or place. Popular celebrities, causes, discoveries, or disasters are examples of common categories of news pegs.

Objectivity: The journalistic concept of presenting the news in a "fair and balanced" manner, such as interviewing "both sides" of a story.

Partisan reportage: Deliberately skewed news stories meant to favor one side of an issue over all others. It is a form of propaganda disguised as journalism.

Pseudo-journalism: Lies, hoaxes, scams, gossip, rumors, and propaganda presented as accurate information. Misinformation may be presented by a partisan or bogus website, or, more likely, through a traditional news outlet.

Soft news: News that is not considered to have direct or consequential impact on citizens, such as movie releases, trends in fashion, and the like.

Source: A person or organization giving information to a journalist.

Vector: A source of misinformation, lies, distortion, or propaganda that infects the information stream.

Yellow journalism: The practice of focusing on trivial and base stories in a sensationalistic fashion.

References

Abbruzzese, J. (2014). "The Full New York Times Innovation Report". *Mashable,* May 16, mashable.com.

Abdo, N. (ed). (1996). *Sociological Thought: Beyond Eurocentric Theory.* Toronto: Canadian Scholars' Press.

Abramowitz, A.I. (2016). "Despite scandals and two unpopular presidential candidates, history shows Hillary Clinton will win". *New York Daily News,* November 1, nydailynews.com.

AFP. (2017). "Celebrities join protesters in large New York rally against Trump". *Times of Israel,* January 20, timesofisrael.com.

Ahsan, S. (2017). "Has Lindsay Lohan converted to Islam? A National Post investigation". *National Post,* January 17, nationalpost.com.

Aitkenhead, D. (2015). "Johann Hari: 'I failed badly. When you harm people, you should shut up, go away and reflect on what happened'". *The Guardian,* January 2, theguardian.com.

Alinksy, S. (1971). *Rules for Radicals: A Practical Primer for Realistic Radicals.* New York: Random House.

Allen, E. (2016). "Chilcot Inquiry: What is it and what did the Iraq War report say?" *The Telegraph,* July 16, telegraph.co.uk.

Allen, J. and Parnes, A. (2017). *Shattered: Inside Hillary Clinton's Doomed Campaign.* New York: Crown.

Allen, W. (2014). "Woody Allen speaks out." *New York Times,* February 7, nytimes.com.

Alpert, L.I. and Sharma, A. (2017). "Politico CEO Reins In Predecessor's Projects". *Wall Street Journal,* March 20, wsj.com.

Al-Yasin, Y. and Dashti, A.A. (2008). "Foreign Countries and US Public Relations Firms: The Case of Three Persian Gulf States". *Journal of Promotion Management,* Vol. 14, No. 3-4, pages 355-374.

Ambler, S. (chair) (2014). *Invisible Women: A call to action. Report on Missing and Murdered Indigenous Women in Canada.* March, 41st Parliament, First Session.

Anderson, D.M. (writer) (2000). Broadcast: "Hype and Glory". *Investigative Reports.*

Annett, E. (2017). "Why we're talking about 'fake news' now". *The Globe and Mail,* February 1, theglobeandmail.com.

Anonymous. (1998). "CHS Electronics Continues Its Spree of Acquisitions". *Bloomberg News,* July 8, latimes.com.

Anonymous. (1994). "Cokie Roberts Reprimanded For Fake Shot". *Orlando Sentinel,* February 16, orlandosentinel.com.

Anonymous. (2001). "IN BRIEF; Around the Island". *New York Times,* March 4, nytimes.com.

Anonymous. (2002). "CBC loses bid to appeal $1 million defamation case". *CBC News,* February 7, cbc.ca.

Anonymous. (2003). "Sky journalist resigns over 'fake' report". *BBC News,* July 18, news.bbc.co.uk.

Anonymous. (2005). "CBS ousts four over Bush Guard story". *CNN,* January 11, cnn.com.

Anonymous. (2006). "FOX NEWS INTERNAL MEMO: 'Be On The Lookout For Any Statements From The Iraqi Insurgents... Thrilled At The Prospect Of A Dem Controlled Congress'". *Huffington Post,* November 14, huffingtonpost.com.

Anonymous. (2013). "Mark Thompson outlines future of *The New York Times in the digital age*". *Reuters Institute*, June 9, reutersinstitute.com.

Anonymous. (2014). "Kamloops Daily News to close". *Kamloops This Week,* January 6, kamloopsthisweek.com.

Anonymous. (2015). "Alison Parker, Adam Ward, Virginia shooting victims, remembered fondly". *CBCnews,* August 26, cbc.ca.

Anonymous. (2016). "Should the government step in to save Canadian media?" *Global News,* February 14, globalnews.ca.

Anonymous. (2016). "Black Press closes Nanaimo Daily News after 141 years". *The Canadian Press,* January 23, cbc.ca.

Anonymous. (2016). "Toronto Star union calls for 3rd-party investigation into reporter's death". *CBC News,* June 7, cbc.ca.

Anonymous. (2016). "The dangerous chill of Chilcot". *The Economist,* July 9, economist.com.

Anonymous. (2016). "France 'must learn to live with terrorism'". *ITV News,* July 15, itv.com.

Anonymous. (2016). "Dean Baquet: The Golden Age of Journalism Is Now!" *New York Times,* September 26, nytimes.com.

Anonymous. (2016). "Rush Limbaugh Urges Listeners Not To 'Fall For' Fact-Checks". *Media Matters,* September 28, mediamatters.org.

Anonymous. (2016). "Background and Documents on Attempts to Frame Assange as a Pedophile and Russian spy". *WikiLeaks,* October 18, wikileaks.org.

Anonymous. (2016). "National Enquirer — The Voice Of America!" *National Enquirer,* November 16, nationalenquirer. com.

Anonymous. (2016). "Frequently Asked Questions". *PropOrNot,* November 26, propornot.com.

Anonymous. (2017). "Journalism That Stands Apart: THE REPORT OF THE 2020 GROUP". *New York Times,* January, nytimes.com.

Anonymous. (2017). "Media Hits New Low for Piss Poor Ethics". *New York Observer,* January 11, observer.com.

Anonymous. (2017). "CNN learns a hard lesson". *Washington Times,* January 15, washingtontimes.com.

Anonymous. (2017). "Arrest Madonna for 'blow up the White House' remark, says Newt Gingrich". *The Guardian,* January 24, theguardian.com.

Anonymous. (2017). "Massive networks of fake accounts found on Twitter". *BBC,* January 24, bbc.com.

Anonymous. (2017). "Fury as Channel 4 News brand 'Serb fascists'". *Britić,* January 27, ebritic.com.

Anonymous. (2017). "Angelina Jolie scrambles to do

damage control". *New York Post,* February 13, nypost.com.

Anonymous. (2017). "Milo Yiannopoulos resigns as editor of Breitbart Tech after video appears to show him endorsing pedophilia". *Washington Post,* February 21, washingtonpost.com.

Anonymous. (2017). "Read President Trump's Interview With TIME on Truth and Falsehoods". *Time,* March 23, time.com.

Anonymous. (2017). "Globe and Mail suspends columnist Leah McLaren after breastfeeding controversy". *Toronto Star,* March 30, thestar.com.

Anonymous. (2017). "Our Dishonest President". *Los Angeles Times,* April 2, latimes.com.

Anonymous. (2017). "For Women, It's Not Just the O'Reilly Problem". *New York Times,* April 22, nytimes.com.

Anonymous. (2017). "What the press still doesn't get about Trump". *Politico,* May/June, politico.com.

Anonymous. (2017). "America's lethal politics". *New York Times,* June 14, nytimes.com.

Argetsinger, A. (2015). "How the Brat Pack got its name — and spoiled celebrity journalism forever". *Washington Post,* August 10, washingtonpost.com.

Ariens, C. (2017). "WikiLeaks Threatens to Sue CNN After Ex-CIA Official Called Julian Assange a Pedophile". *AdWeek,* January 5, adweek.com.

Asch, S.E. (1956). "Studies of independence and conformity: 1. A minority of one against a unanimous majority". *Psychological Monographs,* Vol. 70, No. 9, Whole No. 416.

Aslan, R. (2017). *Tweet,* Twitter, June 3, 6:50 pm, twitter.com.

Aslan, R. (2017). *Tweet,* Twitter, June 3, 7:47 pm, twitter.com.

Associated Press. (2015). "Virginia shooting: Fired reporter kills 2 former co-workers on live TV". *CBC News,* August 26, cbc.ca.

Associated Press. (2015). "Virginia shooting: Vester Flanagan had been ordered to go to workplace counselling". *CBC News,* August 27, cbc.ca.

Associated Press. (2016). "RI official resigns after using man dressed as elderly woman in news conference." *Boston Globe,* January 15, bostonglobe.com.

Associated Press. (2016). "To Clinton, These Swing States Are Starting to Look More Like Safe States". *Fortune,* October 13, fortune.com.

Associated Press. (2016). "Rolling Stone reporter admits she made mistakes in 'Jackie' rape story". *The Guardian,* October 20, theguardian.com.

Associated Press. (2017). "*The Washington Post* rolls out new motto". *Associated Press,* February 22, bigstory.ap.com.

Associated Press. (2017). "Fox News's 'Swedish defence advisor' unknown to country's military officials". *The Guardian,* February 26, theguardian.com.

Associated Press. (2017). "Ted Koppel calmly tells Sean Hannity he's 'bad for America'". *USA Today,* March 27, usatoday.com.

Auletta, K. (2003). *Backstory: Inside the Business of News.* New York: The Penguin Press.

Auletta, K. (2014). "Why Jill Abramson was fired". *The New Yorker,* May 14, newyorker.com.

Bacon, L. and Tkachuk, D. (2006). *Final report on the Canadian News Media.* Standing Senate Committee on Transport and Communications, Ottawa, June.

Bagehot. (2011). "The depressing tale of Johann Hari". *The Economist,* September 15, economist.com.

Bailey, I. (2014). "Kamloops newspaper to close doors after more than 80 years". *The Globe and Mail,* January 9, theglobeandmail.com.

Balakrishnan, A. (2015). "'American Journalism Review' ends online publishing". *USA Today,* July 31, usatoday.com.

Ballingall, A. (2017). "Former Toronto Star publisher John Cruickshank lands diplomatic post in Chicago". *Toronto Star,* March 13, thestar.com.

Banerjee, S. (2017). "Author of Maclean's Quebec malaise piece steps down from post at McGill". *Toronto Star,* March 23, thestar.com.

Baragona, J. (2017). "'You are fake news!': Trump and CNN's Jim Acosta Get Into Shouting Match at Presser". *Mediaite,* January 11, mediaite.com.

Barnes, B. and Ember, S. (2017). "In House of Murdoch, Sons Set About an Elaborate Overhaul". *New York Times,* April 22, nytimes.com.

Barrera, J. (2016). "Author Joseph Boyden's shape-shifting Indigenous identity". *APTN,* December 23, aptnnews.ca.

Barrera, J. (2017). "Similarities between Joseph Boyden story and Ojibway healer's published work trigger questions". *APTN,* February 22, aptnnews.ca.

Barringer, F. (2001). "*Brill's Content* closes; Web Site, inside.com, is cut back". *New York Times,* October 16, nytimes.com.

Barron, R. and Lardieri, A. (2015). "Newspapers Hunt for New Readers on Instagram". *American Journalism Review,* April 7, ajr.org.

Barsamian, D. and Chomsky, N. (2001). *Propaganda and the Public Mind: Conversations with Noam Chomsky.* London: Pluto Press.

Barthel, M. (2016). "Newspapers: Fact sheet". *Pew Research Center,* June 15, journalism.org.

Bates, S. (1987). *If No News, Send Rumors: Anecdotes of American Journalism.* New York: St. Martin's Press.

Battaglio, S. (2017). "President Trump will be a boon and a challenge for the cable news business". *Los Angeles Times,* January 20, latimes.com.

Battersby, M. (2015). "April Fools' hoaxes: From the spaghetti trees to the alarming bras". *The Independent,* April 1, independent.co.uk.

Bauder, D. (2017). "Oliver Stone: Megyn Kelly didn't know her stuff with Putin". *Associated Press,* June 7, hosted.ap.org.

Baum, M.A. (2011). *Soft News Goes to War: Public Opinion and American Foreign Policy in the New Media Age.* Princeton:

Princeton University Press.

Beauchamp, Z. (2017). "A viral Washington Post story about State Department resignations is very misleading". *Vox,* January 27, vox.com.

Beaujon, A. (2012). "Activist contributes to NYT story on former New Orleans cops sentencing". *Poynter,* April 9, poynter.org.

Bedard, P. (2015). "Media graveyard: Daily newspapers down nearly 80%, hard news 'in danger'". *Washington Examiner,* November 11, washingtonexaminer.com.

Belluz, J. (2015). "'Try not to be an idiot': How the editor of the Toronto Star responds to critics". *Vox,* February 11, vox.com.

Belluz, J. (2015). "How the Toronto Star massively botched a story about the HPV vaccine — and corrected the record". *Vox,* February 21, vox.com.

Bensinger, K., Elder, M., and Schoofs, M. (2017). "These reports allege Trump has deep ties to Russia". *BuzzFeed,* January 10, buzzfeed.com.

Berg, M. (2017). "Rachel Maddow Releases Trump Tax Returns". *Forbes,* March 14, forbes.com.

Berg, M. (2017). "Megyn Kelly's NBC debut with Vladimir Putin falls flat". *Forbes,* June 5, forbes.com.

Berger, P.L. and Luckmann, T. (1966). *The Social Construction of Reality: A Treatise in the Sociology of Knowledge.* New York: Anchor Books.

Berman, T. (2017). "Report: *Vice* Music Editor Allegedly Tried to Turn Writers Into Drug Mules". *Spin,* February 2, spin.com.

Bernstein, C. and Woodward, B. (1975). *All the President's Men.* New York: Warner Books.

Beutler, B. (2017). "The Media Failed to Prepare Americans for the Trump Whiplash". *New Republic,* January 24, newrepublic.

Bilton, R. (2014). "Why The New York Times' niche app strategy is flailing". *Digiday,* October 2, digiday.com.

Binckes, J. (2017). "President as media critic: Trump hits CNN host Chris Cuomo for not asking a question he actually asked". *Salon,* February 9, salon.com.

Bird, C. (2016). "A Look at Joe Warmington's Terrible, Shameless Hackery". *The Torontoist,* June 9, torontoist.com.

Black, S. (2017). "Casey Affleck's Oscar Nom and Hollywood's Selective Memory". *Paper,* January 24, papermag.com.

Blatchford, C. (2017). "Christie Blatchford: O'Reilly mess reveals absolute power does corrupt absolutely. So does the desire for some". *National Post,* April 19, nationalpost.com.

Blake, M. (2013). "A bizarre and telling book excerpt from *60 Minutes'* bogus Benghazi source". *Mother Jones,* November 8, motherjones.com.

Blatchford, C. (2017). "Christie Blatchford: O'Reilly mess reveals absolute power does corrupt absolutely. So does the desire for some". *National Post,* April 19, nationalpost.com.

Blatchford, C. (2014). "Christie Blatchford: The horrific tragedy of Jeffrey Baldwin's death should be remembered as more than a Superman costume". *National Post,* July 9, nationalpost. com.

Blatchford, C. (2016). "Christie Blatchford: Defence team a contrast to over-delicate view of women around Ghomeshi trial". *National Post,* February 11, nationalpost.com.

Blum, D. (1985). "Hollywood's Brat Pack". *New York,* June 10, nymag.com.

Boggioni, T. (2017). "Media critic: Press needs to stop acting like Trump's 'botoxed Riefenstahls' and realize he's at war with them". *Raw Story,* February 5, rawstory.com.

Bomey, N. (2017). "Who is David Cay Johnston? What to know about Trump tax return reporter". *USA Today,* March 15, usatoday.com.

Borchers, C. (2016). "Danney Williams is not Bill Clinton's son, no matter what Matt Drudge tells you". *Washington Post,* October 16, washingtonpost.com.

Borchers, C. (2017). "The problem with *BuzzFeed's* defense of publishing the Trump-Russia dossier". *Washington Post,*

January 23, washingtonpost.com.

Borger, J. (2017). "WikiLeaks' impact: an unfiltered look into the world's elite and powerful". *The Guardian,* January 18, theguardian.com.

Bowcott, O. and Watt, H. (2017). "Melania Trump accepts Daily Mail damages and apology in libel case". *The Guardian,* April 12, theguardian.com.

Bradshaw, J. (2015). "Bell head meddled in news coverage". *The Globe and Mail,* March 25, theglobeandmail.com.

Bradshaw, J. and Dobby, C. (2015). "Bell Media president Kevin Crull ousted over journalistic meddling". *The Globe and Mail,* April 9, theglobeandmail.com.

Bradshaw, J. (2016). "*BuzzFeed* Canada to close Parliament Hill bureau". *Globe and Mail,* June 28, theglobeandmail.com.

Bradshaw, J. (2016). "Torstar cuts 52 jobs, drastically reducing tablet edition staff". *The Globe and Mail,* August 9, theglobeandmail.com.

Braestrup, P. (1992). "'Live From Baghdad': 'We're Using Them, They're Using Us'". *New York Times,* January 5, nytimes.com.

Bredin, S. (2015). "The Inside Man". *Ryerson Review of Journalism,* April 7, rrj.ca.

Broad, W. and Wade, N. (1982). *Betrayers of the Truth: Fraud and Deceit in the Halls of Science.* New York: Simon and Schuster.

Brownstein, R. (2016). "Is Donald Trump Outflanking Hillary Clinton?" *The Atlantic,* November 2, theatlantic.com.

Brownstein, R. (2016). "How the Rustbelt Paved Trump's Road to Victory". *The Atlantic,* November 10, theatlantic.com.

Bruser, D. and McLean, J. (2015). "A wonder drug's dark side". *Toronto Star,* February 5, thestar.com.

Brzezinski, M. (2017). *Tweet,* February 22, 1:03 pm, twitter.com.

Buncombe, A. (2011). "A friend's labor of love reveals who killed Daniel Pearl". *The Independent,* January 21, independent. co.uk.

Buncombe, A. (2017). "Alex Jones doubles down on Sandy Hook

conspiracy theory in 'disgusting' Megyn Kelly interview". *The Independent,* June 12, independent.co.uk.

Buncombe, A. (2017). "Alex Jones releases secretly recorded Megyn Kelly tape amid 'hit job' claims." *The Independent,* June 16, independent.co.uk.

Burke, M. (2017). "Tiffany Trump shunned by magazine editors at New York Fashion Week". *New York Daily News,* February 14, nydailynews.com.

Burkes, C. (2015). "New York Times executive editor discusses the future of journalism with LSU students". *The Daily Reveille,* November 30, lsunow.com.

Burrough, B. (2015). "The inside story of the civil war for the soul of NBC News". *Vanity Fair,* April 7, vanityfair.com.

Byerly, C.M. (2011). *Global Report on the Status of Women in the News Media.* International Women's Media Foundation. Washington, DC.

Byers, D. (2016). "Can *BuzzFeed* News survive the shift to video?" *CNN Money,* May 24, money.cnn.com.

Byers, D. (2016). "Fox News staff feared Roger Ailes was monitoring them". *CNN Money,* August 9, money.cnn.com.

Calderone, M. (2008). "Why I also didn't write on John Edwards". *Politico,* August 10, politico.com.

Calderone, M. (2015). "New York Times Touts Virtual Reality As History-Making Journalistic Innovation". *Huffington Post,* November 9, huffingtsonpost.com.

Calderone, M. (2016). "New York Times Eyes Ambitious Overhaul In Quest For 'Journalistic Dominance'". *Huffington Post,* February 4, huffingtonpost.com.

Calderone, M. (2016). "The Wall Street Journal shows how not to handle Donald Trump's false voting claim". *Huffington Post,* November 28, huffingtonpost.com.

Calderone, M. (2017). "*HuffPost* lays off dozens amid corporate cutbacks." *Huffington Post,* June 14, huffingtonpost.com.

Calia, M. (2014). "New York Times to Eliminate Jobs, NYT

Opinion App". *Wall Street Journal,* October 1, wsj.com.

Callahan, M. (2017). "Angelina may have the kids, but Brad has custody of Hollywood". *New York Post,* February 19, nypost. com.

Campbell, K. (2017). "How journalism will protect our democracy in the era of fake news". *Globe and Mail,* February 14, theglobeandmail.com.

Campbell, T. and Friesen, J. (2015). "Why People 'Fly from Facts': Research shows the appeal of untestable beliefs and how they lead to a polarized society". *Scientific American,* March 3, scientificamerican.com.

Campion-Smith, B. and Ballingall, A. (2017). "Media cuts are a threat to Canadian democracy, new report warns". *Toronto Star*, January 26, thestar.com.

Canadian Journalism Foundation. (2017). "The Media as Opposition: Covering Trump in a Post-Truth Era". cjf-fjc.ca.

Canadian Press. (2015). "Francois Bugingo, journalist accused of fabricating stories, admits 'errors of judgment'". *Huffington Post*, May 30, huffingtonpost.com.

Canadian Press. (2016). "Star names new managing editor amid turmoil after reporter's suicide". *St. Catharines Standard,* June 8, stcathatinesstandard.ca.

Canadian Press. (2016). "Atwood, Boyden face backlash over letter over Steven Galloway firing". *Maclean's,* November 16, macleans.ca.

Carmody, D. (1994). "Time Responds to Criticism Over Simpson Cover". *New York Times,* June 25, nytimes.com.

Carpenter, Z. (2013). "A Grim Report on Press Freedoms Under Obama". *The Nation,* October 10, thenation.com.

Carr, D. (2013). "The Pressure to Be the TV News Leader Tarnishes a Big Brand". *New York Times,* April 21, nytimes. com.

Carroll, R. (2016). "Can mythbusters like Snopes.com keep up in a post-truth era?" *The Guardian,* August 1, theguardian.com.

Carroll, R. (2017). *"BuzzFeed* publishes unsubstantiated Trump report, raising ethics questions". *The Guardian,* January 11, theguardian.com.

Carter, B. (2013). "CBS News Defends Its '60 Minutes' Benghazi Report". *New York Times,* November 6, nytimes.com.

Carter, B. (2013). "CBS Report on Benghazi Is Called Into Question". *New York Times,* November 8, nytimes.com.

Carter, G. (2017). "Trump's White House: The Gang that Couldn't Shoot Straight". *Vanity Fair,* February 20, vanityfair.com.

Carter III, H. (2015). "Glenn Greenwald, I'm sorry: Why I changed my mind on Edward Snowden". *Salon,* May 23, salon.com.

CBS Evening News with Scott Pelley. (2017). CBS, February 14, broadcast.

Chait, J. (2016). "The case against the media. By the media". *New York,* July 25, nymag.com.

Chait, J. (2017). "Donald Trump Tries to Explain Economics to *The Economist.* Hilarity Ensues". *New York,* May 11, nymag.com.

Chandra, T. (2017). *NSD/FARA Registration Unit,* #5926. January 30, fara.gov.

Channel 2 News. (2016). WGRZ, December 27, broadcast.

Charman, P. (2017). "How journalists SHOULD handle stress — a new study". *London Press Club,* May 19, londonpressclub.co.uk.

Chen, A. (2016). "The Propaganda about Russian propaganda". *New Yorker,* December 1, newyorker.com.

Chiacu, D. and Lange, J. (2017). "White House vows to fight media 'tooth and nail' over Trump coverage". *Reuters,* January 22, yahoo.com.

Chilcot, J. (2016). *The Report of the Iraq Inquiry: Report of a Committee of Privy Counsellors.* London: William Lea Group, Her Majesty's Stationery Office.

Chomsky, N. (1987). *On Power and Ideology.* Montreal: Black Rose Books.

Chomsky, N. (1989). *Necessary Illusions: Thought Control in Democratic Societies.* Boston: South End Press.

Chown Oved, M. (2014). "Walrus unpaid interns are back — with pay". *Toronto Star,* May 5, thestar.com.

Cirilli, K. (2013). "Kurtz apologizes on CNN for errors". *Politico,* May 5, politico.com.

CNN. (2017). "Disaster Could Put Obama Cabinet Member in Oval Office". *Developing Story,* January 19, broadcast.

Cohan, W.D. (2016). "The inside story of why Arianna Huffington left *The Huffington Post*". *Vanity Fair,* September 8, vanityfair.com.

Cohn, N. (2016). "Why the Surprise Over 'Brexit'? Don't Blame the Polls". *New York Times,* June 24, nytimes.com.

Cohn, N. (2016). "Fewer Polls This Year, but They Point in Same Direction: A Clear Clinton Lead". *New York Times,* October 17, nytimes.com.

Cohn, N. (2016). "Polling Still Shows Hillary Clinton With a Lead, but Not a Safe One". *New York Times,* November 4, nytimes.com.

Collins, E. (2016). "CNN: 'Completely uncomfortable' with Brazile-Clinton campaign contacts". *USA Today,* October 31, usatoday.com.

Collins, G. (2017). "Trump's Inauguration Was No Woodstock". *New York Times,* January 20, nytimes.com.

Collins, R. (1982). *Sociological Insight: An Introduction to Non-Obvious Sociology.* New York: Oxford University Press.

Concha, J. (2017). "*BuzzFeed's* publication of Trump report violated journalistic ethics". *The Hill,* January 11, thehill.com.

Concha, J. (2017). "CNN looking for reporter to cover 'wave' of 'fake news'". *The Hill,* January 19, thehill.com.

Concha, J. (2017). "Drudge tweet could mark end of era at Fox". *The Hill,* April 18, the.hill.com.

Continetti, M. (2017). "Donald Trump and the New American Patriotism". *Washington Free Beacon,* January 20, freebeacon.

com.

Cook, J. and Nolan, H. (2011). "Roger Ailes Caught Spying on the Reporters at His Small-Town Newspaper". *Gawker,* April 18, gawker.com.

Cook, J. (2013). "A Judge Told Us to Take Down Our Hulk Hogan Sex Tape Post. We Won't". *Gawker,* April 25, gawker.com.

Coronel, S., Coll, S., and Kravitz, D. (2015). "*Rolling Stone's* investigation: 'A failure that was avoidable'". *Columbia Journalism Review,* April 5, cjr.org.

Corcoran, T. (2016). "Terence Corcoran: Government to the newspaper industry's rescue? No thanks". *National Post,* February 6, nationalpost.com.

Coronel, S., Coll, S., and Kravitz, D. (2015). "*Rolling Stone's* investigation: 'A failure that was avoidable'". *Columbia Journalism Review,* April 5, cjr.org.

Cosh, C. (2012). "Globe and Mail, or Cut and Paste?" *Maclean's,* September 23, macleans.ca.

Craig, S. (2016). "Rogers makes major retreat from print media, taking four titles online, shopping others". *National Post,* September 30, nationalpost.com.

Craig, S. (2016). "Toronto Star announces newsroom layoffs, downsizing at tablet app Star Touch". *National Post,* August 9, nationalpost.com.

Craig, S. and Humphreys, A. (2017). "How a former editor allegedly used *Vice* Canada to recruit drug mules for a global smuggling ring". *National Post,* February 2, nationalpost.com.

Craig, S. (2017). "Globe spikes Leah McLaren's column on trying to breastfeed MP Michael Chong's baby 'to see what it felt like'". *National Post,* March 27, nationalpost.com.

Craig, S. (2017). "Torstar Corp reports $24.4 million loss on declining newspaper and digital revenues". *National Post,* May 3, nationalpost.com.

Crockett, E. (2016). "Why Misogyny won". *Vox,* November 15, vox.com.

Crockett, E. (2017). "The 'Women's March on Washington,' explained". *Vox,* January 21, vox.com.

Crosariol, B. (2004). "Post drops columnist after apology". *The Globe and Mail,* December 3, theglobeandmail.com.

Currier, C. (2017). "Secret Rules make it pretty easy for the FBI to spy on journalists". *The Intercept,* January 31, the intercept. com.

Cush, A. (2017). "Here's What Was Actually Revealed in Rachel Maddow's Overhyped Trump Tax Return Segment". *Spin,* March 15, spin.com.

Dale, D. (2017). "Donald Trump said 17 false things at press conference where he called media 'dishonest'". *Toronto Star,* February 17, thestar.com.

Dale, D. (2017). "Donald Trump voters: We like the president's lies". *Toronto Star,* March 26, thestar.com.

Dalglish, L. (2015). "American Journalism Review To Cease Online Publication". *American Journalism Review,* August 3, ajr.org.

Darbyshire, P. (2016). "CanLit stars pen open letter blasting UBC over the Steven Galloway affair". *Vancouver Sun,* November 15, vancouversun.com.

Datoc, C. (2017). "Paul Ryan Shuts Down CBS Reporter — 'We're Not Here To Debate...'" *The Daily Caller,* January 31, dailycaller.com.

Daulerio, A.J. (2012). "Even for a Minute, Watching Hulk Hogan Have Sex in a Canopy Bed is Not Safe For Work but Watch it Anyway". *Gawker,* October 4, gawker.com.

Davidoff Solomon, S. (2010). "Anti-Merger Activism Spurs Pills". *New York Times,* December 17, nytimes.com.

Davidson, A. (2013). "'60 Minutes' and the Benghazi Trap". *New Yorker,* November 12, newyorker.com.

Davis, A. (2000). "Public relations, business news and the reproduction of corporate elite power". *Journalism,* Vol. 1 (3), pages 282-304.

Davis, A. (2003). *Public Relations Democracy: Public Relations, Politics, and the Mass Media in Britain.* Manchester: Manchester University Press.

Davis, A. (2007). "Investigating Journalist Influences on Political Issue Agendas at Westminster". *Political Communication,* May 18, 24:2, pages 181-199.

Davis, A. (2017). Personal Interview.

Davis, N. (2008). *Flat Earth News: An Award-winning Reporter Exposes Falsehood, Distortion and Propaganda in the Global Media.* London: Chatto & Windus.

de Courcy, J. (1993). "Manipulating the Media". *Intelligence Digest,* February 4, 1-2.

Dedman, B. (2007). "Reading Hillary Rodham's hidden thesis". *NBC News,* May 9, nbcnews.com.

Delacourt, S. (2016). "How big data and thinking small could help save journalism: Delacourt". *Toronto Star,* February 5, the star.com.

Democracy Now! (2017). "Noam Chomsky". PBS, April 4, broadcast.

de Moraes, L. (2017). "Rachel Maddow Bags Biggest Audience Ever With Donald Trump Tax Document". *Deadline Hollywood,* March 16, deadline.com.

de Morares, L. (2017). "Megyn Kelly torched for giving NBC air time to Sandy Hook truther Alex Jones". *Deadline Hollywood,* June 12, deadline.com.

Denton, N. (2016). "How things work". *Gawker,* August 22, gawker.com.

De Vynck, G. (2016). "Newspapers Wither in Canada With Few Billionaires to Save Them". *Bloomberg News,* February 17, bloomberg.com.

DeYoung, K. (2013). "60 Minutes' broadcast helps propel new round of back-and-forth on Benghazi". *Washington Post,* October 31, washingtonpost.com.

Dockterman, E. (2017). "What to Know About the Casey Affleck

Oscar Controversy". *Time,* January 25, time.com.

Doctor, K. (2016). "The New York Times' Dean Baquet on calling out lies, embracing video, and building a more digital newsroom". *Nieman Lab,* October 6, niemanlab.org.

Doctorow, C. (2017). "Wikipedia policy declares the Daily Mail to be 'unreliable' and not suited for citation". *Boing Boing,* February 9, boingboing.com.

Donnelly, M. (2011). "Rosie O'Donnell doesn't get Kardashians: 'the new Gabor sisters'". *Los Angeles Times,* November 8, latimes.com.

Donovan, K. (2015). "CBC host Evan Solomon fired after Star investigation finds he took secret cut of art deals". *Toronto Star,* June 9, thestar.com.

Doolittle, R. (2013). "Rob Ford crack video story started with an anonymous early morning phone call to a reporter". *Toronto Star,* November 6, thestar.com.

Dowd, M. (2017). "Free Melania — From Our Expectations". *New York Times,* February 4, nytimes.com.

Drange, M. (2016). "Peter Thiel's War On Gawker: A Timeline". *Forbes,* June 21, forbes.com.

Duboff, J. (2014). "Ronan Farrow tweets his displeasure with Woody Allen at Golden Globes tribute". *Vanity Fair,* January 13, vanityfair.com.

Dutton, K. (2012). *The Wisdom of Psychopaths: What Saints, Spies, and Serial Killers Can Teach Us About Success.* London: Heinemann.

Easley, J. (2016). "Trump's media feud enters new era". *The Hill,* November 25, thehill.com.

Edsall, T.B. (2017). "How the Internet Threatens Democracy". *New York Times,* March 2, nytimes,com.

Eichensehr, M. (2015). "Happily, News Orgs Find Success With Humorous Video". *American Journalism Review,* April 21, ajr. org.

Eil, P. (2016). "Remember, America: Hating the press is not

American". *Columbia Journalism Review*, November 30, cjr.org.

Elash, A. (2014). "The Rise and Fall of Mike Duffy". *The Fifth Estate*, March 14, cbc.ca.

Elie, P. (2017). "Why Writers Lie (and Plagiarize and Fabricate and Stretch the Truth and...)". *Vanity Fair*, March 10, vanityfair.com.

Elliott, P. (2016). "How Hillary Clinton Lost". *Time*, November 10, time.com.

Ellison, S. (2016). "Can anyone save The New York Times from itself?" *Vanity Fair*, June 1, vanityfair.com.

Ellison, S. (2017). "Exclusive: After Bill O'Reilly's ouster, Fox executives fear 'there's more to come.'" *Vanity Fair*, April 19, vanityfair.com.

Ellul, J. (1965). *Propaganda: The Formation of Men's Attitudes*. New York: Vintage.

Ember, S. and Grynbaum, M.M. (2017). "*BuzzFeed* posts unverified claims on Trump, stirring debate". *New York Times*, January 10, nytimes.com.

English, K. (2015). "Public editor criticizes the Star's Gardasil story". *Toronto Star*, February 13, thestar.com.

English, K. (2015). "Catherine Porter, Ezra Levant and journalism standards". *Toronto Star*, July 17, thestar.com.

English, K. (2016). "When a private tragedy becomes a public spectacle: Public Editor". *Toronto Star*, June 7, thestar.com.

English, K. (2017). "What's the public interest in the future of Canadian media?: Public Editor". *Toronto Star*, January 27, thestar.com.

English, K. (2017). "The facts about fake news: Public Editor". *Toronto Star*, February 17, thestar.com.

English, K. (2017). "Democracy demands media literacy: Public Editor". *Toronto Star*, March 3, thestar.com.

English, K. (2017). "Journalists shouldn't become the news: Public Editor". *Toronto Star*, May 4, thestar.com.

Erdely, S. (2014). "A Rape on Campus: A Brutal Assault and

Struggle for Justice at UVA". *Rolling Stone,* November 19, rollingstone.com.

Eustachewich, L. (2017). "Roger Ailes, former chief of Fox News, dies at 77". *New York Post,* May 18, nypost.com.

Face the Nation. (2017). NBC Television, January 1, broadcast.

Fager, J., Ortiz, A. (2013). *Memo regarding 60 Minutes' Benghazi report.*

Fang, L. (2015). "Saudi Arabia Continues Hiring Spree of American Lobbyists, Public Relations Experts". *The Intercept,* October 5, theintercept.com.

Farhi, P. and Kenber, B. (2013). "Time's Stengel latest in long line of reporters who jumped to jobs in Obama administration". *Washington Post,* September 25, washingtonpost.com.

Farhi, P. (2014). "Sabrina Rubin Erdely, woman behind Rolling Stone's explosive U-Va. alleged rape story". *Washington Post,* November 28, washingtonpost.com.

Farhi, P. (2016). "Donald Trump meets with TV news execs and journalists in private meeting — and lets them have it". *Washington Post,* November 22, washingtonpost.com.

Farhi, P. (2017). "Megyn Kelly leaving Fox News for NBC". *Washington Post,* January 3, washingtonpost.com.

Farhi, P. (2017). "*The Washington Post*'s new slogan turns out to be an old saying". *Washington Post,* February 24, washingtonpost.com.

Farrow, D. (2014). "An open letter from Dylan Farrow". *New York Times,* February 1, nytimes.com.

Farrow, R. (2014). *Tweet,* January 12, 11:15 pm, twitter.com.

Farsetta, D. (2004). "The Return of Karen Ryan". *PR Watch,* October 10, prwatch.org.

Feldman, C. and Swanson, E. (2016). "Poll: Vast majority of Americans don't trust the news media". *Associated Press,* April 17, ap.org.

Fenton, T. (2005). *Bad News: The Decline of Reporting, the Business of News, and the Danger to Us All.* New York: ReganBooks.

Ferguson, C. (2015). "A rare event: Toronto Star retracts fear-mongering vaccine story". *Retraction Watch,* February 23, retractionwatch.com.

Filipovic, J. (2017). "The All-Male Photo Op Isn't a Gaffe. It's a Strategy". *New York Times,* March 27, nytimes.com.

Fischer, B. (2017). "Angelina Jolie Faces Eternal Public Relations Disaster: Career Destroyed Following Brad Pitt Divorce?" *Celebrity Dirty Laundry,* February 18, celebritydirtylaundry. com.

Fiske, J. (1987). *Television Culture.* London: Routledge.

Fiske, S. and Taylor, S. (1984). *Social Cognition.* Boston: Addison-Wesley Publishers.

Flint, J. and Rothfeld, M. (2017). "Scope of federal probe into Fox News broadens". *Wall Street Journal,* May 4, wsj.com.

Frates, K. (2017). "Thanks, Obama: Hillary Found A New Reason For Her Loss To Trump". *The Daily Caller,* January 31, dailycaller.com.

Friend, D. (2015). "CHCH cancels news for a day in major restructuring". *Toronto Sun,* December 11, torontosun.com.

Friend, T. (2005). "The Shroud of Marin". *The New Yorker,* August 29, newyorker.com.

Friendly, F. (1967). *Due to Circumstances Beyond Our Control...* New York: Times Books.

Friscolanti, M. (2017). "Why Andrew Potter lost his 'dream job' at McGill: High-profile writer forced out over a Maclean's column in what's being called an attack on academic freedom". *Maclean's,* March 23, macleans.ca.

Gaines, J.R. (1994). "To our readers". *Time,* July 4, time.com.

Galloway, G. (2004). "Writer fabricated names, quotes, *National Post* says". *The Globe and Mail,* July 3, theglobeandmail.com.

Galupo, S. (2017). "Is Trumpism the new punk rock?" *The Week,* March 2, theweek.com.

Garrahan, M. (2017). "Murdoch & Sons: Lachlan, James and Rupert's $62bn empire". *Financial Times,* January 26, ft.com.

Garner, M. (2015). "Top 10 Rich Kids of Instagram — Who to Follow". *The Street*, July 1, the street.com.

Garrahan, M. (2017). "Murdoch & Sons: Lachlan, James and Rupert's $62bn empire". *Financial Times*, January 26, ft.com.

Garvin, G. (2017). "From Opa-locka to Fox News, the meteoric rise and fall of Bill O'Reilly". *Miami Herald*, April 19, miamiherald.com.

Gentzkow, M. and Shapiro, J.M. (2008). "Competition and Truth in the Market for News". *Journal of Economic Perspectives*, Spring, Vol. 22, No. 2, pages 133-154.

Ghosh, S. (2017). "David Cay Johnston speculates Trump emailed him the tax documents as a distraction". *Raw Story*, March 15, raw story.com.

Giaritelli, A. (2017). "Mike Pence demands AP apologize for publishing, refusing to take down story showing his wife's email address". *Washington Examiner*, March 4, washingtonexaminer.com.

Gibbs, N. (1994). "O.J. Simpson: End of the run." *Time*, June 27, time.com.

Gibbs, N. (2003). "At Home: The Private Jessica Lynch". *Time*. November 17, time.com.

Gibson, J. (1999). "News colleagues pay tribute to 'one of ours'". *The Guardian*, April 27, theguardian.com.

Gill, I. (2016). *No News is Bad News: Canada's Media Collapse— and What Comes Next*. Vancouver: Greystone Books.

Gillette, F. (2016). "Tabloid's shocking love affair with Trump revealed!" *Bloomberg*, September 29, bloomberg.com.

Gilmore, J. (2005). *L.A. Despair: A Landscape of Crimes & Bad Times*. Los Angeles: Amok.

Gilmore, S. (2017). "On Quebec and Andrew Potter: Tread carefully, Canada". *Maclean's*, March 23, macleans.com.

Glaser, A. (2017). "Silicon Valley billionaires are 'prepping' to survive in underground bunkers". *Recode*, January 23, recode. net.

Glasser, S.B. (2016). "Covering politics in a 'post-truth' America". *Brookings,* December 2, brookings.edu.

Goffman, E. (1963). *Stigma: Notes on the management of spoiled identity.* New York: Penguin.

Gold, H. (2016). "*Vice* expands Josh Tyrangiel's role, will lay off around 15 staffers". *Politico,* May 24, politico.com.

Gold, H. (2017). "New York Times, Wall Street Journal editors take on Trump and the media". *Politico,* January 17, politico.com.

Gold, H. (2017). "White House ices out CNN". *Politico,* January 31, politico.com.

Gomez, L. (2017). "It's official: Bill O'Reilly is done at Fox News". *San Diego Union-Tribune,* April 18, sandiegouniontribune.com.

Goodman, A. (2015). "NY Times Editor Calls Journo Prof 'A-hole' for Criticizing Cartoon Decision". *Washington Free Beacon,* January 9, free beacon.com.

Goodwin, M. (2017). "Sorry media — this press conference played very different with Trump's supporters". *New York Post,* February 16, nypost.com.

Gould, J. (1957). "TV: C.B.S. Exclusive; Interview With Khrushchev, Filmed in Kremlin, *New York Times,* June 3, page 41, nytimes.com.

Graham, K. (1997). *Personal History.* New York: Vintage.

Graham, R.F. (2016). "DNC staffers wrote questions for CNN anchor Wolf Blitzer when he interviewed Trump, new batch of 8,000 WikiLeaks emails reveals". *The Daily Mail,* November 7, dailymail.co.uk.

Grant, A. (2016). "Guelph Mercury stops publishing print edition". *CBC News,* January 25, cbc.ca.

Graves, L. (2012). "ALEC Goes After the Center for Media and Democracy". *PR Watch,* August 29, prwatch.org.

Gray, K. (ed). (2015). *The Status of Women in the US Media 2015.* Women's Media Center, New York.

Greenslade, R. (2011). "Pension plunderer Robert Maxwell remembered 20 years after his death". *The Guardian,* November 3, theguardian.com.

Greenslade, R. (2016). "Two newspaper closures as Canada's media crisis deepens". *The Guardian,* January 26, theguardian. com.

Greenslade, R. (2016). "Canada's Toronto Star cuts 45 newsroom jobs after £14m loss". *The Guardian,* August 10, theguardian. com.

Greenspon, E. (2017). "How to fix the ever-weakening state of the news media". *Globe and Mail,* January 26, theglobeandmail. com.

Greenwald, G. (2012). "CNN and the business of state-sponsored TV news". *The Guardian,* September 4, the guardian.co.uk.

Greenwald, G. (2012). "US media angrily marvels at the lack of Muslim gratitude". *The Guardian,* September 14, theguardian. com.

Greenwald, G. (2012). "US investigates possible WikiLeaks leaker for 'communicating with the enemy'". *The Guardian,* September 27, theguardian.com.

Greenwald, G. (2017). "Key Democratic Officials Now Warning Base Not to Expect Evidence of Trump/Russia Collusion". *The Intercept,* March 16, the intercept.com.

Griffin, A. (2014). "Where Are the Women?" *Nieman Reports,* September 11, nieimanreports.org.

Griffin, A. (2017). "US in the middle of coup by Donald Trump, Michael Moore warns". *The Independent,* January 31, independent.co.uk.

Griffith, C. (2015). "The privileged lives of the real 'Rich Kids of Instagram' — including Tiffany Trump". *Dujour,* August 20, dujour.com.

Grimm, J. (2012). "Why 'there has never been a better time to be in journalism'". *Poynter,* December 11, poynter.org.

Griswold, A. (2017). "Chuck Todd: Donald Trump's

Delegitimization of the press is 'Un-American,' 'not a laughing matter.'" *Mediaite,* February 16, mediaite.com.

Gros, C. (2007). "New York Times editor warns newspapers facing Web challenges". *The Guardian,* November 29, theguardian. com.

Grynbaum, M.M. (2017). "Donald Trump's news session starts war with and within media". *New York Times,* January 11, nytimes.com.

Grynbaum, M.M. (2017). "Trump teams considers moving press corps, alarming reporters". *New York Times,* January 15, nytimes.com.

Grynbaum, M.M. (2017). "New York Times, CNN and Politico barred from briefing by Trump's press secretary". *New York Times,* February 24, nytimes.com.

Grynbaum, M.M. and Koblin, J. (2017). "For Solace and Solidarity in the Trump Age, Liberals Turn the TV Back On". *New York Times*, March 12, nytimes.com.

Grynbaum, M.M. (2017). "Rachel Maddow Lands a Scoop, Then Makes Viewers Wait". *New York Times,* March 15, nytimes. com.

Grynbaum, M.M. (2017). "After London Attack, Trump Again the Center of Partisan Media Combat". *New York Times,* June 4, nytimes.com.

Guarnieri, G. (2016). "Rolling Stone, Sabrina Rubin Erdely deemed liable in dean's defamation suit for University of Virginia rape story". *Salon,* November 4, salon.com.

Gunter, J. (2015). "Toronto Star claims HPV vaccine unsafe. Science says the Toronto Star is wrong". *Dr. Jen Gunter,* February 5, drjengunter.wordpress.com.

Gupta-Sunderji, M. (2014). "Four things millennials hate about you". *The Globe and Mail,* March 30, theglobeandmail.com.

Guthrie, M. (2015). "Dan Rather Reflects on His Dramatic CBS Exit That Inspired 'Truth': 'I Have a Lot of Wounds'". *The Hollywood Reporter*, October 7, hollywoodreporter.com.

Guthrie, M. (2017). "Fox News Confirms That Bill O'Reilly Won't Return to Air". *The Hollywood Reporter*, April 19, hollywoodreporter.com.

Guthrie, R.V. (1976). *Even the Rat Was White: A Historical View of Psychology*. New York: Harper and Row.

Haberman, M. and Thrush, G. (2017). "Trump Reaches Beyond West Wing for Counsel". *New York Times*, April 22, nytimes.com.

Hagan, J. (2012). "Truth or Consequences". *Texas Monthly*, May, texasmonthly.com.

Hagan, J. (2014). "Benghazi and the Bombshell". *New York*, May 4, nymag.com.

Haggin, P. (2017). "Social Publisher Medium Cuts One-Third of Staff". *Wall Street Journal*, January 4, wsj.com.

Hall, K.G., Goldstein, D., and Gordon, G. (2017). "*BuzzFeed* sued over its publication of uncorroborated Trump dossier". *McClatchy DC*, February 3, mcclatchydc.com.

Hallin, D. (2017). Personal Interview.

Halper, D. (2017). "Trump goes on marathon rant against the media". *New York Post*, February 16, nypost.com.

Hannay, M. (2017). "What does Medium.com's profit model pivot say about the future of online advertising?" *Marketing Land*, January 25, marketingland.com.

Hanretty, C. (2016). "Here's why pollsters and pundits got Brexit wrong". *Washington Post*, June 24, washingtonpost.com.

Hari, J. (2011). "Johann Hari: A personal apology". *The Independent*, September 14, independent.co.uk.

Harrington, M. and Herzlich, J. (2004). "Ex-Symbol CEO waiting out charges in Sweden". *Chicago Tribune*, July 4, chicagotribune.com.

Harvey, E. (2017). "Condé Nast Cuts the Title 'Publisher' in Sales Shakeup". *Publishing Executive*, January 27, pubexec.com.

Hasson, P. (2017). "Trump Inaugural Address Focuses On 'We,' Leaves Himself Out Of Speech Almost Entirely". *Associated*

Press, January 20, dailycaller.com.

Haughney, C. (2012). "Lemann to Step Down as Dean of Journalism School at Columbia". *New York Times*, October 9, nytimes.com.

Hawkins, J. (2012). "12 Ways To Use Saul Alinsky's Rules For Radicals Against Liberals". *Townhall*, April 13, townhall.com.

Hazen, D. (2016). "Robert Reich: Don't Worry, Hillary Clinton will win the election". Salon, November 8, salon.com.

Hébert, C. (2014). "Justin Trudeau is Canada's first war casualty: Hébert." *Toronto Star*, October 8, thestar.com.

Hébert, C. (2017). "It was shoddy journalism that cost Andrew Potter his job at McGill: Hébert". Toronto Star, March 24, thestar.com.

Hedges, C. (2008). "The Internet Is No Substitute for the Dying Newspaper Industry". *Alternet*, July 21, alternet.org.

Heer, J. (2016). "What were blogs?" *The New Republic*, August 24, newrepublic.com.

Hemlock, D. (1997). "Chs Electronics Plans To Buy 6 Smaller Rivals". *Sun-Sentinel*, November 18, sun-sentinel.com.

Hemmer, N. (2016). "Are we witnessing the end of the Fox News era?" *Vox*, November 4, vox.com.

Henwood, D. (2014). "Stop Hillary!" *Harper's*, November, harpers.org.

Herbert, C. (2017). Tweet. January 12, 3:40 pm, twitter.com.

Herman, E.S. and Chomsky, N. (1988). *Manufacturing Consent: The Political Economy of the Mass Media*. New York: Pantheon Books.

Herrman, J. (2016). "Media Websites battle faltering ad revenue and traffic". New York Times, April 17, nytimes.com.

Hess, A. (2017). "Trump, Twitter and the Art of His Deal". *New York Times*, January 15, nytimes.com.

Hill, A. (2012). "Sexist stereotypes dominate front pages of British newspapers, research finds". *The Guardian*, October 14, theguardian.com.

Hiltzik, M. (2015). "How a major newspaper bungled a vaccine story, then smeared its critics". *Los Angeles Times,* February 13, latimes.com.

Hiltzik, M. (2015). "Actually, that 'off target' 1995 anti-Internet column was amazingly on-target". *Los Angeles Times,* March 2, latimes.com.

Hiltzik, M. (2015). "Stephen Glass is still retracting his fabricated stories — 18 years later". *Los Angeles Times,* December 15, lattices.com.

Hinckley, D. (2013). "Lara Logan, producer ordered to take leave in aftermath of '60 Minutes' Benghazi reporting scandal". *New York Daily News,* November 26, nydailynews.com.

Ho, C. (2016). "Saudi government has vast network of PR, lobby firms in US". *The Washington Post,* April 20, washingtonpost. com.

Hoffman, K. (2015). "The Gardasil Girls: How Toronto Star story on young women hurt public trust in vaccine". *CBCnews,* February 14, cbc.ca.

Holcomb, J. (2014). "5 facts about Fox News". *Pew Research Center,* January 14, pewresearch.org.

Holt, R.R. and Silverstein, B. (1989). "On the Psychology of Enemy Images: Introduction and Overview". *Journal of Social Issues,* Vol. 45, No. 2, pages 1-11.

Holub, C. (2016). "Lorne Michaels Reveals Alec Baldwin Playing Donald Trump Was Tina Fey's Idea". *Fortune,* October 2, fortune.com.

Hong, J. (2017). "MP Michael Chong calls writer's attempt to breastfeed his baby 'odd' but inconsequential". *Toronto Star,* March 27, thestar.com.

Hopkins, K. (2017). *Tweet,* May 23, 7:24 am, twitter.com.

Houpt, S. (2014). "Unpaid internships at magazines new target of Ontario labor ministry". *The Globe and Mail,* March 27, theglobeandmail.com.

Houpt, S. (2015). "Following conflict-of-interest allegations, CBC bans on-air journalists from making paid appearances". *The Globe and Mail,* January 23, theglobeandmail.com.

Houpt, S. (2015). "Amanda Lang leaving CBC". *The Globe and Mail,* October 13, theglobeandmail.com.

Howard, M. (2013). "12 most despicable things Fox News did in 2012". *Salon,* January 5, salon.com.

Howell, T. (1997). "The Writers' War Board: US Domestic Propaganda in World War II". *The Historian,* Summer, Vol. 59, No. 4, pages 795-813.

Hoyt, M. (2015). "The end of *American Journalism Review* and what it means for media criticism". *Columbia Journalism Review,* August 24, cjr.org.

Huang, J. (2015). "Brian Williams returns to the airwaves". *USA Today,* September 22, usatoday.com.

Huddleston, Jr., T. (2016). "Here's Why CNN Became a Lightning Rod for Accusations of Media Bias". *Fortune,* December 3, fortune.com.

Hudes, S. (2017). "Canadian journalism urged to tackle the 'culture of free' to survive". *Toronto Star,* January 26, thestar.com.

Hume, M. (2016). "Author Ian Gill: What comes after Canada's media collapse?" *The Globe and Mail,* October 9, theglobeandmail.com.

Humphreys, A. and Craig, S. (2017). "Police open investigation into allegations ex-*Vice* Canada editor recruited drug mules for smuggling ring". *National Post,* February 10, nationalpost.com.

Humphreys, A., Craig, S., and Wellbank, P. (2017). "How a New York-based model was recruited to smuggle $3.7M worth of cocaine by an ex-*Vice* Canada editor". *National Post,* March 1, nationalpost.com.

Hundley, J. (2003). "The dearly undeparted". *Los Angeles Times,* June 19, latimes.com.

Hunter, D. (2017). "Journalists Meltdown, Cry Over Trump

Refugee Executive Order". *Daily Caller*, January 28, dailycaller. com.

Ingram, M. (2017). "*Vice* Media Said to Be Raising More Cash as Prelude to Possible IPO". *Fortune*, May 12, fortune.com.

Ioffe, J. (2016). *Tweet*, Twitter, December 14, 1:44 pm, 3:47 pm, twitter.com.

Jackson, J. (1999). *Newspaper Ownership in Canada: An Overview of the Davey Committee and Kent Commission Studies*. PRB 99-35e, December 17.

Jackson, J.B. (1980). *The Necessity of Ruins: And Other Topics*. Amherst: The University of Massachusetts Press.

James, A. (2017). "How Kellyanne Conway stymies reporters". *Boing Boing*, February 16, boingboing.com.

Jamieson, A. (2017). "'You are fake news': Trump attacks CNN and *BuzzFeed* at press conference". *The Guardian*, January 11, theguardian.com.

Jarvey, N. (2016). "Gawker.com to shut down next week". *The Hollywood Reporter*, August 18, hollywoodreporter.com.

Jarvik, L. (1997). *PBS: Behind the Screen*. Rocklin: Forum.

Jensen, E. (2016). "When Is A Friendship A Conflict Of Interest?" *NPR*, February 26, npr.org.

Johnson, J. and Gold, M. (2017). "Donald Trump just called the media 'the enemy of the American people'". *Washington Post*, February 17, washingtonpost.com.

Johnson, J. and Weigel, D. (2017). "Trump supporters see a successful president — and are frustrated with critics who don't". *Washington Post*, February 19, washingtonpost.com.

Johnson, R. (2017). "Angelina Jolie's image issues not going away, PR expert claims". *New York Post*, February 16, nypost. com.

Johnston, M. (2017). "Q&A: Paul Godfrey, the CEO who's presiding over the Postmedia newspaper chain's rapid decline". *Toronto Life*, February 7, torontolife.com.

Jowett, G.S. (1987). "Propaganda and Communication: The Reemergence of a Research Tradition". *Journal of Communication,* Winter, pages 97-114.

Kalb, M. (1998). "The rise of the new news: A case study of two root causes of the modern scandal coverage". Discussion paper D-34, Harvard Kennedy School's Shorenstein Center on Media, Politics and Public Policy, October, shorensteincenter. org.

Kampfner, J. (2003). "The Truth about Jessica". *The Guardian,* May 15, theguardian.com.

Kaplan, D. (2017). "Rachel Maddow's ratings may be explosive after her bombshell Trump tax return reveal". *New York Daily News,* March 14, nydailynews.com.

Kaplan, S. (2015). "Botched exposé of HPV vaccine's 'dark side' reveals dark side of news business". *Washington Post.* February 25, washingtonpost.com.

Kay, J. (2014). "Jonathan Kay: Woody Allen versus Mia Farrow — who's the real monster?" *National Post,* February 7, nationalpost.com.

Kay, J. (2016). "Show Us the Suicide Note". *The Walrus,* June 8, thewalrus.ca.

Keen, S. (1988). *Faces of the Enemy: Reflections of the hostile imagination.* San Francisco: Harper & Row.

Kellam, M. (2011). "Offer made on Glendale cemetery". *Los Angeles Times,* April 25, latimes.com.

Kelly, C. (2016). "The shooting of Philando Castile: What they're saying." *Star Tribune,* July 8, startribune.com.

Kelly, K.J. (2017). "Gannett slashes more than 140 jobs at NJ newspaper group". *New York Post,* January 23, nypost.com.

Kelly, K.J. (2017). "*Vice* Media passes on buying *Us Weekly*". *New York Post,* January 24, nypost.com.

Kennedy, D. (1995). "Truth or dare: The strange case of Ruth Shalit and the *Washington Post*". *Boston Phoenix,* September 29, bostonphoenix.com.

Kennedy, D. (2016). "Print is dying, digital is no savior: the long, ugly decline of the newspaper business continues apace". *WGBH*, January 26, news.wgbh.org.

Kerbel, M.R. (2000). *If It Bleeds, It Leads: An Anatomy of Television News*. Boulder: Westview.

Kerner, N. and Pressman, G. (2007). *Chasing Cool: Standing Out in Today's Cluttered Marketplace*. New York: Atria Books.

Kettle, M. (2016). "Hillary Clinton will win. But what kind of president will she be?" *The Guardian*, October 27, theguardian. com.

Kheiriddin, T. (2017). "Fake news or state news? It's a false choice". *iPolitics*, February 6, ipolitics.com.

Kind, F. (2017). "Expert: Ange may never bounce back". *Be Entertainment* (Yahoo Australia), February 17, au.be.yahoo. com.

King, S. (2002). "Celebrating the Dead Is No Grave Undertaking". *Los Angeles Times*, May 18, lattices.com.

Kingston, A. (2015). "The strange downfall of Evan Solomon". *Maclean's*, June 19, macleans.ca.

Kinsley, M. (2015). "Parsing the Plagiarism of Fareed Zakaria". *Vanity Fair*, February 5, vanityfair.com.

Kirby, J. (2016). "Roger Ailes Reportedly Threatened Physical Violence Against *New York*'s Gabriel Sherman". *New York* magazine, August 10, nymag.com.

Kissel, M. (2013). "The decline of print doesn't mean the end of journalism". *The Guardian*, October 29, theguardian.com.

Kitty, A. (1998). "Objectivity in Journalism: Should we be skeptical?" *Skeptic*, Vol. 6, No. 1, pages 54-61.

Kitty, A. (1998). "Oh, Canada!" *Presstime*, September, pages 37-39.

Kitty, A. (1998). "When Personal Problems Undermine Good Journalism". *Editor & Publisher*, December 12, Vol. 131, Issue 50, page 70.

Kitty, A. (1999). "Canadians to debut new pricing policies". *Presstime*, March, pages 16-17.

Kitty, A. (1999). "The Daily News". *Presstime,* October, pages 26-27.

Kitty, A. (2000). "Horizons Operations Ltd". *Presstime,* February, pages 30-31.

Kitty, A. (2000). "Time for a Change: Thomson Corporation shifts its focus, making plans to sell its newspapers as the company moves into the online information business". *Quill,* June 5, pages 14-17.

Kitty, A. (2000). "Up North". *Presstime,* September, pages 55-58.

Kitty, A. (2001). "The *Globe and Mail,* Toronto". *Presstime,* January, pages 30-31.

Kitty, A. (2001). "CBC chooses its strategy: a more Canadian channel". *Current,* June 11, pages B1, B30-32.

Kitty, A. (2001). "Sales, Canadian-Style: Campaigns romance the young as the single-copy category grows". *Presstime,* May, pages 39-45.

Kitty, A. (2003). "Everything I know about journalism I learned in Mac psych". *McMaster Times,* Vol. 18, No. 3, pages 32-28.

Kitty, A. (2003). "Appeals to Authority in Journalism". *Critical Review,* 15, 3-4, pages 347-357.

Kitty, A. (2005). *Don't Believe It!: How lies become news.* New York: The Disinformation Company.

Kitty, A. (2005). *OutFoxed: Rupert Murdoch's War on Journalism.* New York: The Disinformation Company.

Kludt, T. (2017). "Milo Yiannopoulos resigns from Breitbart amid child sex comments". *CNN,* February 21, cnn.com.

Knox, M. (2012). "John Moody Returns to Fox News as Executive Editor; Michael Clemente Promoted to EVP". *Adweek,* June 6, adweek.com.

Koblin, J., and Grynbaum, M.M. (2017). "Anchor becomes the news as Megyn Kelly leaves Fox News for NBC". *New York Times,* January 3, nytimes.com.

Koblin, J. (2017). "With Bill O'Reilly Out, Fox Rivals See a Chance to Move In". *New York Times,* April 23, nytimes.com.

Köhler, N. (2016). "The ennui of Mike Duffy's red-chamber redemption". *Maclean's,* May 3, macleans.ca.

Kopun, F. (2017). "Torstar taps a seasoned marketer, turnaround agent as president and CEO". *Toronto Star,* March 3, thestar. com.

Kosoff, M. (2016). "*BuzzFeed* Slashes Revenue Forecast: Is This the Beginning of the End of the Millennial Media Bubble?" *Vanity Fair,* April 12, vanityfair.com.

Kovach, S. (2017). "The iPad was supposed to revolutionize news, books, and computers. So what happened?" *Business Insider,* June 4, businessinsider.com.

Krayden, D. (2017). "Donna Brazile Admits Dems 'Got Cocky' In 2016 Election". *Daily Caller,* January 14, dailycaller.com.

Krugman, P. (2017). "Donald the Unready". *New York Times,* January 20, nytimes.com.

Krupkin, T. (2016). "Jewish-American Journalist Fired Over Obscene Tweet About Donald and Ivanka Trump". *Haaretz,* December 15, haaretz.com.

Krupkin, T. (2017). "Who Is Juan Thompson, the Man Accused of Making Bomb Threats Against Jewish Institutions?" *Haaretz,* March 3, haaretz.com.

Kuczynski, A. (2000). "On CBS News, Some of What You See Isn't There". *New York Times,* January 12, nytimes.com.

Kurtz, H. (1994). *Media Circus: The Trouble with American Newspapers.* New York: Times Books.

Kurtz, H. (1998). *Spin Cycle: Inside the Clinton Propaganda Machine.* New York: The Free Press.

Kurtz, H. (2003). "Rick Bragg quits at New York Times". *Washington Post,* May 29, washingtonpost.com.

Kurtz, H. (2007). "Journal's Pains Reflect Media's Malaise". *Washington Post,* August 22, washingtonpost.com.

Ladd, J.M. (2012). *Why Americans Hate the Media and How It Matters.* Princeton: Princeton University Press.

Lafrance, A. (2017). "The Mark Zuckerberg Manifesto Is a

Blueprint for Destroying Journalism". *The Atlantic,* February 17, theatlantic.com.

Lakoff, R. (2016). "Hillary Clinton's Emailgate Is an Attack on Women". *Time,* October 31, time.com.

Laurance, B. and Hooper, J. (1991). "Maxwell's body found in sea". *The Guardian,* November 6, theguardian.com.

Lauter, D. (2016). "Even elite campaign aides still aren't sure why Donald Trump succeeded". *Los Angeles Times,* December 2, latimes.com.

Lavrusik, V. (2010). "The future of social media in journalism". *Mashable,* September 13, mashable.com.

LeBlanc, D. (2017). "Ottawa facing growing calls to bolster media industry". *Globe and Mail,* January 24, theglobeandmail.com.

LeBlanc, D. (2017). "Canadian media industry needs major federal cash injection: report". *Globe and Mail,* January 26, theglobeandmail.com.

Lederman, M. (2016). "Postmedia cut about 90 jobs and merged newsrooms in four cities as it steps up plans to slash costs amid mounting revenue losses". *The Globe and Mail,* January 22, theglobeandmail.com.

Lederman, M. (2017). "Under a cloud: How UBC's Steven Galloway affair has haunted a campus and changed lives". *The Globe and Mail,* January 5, globeandmail.com.

Lehman, S. (2016). "Times editor Dean Baquet on calling out Donald Trump's lies". *New York Times,* September 23, nytimes.com.

Levant, E. (2015). "Ezra Levant begs to differ". *Toronto Star*, July 7, thestar.com.

Levant, E. (2016). "'Toronto Star run by a bunch of sexist pigs'? Young reporter's suicide reveals MORE Media Party hypocrisy on feminism". *The Rebel,* June 8, therebel.media.

Lever, R. (2017). "How algorithms (secretly) run the world". AFP, February 11, yahoo.com.

Levin, S. (2017). "President paid $38m in 2005, leaked document reveals — as it happened". *The Guardian,* March 15, theguardian.com.

Levy, S. (2012). "Can an algorithm write a better news story than a human reporter?" *Wired,* April 24, wired.com.

Lewin, T. (1986). "Winans Conviction Upheld". *New York Times,* May 28, nytimes.com.

Libin, K. (2017). "Kevin Libin: The only Fake News the government wants you to see is Government Fake News". *National Post,* January 24, nationalpost.com.

Libin, K. (2017). "Kevin Libin: The Liberal government's media blacklist offers the exciting promise of a whole new Sponsorship Scandal". *National Post,* February 6, nationalpost. com.

Lichterman, J. and Ellis, J. (2014). "A mixed bag on apps: What *The New York Times* learned with NYT Opinion and NYT Now". *Nieman Lab,* October 1, niemanlab.org.

Lieber, D. (2015). "Watchdog: Massive Ponzi scheme hit Texas hard". *Dallas News,* March, dallasnews.com.

Loftus, E.F. and Palmer, J.C. (1974). "Reconstruction of auto-mobile destruction: An example of the interaction between language and memory". *Journal of Verbal Learning and Verbal Behavior*, 13, 585-589.

Loofbourow, L. (2016). "What I'll miss about *Gawker*". *The Week,* August 19, theweek.com.

Lorek, L.A. (1998). "Bigger Chip Of Pc Pie". *The Sun-Sentinel,* May 9, sun-sentinel.com.

Lu, V. (2013). "Sun Media closing 11 papers, cutting 360 jobs". *Toronto Star,* July 16, thestar.com.

Lu, V. (2016). "Bleak times for local journalism in Canada". *Toronto Star,* January 29, the star.com.

Lucas, F. (2015). "'Revolving Door': More Than Two Dozen Journalists Have Joined the Obama Administration, but Is It Really Anything New?" *The Blaze,* March 29, theblaze.com.

Luna, F. (2017). "A top media critic went on CNN to blast

journalists for freaking out over President Trump's every move". *Rare,* February 6, rare.com.

Mabe, C. (2010). "Why blogging, websites and the Internet will never replace newspapers". Open Page *(The Florida Center for the Literary Arts)*, December 14, flcenterlitarts.wordpress.com.

MacArthur, J.R. (1992). "Remember Nayirah, Witness for Kuwait?" *New York Times,* January 6, page A17.

MacArthur, J.R. (1993). *Second Front: Censorship and Propaganda in the Gulf War.* New York: Hill & Wang.

MacKenzie, M. (2016). "Rolling Stone and Reporter-Fabricator Sabrina Erdely Guilty of Malice and Defamation". *American Spectator,* November 4, spectator.org.

Mackey, R. (2017). "Fox News Interview With Fake Expert on Sweden Further Baffles Swedes". *The Intercept,* February 25, theintercept.com.

MacLellan, L. (2016). "A Trump presidency is forcing an entire generation of journalists to rethink what 'journalism' even means". *Quartz,* November 10, qz.com.

Maddaus, G. (2016). "Roger Ailes Allegations Move From Sex to Surveillance". *Variety,* August 10, variety.com.

Madrigal, A.C. (2013). "What Is Medium?" *The Atlantic,* August 23, theatlantic.com.

Mallick, H. (2015). "Vaccine debate is one we shouldn't even be having: Mallick". *Toronto Star,* February 6, thestar.com.

Maloy, S. (2014). "CBS' Lara Logan problem: Why is disgraced reporter returning to '60 Minutes'?" *Salon,* June 5, salon.com.

Mance, H. (2016). "Britain has had enough of experts, says Gove Brexit campaigner offers to have disputed EU contribution figure audited". June 3, ft.com.

Manhattan, A. (1986). *The Vatican's Holocaust: The sensational account of the most horrifying religious massacre of the 20th century.* Springfield: Ozark Books.

Mannheim, K. (1936). *Ideology and Utopia.* San Diego: Harvest.

Margolick, D. (2016). "Nick Denton, Peter Thiel, and the plot to murder *Gawker*". *Vanity Fair,* November 6, vanityfair.com.

Marin, C. (2004). "Outing Karen Ryan, the 'journalist'". *Chicago Tribune,* March 24, chicagotribune.com.

Marshall, J.P. (2013). "The Mess of Information and the Order of Doubt". *Global Media Journal, Australian Edition,* Vol. 7, Issue 1.

Martin, L. (2016). "Canada's media: A crisis that cries out for a public inquiry". *The Globe and Mail,* February 2, theglobeandmail.com.

Mascaro, L. (2017). "Trump's inauguration, just like his campaign, breaks Washington norms". *Los Angeles Times,* January 20, latimes.com.

Mason, J. (2017). "Why the White House Press Matters". *US News and World Report,* January 19, usnews.com.

Massa, G. (2017). "Is Trump coverage giving you social media fatigue?" *CityTV News,* February 2, citynews.ca.

Mazur, K. (2017). "Want to make a lie seem true? Say it again. And Again. And Again". *Wired,* February 11, wired.com.

Mcallister, J.F.O. (1992). "Must it go on?" *Time,* August 17, time. com.

McElwee, S., McDermott, M., and Jordan, W. (2017). "4 pieces of evidence showing FBI Director James Comey cost Clinton the election". *Vox,* January 11, vox.com.

McGregor, J. (2017). "Reddit is Being Manipulated By Big Financial Services Companies". *Forbes,* February 20, forbes. com.

McHugh, K. (2017). *Tweet,* June 3, 4:55 pm, twitter.com.

McKenzie, D. (2017). "Maclean's piece calls Quebec 'pathologically alienated,' politicians erupt". *Toronto Star,* March 22, the star.com.

McKnight, Z. and Nursall, K. (2014). "Ministry of Labour cracks down on unpaid magazine internships. *Toronto Star,* March 27, thestar.com.

McLaren, L. (2014). "An open letter to Peter MacKay's wife". *The*

Globe and Mail, June 25, theglobeandmail.com.

McLaren, L. (2017). "Leah McLaren: The joy (and politics) of breastfeeding someone else's baby". *The Globe and Mail,* March 22, theglobeandmail.com.

McLaughlin, S. (2017). "DNC chairman candidate blames Hillary Clinton's loss on Sen. Tim Kaine". *The Washington Times,* January 28, washingtontimes.com.

McLuhan, M. (1964). *Understanding Media: The Extensions of Man.* New York: Pantheon.

McMahon, T. (2014). "Who belongs to Canada's middle class?" *Maclean's,* February 26, macleans.ca.

McKnight, Z. (2015). "CBC host Evan Solomon scandal 'mystifying': journalism ethics expert". *Maclean's,* June 10, macleans.ca.

McNeal, S. (2016). "People Are Worried About Melania Trump After Seeing These 'Sad' Pics." *BuzzFeed,* January 23, buzzfeed.com.

McNish, J. and Sinclair, S. (2004). *Wrong Way: The Fall of Conrad Black.* Toronto: Viking Canada.

McParland, K. (2016). "The cause of the crisis in newspapers is not a mystery. So why investigate it?" *National Post,* February 3, nationalpost.com.

McQueeney, R. (2017). "Will *Vice* Media IPO in 2017? Everything Investors Need To Know". *Nasdaq,* December 21, nasdaq.com.

Mele, C. (2017). "Fatigued by the News? Experts Suggest How to Adjust Your Media Diet". *New York Times,* February 1, nytimes.com.

Melton, H.K. and Wallace, R. (2009). *The Official CIA Manual of Trickery and Deception.* New York: William Morrow.

Mendleson, R. (2017). "Jonathan Kay resigns as editor of The Walrus amid 'appropriation prize' backlash". *Toronto Star,* May 14, thestar.com.

Menegus, B. (2016). "Reddit is tearing itself apart". *Gizmodo,* November 11, gizmodo.com.

Merlino, J. (1993). *Les vérités yougoslaves ne sont pas toutes bonnes á dire.* Paris: Albin Michel Paris.

Mertl, S. (2014). "Ontario cracks down on unpaid internships at prominent Canadian magazines". *Daily Brew,* March 27, ca.news.yahoo.com.

Miller, M. (2001). "Veterans Hope to Fund Bob Hope Monument". *Los Angeles Times,* September 10, latimes.com.

Mills, L. (2017). "Russia says it has no compromising material on Trump". *Wall Street Journal,* January 11, wsj.org.

Missal, M.J. and Coe Lanpher, L. (2005). *Report of the Independent Review Panel Dick Thornburgh and Louis D. Boccardi on the September 8, 2004 60 Minutes Wednesday Segment 'For the Record' Concerning President Bush's Texas Air National Guard Service.* January 5.

Mlodinow, L. (2008). *The Drunkard's Walk: How randomness rules our lives.* New York: Vintage.

Mohan, B. (1997). "The Professional Quest for Truth: Paradigm, Paradox, and Praxis". *International Journal of Contemporary Sociology,* Vol. 34, No. 1, pages 51-63.

Molloy, T. (2017). "Trump Tax Returns Reporter Tells Rachel Maddow Trump May Have Leaked Own Tax Returns". *The Wrap,* March 14, thewrap.com.

Moody, J. (2004). *Memo to Fox News Channel employees,* April 6.

Moody, J. (2004). *Memo to Fox News Channel employees,* April 28.

Morford, M. (2003). "The Big Lie Of Jessica Lynch". *Common Dreams,* September 5, commondreams.org.

Morning Joe. (2017). MSNBC News, February 22, broadcast.

Morris, D. (1977). *Manwatching: A field guide to human behavior.* New York: Abrams.

Morris, S. (2003). "Sky News reporter who faked war report found hanged". *The Guardian,* October 7, theguardian.com.

Morrison, S. (2016). "Obama undermined press freedom. Now he wants a strong media to stop Trump?" *The Guardian,* March 30, the guardian.com.

Morse, B. (2017). "CNN apologizes to WikiLeaks after threatening to sue over commentator calling Assange a pedophile". *The Blaze,* January 4, theblaze.com.

Moses, L. (2017). "Facebook faces increased publisher resistance to Instant Articles". *Digiday,* April 11, digiday.com.

Mott, L.M. (1962). *The News in America.* Cambridge: Harvard University Press.

Mount, D. et al. (2016). "An open letter to UBC: Steven Galloway's right to due process." *UBC Accountable,* November 14, ubcaccountable.com.

Moyers, B. (2017). "10 Investigative Reporting Outlets to Follow". *Bill Moyers,* January 13, billmoyers.com.

MSNBC. (2017). "Breaking News". *Hardball.* February 24.

MSNBC. (2017). "Opening Segment". *The Rachel Maddow Show.* March 14.

Mullin, B. (2015). "CJR cuts print schedule to two issues per year". *Poynter,* October 14, poynter.org.

Mundy, A. (1992). "Is the press any match for powerhouse PR?" *Columbia Journalism Review,* September/October, pages 27-34.

Myers, S. (2012). "DealBook columnist apologizes for consulting on business deal he wrote about". *Poynter,* January 24, poynter.org.

Nadin, M. (2002). *Anticipation: The end is where we start from.* Baden: Lars Müller Publishers.

Nazaryan, A. (2017). "Right-wing media critics slam *BuzzFeed* over Trump assassination joke". *Newsweek*, May 4, newsweek.com.

NBC Nightly News. (2017). *Tweet,* Twitter, May 3, 1:44 pm, 7:21 pm, twitter.com.

Nelson, J. (1989). *The Sultans of Sleaze: Public Relations and the Media.* Toronto: Between the Lines.

Neustaedter, C. (2017). "PPF releases The Shattered Mirror: News, Democracy and Trust in the Digital Age". *Public Policy Forum,* January 26, ppforum.ca. Press Release.

New Day. (2016). CNN, October 16, broadcast.

New Day. (2017). CNN, February 9, broadcast.

News 4. (2016). WIVB, December 27, broadcast.

N.L. (2014). "Singled Out?" *The Economist,* February 6, conomist. com.

Nolte, J. (2017). "CNN Is Hitler: Beware Anderson Cooper's Gaystapo". *The Daily Wire,* June 17, dailywire.com.

Noonan, P. (2017). "President Trump Declares Independence". *Wall Street Journal,* January 20, wsj.com.

Norton, B. and Greenwald, G. (2016). "Washington Post Disgracefully Promotes a McCarthyite Blacklist From a New, Hidden, and Very Shady Group". *The Intercept,* November 26, theintercept.com.

O'Connell, M. (2017). "Rachel Maddow Tops Cable News as Ratings Thrive". *The Hollywood Reporter,* March 13, hollywoodreporter.com.

O'Connell, M. (2017). "TV Ratings: Bill O'Reilly Audience Grows Amid Scandal". *The Hollywood Reporter,* April 5, hollywoodreporter.com.

Omar, M. (2015). "Toronto Star Gardasil Story Pulled From Paper's Website: Publisher's Note". *Huffington Post,* February 21, huffingtonpost.com.

Oremus, W. (2017). "How Megyn Kelly's Alex Jones Interview Could Go Wrong, and How It Could Go Right". *Slate,* June 15, slate.com.

Ortiz, A. (2013). *Memo regarding 60 Minutes' Benghazi report.*

Ortiz, E. (2017). "Megyn Kelly defends interview with Infowars host Alex Jones". *NBC News,* June 13, nbcnews.com.

Osnos, E. (2017). "Doomsday Prep for the Super-Rich." *New Yorker,* January 30, newyorker.com.

Osumi, M. (2016). "Exposing government's lack of action may save Yasuda's life: security consultant". *Japan Times,* March 18, japantimes.com.

Owen, J. (2016). "'We're in a Golden Age of Journalism' says

NYT Executive Editor". October 1, johnowenjournalist.com.

Pace, R.D. (2015). "Saudi Arabia Hires Edelman & The Podesta Group". *Everything-PR*, October 5, everything-pr.com.

Paddon, N. (2015). "CHCH TV suspends newscasts amid bankruptcy and restructuring moves". *Hamilton Spectator*, December 12, thespec.com.

Paine, A. and Jobson, R. (2003). "TV war reporter kills himself". *Evening Standard,* October 5, standard.co.uk.

Panorama. (1957). BBC News, April 1, broadcast.

Paris, E. (1961). *Genocide in Satellite Croatia, 1941-1945: A record of racial and religious persecutions and massacres.* Chicago: The American Institute for Balkan Affairs.

Parker, R. (2017). "New York Times Reporter Reprimanded for 'Hooker' Comment About Melania Trump". *The Hollywood Reporter,* February 13, hollywoodreporter.com.

Parker-Pope, T. (1997). "Hill & Knowlton Will Polish Its Own Controversial Image". *Wall Street Journal,* February 19, wsj.com.

Paskin, W. (2017). "Rachel Maddow Turned a Scoop on Donald Trump's Taxes Into a Cynical, Self-Defeating Spectacle". *Slate*, March 15, slate.com.

Patrick, R. (2013). "Funeral scam figures get prison sentences in St. Louis federal court". *St. Louis Post-Dispatch,* November 14, stltoday.com.

Patterson, T.E. (2017). *News Coverage of Donald Trump's First 100 Days.* Harvard Kennedy School's Shorenstein Center on Media, Politics and Public Policy, May 19, shorensteincenter.org.

Paulos, J.A. (1995). *A Mathematician Reads the Newspaper.* New York: Basic Books.

Pearce, M. and Finnegan, M. (2017). "The mainstream and conservative media are living in different worlds. So are those who read them". *Los Angeles Times,* April 10, latimes.com.

Pedwell, T. (2017). "Report to offer 'ideas' for stemming crisis in

Canada's media sector: author". *The Canadian Press,* January 25.

Perkel, C. (2014). "Crackdown on unpaid media internships in Ontario starts with major magazines: Toronto Life and The Walrus forced to limit stints to students working for credit". March 27, *The Canadian Press.*

Perkel, C. (2017). "*Vice* journalist's fight to keep messaging logs of man accused of terrorist offences from RCMP back in court". *The Canadian Press,* February 6, thestar.com.

Pfeiffer, A. (2017). "Errors From The Press Are Piling Up In The Opening Weeks Of The Trump Administration". *Daily Caller,* February 4, dailycaller.com.

Pierce, C.P. (2017). "What We Can All Learn from Maddow's Trump Taxes Broadcast". *Esquire,* March 15, esquire.com.

Pilkington, E. (2016). "Trump v the media: did his tactics mortally wound the fourth estate?" *The Guardian,* November 22, theguardian.com.

Pindell, J. (2017). "3 ways Rachel Maddow helped, yes helped, Donald Trump last night". *Boston Globe,* March 15, bostonglobe.com.

Plotkin, H. (2002). *The Imagined World Made Real: Towards a natural science of culture.* London: Penguin.

Plotz, D. (2014). "David Plotz: We are in a golden age for journalism". *National Post,* May 27, nationalpost.com.

Poisson, J. (2017). "How Toronto Star reporter Daniel Dale fact-checks Trump". *Toronto Star,* June 16, thestar.com.

Porter, E. (2009). "Drudge Has Lost His Touch: Technology, the competition, and the times have passed him". *Columbia Journalism Review,* September/October, cjr.org.

Pompeo, J. (2015). "Meet Nate Cohn, New York Times' new young gun on data". *Politico,* January 6, politico.com.

Pompeo, J. (2017). "Upset in WSJ newsroom over editor's directive to avoid 'majority Muslim' in immigration ban coverage". *Politico,* January 31, politico.com.

Ponce de Leon, C.L. (2015). "'Perilously close to propaganda': How Fox News shilled for Iraq War, and Jon Stewart returned sanity". *Salon,* May 23, salon.com.

Poniewozik, J. (2013). "CBS's Benghazi Apology: Sorry Is the Hardest, or At Least Slowest, Word". *Time,* November 15, time.com.

Ponsford, D. (2017). "*Guardian* pulls out of Facebook Instant Articles over 'woeful' return as UK ad revenue for US giant booms". *Press Gazette,* April 26, pressgazette.co.uk.

Pope, K. (2017). "An open letter to Trump from the US press corps". *Columbia Journalism Review,* January 17, cjr.org.

Porter, C. (2015). "My daughter's run-in with Ezra Levant at her first protest: Porter". *Toronto Star,* July 6, thestar.com.

Porter, C. (2015). "I made mistakes in my Ezra Levant column: Porter". *Toronto Star,* July 21, thestar.com.

Porter, R. (2017). "Updating Alinsky's 'Rules for Radicals' for the Trump Era". *Real Clear Politics,* January 23, realclearpolitics. com.

Porter, S., Yuille, J.C., and Lehman, D.R. (1999). "The Nature of Real, Implanted, and Fabricated Memories for Emotional Childhood Events: Implications for the recovered memory debate". *Law and Human Behavior,* October, Vol. 23, No. 5, pages 517-537.

Potter, A. (2017). "How a snowstorm exposed Quebec's real problem: social malaise". *Maclean's,* March 20, macleans.ca.

Prince, S.J. (2017). "MSNBC's Mika Brzezinski: 'Our Job' Is to Control 'What People Think' [VIDEO]". *Heavy,* February 22, heavy.com.

Public Policy Forum. (2017). *The Shattered Mirror: News, Democracy and Trust in the Digital Age.* January, Ottawa.

Quigley, A. (2017). "NBC Normalizing Alex Jones's fake news with Megyn Kelly interview, a Sandy Hook parent charges". *Newsweek,* June 12, newsweek.com.

Quill, G. (2012). "Plagiarism and fabrication charges undermine news media credibility". *Toronto Star*, August 9, thestar.com.

Rahn, W. (2016). "Commentary: The unbearable smugness of the press". *CBS News,* November 10, cbsnews.com.

Rather, D. (2017). Facebook Posting, April 7, facebook.com.

Rathi, A. (2015). "Why there has never been a better time to trust journalism". *Quartz,* August 4, qz.com.

Redden, M. (2016). "How one lawsuit unleashed a cascade of allegations against Roger Ailes". *The Guardian,* July 22, theguardian.com.

Reed Lajoux, A. (1986). "Trading Secrets: Seduction and Scandal at the Wall Street Journal *by R. Foster Winans*". *Los Angeles Times,* October 19, latimes.com.

Reilly, K. (2017). "Madonna on Donald Trump's Inauguration: 'We Can Only Go Up From Here'". *Time,* January 20, time.com.

Reilly, K. (2017). "White Woman Whose Harassment Claim Led to Emmett Till's Lynching: 'That Part's Not True'". *Time,* January 27, time.com.

Resnick, G. (2017). "WikiLeaks declares war on *The Intercept*". *The Daily Beast*, June 6, thedailybeast.com.

Reuters. (2017). "Covering Trump the Reuters Way". *Reuters,* January 31, reuters.com.

Rich, F. (2017). "No Sympathy for the Hillbilly". *New York* magazine, March 19, nymag.com.

Richards, B. (2017). Personal Interview.

Richardson, T. (2014). "Rolling Stone statement: 'There now appear to be discrepancies'". *Washington Post*, December 5, washingtonpost.com.

Riddell, K. (2016). "Mainstream media maligned: 10 examples of blatant bias". *Washington Times,* November 8, washingtontimes.com.

Riddell, K. (2017). "Mainstream media whines as Trump calls on less established news outlets". *Washington Times,* February 13, washingtontimes.com.

Rider, D. (2017). "A Rob-Ford-beat reporter's advice to the scribes covering Donald Trump: Rider". *Toronto Star,* January 20, thestar.com.

Rieder, R. (2012). "An Important City without a Daily Paper". *American Journalism Review,* June/July, ajr.org.

Rieder, R. (2015). "Rieder: NBC's terrible Brian Williams decision". *USA Today,* June 18, usatoday.com.

Rieder, R. (2015). "Rieder: Real-world consequences of journalism scandals". *USA Today,* July 3, usatoday.com.

Riendeau, D. (2017). "Alberta Magazine Publisher Having Trouble Paying Its Employees". *Canadaland,* March 21, canadaland.com.

Riley, J. (2014). "Feds seek $12M from fugitive LI tech exec". *Newsday,* January 17, newsday.com.

Risen, J. (2016). "If Donald Trump Targets Journalists, Thank Obama". *New York Times,* December 30, nytimes.com.

Rivers, W. (1970). *The Adversaries; Politics and the Press.* Boston: Beacon.

Robinson, A. and McGuinness, A. (2017). "Melania Trump accepts damages from Daily Mail over model claims". *Sky News*, April 12, sky.com.

Robinson, J. (2011). "NoW phone-hacking scandal: News Corp's 'rogue reporter' defence unravels". *The Guardian,* January 17, theguardian.com.

Rodham, H.D. (1969). "'There is only the fight...' An analysis of the Alinsky model." *Senior thesis.* May 2, hillaryclintonquarterly. com.

Rogers, E. (2017). "Trump won the battle at his news conference, but the war's not over". *Washington Post*, February 17, washingtonpost.com.

Rogin, J. (2017). "The State Department's entire senior administrative team just resigned". *Washington Post,* January 26, washingtonpost.com.

Romenesko, J. (2003). "New Yorker's Lemann considering

Columbia j-school job". *Poynter,* April 8, poynter.org.

Romenesko, J. (2003). "The New Yorker's Lemann named Columbia j-school dean". *Poynter,* April 16, poynter.org.

Romenesko, J. (2003). "Advice for Lemann: Drop the highfalutin stuff, teach basics". *Poynter,* May 28, poynter.org.

Romenesko, J. (2004). "Toronto Star reporter caught lifting Village Voice passages". *Pointer,* April 15, pointer.org.

Romney, L. (2011). "Two convicted of murder in shooting of Oakland journalist". *Los Angeles Times,* June 10, latimes.com.

Ross, C. (2016). "Court Docs: Rolling Stone Recently Fired Author Of Debunked Campus Gang Rape Article". *The Daily Caller,* July 22, dailycaller.com.

Roth, Z. (2004). "Karen Ryan, Revisited". *Columbia Journalism Review,* April 20, cjr.org.

Rugaber, C.S. (2017). "Correction: Trump-Manufacturing story". *AP The Big Story,* February 24, bigstory.ap.com.

Rutenberg, J. (2017). "Roger Ailes: The Man Who Mined a Divided America". *New York Times,* May 18, nytimes.com.

Rutenberg, J. (2014). "Megyn Kelly, Alex Jones and a Fine Line Between News and Promotion". *New York Times,* June 14, nytimes.com.

Saba, J. (2009). "NAA cuts 50% of staff; halts *Presstime*". *Adweek,* April 29, adweek.com.

Sagan, A. (2016). "Rogers Media to cut workforce 4%: 200 TV, radio, publishing and admin jobs". *Montreal Gazette,* January 24, montrealgazette.com.

Sager, M. (2016). "The fabulist who changed journalism". *Columbia Journalism Review,* Spring, cjr.org.

Sailer, S. (2016). "Sabrina Rubin Erdely's Malice in Blunderland". *Taki's Magazine,* October 26, takimag.com.

Salemi, V. (2013). "Journalism Is Among Top 10 Occupations to Most Likely Attract Psychopaths". *Adweek,* January 4, adweek.com.

Sande, G.N., Goethals, G.R., Ferrari, L., and Worth, L.T. (1989).

"Value-Guided Attributions: Maintaining the Moral Self-Image and the Diabolical Enemy-Image". *Journal of Social Issues*, Vol. 45, No. 2, pages 903-913.

Saperstein, T. (2014). "The Future of Print: Newspapers Struggle to Survive in the Age of Technology". *Harvard Political Review,* December 6, harvardpolitics.com.

Sargent, J. (2014). "Taylor Swift's Parents Are Assholes". *Gawker,* April 9, gawker.com.

Scarry, E. (2015). "Politico reporter downplays 'clumsy' Chelsea Clinton request". *Washington Examiner,* November 30, washingtonexaminer.com.

Scarry, E. (2016). "Jake Tapper defends his 'polite' note to Podesta". *Washington Examiner,* October 11, washingtonexaminer.com.

Scarry, E. (2017). "Media say hacked emails are critical, but can't say why". *Washington Examiner,* January 10, washingtonexaminer.com.

Scheflin, A.W. and Opton, E.M. (1978). *The Mind Manipulators.* New York: Paddington Press.

Schieffer, B. (2014). "Nikita Khrushchev and *Face the Nation's* biggest scoop". *CBS News*, March 2, cbsnews.com.

Schindehette, S. (1991). "As Bombs Fell on Baghdad, Three CNN Reporters Scored a Coup". *People,* February 4, people.com.

Schow, A. (2014). "New York Times publisher fires back, calls claim that Jill Abramson was paid less 'not true'". *Washington Examiner,* May 15, washingtonexaminer.com.

Schow, A. (2017). "Rolling Stone rape hoaxer ordered to comply with second lawsuit". *Watchdog,* January 31, watchdog.com.

Schwartz, R., Naaman, M., and Teodoro, R. (2015). "Editorial Algorithms: Using Social Media to Discover and Report Local News". *Association for the Advancement of Artificial Intelligence,* aaah.org.

Scocca, T. (2014). "Why Be a Neocon? Because You Like Being Very Wrong About Everything". *Gawker,* April 9, gawker.com.

Scocca, T. (2016). "*Gawker* Was Murdered by Gaslight". *Gawker,* August 22, gawker.com.

Scott, E. (2017). "Kay Ivey takes Alabama governor's seat after Bentley scandal". CNN, April 11, cnn.com.

Seipel, B. (2017). "CNN's Zakaria: Trump got to the Presidency by 'bulls--tting'". *The Hill,* March 18, the hill.com.

Selley, C. (2016). "Chris Selley: *The Toronto Star* was right to reconsider Raveena Aulakh's request to be forgotten". *National Post,* June 9, nationalpost.com.

Shabad, R. (2013). "Publisher halts books by Benghazi witness". *The Hill,* November 8, thehill.com.

Shafer, J. and Doherty, T. (2017). "The media bubble is worse than you think". *Politico,* May/June, politico.com.

Shanker, D. (2017). "How to Stay Sane in a World of Crazy News". *Bloomberg News,* February 16, bloomberg.com.

Shapiro, T.R. (2014). "Key elements of Rolling Stone's U-Va. gang rape allegations in doubt". *Washington Post,* December 5, washingtonpost.com.

Shapiro, T.R. (2016). "In her own words: Rolling Stone's Sabrina Rubin Erdely on experience with 'Jackie'". *Washington Post,* July 3, washingtonpost.com.

Shapiro, T.R. (2016). "Jury finds reporter, Rolling Stone responsible for defaming U-Va. dean with gang rape story". *Washington Post,* November 4, washingtonpost.com.

Shapiro, T.R. and Brown, E. (2017). "Rolling Stone settles with former U-Va. dean in defamation case". *Washington Post,* April 11, washingtonpost.com.

Shapiro, T.R. (2017). "Fraternity chapter at U-Va. to settle suit against Rolling Stone for $1.65 million". *Washington Post,* June 13, washingtonpost.com.

Shattuck, T. (2017). "Shattuck: Rachel Maddow left with nothing after fake news report". *Boston Herald,* March 15, bostonherald.com.

Sheffield, H. (2015). "The 10 jobs that attract the most

psychopaths". *The Independent,* December 15, independent. co.uk.

Shepard, A.C. (1995). "Too Much Too Soon? (interview)". *American Journalism Review,* December, ajr.org.

Sherman, G. (2016). "6 More Women Allege That Roger Ailes Sexually Harassed Them". *New York,* July 9, nymag.com.

Sherman, G. (2016). "How Fox News Fired and Silenced a Female Reporter Who Alleged Sexual Harassment". *New York* magazine, July 23, nymag.com.

Sherman, G. (2016). "Roger Ailes Used Fox News Budget to Finance 'Black Room' Campaigns Against His Enemies". *New York,* August 7, nymag.com.

Sherman, G. (2016). "The Revenge of Roger's Angels: How Fox News women took down the most powerful, and predatory, man in media". *New York,* September 2, nymag.com.

Sherman, G. (2017). "Fox News Is Dropping Its 'Fair & Balanced' Slogan". *New York,* June 14, nymag.com.

Shivani, A. (2017). "America last: The case for moral disengagement from politics in the age of Trump". *Salon,* February 26, salon.com.

Sholars, M. (2017). "Desmond Cole Will Be Fine; The Canadian Media? Not So Much". *Huffington Post,* May 4, huffingtonpost. ca.

Shufelt, T. (2016). "Guelph Mercury newspaper to close amid financial pressures". *The Globe and Mail,* January 25, theglobeandmail.com.

Sifakis, C. (1993). *Hoaxes and Scams: A compendium of deceptions, ruses, and swindles.* London: Michael O'Mara Books.

Signorile, M. (2016). "*Gawker* Didn't 'Out' Peter Thiel — Nor Did It Wrong Him in Any Way". *Huffington Post,* May 26, huffingtonpost.com.

Silverman, C. (2014). "The year in media errors and corrections 2014". *Poynter,* December 18, poynter.org.

Silverstein, B. (1987). "Toward a Science of Propaganda". *Political*

Psychology, Vol. 8, No. 1, March, pages 49-59.

Silverstein, B. (1989). "Enemy Images: The Psychology of US Attitudes and Cognitions Regarding the Soviet Union". *American Psychologist,* 44, June, pages 903-913.

Silverstein, B. and Flamenbaum, C. (1989). "Biases in the Perception and Cognition of the Actions of Enemies". *Journal of Social Issues,* Vol. 45, No. 2, pages 51-72.

Silvester, C. (2011). "News Corp. Phone-Hacking Scandal Gets New Legs". *Adweek,* April 6, adweek.com.

Simo, F. (2017). "Announcing The Facebook Journalism Project". Facebook, January 11, facebook.com.

Simo, F. (2017). "Introducing: The Facebook Journalism Project". Facebook, January 11, facebook.com.

Simon, J. (2015). "Barack Obama's press freedom legacy". *Columbia Journalism Review,* April 3, cjr.org.

Sinclair, H. (2017). *"New York Times* corrects editorial that linked Sarah Palin to Gabby Giffords' shooting". *Newsweek,* June 15, newsweek.com.

Sink, J., Talev, M., and Olorunnipa, T. (2017). "Trump Aide Says Press Secretary Used 'Alternative Facts'". *Bloomberg,* January 21, bloomberg.com.

Sink, J., Talev, M., and Pettypiece, S. (2017). "Trump Spokesman Accuses Media of False Inaugural Reporting". *Bloomberg,* January 21, bloomberg.com.

Sismondo, S. (2009). "Ghosts in the Machine: publication planning in the medical sciences". *Social Studies of Science,* Vol. 39, No. 2, April 2009, pages 171-198.

60 Minutes. (1992). "Nayirah". CBS Television, September 6, broadcast.

60 Minutes. (2013). "Benghazi". CBS Television, October 27, broadcast.

60 Minutes. (2017). "Cuban rum wars". CBS Television, January 1, broadcast.

60 Minutes. (2017). "Julia". CBS Television, March 19, broadcast.

60 Minutes. (2017). "Fake News". CBS Television, March 26, broadcast.

Slatterly, D. (2017). "Bo Dietl admits to digging up dirt for Fox News". *New York Daily News*, May 5, nydailynews.com.

Slotnik, D.E. (2016). "The Intercept Says Reporter Falsified Quotations". *The New York Times*, February 2, nytimes.com.

Smith, A. (2017). "CNN host Chris Cuomo to Trump: Being called 'fake news' is 'like an ethnic disparagement' for journalists". *Business Insider*, February 9, businessinsider.com.

Smith, B. (2017). "Why *BuzzFeed* News published the dossier". *New York Times*, January 23, nytimes.com.

Smith, C. (2016). "Toronto Star ripped asunder by deceased environmental reporter Raveena Aulakh's revelations". *Georgia Straight*, June 8, straight.com.

Smith, G. (2017). "Facebook, Snapchat Deals Produce Meager Results for News Outlets". *Bloomberg*, January 24, bloomberg. com.

Smith, S. (2015). "Canadian Journalist Francois Bugingo Suspended, Accused of Fabrication". *iMediaEthics*, May 23, imediaethics.org.

Smith, S. (2015). "Harper's Issues its First Retraction, Stephen Glass Faked at least 71% of 'Prophets and Losses'". *iMediaEthics*, December 17, imediaethics.org.

Solnik, C. (2004). "2004: High-profile cases, low mortgage rates". *Long Island Business News*, December 10, libn.com.

Solomon Wood, L. (2017). "Quality journalism has never been more important. Will you support it?" *National Observer*, February 10, nationalobserver.com.

Solomont, E.B. (2013). "Exclusive: Cassity pleads guilty to federal charges". *St. Louis Business Journal*, June 3, bizjournals.com.

Solon, O. (2016). "In firing human editors, Facebook has lost the fight against fake news". *The Guardian*, August 28, theguardian.com.

Sommerfeldt, C. (2017). "CNN apologizes to Assange after

commentator calls him 'pedophile". *New York Daily News,* January 5, nydailynews.com.

Sonderman, J. (2012). "What's next for Columbia's Journalism School as Dean Nicholas Lemann steps down". *Poynter,* October 10, poynter.org.

Spayd, E. (2015). "A note to CJR's readers". *Columbia Journalism Review,* October 14, cjr.org.

Sproule, J.M. (1998). "Propaganda, History, and Orthodoxy". *SSMC Review and Criticism*, December, 457-459.

Spurr, B. (2011). "A brief history of Canadian news scandals". *Now,* July 10, nowtoronto.com.

Squitieri, J. (2017). "Mukasey: White House did not violate rule limiting contact with DOJ". *CNN,* February 27, cnn.com.

Stanford, P. (2011). "Whatever happened to the Maxwells?" *The Telegraph,* March 11, telegraph.co.uk.

Stauber, J. and Rampton, S. (1995). *Toxic Sludge Is Good For You: Lies, Damn Lies and the Public Relations Industry.* Monroe: Common Courage Press.

Stead, S. (2017). "Public Editor: Error in RCMP story shows lessons to be learned". *The Globe and Mail,* February 14, theglobeandmail.com.

Steel, E. and Schmidt, M.S. (2017). "Bill O'Reilly Thrives at Fox News, Even as Harassment Settlements Add Up". *New York Times,* April 1, nytimes.com.

Schmidt, M.S. (2017). "The Murdochs Assess the O'Reilly Damage". *New York Times,* April 12, nytimes.com.

Steel, E. and Schmidt. M.S. (2017). "Bill O'Reilly Is Forced Out at Fox News". *New York Times,* April 19, nytimes.com.

Stefansky, E. (2017). "Watch Ted Koppel tell Sean Hannity that he's 'bad for America'". *Vanity Fair,* March 26, vanityfair.com.

Stein, J. (2013). "Lara Logan's Mystery Man". *Newsweek,* November 22, newsweek.com.

Stein, S. (2016). "The Clinton Campaign Was Undone By Its Own Neglect And A Touch Of Arrogance, Staffers Say". *Huffington*

Post, November 16, huffingtonpost.com.

Steinberg, B. and Littleton, C. (2017). "Bill O'Reilly Sexual Harassment Scandal, Advertiser Defections a Test for Fox News' Future". *Variety,* April 11, variety.com.

Steinberg, B. (2017). "Scott Pelley to leave as anchor of 'CBS Evening News'". *Variety,* May 30, variety.com.

Steinberg, B. (2017). "Cable News Wars: Inside the Unprecedented Battle for Viewers in Trump Era". *Variety.* June 13, variety.com.

Steinberg, B. (2017). "CNN Presses 'New Day' to Hit Hard in the Morning". *Variety,* June 15, variety.com.

Steinberg, J. (2013). "Times reporter steps down amid criticism". *New York Times,* May 29, nytimes.com.

Stelter, B. (2016). "Revealed: Fox News' 400-page oppo file on Gabriel Sherman". *CNN,* August 26, cnn.com.

Stelter, B. (2017). "Source: Fox News and Bill O'Reilly are talking exit". *CNN,* April 18, cnn.com.

Stevens, H. (2017). "Megyn Kelly's Alex Jones interview is callous and unwarranted". *Chicago Tribune,* June 13, chicagotribune.com.

Stockman, R. (2017). "Hospital CEO Wins Major Court Victory After Accusing CNN of False Reporting". *Law Newz,* February 15, lawnewz.com.

Stoll, C. (1995). "Why the web won't be nirvana". *Newsweek,* February 26, newsweek.com.

Stone, M. and Jacobs, S. (2015). "The 'Insta-famous' sons and daughters of New York's elite let me into their circle — here's what it was like". *Business Insider,* September 21, businessinsider.com.

Stone, P. and Gordon, G. (2017). "FBI's Russian-influence probe includes a look at far-right news sites". *McClatchy,* March 20, mcclatchydc.com.

Stout, K. (2016). "How Guilty Should I Feel?" *Gawker,* August 22, gawker.com.

Straus, E. (2015). "Ted Koppel: Brian Williams 'Has More Than Paid the Price'". *Time,* October 22, time.com.

Strugatch, W. (2000). "IN BRIEF". *New York Times,* November 19, nytimes.com.

Strugatch, W. (2001). "L.I. @ WORK". *New York Times,* July 22, times.com.

Sullivan, A. (2017). "Maybe America Wasn't Crazy to Elect Donald Trump". *New York,* April 28, nymag.com.

Sullivan, M. (2015). "Dean Baquet's 'Charting the Future' Note to Times Staff". *New York Times,* January 6, nytimes.com.

Sullivan, M. (2015). "A 'Darker Narrative' of Print's Future From Clay Shirky". *New York Times,* April 10, nytimes.com.

Sullivan, M. (2017). "Cancel dinner plans. Send 'nerd prom' to the history books". *Washington Post,* February 5, washingtonpost.com.

Sullivan, M. (2016). "What TV journalists did wrong — and The New York Times did right — in meeting with Trump". *Washington Post,* November 22, washingtonpost.com.

Sullivan, M. (2017). "Rachel Maddow had a decent scoop. Here's what she did wrong with it". *Washington Post,* March 15, washingtonpost.com.

Sullivan, M. (2017). "Is media coverage of Trump too negative? You're asking the wrong question". *Washington Post,* June 11, washingtonpost.com.

Sunday Night with Megyn Kelly. (2017). NBC Television, June 4, broadcast.

Sun Tzu, and Griffith, S.B. (1964). *The Art of War.* Oxford: Clarendon Press.

Superville, D. and Thomas, K. (2017). "Defensive Donald Trump calls media 'out of control' at free-wheeling news conference". *Associated Press* via the *National Post,* February 16, nationalpost.com.

Sutton, K. (2016). "NYT executive editor: CNN and Fox News are 'bad for democracy'". *Politico,* October 28, politico.com.

Swift, A. (2016). "Americans' trust in mass media sinks to new low". *Gallop,* September 14, gallop.com.

Szigeti, A. (2014). "Not criminally responsible law erects hurdles for mentally ill". *Toronto Star,* June 29, thestar.com.

Tagliaferro, L. (1996). "Long Island Q&A: Tomo Razmilovic; Moving From Bar Codes to Advances in Communications". *New York Times,* May 19, nytimes.com.

Taibbi, M. (2016). "The 'Washington Post' 'Blacklist' Story Is Shameful and Disgusting: The capital's paper of record crashes legacy media on an iceberg". *Rolling Stone,* November 28, rollingstone.com.

Tamarkin, B. (1993). *Rumor Has it: A curio of lies, hoaxes, and hearsay.* New York: Prentice Hall.

Tannahill, J. (2015). "Saudi Arabia's PR Firm Edelman Also Has a Questionable Record On Climate Change". *Everything PR,* November 23, everything-pr.com.

Taylor, A. (2017). "Who is Nils Bildt? Fox News' Swedish 'security adviser' has heads scratching". *Washington Post,* February 26, washingtonpost.com.

Thomas, O. (2007). "Peter Thiel is totally gay, people". *Gawker,* December 19, gawker.com.

Thompson, D. (2016). "Why do Americans distrust the media?" *The Atlantic,* September 16, theatlantic.com.

Thorsell, W. (2016). "A former Globe & Mail editor argues that newspapers have forgotten what they want from readers". *Maclean's,* February 16, macleans.ca.

Tieleman, B. (2016). "Journalists Jumping to BC Liberal Jobs a Problem for Media Credibility". *The Tyee,* November 22, thetyee.ca.

Tilly, C. (2006). *Why: What happens when people give reasons...and why.* Princeton: Princeton University Press.

Timberg, C. (2016). "Russian propaganda effort helped spread 'fake news' during election, experts say". *Washington Post,* November 24, washingtonpost.com.

Timm, T. (2016). "How the Obama administration laid the groundwork for Trump's coming crackdown on the press". *Freedom of the Press Foundation,* December 13, freedom.press.

Timson, J. (2017). "Leah McLaren and the perils of personal journalism: Timson". *Toronto Star,* March 30, thestar.com.

Todd, C. (2017). *Tweet,* Twitter, February 16, 1:44 pm, twitter.com.

Tolentino, J. (2017). "The somehow controversial women's march on Washington". *New Yorker,* January 18, newyorker.com.

Topping, A. (2017). "Katie Hopkins leaves LBC radio show after 'final solution' tweet". *The Guardian,* May 26, theguardian.com.

Townsend, T. (2017). "Google has banned 200 publishers since it passed a new policy against fake news". *Recode,* January 25, recode.com.

Trex, E. (2010). "7 Stories The National Enquirer Actually Got Right". *Mental Floss,* March 25, mentalfloss.com.

Tripp, M. (2017). "Fake News: Will a backlash bring renewed interest to reputable outlets?" *Martin Tripp Associates,* January 31, trippassociates.co.uk.

Tritten, T.J. (2015). "NBC's Brian Williams recants Iraq story after soldiers protest". *Stars and Stripes,* February 4, stripes.com.

Tritten, T.J. (2015). "Brian Williams' apology draws mixed reviews from mission vets". *Stars and Stripes,* February 5, stripes.com.

Trotter, J.K. (2013). "Lara Logan's Husband Was a Propagandist for the US Military". *Gawker,* November 11, gawker.com.

Trotter, J.K. (2014). "Fox News Boss Roger Ailes Treats Cops as His Personal Minions". *Gawker,* September 15, gawker.com.

Trotter, J.K. (2016). "This Is Why Billionaire Peter Thiel Wants to End *Gawker*". *Gawker,* May 26, gawker.com.

Trotter, J.K. (2016). "Peter Thiel's Lawyer Threatens Deadspin Over Feature on 'Betting Expert' RJ Bell". *Gawker,* June 5, gawker.com.

Trotter, J.K. (2016). "Report: Roger Ailes Used Fox News Money to Spy on *Gawker* Staffers". *Gawker,* August 7, gawker.com.

Uberti, D. (2014). "The worst journalism of 2014". *Columbia Journalism Review,* December 22, cjr.org.

Uberti, D. and Vernon, P. (2017). "The coming storm for journalism under Trump". *Columbia Journalism Review,* January 19, cjr.org.

United States District Court for the Northern District of Georgia Atlanta Division. (2017). Davide M. Carbone v. Cable New Network, February 15, Civil Action No. 1:16-CV-1720-ODE.

Uygur, C. (2006). "Will John Moody be Forced Out of Fox Like Dan Rather from CBS?" *Huffington Post,* November 15, huffingtonpost.com.

Verhoeven, B. (2017). "New York Times Reporter Apologizes for Calling Melania Trump a 'Hooker'". *The Wrap,* February 14, thewrap.com.

Vicente, K. (2004). *The Human Factor: Revolutionizing the way we live with technology.* Toronto: Vintage Canada.

Victor, D. (2017). "'I said nothing wrong': Breitbart news editor says she was fired over anti-Muslim tweets". *New York Times,* June 6, nytimes.com.

Viebeck, E. and Gold, M. (2017). "Once led by Steve Bannon, Breitbart is owned by family that poured millions into getting Trump elected". *Washington Post,* February 25, washingtonpost.com.

Vincent, D. (1996). "A dying mother says thank you." *Toronto Star,* April 10, page A1.

Vinograd, C. (2015). "WDBJ7 Reporter Alison Parker, Photographer Adam Ward Killed on Live TV". *NBC News,* August 26, nbcnews.com.

Visser, J. (2012). "'Editorial oversight': Globe issues new mea culpa after columnist Leah McLaren writes article trying to sell her house". *National Post,* September 27, nationalpost.

com.

Volokh, E. (2016). "'Remember, it's illegal to possess' WikiLeaks Clinton emails, but 'it's different for the media,' says CNN's Chris Cuomo". *Washington Post,* October 17, washingtonpost. com.

Wainman, L. (2015). "Inside power lobbyist, philanthropist and contemporary art collector Tony Podesta's Kalorama home". *Washington Life* magazine, June 5, washingtonlife.com.

Waldron, K. (1992). "Spin doctors of war". *New Statesman and Society,* July, 5 (215), pages 12-13.

Walker, T. (2016). "Four items from the Podesta emails that could hurt Hillary Clinton at the debate - and one that could hurt Donald Trump". *The Independent,* October 19, independent. co.uk.

Warren, J. (2016). "The winner of last night's debate? Lester Holt". *Poynter,* September 27, pointer.org.

Warren, J. (2016). "Is the *National Enquirer* in bed with Donald Trump?" *Vanity Fair,* September 30, vanityfair.com.

Warren, J. (2016). "Clinton will win by one of the largest margins in recent history". *The Toronto Sun,* October 22, torontosun. com.

Warren, J. (2017). "Why Meryl Streep's defense of the media could backfire". *Poynter,* January 10, poynter.org.

Warren, J. (2017). "The White House Press Corps is fighting a losing battle". *Vanity Fair,* January 17, vanityfair.com.

Warzel, C. (2017). "The New Twitter Detectives Want To Bring Down Trump Without Becoming Alex Jones". *BuzzFeed,* February 12, buzzfeed.com.

Warzel, C. (2017). "Alex Jones Scoops Megyn Kelly And Proves The Media Isn't Ready For The Trolls". *BuzzFeed,* June 16, buzzfeed.com.

Weaver, H. (2017). "Meryl Streep's Powerful, Anti-Trump Golden Globes Speech: Read the Whole Thing Here". *Vanity Fair,* January 8, vanityfair.com.

Weigel, D. (2016). "Why 'dump all those emails' doesn't mean what Drudge thinks it does". *Washington Post,* November 1, washingtonpost.com.

Weigel, D. and Costa, R. (2017). "Milo Yiannopoulos uninvited from American conservatives' conference over video 'condoning pedophilia'". *Washington Post,* February 20, washingtonpost.com.

Weinberg, S. (1996). *The Reporter's Handbook: an investigator's guide to documents and techniques.* New York: St. Martin's Press.

Weiner, J. (2013). "Dylan Davies, the Benghazi security officer who tricked *60 Minutes,* forgot to also trick the FBI". *Vanity Fair,* November 8, vanityfair.com.

Wells, G.L., and Bradfield, A.L. (1998). "'Good, you identified the suspect': Feedback to eyewitnesses distorts their reports of the witnessing experience." *Journal of Applied Psychology,* 83, pages 360-376.

Wemple, E. (2015). "The Brian Williams scandal is an NBC News-wide scandal". *Washington Post,* February 5, washingtonpost.com.

Wemple, E. (2015). "Charlottesville police make clear that Rolling Stone story is a complete crock". *Washington Post,* March 23, washingtonpost.com.

Wemple, E. (2016). "New York Times top editor Dean Baquet savages CNN, Fox News". *Washington Post,* October 28, washingtonpost.com.

Wemple, E. (2017). "Washington Post publishes editor's note to address 'duplicated' passages from Government Executive". *Washington Post,* January 19, washingtonpost.com.

Wemple, E. (2017). "Roger Ailes is dead. His scourge will live for decades". *Washington Post,* May 18, washingtonpost.com.

Werber, C. (2016). "Facebook is predicting the end of the written word". *Quartz,* June 14, qz.com.

Wherry, A. (2013). "Middle Class Bias". *Maclean's,* February 21, macleans.ca.

White, A. (2017). "Is Angelina Jolie done with Hollywood? And does Hollywood even care?" *The Telegraph*, February 20, telegraph.co.uk.

Will, G.F. (2014). "George Will: Colleges become the victims of progressivism". *Washington Post*, June 6, washingtonpost.com.

Will, G.F. (2017). "Trump and academia actually have a lot in common". *Washington Post,* January 27, washingtonpost.com.

Willcocks, P. (2016). "Big Loser in Wente Plagiarism? Globe's Reputation". *The Tyee,* April 26, thetyee.ca.

Wolbrecht, C. (2017). "Don't overlook the feminist triumph of Clinton's run". *Vox,* January 21, vox.com.

Wolcott, J. (2016). "How Trump trumped *The New York Times, CNN,* and the rest of the media in 2016". *Vanity Fair,* December 28, vanityfair.com.

Wolff, M. (2017). "Michael Wolff: It's James Murdoch's Fox News Now". *Hollywood Reporter,* April 20, hollywoodreporter.com.

Wolff, M. (2017). "Michael Wolff on Roger Ailes' Final Days and a Complicated Murdoch Relationship". *Hollywood Reporter,* May 18, hollywoodreporter.com.

Wong, J.C. (2014). "A Very Serious Problem With Very Serious Journalism". *The Nation,* March 27, thenation.com.

Woodward, B. (2005). *The Secret Man: The story of Watergate's Deep Throat.* New York: Simon and Schuster.

Wright, T. (2013). "Chrétien says he 'had the good sense' not to appoint Duffy to Senate". *The (Charlottetown) Guardian,* October 30, theguardian.pe.ca.

Yarow, J. (2017). "Op-Ed: Donald Trump just got a nice victory, thanks, of all people, to Rachel Maddow". *CNBC,* March 15, cnbc.com.

York, B. (2016). "Byron York: Trump win confounds critics who thought gaffes would do him in". *Washington Examiner,* February 21, washingtonexaminer.com.

Youssef, N.A. (2013). "Questions about '60 Minutes' Benghazi story go beyond Dylan Davies interview; CBS conducting 'journalistic review'". *McClatchy DC,* November 13, mcclatchydc.com.

Zelizer, J. (2016). "Bill Clinton's nearly forgotten 1992 sex scandal". *CNN,* April 6, cnn.com.

Zetter, K. (2013). "Obama Administration secretly obtains phone records of AP journalists". *Wired,* May 13, wired.com.

Zimbardo, P.G. (1975). "Transforming Experimental Research into Advocacy for Social Change. *Applying Social Psychology: Implications for Research, Practice, and Training,* 33-66.

Zuckerberg, M. (2017). "Building Global Community". Facebook, February 16, facebook.com.

Zur, O. (1991). "The Love of Hating: The Psychology of Enmity". *History of European Ideas,* Vol. 13, No. 4, pages 345-369.

Zero Books

CULTURE, SOCIETY & POLITICS

Recent bestsellers from Zero Books are:

In the Dust of This Planet
Horror of Philosophy vol. 1
Eugene Thacker
In the first of a series of three books on the Horror of
Philosophy, *In the Dust of This Planet* offers the genre of horror
as a way of thinking about the unthinkable.
Paperback: 978-1-84694-676-9 ebook: 978-1-78099-010-1

Capitalist Realism
Is there no alternative?
Mark Fisher
An analysis of the ways in which capitalism has presented itself
as the only realistic political-economic system.
Paperback: 978-1-84694-317-1 ebook: 978-1-78099-734-6

Rebel Rebel
Chris O'Leary
David Bowie: every single song. Everything you want to know,
everything you didn't know.
Paperback: 978-1-78099-244-0 ebook: 978-1-78099-713-1

Cartographies of the Absolute
Alberto Toscano, Jeff Kinkle
An aesthetics of the economy for the twenty-first century.
Paperback: 978-1-78099-275-4 ebook: 978-1-78279-973-3

Malign Velocities
Accelerationism and Capitalism
Benjamin Noys
Longlisted for the Bread and Roses Prize 2015, *Malign Velocities* argues against the need for speed, tracking acceleration as the symptom of the ongoing crises of capitalism.
Paperback: 978-1-78279-300-7 ebook: 978-1-78279-299-4

Meat Market
Female flesh under Capitalism
Laurie Penny
A feminist dissection of women's bodies as the fleshy fulcrum of capitalist cannibalism, whereby women are both consumers and consumed.
Paperback: 978-1-84694-521-2 ebook: 978-1-84694-782-7

Poor but Sexy
Culture Clashes in Europe East and West
Agata Pyzik
How the East stayed East and the West stayed West.
Paperback: 978-1-78099-394-2 ebook: 978-1-78099-395-9

Romeo and Juliet in Palestine
Teaching Under Occupation
Tom Sperlinger
Life in the West Bank, the nature of pedagogy and the role of a university under occupation.
Paperback: 978-1-78279-637-4 ebook: 978-1-78279-636-7

Sweetening the Pill
or How We Got Hooked on Hormonal Birth Control
Holly Grigg-Spall
Has contraception liberated or oppressed women? *Sweetening the Pill* breaks the silence on the dark side of hormonal contraception.
Paperback: 978-1-78099-607-3 ebook: 978-1-78099-608-0

Why Are We The Good Guys?
Reclaiming Your Mind from the Delusions of Propaganda
David Cromwell
A provocative challenge to the standard ideology that Western power is a benevolent force in the world.
Paperback: 978-1-78099-365-2 ebook: 978-1-78099-366-9

Readers of ebooks can buy or view any of these bestsellers by clicking on the live link in the title. Most titles are published in paperback and as an ebook. Paperbacks are available in traditional bookshops. Both print and ebook formats are available online.

Find more titles and sign up to our readers' newsletter at http://www.johnhuntpublishing.com/culture-and-politics

Follow us on Facebook
at https://www.facebook.com/ZeroBooks

and Twitter at https://twitter.com/Zer0Books